MAN'S UNCONQUERABLE MIND

MAN'S UNCONQUERABLE MIND

*Studies of English Writers, from Bede to
A. E. Housman and W. P. Ker*

by

R. W. CHAMBERS

*Quain Professor of English in
University College, London*

It is not to be thought of that . . . this most
famous Stream . . . should perish

JONATHAN CAPE
THIRTY BEDFORD SQUARE
LONDON

FIRST PUBLISHED MARCH 1939
REPRINTED SEPTEMBER 1939
REISSUED 1952
REPRINTED 1955

PRINTED IN GREAT BRITAIN BY
LOWE & BRYDONE (PRINTERS) LIMITED
BOUND BY A. W. BAIN & CO. LTD., LONDON

CONTENTS

ILLUSTRATIONS

ACKNOWLEDGEMENTS

I HAVE to thank the following bodies and persons for permission to reprint: the British Academy for my lectures on Bede and Shakespeare, and portions of the obituary notice on W. P. Ker; Messrs. Constable & Co., for my 'Foreword' to Sir Archibald Strong's translation of *Beowulf*; Messrs. Ivor Nicholson & Watson for my contribution on Thomas More to *Great Tudors*; *The Times Literary Supplement*, for what I have written on William Tyndale; the English Association, for my lecture on 'Ruskin (and others) on Byron', and for a contribution on Langland to vol. IX of its *Essays and Studies*; the editors of the *Modern Language Review* and *London Mediaeval Studies*, for contributions to those periodicals; and the editor of the University College magazine for various contributions relating to A. E. Housman, made to that magazine.

I have also to thank Mr. R. E. Mortimer Wheeler for permission to reproduce his caricature of A. E. Housman, which appeared in the U.C.L. Magazine; and the authorities of the British Museum for permission to reproduce passages in facsimile from Tyndale's *New Testament*, 1525, and from *The Book of Sir Thomas More*.

Further, I have to thank the Cambridge University Press and Mr. Edward A. Platt for permitting the reprint from A. E. Housman's Preface to Platt's *Nine Essays*; Mr. Guy Boas and the Proprietors of *Punch* for permission to quote his lines on 'Shakespeare's Ghost'; the executors of the late A. E. Housman and the Richards Press for permission to quote, especially No. xxiii of *A Shropshire Lad*; the executors of the late G. K. Chesterton for permission to quote two verses from *The Ballad of the White Horse*; and Messrs. George Allen and Unwin for permission to quote from their monumental authorized edition of Ruskin's Works.

For permission to quote from the *Alpine Journal* the account of W. P. Ker as a mountaineer, to many friends of Ker for permitting quotation of letters and reminiscences, to Mrs. Katharine E. Symons and Mr. Laurence Housman for reading the typescript of what I have written about their brother, and for making valuable suggestions, I express my great gratitude.

To my younger god-children:

*Rosemary Sisson, Bridget Hamel, David Butler,
Jane Bruce Dickins, Weland Stone*

Dear Gossips,

I have promised to take you to hear sermons, and I have never taken any one of you to hear one. I will ask you to listen instead to some English writers.

Members of the younger generation are often told to-day that they have cause against earlier ages, which have left them so many problems to meet as they grow older. They must see to it that their children do not have cause against them. They will find helpers: poets like Shakespeare or Langland, scholars like More or Tyndale, Bede or Ker, and others, a mighty company. 'Great men have been among us,' and

What we have loved
Others will love.

R. W. C.

MAN'S UNCONQUERABLE MIND

                              Thou hast great allies;
Thy friends are exultations, agonies,
And love, and man's unconquerable mind.

It is not to be thought of that the Flood
Of British freedom, which, to the open sea
Of the world's praise, from dark antiquity
Hath flowed, 'with pomp of waters, unwithstood',
Road by which all might come and go that would,
And bear our freights of worth to foreign lands;
That this most famous Stream in bogs and sands
Should perish; and to evil and to good
Be lost for ever. In our halls is hung
Armoury of the invincible Knights of old;
We must live free or die, who speak the tongue
That Shakespeare spake. . . .

                    WILLIAM WORDSWORTH in *The Morning Post*,
                         2 February and 16 April, 1803.

TO THE READER

In time of danger and responsibility many people of many nations have drawn comfort from their great writers. At least one French scholar-soldier, and probably scores of his fellow-countrymen, found encouragement in the trenches by thinking of the words which the good Count of Soissons spoke to Join-ville during the grim fighting near Mansourah: 'Seneschal, we shall yet talk of this day, you and I, in the drawing room among the ladies.' And English literature is as full of words of encouragement as that of any nation. Earl Baldwin found in *Piers Plowman* 'the Englishman immutable and eternal'. Carlyle saw Shakespeare 'shine over us all, as the noblest, gentlest, yet strongest of rallying signs, indestructible.'

Nevertheless, it is fashionable to represent both these poets as victims of discouragement and disillusionment, overwhelmed by the sorrows of their age. It is the chief object of this book to acclaim their 'victorious strength'.

When Baldwin perceived in *Piers Plowman* 'the same English-man with whom you have to work to-day — the same English-man in his strength and in his weakness, in his heroism and in his humour', he was, I believe, the first to stress, as it deserves, the heroism of the poem. The author is still generally held to have been what John Richard Green held him to have been, a victim of depression: 'the gaunt poet of the poor', who 'sings as a man conscious of his loneliness, and without hope', with 'narrow intensity', 'a deep undertone of sadness', and 'a terrible despair'. But that is not the whole truth. It can be shown that the poet, in his spirit, as in his metre and vocabulary, is the successor of the Old English heroic poets. He sees 'all the wealth of this world, and the woe both', and refuses to be flattered by the one or intimidated by the other. He confesses to moments of weakness, even to long periods during which he abandons his great quest; he has lost time, but he has not lost hope.

He will never give in. He makes the whole scheme of man's

salvation his subject, and produces a religious epic, the English counterpart of the *Divine Comedy*.

To Carlyle, ninety-eight years ago, Shakespeare was 'the hero as poet'. Carlyle saw his 'placid joyous strength', his 'calm creative perspicacity', his 'tolerance', his 'truthfulness': 'No *twisted*, poor convex-concave mirror, reflecting all objects with its own convexities and concavities; a perfectly *level* mirror;—that is to say withal . . . a good man'. But nowadays it *is* precisely as this convex-concave mirror that we are often invited to contemplate Shakespeare. Very useful work has been done in fixing the chronology of Shakespeare's plays, and we now know that in the opening years of the reign of James I, 1603-08, he produced most of his greatest tragedies: *Othello*, *Lear*, *Macbeth*, *Antony and Cleopatra*, *Coriolanus*, and one comedy, *Measure for Measure*. We know that later, after this period of Tragedy and of a Comedy which is full of tragic feeling, comes the final period of the 'Romances'. Hence it is very generally argued that during the early Jacobean years Shakespeare was in a mood of gloom and dejection, cynicism and disgust, till a sudden conversion raised him from 'the depths' on to 'the heights', from Tragedy to Romance.

And now that English is so important a part of the teaching of our schools, many tens of thousands of school boys and girls have been taught for generations that in these early Jacobean years Shakespeare wrote 'in darkness of spirit', because 'public and private ill then weighed heavily upon him'. Yet to assume that when Shakespeare wrote *Macbeth*, he must have been as disillusioned as Macbeth, is to assume that his art *is* a convex-concave mirror, reflecting all objects with its own convexities and concavities. May we not find more help in Carlyle's conception? Of course Shakespeare must have suffered: 'How could a man delineate a Hamlet, a Coriolanus, a Macbeth, so many suffering heroic hearts, if his own heroic heart had never suffered?' As Carlyle reads Shakespeare, it is Shakespeare's own heroic heart which will not allow him to forget that Macbeth, despite all the disillusionment that his crime has brought upon him, is heroic. 'It is truly a lordly spectacle how this great soul takes in all kinds of men and objects, a Falstaff, an Othello, a Juliet, a Coriolanus; sets them all forth to us in their round completeness; *loving, just, and equal brother of all.*'

Measure for Measure is the touchstone to show which view is correct. It is claimed that this 'acrid' play (which we can date exactly) is evidence of Shakespeare's Jacobean cynicism about 1604. Upon it must turn our belief in Shakespeare's long period of 'disillusionment', and I have therefore chosen it for special study.

I believe that *Piers Plowman* and *Measure for Measure* are the two things most widely misunderstood in English Literature, with the one exception of the work of Jonathan Swift. I had hoped to print two lectures depicting Swift as yet another 'suffering heroic heart'. Almost every year for thirty years since 1904, I have tried thus to show to students the alleged hater of his kind. But this book is long enough already, and I leave Swift in abler hands than mine.

Oliver Elton has asked us to dream of our poetry for a moment 'as all written by a single poet of unimaginable gifts, and older than Methuselah'. May we not dream of all our literature, whether in prose or verse, in modern English, in early English, or in Latin, as the work of one spirit? We see that spirit when Bede preserved the continuity of civilization, and *Beowulf* consecrated valour. It inspired men as different as Tyndale and 'unbending More', Byron and Ruskin. It inspired also those modern scholars, with some account of whom this book closes, scholars who 'friend us' 'in the dark and cloudy day', when some are again fearing 'that there will be no long posterity for learning'.[1]

From the august roll of English writers, other names might have been chosen equally well to illustrate that spirit: these were determined for me principally by the fact that between 1924 and 1936 certain anniversaries came round: the hundredth, four hundredth, twelve hundredth, as the case might be. A bundle of lectures and essays, the result of such chronological accident, may seem to have no more unity than the memoranda out of which Mr. Dick constructed his kite. Yet even to those discourses of Mr. Dick, the recurrence of the head of King

---

[1] HOUSMAN, *Shropshire Lad*, lxii; MANILIUS, v, xxxvi.

Charles the First gave a certain consistency: and Mr. Dick and I may both say of our 'manner of diffusing the facts': 'It's according to the circumstances and so forth; but I take my chance of that.'

When that great man, Henry Morley, set to work to write the history of English Literature in twenty volumes, he described his object as being 'to tell the story of the English mind'. Morley's *English Writers* is one of the best attempts ever made to do this. But Henry Morley had come too late to his task, after a lifetime of struggle. 'The blind fury with th' abhorred shears' intervened. *English Writers* was left unfinished.

The problem remains: a brief history of English Literature tends to become a mere succession of names and dates, interspersed perhaps with an assertion of the writer's preferences for this author over that. A long history of English Literature exceeds the powers of any one man — Henry Morley outlined the combination of gifts necessary for it, and ended with the statement that, should a man possessing all these gifts be born, he assuredly would not devote them to writing a history of English Literature.

All that most of us can aspire to do, is to make isolated contributions, by editing an author, or writing a biography or a number of scattered essays.

These studies are controversial, except for the first and the last. An invitation from the British Academy to speak on Bede as a Master Mind, on the occasion of his twelve hundredth anniversary; an invitation from University College, London, to speak on the history of the study of literature in that College, on the centenary of its foundation — these were not controversial occasions.

But nearly all the other essays are necessarily so. The history of English literature is so well-worn a theme that there seems no reason why a man should write about it unless he finds some subject upon which he thinks that he can throw fresh light. Now there are some historians of literature who can do this almost without controversy — men who can state something which is new, but the truth of which the reader nevertheless feels to be evident, without argument. True wit, Dr. Johnson said, is that which 'though not obvious, is upon its first production, acknowledged to be just; that, which he that never found it, wonders how he missed.' Such wit was possessed by W. P. Ker. But with most of us it is not so. And I should not have ventured to speak or write on the topics which follow had I not believed that they were subject to misunderstandings, and that argument might throw light upon them.

There has been, and still is, much misunderstanding about Thomas More, and the part he played in what may be claimed as the most heroic episode in English history: the greatest assertion *in our literature* of the right of the individual conscience against totalitarian tyranny. There had been before More, and there were to be after him, many martyrs as noble as he. But they had been comparatively inarticulate. More's letters and writings in the Tower plead against the loving persuasions of daughter and friends, with a 'sweet reasonableness' which we can only parallel when we go back to the Socratic *Apology* and its group. More refuses to argue in favour of the truth of the cause for which he dies. He argues in favour of a man dying for what he believes to be the truth. Intolerant More had sometimes been in earlier days. There was no intolerance at the end.

In William Tyndale we have a man, the equal of More in 'plain heroic magnitude of mind', and one whose influence upon English literature has been greater than that of any other man — and will be, so long as we read our *Bible*. It seemed right, on the fourth centenary of his martyrdom, to make some estimate, however unworthy, of his place in English literature.

It is a fact worth stressing that in Protestant London, after Queen Elizabeth had been excommunicated by the Pope, and when priests were from time to time being executed for saying Mass, a body of playwrights (all presumably Protestants, and one certainly a most violent Protestant) should have proposed to stage a play glorifying Thomas More, and telling how

> A very learned worthy gentleman
> Seals error with his blood.

What matters to the dramatists is that More dies for what he believes to be the truth (error though it may be) with the words

No eye salute my trunk with a sad tear,
Our birth to heaven should be thus: void of fear.

Of course the play was not allowed to be acted. That a number of working playwrights took the trouble to write it, is a glorious fact. But if, as I think can be proved, Shakespeare added to that play its greatest scene, then it is worth while spending some time to try to prove *that*.

Ruskin, from his childhood, read and loved Byron; and he helps us to see Byron rather as a heroic poet than as the misanthropic villain which some modern critics would make him.

Finally, there seems to be something worth our attention to-day in the way in which modern scholarship is seeking to restore on a vaster scale that community of outlook which belonged to the scholarship of England in the days of Bede, and which continued, until the growth of nationalism and the wars of religion rent asunder the community of learning in Western Europe. Bacon complained how knowledge had been parcelled out among the nations: learning, he said, 'would be yet more advanced, if there were more intelligence mutual between the Universities of Europe than there now is'. Yet little was done to further Bacon's wish, and in the Universities of England knowledge, about 1827, had become peculiarly insular: scholars, having, in the words of A. E. Housman, 'turned their backs on Europe and science and the past, sat down to banquet on mutual approbation, and to perish without a name'.

It may be permitted to one who owes all his education to University College, London, to look upon the foundation of that College as having marked an epoch in the reunion of learning in Europe. The experience of the universities of Germany was kept in mind by our founders. For the first time in England, chairs were founded in French, German, Italian and English. The names of Rosen and Panizzi and many others amongst our earliest professors show that our founders did not turn their backs on Europe, and a movement was started which has gone far to carry out the vision of Bacon:

And surely as nature createth brotherhood in families, and arts mechanical contract brotherhoods in communalties, and the anointment of God superinduceth a brotherhood in kings and bishops, so in like manner there cannot but be a fraternity in learning and illumination.

This fraternity in learning and illumination is one of the things to which a distracted Europe must look for the healing of its wounds.

So these studies, beginning at Bede, close with the names of three great teachers of University College, London: Arthur Platt, A. E. Housman and W. P. Ker. It was in Germany, rather than at home, that Ker's vast learning was first fully appreciated. He was interested in all the literatures and dialects of Western Europe, of Spain, Portugal, Provence, France, Italy, Germany. He was equally at home with Icelandic farmers and Swiss peasants. But above all he strove to make us understand the part which Scandinavia had played in the world, and the meaning of the Heroic Age, which was realized in so remarkable a way in the ancient Norse literature. He was one of the greatest exponents of that age, because his own spirit was that of his epic hero: 'A gentleman adventurer on board his own ship, following out his own ideas, carrying his men with him by his own power of mind and temper.'

A critic may say that a book stands self-condemned, if it looks for the heroic in English literature, but has no chapter devoted to Milton or Wordsworth or Scott. Yet I hope that reminiscences of them, and of other heroic souls, Homer and Dante, will be found running through these essays, appearing almost as frequently as the head of Sir Thomas More. And so, like Mr. Dick, 'casting anything but a confident look at his manuscript', I send mine to Mr. Jonathan Cape, to be submitted ultimately, dear reader, to your eyes. And, as I do so, my own eye falls upon some comfortable words of Thomas Carlyle, which might serve as a motto for this book:

One comfort is, that Great Men, taken up in any way, are profitable company. We cannot look, however imperfectly, upon a great man, without gaining something by him. He is the living light-fountain, which it is good and pleasant to be near ... On any terms whatsoever, you will not grudge to wander in such neighbourhood for a while ... How happy, could I but, in any measure, in such times as these, make manifest to you the meanings of Heroism; the divine relation (for I may well call it such) which in all times unites a Great Man to other men.

University College, London
 30 Jan., 1939

I

BEDE

*Annual lecture on a Master Mind, Henriette Hertz Trust,
of the British Academy*[1]

OURS is an age in which those who delight in such things delight to take a 'master mind' and to throw him down from his pedestal. My friend and predecessor in this series, Tenney Frank, speaking of Cicero as a master mind, had to vindicate against cavillers his hero's claim to that title. Indeed, said Professor Frank, 'the first poet of Greece is perhaps the only human being who has attained an undisputed place of honour'. Yet even here he was too optimistic. I was brought up on Mahaffy's *History of Greek Literature*, and Mahaffy and Sayce between them taught me that Homer was *not* a human being, but a collection of interpolations, 'fitted together', which is what the name *Homêros* means, so that 'with a closer insight into the structure of the epic poems', we must depose him from his pedestal and give the first place to Aeschylus.[2] All my lifetime Homer has been slowly climbing back on to his pedestal again. But he has not yet been selected for the 'master mind' lecture. He lacks one important qualification for public recognition as a master mind: a fixed date of death, which will ensure his merits being officially brought under the notice of the Academy at least once every century.

Bede is more fortunate. We can say with fair certainty that he died at the hour of Vespers, on Wednesday, 25 May 735, the eve of Ascension Day. Anyway, it seems that he did not die before that date, so we are on the safe side in keeping his twelve hundredth anniversary a little late. To-day, the 27th of May, is, of course, his day in the Church's calendar.

In a broader sense, it is to his date that Bede owes his

[1] Read 27 May 1936.
[2] *History of Classical Greek Literature* (3rd edit., 1891), I, i, 284; I, ii, 51.

supreme position. His life was preceded, and it was followed, by a period of great darkness. The seventh century, in which Bede was born, has been called 'the nadir of the human mind'; or at least a great historian of to-day, George Sarton, has censured a great historian of a century ago, Henry Hallam, for so calling it.[1] Sarton has pointed out that, though things were bad in Europe, the early seventh century was a golden age in Arabia, in Tibet, in China, and in Japan. Hallam hardly deserves the censure of his critic, for what he really said was that the seventh century was the nadir of the human mind in Europe. Two pages later, however, Hallam does so far abandon caution as to say that 'the Venerable Bede may perhaps be reckoned superior to any man *the world* then possessed'. Hallam would have been on safer ground if here also he had said 'Europe'. To-day, as we pass through any great museum, the marvels of the T'ang dynasty warn the most careless of us not to suppose that 'Europe' and 'the world' are synonymous. But of these things Hallam could know nothing; they were hidden in recesses of China and Japan then inaccessible to Westerners.

Amid the European darkness of the seventh and eighth centuries Bede's life 'throws its beams' far; it shines, as the editor of Bede's Historical Works, Charles Plummer, has said, like

a good deed in a naughty world.

Or rather, *we* will say, 'like a good deed in a naughty Europe'.

Bede is the most striking example of the truth which Oderisi of Gubbio[2] uttered to Dante, as they paced, crouching together, round the first circle of Purgatory, the circle of the Proud:

Oh vain glory of human powers! How short a time does it remain green upon the top, *if it be not followed by ages of darkness.* Cimabue thought to hold the field in painting; now Giotto has the cry . . . Even so has one Guido taken from the other the glory of our tongue . . . And for thee, if

---

[1] GEORGE SARTON, *Introduction to the History of Science*, i, p. 460, 1927. Compare HALLAM, *Literature of Europe*, i, p. 5, footnote, 1837.
[2] *Purgatorio*, xi.

thou livest to be old, how, ere a thousand years be passed, will thy fame be more than if thou hadst died a babe; which thousand years yet, to eternity, is a shorter space than the twinkling of an eye.

This shows, incidentally, how much Dante underestimated his own fame. The six hundred years following Dante's death have been no ages of darkness, yet, so far as anything can be predicted, it seems safe to predict that, a thousand years after his birth, Dante's glory will remain undimmed. Dante tells us how he was burdened by thinking of the heavy load of penance which he would have to carry in Purgatory for his pride.[1] For my part, I find myself amazed at his modesty.[2]

But Bede had a humbler mind than Dante. He was an expert in Chronology, and he knew that he was living in the Sixth, and Last, Age of the World. For the first Five Ages, those before Christ, Bede's reckoning did not differ materially from the results arrived at by Archbishop Usher, which are still in the margins of our bibles. These Ages, according to Bede, together covered 3952 years, only fifty-two less than Usher allowed. The last of these five pre-Christian Ages (from the destruction of Solomon's Temple at Jerusalem by Nebuchadnezzar to the Coming of our Lord in the flesh) was the epoch in which, Bede asserted, the world had grown old. The Sixth Age was to stretch from the Incarnation of Christ to the Day of Doom: it was, according to Bede, the age of complete decrepitude, as befitted the epoch which was to end in the destruction of all.[3] Bede deprecated inquiry as to how long this last age of decrepitude would continue; but assuredly he would not, like Dante, have thought in terms of thousands of years. Dante's idea of successive painters, poets, scholars, each surpassing and obscuring the fame of his predecessor, shows how much the outlook of the European spirit had grown since the Dark Age of Bede.

[1] *Purgatorio*, xiii, 136-8. Yet in *Paradiso*, xxx, 131-2, Dante sees but few thrones still unfilled; indicating a brief future for history.

[2] Mr. T. S. Eliot tells me that I am wrong here. It was not Dante's modesty, he says. It was his miscalculation.

[3] Mon. Germ. Hist., *Chronica Minora*, ed. Th. Mommsen, iii, p. 248, Berlin, 1898.

The Dark Age continued for many centuries after Bede, and so Bede, as generation followed generation, had few rivals to fear in the West. George Sarton, in the first volume of his mighty *Introduction to the History of Science*, gives the name of one great man to each half-century of his survey, and, with some hesitation, he names the first half of the eighth century after Bede. 'This was my last chance,' he says, 'in this volume, of giving a Christian title to a chapter.' Not till the great revival which took place after the year 1100 does the West again begin to take the lead. The two half-centuries before Bede, Sarton names after two Chinese travellers. The seven half-centuries after Bede, he names from seven sages of the Moslem world. So that, during a period of 500 years, from A.D. 600 to A.D. 1100, Bede is the only master mind of Christendom whom Sarton thinks worthy of a supreme place.

But though Bede lived in what was, so far as Europe was concerned, a dark age, there is nothing dark about *him*. In the words of W. P. Ker, 'Bede has taken his place through simple strength of mind and character':

> He did not, in his reading or writing, go beyond the sources or the models that were commonly accessible. For all that, the impression he leaves is that of something different from his age, an exceptional talent escaping from limitations and hindrances. There is no period in the history of Britain or of the English Church in which Bede is antiquated; in every generation he speaks familiarly. The seventeenth century is less intelligible to the eighteenth, the eighteenth century more in opposition to the nineteenth, than Bede to any one of them; his good sense is everywhere at home ... The reputation of Bede seems always to have been exempt from the common rationalist criticism, and this although his books are full of the things a Voltairian student objects to.[1]

Ker goes on to speak of matters where Bede is intolerant. Yet he says:

> Like Dr. Johnson's refusal to countenance a Presbyterian church in Scotland, the severity of Bede has been taken

---

[1] *The Dark Ages*, 1904, p. 141.

lightly by the most sensitive, and has failed to make him enemies, even among the fiercest advocates of Christian charity and impartial toleration. It appears to be felt that he is a great man. The volume of his book is too much for carpers and cavillers.

Or, if we may translate the classic periods of 'W.P.' into the vulgarisms of to-day, we may say that even Lytton Strachey would have found it difficult to debunk the Venerable Bede. True, there *is* a volume entitled *The Venerable Bede expurgated, expounded, and exposed*, but the satire of that moderately amusing book is aimed, not at Bede, but at Anglican clergy who dare to claim him as their own.

Therefore, when the Academy did me the honour of asking me to give a lecture on the Master Mind Foundation, and chose Bede as the subject, I could only obey, although with many doubts as to my ability to deal with him. There is something which overawes us, in the contemplation of this unchanging reputation, in a world where everything else seems to be open to challenge and dispute, a challenge of which I, at least, am reminded every time I enter the British Museum Reading Room. All my life, when overcome by the atmosphere of that room, I have been accustomed to get up and walk along the Roman gallery, where the long line of Roman Emperors stood on their polished pedestals, till I finished opposite the bust of Julius Caesar. There, I said to myself, are the features of the foremost man of all this world, fashioned from the life by some master-craftsman of the first century B.C. And I returned refreshed to my work. In accordance with the spirit of our age, the polished pedestals have all been swept away; a sadly diminished line of Emperors now stands, in the Roman gallery, on a shelf reminiscent of a cocktail bar. Julius Caesar has been expelled. He now faces us, as we enter the Reading Room, with an inscription, *Julius Caesar, Ideal portrait of the 18th century. Rome, bought 1818.*

And so he, who insisted that his wife must be above suspicion, now only serves to warn the unsuspicious Englishman against buying sham antiques abroad. There is change and decay in all the galleries of the Museum. No longer can we see the Etruscan lady deliver, with uplifted finger, an everlasting curtain-lecture to her recumbent spouse. I believe that after the night watchman has done his rounds, from one monument of Antiquity to another, there passes

A timid voice, that asks in whispers
'Who next will drop and disappear?'

Yet there *are* works of art in the Museum which have nothing to fear from any hostile critic; and two supreme ones have a special bearing on the Age of Bede. The Chinese pottery statue of a Buddhist apostle sits in the centre of the King Edward VII Gallery, rather more than life-size. In his grand simplicity, utterly remote from all earthly affairs, the apostle gazes into eternity. If our art-critics are right in their dates, he shows us what the Far East could do in the Age of Bede. He serves as a symbol to remind us once again that the darkest period of Western civilization coincides with the glories of the T'ang dynasty in China. Dynasties might have changed, and empires fallen, and the meditations of the Chinese sage, from whom that portrait was modelled (for a portrait it must assuredly be), would have been as little disturbed thereby as have been the features of his porcelain image. Like the sage of Bacon's New Atlantis, he has an aspect as though he pitied men. He belongs, we are told, to an age when inspiration was fresh, and Chinese Buddhist art young and virile.

The other great monument of the Age of Bede in the British Museum we can date exactly. It, again, is a monument of a young and virile art. It is the Lindisfarne Book, made on Holy Island by Bede's friend Eadfirth. The Lindisfarne Book is apparently the first great surviving masterpiece of the school to which it belongs. Its perfection has so surprised one eminent Celtic expert[1] that he has persuaded himself that the book was really written about 120 years later (and, of course, in Ireland), shortly after which it fell into English hands, 'doubtless by

[1] Prof. R. A. S. MACALISTER, in *Essays and Studies presented to William Ridgeway*, Cambridge, 1913.

some nefarious means'. But the Celtic expert forgot that the Lindisfarne Book is not only a masterpiece of design. It is a text of the Latin gospels, and, as such, has a very definite textual history; it has a liturgical history likewise, and these make it clear that the inscription which the Lindisfarne Book bears is not to be disputed, when it says that the book was written by Eadfirth, Bishop of Lindisfarne, in honour of God and St. Cuthbert. Eadfirth also showed his veneration for St. Cuthbert by causing a Latin life to be made by some anonymous writer. Not satisfied with this, he asked Bede to write a second *Life*. Bede did so, and revised it carefully, after conference with those who had known the Saint. He then so far departed from his usual custom of seclusion within his own monasteries of Monkwearmouth and Jarrow, that he himself took the *Life* to Lindisfarne, some fifty miles away. There, for two days, it was diligently scrutinized by the brethren. They could find no fault in it, and Bede dedicated it to Eadfirth.

At the time when Bede visited Holy Island, Bishop Eadfirth had probably finished his long task of writing and illuminating the Lindisfarne Book.[1] It seems unlikely that, when Bede brought to Lindisfarne his tribute to St. Cuthbert, the Bishop would have failed in return to show Bede *his* tribute. So we may think that Bede and the Bishop bent their tonsured heads over the leaves of the Lindisfarne Book, and followed the intricate subtleties of the ornamentation, so delicate that the eye can scarcely trace them, and that we wonder how any brain devised them.

The figure of the Buddhist apostle and the designs of the Lindisfarne Book are both, in their way, as near perfection as work of man can be. Compared with the Chinese apostle the Lindisfarne Book belongs to a primitive — almost barbaric — culture. But it is the most beautiful thing the West could do in that age, just as Bede is the greatest product of the West in knowledge. When we think of this meeting, in a humble shack on Holy Island, of the greatest scholar and the greatest

[1] In the *De temporum ratione* (725) Bede speaks of having written the prose *Life of St. Cuthbert* recently (*nuper*). This seems to preclude a date much earlier than about 720 for Bede's visit to Holy Island. And Eadfirth died in 721.

artist of the West, we may ask, How did it come that one small English district produced both?

Bede, the scholar, following knowledge, Eadfirth, the craftsman, creating beauty, Cuthbert, the saint, seeking God, were all alive together, pursuing their quest in one remote corner of England.

How did it come, that just when learning and civilization seemed to be dying out on the continent of Western Europe, they flourished among the Celts of Ireland and the Angles, Saxons, and Jutes of England — tribes who had never before known Roman discipline or Greek learning? Whilst Bede as Chronologist was conscious of living in the last, final age of the world, Bede as Geographer was equally conscious of living in the last, uttermost regions. He speaks of Ireland and Britain as the two remotest isles of the ocean.[1] Like his abbot, Ceolfrid, he felt that he was living 'in the extreme limits'. How did this monastery on the outskirts become the refuge, not only of the English spirit, but also of the European spirit, in the eighth century?

Two centuries before, under the magnanimous rule of Theodoric, Italy had still been the centre of Western culture. It was in Italy that Boethius, Cassiodorus, and St. Benedict had planted, amid the ruins of the Roman world, the beginnings of a new world which was to exceed the old in glory. These Italians were the Founders of the Middle Ages. And even in Britain there had been a temporary rally of Christian and Roman civilization; at Mount Badon the harassed Roman-Britons enjoyed that brief taste of victory, the distant reverberations of which have echoed through the ages in the stories of King Arthur and his knights. But the sixth century, despite its fair beginning, closed in disaster for the Roman world. When Gregory the Great died, the Lombards had been devastating Italy for a generation. From the walls of Rome, Gregory had to watch the 'unutterable Lombards' driving rows of captured Romans over the Campagna, on their way to slavery among the Franks. Yet Pope Gregory had such pity for the barbarian

---

[1] *Ecclesiastical History*, iii, 25. (A speech placed in the mouth of Wilfrid, at the Council of Whitby.)

world outside those walls that he dispatched St. Augustine on his mission to England. Like Columbus later, Gregory little realized what he was doing. Gregory merely hoped to snatch a few more souls from perdition before the Coming of Antichrist and the Day of Doom ended an unfortunate business which, thanks to Adam and Eve, the Serpent and the apple, had gone wrong from the first. For, as he explained in his letter to King Ethelbert of Kent, the end of the world was approaching, and would shortly be upon us.[1]

Yet, in reality, Pope Gregory was 'calling in a new world to redress the balance of the old'.

For, at the moment, civilization had little chance in Romanized Western Europe. The conquering barbarians were quarrelling over the loot of the Roman Empire till they lost whatever barbaric virtues they had formerly possessed when they lived in the more austere surroundings of their native forests and swamps. A good idea of life in Western Europe can be drawn from the two historians who are nearest in date to Bede, Gregory of Tours for the *History of the Franks*, and Paul the Deacon for the *History of the Lombards*.

What the ruling Frankish kings and queens were like we may gather from the way in which Queen Fredegund suppressed her naughty daughter Rigunth. Growing tired of the impertinences of her daughter, Fredegund invited her to share the crown jewels, which were kept in a huge chest. She handed out one after another, and at length, pretending to be tired, she said, 'Take them out for yourself, my dear.' The daughter put her arm into the chest, and the mother brought down the lid with all her might upon the head of her unruly offspring, and pressed her throat against the edge of the chest, till her daughter's eyes were starting out of her head. The murder was prevented by a handmaid calling for help: 'Her Royal Highness the Queen is suffocating Her Royal Highness the Princess.'[2] This is not an unfair example of the manners and morals of the reigning house in Merovingian France, though there were exceptions like the worthy King Guntram, 'whose memory is stained by only one or two murders'.

[1] *Ecclesiastical History*, i, 32.   [2] *History of the Franks*, ix, 34.

Paul's *History of the Lombards* is not as sordid as Gregory's *History of the Franks*. The Lombards had a certain rough chivalry, but they were altogether barbarous. Alboin, their king, slew the king of a rival Teutonic tribe, the Gepids, and made a drinking-cup of his skull. With typical inconsequence he also wedded Rosamund, the daughter of the king he had slain. The queen managed to avert her eyes from the gruesome table ornament, and all went well for a time. But it befell on a day that Alboin sat at the banquet longer than was proper, and filling the cup with wine, bade his cup-bearer carry it to the queen and tell her to drink with her father.[1] That was more than Queen Rosamund could stand, and Alboin's reign ended suddenly in 572 or 573. He was succeeded by other Lombard rulers, equally barbarous and less picturesque.

Even before the barbarians had gained such complete mastery, the Roman world had been oppressed by a sense of its age. A fifth-century historian tells us that 'Rome is falling more from the weakness of age than from external violence'.[2] What must the depression have become when Romans had to flatter masters like Alboin and mistresses like Fredegund? The only way of escape was the way of complete renunciation. Gregory of Tours[3] tells of a recluse who ate nothing but bread (upon which he condescended to put a little salt), who drank only water (which, however, he allowed himself to sweeten with a little honey), who never slept, ceasing from prayer only to read or write, and who perpetually wore a hair shirt. Such a man was likely to get the reputation of working miracles. And, miracles or no, he dominated his surroundings: he was respected, and feared, by Roman and barbarian, by good and bad alike. Yet the path of complete renunciation is too difficult for many men and women to follow, and the barbarians who overran the Roman Empire found that most Christians were not like that. Therefore the mingling of barbarian and Roman within the Roman Empire resulted in that degradation which often follows when two different cultures and languages are violently brought together. Each nation finds that the task of

---

[1] *History of the Lombards*, ii, 28.   [2] Orosius, ed. Zangemeister, II, vi, 14.
[3] *History of the Franks*, v, 5 (10).

learning from the others their irregular manners is easier than that of learning their irregular verbs, and generations pass before either morality or grammar becomes stabilized again.

That accounts for the superiority, both in its grammar and its subject matter, of Bede's *Ecclesiastical History of the English People* over Gregory's *History of the Franks*. For when Romanized Christians went forth to convert Irish or English in their own homes, they found conditions very different from those within the decaying Roman world. The missionaries encountered barbarians living according to the standard which their ancestors had followed for hundreds, perhaps thousands, of years. The barbarians had established themselves in Britain by massacre; they had reduced to serfdom and subjection most of the original inhabitants whom they had not killed. But they were *not* a mere effete aristocracy, living amid the loot of an alien civilization destined ultimately to absorb them. It is true that there were in England some small remains of Roman civilization, and that those remains were useful to the missionaries. But the point is that the Christian evangelists found the native Teutonic culture intact. And on their side the missionaries who came among the heathen English were chosen men, trained in saintliness or obedience. No others would have undertaken so thankless a task. Also, they were often men of learning. Here, then, Roman, Celt, and Teuton, Christian and Heathen, met, each at his best. And there were things in the new Christian teaching which harmonized with the Germanic heroic traditions.

The essential virtue of the Old Germanic system was loyalty, as, of course, it often is where life is organized on the basis of a tribe or clan, to whose welfare the chief is vital. The chief surrounded himself with a band of young companions who were pledged to live and die with him. It was a lifelong disgrace, Tacitus tells us, for the companion to return alive from the field on which his lord had fallen. This loyalty to a person was the bond of Germanic civilization; not the Roman or Greek conception of loyalty to a community: not 'The Republic', but 'My Chief'.

Abstract conceptions of Theology or Philosophy would have

been difficult for the primitive English to grasp. But they were ready to listen to the story of 'the young hero, that was God Almighty, strong and stout of heart'. Let us remember the deep words of St. Augustine in the *Confessions*, where he tells how he found certain books of the Platonists, 'and therein I read, not indeed in those words, but with that meaning: "In the beginning was the Word, and the Word was with God, and the Word was God." . . . *But that the Word was made Flesh, and dwelt among us, that I read not there.*'[1]

Whilst all traditions in Western Europe seemed in danger of breaking down, these two traditions of loyalty to Christ and loyalty to the chief fortified each other, whenever the chief became a true Christian convert. Such men can only have been few in number, amid the masses of superstitious heathen, and equally superstitious Christians. But they were the men who mattered.

It was the great good fortune of Bede to be born into a society, in the first freshness of its conversion, which understood those two personal loyalties. The glory of it lasted only for a generation — but Bede caught it before it perished, and enshrined it in his *Ecclesiastical History*, to endure as long as the story of England endures. The *Ecclesiastical History* is the greatest, but not the only, expression of it. In the Old English poem, *The Dream of the Rood* (which certainly belongs to the age of Bede), we have a perfect fusion of the loyalty of the Germanic companion to his lord, and the loyalty of the Christian to Christ, and the mystery of a creation groaning and travailing in pain at the foot of the Cross; not the historic cross of Calvary, but a marvel beyond man's understanding. And all this in the style, phraseology, and metre of Germanic heathen heroic poetry, familiar to the companions as they drank beer in the lord's hall at night. We know that Bede was skilled in English poetry, and the English verses which he composed on his death-bed have survived. Bede tells in the *Ecclesiastical History* how Cædmon first combined Christian teaching with the style of the old heathen lays; Bede's elder contemporary and fellow in learning, Aldhelm, did the same in the south of England;

[1] vii, 9.

and *Beowulf*, with many another Old English poem, remains as a monument of the fusion.

It was the same combination of loyalties which had led, some years after Bede's birth, to the foundation of the monastery in which he was to work, and without which he would not have been the man he was. There was among the retinue of King Oswy of Bernicia a certain young noble named Biscop. Biscop must have seen a good deal of hard fighting in the early days of his king. When Biscop was twenty-five, Oswy offered him an estate on which he might marry and settle down — just as Hygelac did to Beowulf after he had slain Grendel. It was the usual reward to a young warrior who had proved his worth, and was entitled to pass from the *geoguth*, the young companions, to the *duguth*, the veterans. But, instead, Biscop abandoned the world, went on the pilgrimage to Rome, and set himself to learn all that a monk should know. He sojourned altogether in seventeen monasteries at different times of his life, 'committing to memory whatever he found most profitable in each'. Biscop, who had taken the name Benedict after the founder of the monastic rule which he followed, at length returned to Northumbria, and King Ecgfrid (son of Oswy) gave him a large estate upon which he founded the monastery of Monkwearmouth. The monastery was about five years old when Bede, a boy of seven, entered it. For a dozen years Biscop was Bede's teacher and master. When Ecgfrid gave Biscop a further grant of land, upon which he founded the monastery of Jarrow, the young Bede was transferred there.

Biscop made his monasteries centres of art and learning. He journeyed five times from England to Rome, every time bringing back many books and works of art. Biscop imported builders and glaziers from France, but, as anyone realizes who examines what is left to-day, his buildings were minute if compared with the great structures of later monasticism. In their simplicity, the remains of Biscop's building remind us of the earliest Franciscan sanctuaries. A small church was surrounded by the small huts or cells of the brethren. There were many brethren: by the middle of Bede's life he tells us that there were about six hundred in the two monasteries.

The terrible mortality when the plague fell on these communities shows how unhealthy they must have been. But treasures like the Codex Amiatinus and the Lindisfarne Book survive to show also that no labour was spared in order to make their equipment beautiful.

All this helps us to understand how, in the seventh century, Christian civilization found a refuge in Northumbria. There was the background of the primitive warrior life, not much altered from what it had been in the days of the *Germania* of Tacitus. That was the soldierly education which men like Biscop or Eostorwine received till they were twenty-four or twenty-five. To these still uncorrupted barbarians came Celtic missionaries of the type of the saintly Aidan. Most important of all, the Roman missionaries brought the ordered life of the Benedictine rule.

And so the tone of Bede's *Ecclesiastical History* is altogether different from that of Gregory's *History of the Franks* or Paul's *History of the Lombards*. The tale of Oswin of Deira, which I am going to read from Bede is typical of Bede's *History*, just as the tales of Fredegund half-strangling her daughter Rigunth, or Rosamund contriving the death of her husband Alboin, are typical of the continental histories.

I give the passage in the beautiful English of an Elizabethan exile. He translated *The History of the Church of England, compiled by Venerable Bede, Englishman*, in the conviction that, though a recusant refugee, he was preserving the true English tradition.

King Oswin was of countenance beautiful, of stature high, in talk courteous and gentle, in all points civil and amiable: no less honourable and bountiful to the noble, than free and liberal to persons of low degree. Whereby it happened, that for his outward personage, inward heart, and princely port, he had the love of all men. Especially the nobility of all countries frequented his court, and coveted to be received in his service.

Among other his rare virtues, and princely qualities, his humility and passing lowliness excelled. Whereof we will be contented to recite one most worthy example.

He had given to Bishop Aidan a very fair and proper gelding, which that virtuous bishop (though he used most to travel on foot) might use to pass over waters and ditches, or when any other necessity constrained. It fortuned shortly after, a certain poor weak man met the bishop, and craved an alms of him. The bishop, as he was a passing pitiful man, and a very father to needy persons, lighted off, and gave the poor man the gelding, gorgeously trapped as it was.

The king hearing after hereof, talked of it with the bishop, as they were entering the palace to dinner, and said, 'What meant you, my lord, to give away to the beggar that fair gelding, which we gave you for your own use? Have we no other horses of less price, and other kinds of rewards to bestow upon the poor, but that you must give away that princely horse, which we gave you for your own riding?' To whom the bishop answered, 'Why talketh your grace thus? Is that son of a mare dearer in your sight than that son of God?'

Which being said, they entered for to dine. The bishop took his place appointed, but the king, coming then from hunting, would stand a while by the fire to warm him. Where standing, and musing with himself upon the words which the bishop had spoken unto him, suddenly he put off his sword, giving it to his servant, and came in great haste to the bishop: falling down at his feet, and beseeching him not to be displeased with him for the words he had spoken unto him, saying he would never more speak of it, nor measure any more hereafter what or how much the bishop should bestow of his goods upon the sons of God.

At which sight the bishop, being much astonied, arose suddenly and lifted up the king, telling him that he should quickly be pleased, if it would please him to sit down, and cast away all heaviness.

Afterward, the king being at the bishop's request merry, the bishop contrariwise began to be heavy and sorry; in such sort, that the tears trickled down by his cheeks. Of whom, when his chaplain in his mother tongue (which the king and his court understood not) had demanded why he wept: 'I know,' said he, 'that the king shall not live long. For never before this time have I seen an humble king.

¹ They were both, of course, of Irish stock.

37

Whereby I perceive, that he shall speedily be taken out of this life: for this people is not worthy to have such a prince and governor.'

Shortly after, the bishop's dreadful abodement was fulfilled, with the king's cruel death, as we have before declared. Bishop Aidan himself also was taken away out of this world, and received of God the everlasting rewards of his labours, even on the twelfth day after the king, whom he so much loved, was slain.[1]

Bede's life shows what a fine thing Benedictine monasticism could be in early eighth-century England. But the words which Dante puts into the mouth of St. Benedict in Paradise were to prove true: 'So easily seduced is mortal flesh, that a good beginning on earth lasts not so long as the time between the first springing up of an oak, and its bearing an acorn.'[2] When Bede was a boy of twelve or thirteen the reckless aggression of King Ecgfrid ruined the Northumbrian kingdom. The anonymous *Life of St. Cuthbert* tells how Ecgfrid was ravaging the land of the Picts in the far north, and his queen, attended by St. Cuthbert, was awaiting the issue of the war in the city of Carlisle. The governor of the city was showing them an old Roman fountain constructed in wondrous wise, when Cuthbert exclaimed, 'Oh, Oh, Oh, I deem that the war is finished, and that judgment has been pronounced against our soldiers in their warfare. Oh my children, consider how beyond scrutiny are the judgments of God.' In a few days came the news of the death of Ecgfrid and all his army at Nechtansmere. From this defeat Bede at a later period dated Northumbrian decay: 'The prowess of the dominion of the English began to ebb and recede.' The year after the death of Ecgfrid came the visitation of plague, which carried away from the monastery of Jarrow all who could read, or preach, or recite the antiphons, except Ceolfrid the abbot, and one small lad, nourished and taught by him. In the anonymous *History of the Abbots* the moving story is told of how the abbot and the lad carried on the services

---

[1] From the translation of the *Ecclesiastical History*, by Thomas Stapleton, 1565, Book III, cap. 14, revised. The writing of 'Oswiu' for 'Oswin', and other minor inaccuracies, have been corrected.

[2] *Paradiso*, xxii, 85-7.

unaided. The small lad was certainly[1] Bede himself. I mention these anonymous historical works because, with Eddi's *Life of Wilfrid*, they show us that there was already a school of historical writing in Northumbria before Bede produced his masterpiece.

It has been said that, 'some day, scandal mongers and disintegrating critics may become aware that they have produced most accurate autobiographies'.[2] In his *History* and in his *Lives of the Abbots* Bede has, unconsciously, written his own autobiography. But it adds to our understanding of his character when we realize that Bede's world had already begun to decay when he was a boy of thirteen. Although for another twenty years King Aldfrid ruled the defeated Northumbrian realm competently within its narrower boundaries, after his death, which took place when Bede was about thirty-three, the state of Northumbria became deplorable. Bede's enormous labours were carried on amid a general decline of Northumbrian civilization. Yet Bede only occasionally refers to the decadence of his age. It was not till the last year of his life that Bede spoke out. A young man of royal birth, probably a pupil of his own, Egbert, had just been appointed Archbishop of York. In a letter of advice to him, Bede deals fully with the abuses which had grown in the thirty troubled years since the death of Aldfrid. He is particularly shocked at the bogus monasteries which were everywhere springing up, filled by pseudo-monks whose only object was to avoid military duties and to live in idleness. Bede is for drastic remedies. Even monasteries of professed monks ought to be dissolved or converted if the monks do not live according to their vows:

And because there are very many places of this kind which, as the common saying is, are useful to neither God nor man, because neither is the religious life observed in them, according to the law of God, nor do they have in them

[1] Bede was nourished and taught at Jarrow by Ceolfrid. If only one trained lad was left there, it can only have been Bede.
[2] RAND, *Founders of the Middle Ages*, p. 73. Prof. Rand's book places under a great debt all who are interested in the continuity of civilization, and more particularly the transition from Classical times to the Dark Ages.

soldiers or thanes of the secular powers to defend our people from the barbarians; if any one were to turn such monasteries into bishoprics, he would be doing a virtuous act. Your Holiness, with the help of the devout king of our nation, ought to tear in pieces the unrighteous charters of former princes, and to provide things useful to our country, lest either religion die out in our day, or else the number of our armed men diminishes, so that there are none left to defend our borders from barbarian invasion.

Bede complains that monasteries have grown so numerous that there are no lands upon which time-expired soldiers can be settled. Such soldiers are compelled either to emigrate over-sea, leaving their native land unprotected, or else to live idle and unmarried, growing more and more demoralized.

But, even worse than these many monasteries of unworthy monks, says Bede, are the sham monasteries of laymen, who escape their secular duties without even making any attempt to live the monastic life. [1]

The young archbishop was not able to carry through all the reforms which Bede desired; but he founded the Cathedral school at York and taught in it. It was an epoch-making act — for thereby he passed on the learning of his friend and master, Bede, to his friend and scholar, Alcuin, and through him to the Carolingians and the Middle Ages.

Bede was already ill when he wrote the letter to Egbert — it has been called his swan-song. For eight weeks before his death he was weak, breathing with difficulty, though without much pain. He continued his routine life of teaching, thanks-giving, singing of psalms and antiphons, and he made a small poem in English ('for he was learned in our native poetry'). He dictated part of a translation of St. John's Gospel, and some extracts from Bishop Isidore, 'for he said, I do not want my boys to read a lie, or labour in vain after I am gone'. On the Tuesday before Ascension Day his breathing became much more difficult; yet he continued to dictate, urging his disciples to 'learn speedily'. On the Wednesday, at the ninth hour,

[1] *Epistle to Egbert*, 11, 12.

he had reached the last chapter of the task he had set himself. Then he summoned the priests of the monastery, to distribute among them 'such gifts as God has given me'.

Bede's closing days remind us of those of Richard Hooker: 'Are my books and written papers safe? No other loss can trouble me.' But Bede the monk possessed no private books; his parting gifts to his friends were 'some pepper, napkins, and incense'. It is one of the stories which can never grow hackneyed, how, having distributed these possessions, Bede passed the day in gladness till evening, and dictated to the scribe the last sentence remaining to be written. To the boy's words that it was finished he replied, 'Thou hast spoken truth, it is finished,' and after saying, 'it much pleases me to sit opposite my holy place, where I was wont to pray', he repeated the doxology, and died.

From the time when Benedict Biscop, in or about 653, made his decision to abandon the world, and to become a monk, to the death of Bede in 735 — in these 82 years the two men had done a work which was to leave its mark for ever on civilization. It had come to pass that learning, dying or dead throughout Western Europe, found a new home in Canterbury and York, and on the banks of Wear and Tyne. At Monkwearmouth and Jarrow, Abbot Ceolfrid caused stately manuscripts to be made: one of these he carried with him on that pilgrimage to Rome which he was destined never to complete. This manuscript remains to-day a principal treasure of the great Laurentian library at Florence. This gift, intended for St. Peter's at Rome, as its dedication stated, by 'Ceolfrid, an abbot from the extreme limits of thé English', is typical of the movement of scholarship. England and Ireland were too remote from the centre of things to retain for ever the honour of being the homes of European learning. But English and Irish learning did not decay till the torch had been passed on to the great Continental schools.

It is small wonder that King Alfred looked back upon this age with regret: an age 'when men came from abroad to England in search of wisdom and learning: and now we have to search for wisdom and learning abroad'.

Bede may not be as great a historian as Thucydides, but the events which he records have been more important to the world than the issue of the Peloponnesian war. His subject — the *Ecclesiastical History of the English People* — is the bringing back of Britain into the community of civilized nations. Everywhere else Christendom was giving way. It is interesting to parallel the triumphs which form the subject of Bede's *History* with the losses which were taking place elsewhere. The reign of Bede's greatest hero, the pious Oswald (634-42), almost coincides with that of the Caliph Omar (634-44). Northumbria was won back for Christendom exactly when Syria, Palestine and Egypt were lost: we have the gain of York to set against the loss of Damascus, Jerusalem and Alexandria. Within a year of the birth of Bede, the Saracens had reached the gates of Constantinople: in the same year Archbishop Theodore held at Hertford that first meeting of the united English Church which constitutes the first national act of a united England. Bede was a young deacon when Africa was lost to Christendom, and the Mediterranean ceased to be the central sea of the Christian world: the contemporary event which fell to Bede to record is the conversion of the Frisians and Continental Saxons by English missionaries: a little before Carthage was taken by the Saracens the Northumbrian Willibrord had been consecrated at Rome the first Archbishop of Utrecht. Bede was in middle life when Spain was overrun by the Moslems: just at that time Abbot Ceolfrid, Bede's chief, was sending architects and scholars that the rude Picts might be edified, and, as Bede records, brought into the custom of the Holy Roman Apostolic Church. When Bede was finishing his *History*, the Saracens had reached the centre of France. Then came the turn of the tide. At the end of his story, a year after it was finished, Bede inserted what seems to be a reference to the great victory of Charles Martel over the Saracens, which saved France from utter devastation.

There is something very appropriate in this final reference. Bede taught Egbert, and Egbert taught Alcuin, so we may regard Alcuin as Bede's spiritual grandson. Bede's spiritual grandson was to serve the grandson of Charles Martel in the

re-establishment of learning in Europe. With Charles the Great
the period of the Darkness is over: Civilization is once again
slowly marching forward.

The Saracens too had *their* civilization, which was destined
to outshine that of Christendom for generations to come.
But the civilization which began in Palestine and Greece, and
of which our civilization is the continuation, is, as Cardinal
Newman boldly claimed, 'so distinctive and luminous in its
character, so imperial in its extent, so imposing in its duration,
and so utterly without rival on the face of the earth', that we
may give to it 'the abstract term Civilization'. There are some
of us who, in spite of the depression which has set in since the
end of the War, have enough of Mid-Victorian confidence and
optimism still to share Newman's view. To us, then, the
seventh century must be the era when two-thirds of the
Mediterranean coast lands were lost to Civilization, and when
the coast of the North Sea was won. The full effect of the change
was not obvious for many ages. But the distribution of European culture, the centre of gravity of the civilized world, had
been altered; with the result that Civilization ceased to be
thalassic and became oceanic.

It is satisfactory to know that Bede lived to rejoice over the
news of the great victory of Charles Martel at Tours, and to
record how the Saracens had incurred the just judgment of
God for devastating Gaul; though he could not know how
epoch-making that judgment was to prove. Many years
before, Bede had lamented that these sons of Ishmael, the
Saracens, of old had dwelt in the desert, but now, 'the hated
foes of all, with their hands against every man, and every
man's hand against them, they are holding under their rule
Africa from one end to the other, most of Asia, and part of
Europe'. But it was his pleasanter task to tell of the victories
of the Cross in England: and there is no tale in the whole of
English history of which we should be so proud. Further,
Bede's manner of telling this story is beyond all praise. He
begins by giving an account of his authorities and sources of
information — a practice which marks an epoch in the scientific
writing of history. Bede is the father of English History, and

we must reckon with him if we want to understand the origins of our own civilization.

The conversion of England had its immediate repercussion abroad in the amazing missionary efforts of the Englishmen, Willibrord and Boniface and their companions, among the heathen German tribes of the Continent, which first changed the face of Germany, and then had such influence upon Gaul as to make possible the Carolingian Renaissance. It is remarkable how constantly the missionaries write back to England for the works of Bede:

> We, labouring to plant the seeds of the Gospel among the wild and ignorant Germans, beg you to send us something of the writings of Bede the monk, who of late was shining among you like a lantern, with knowledge of the Scriptures. And if you could send us a bell also, it would be a great comfort to us in our exile.[1]

Or

> We beg that you will comfort us by doing as you have done before, by sending us some ray from that lantern of the Church enlightened by the Holy Spirit in your land — Bede. And we are sending by the bearer two small vats of wine, that you may have a day of joy with your monks.[2]

Or

> I beg that you will send us, for a comfort in our exile, any one of these works, which Bede the priest of blessed memory wrote. [A list follows.] I am asking much, but it will not seem much to your charity.[3]

Or

> I am sick, and like to leave this vale of tears. I beg, as a consolation both of my exile and my illness, for the books of Bede of blessed memory on the building of the Temple, or on the Song of Songs, or his epigrams in heroic or elegiac verse — all, if possible, but, if not, the three books on the

---

[1] Boniface to Huetberht, Abbot of Wearmouth and Jarrow; JAFFÉ, *Monumenta Moguntina*, 180.
[2] Boniface to Egbert, Archbishop of York; JAFFÉ, *Mon. Mog.*, 250.
[3] Lull to the Archbishop of York; JAFFÉ, *Mon. Mog.*, 288.

building of the Temple. Perhaps what I ask is difficult, but I think nothing will be difficult to your charity.[1]

Such is the constant appeal of the missionaries, Boniface, Lull, and the rest, writing home to the abbots of Monkwearmouth and to Egbert at York. The English ecclesiastics do what they can to supply the need — the abbot of Monkwearmouth laments that he cannot send more of Bede's writings: he has put his boys to work, but it has been a horrible winter, with cold and frost and storms, which have numbed the hand of the writer.[2]

It is thanks to the labours of Boniface and Alcuin, and the inspiration of Bede, that discipline and learning were re-established on the Continent. In England the worst time had still to come, when the whole country was harried by the Vikings, but on the Continent learning, however depressed, never sank again as low as it had done before Bede, and those whom he inspired, began their labours.

When, at the end of the ninth century, King Alfred had at last checked the Viking raids in England, one of the works he promoted was the translation of Bede's *History* into English. England, therefore, was the first of the nations of Western Europe to have a great history written in the vernacular. But the book was multiplied much more frequently in Latin, and William of Malmesbury looked back to the *Ecclesiastical History* as a model when, four centuries after Bede's time, he re-established in England Bede's tradition of Latin historiography.

How great had been the popularity of Bede's *History*, during the period which intervenes between Bede and William of Malmesbury, is proved by the large number of early manuscripts which have survived, despite all the destruction wrought by Vikings and others. Two of these earliest manuscripts contain chronological notes, which enable us to date them. The oldest, which was written on the Continent, though it is now at Cambridge, was made within some two years of Bede's death.

---

[1] Lull to Cuthbert, Abbot of Wearmouth and Jarrow; JAFFÉ, *Mon. Mog.*, 289.

[2] Cuthbert to Lull, JAFFÉ, *Mon. Mog.*, 300. Cuthbert is, of course, the man who, at an earlier date, had been present at Bede's death, and has left us the account of it summarized above (pp. 40-1).

The second oldest, written within eleven years of Bede's death, was once at Corbie, and is now in Leningrad.[1] It has been generally overlooked, and is not mentioned either by Plummer or Dr. James. Yet it would seem to be of great importance.

Nowadays the medieval veneration of saints' relics is being revived, and the uncorrupted body of Lenin is worshipped by crowds of pilgrims in Moscow, just as that of Cuthbert was of old revered in Lindisfarne and Durham. Could not the trade in relics also be resuscitated? Our Government might then acquire the Leningrad manuscript for the British Museum, in exchange for the bones of Karl Marx, now resting in Highgate Cemetery.

The Durham library claimed, in the Middle Ages, to have four manuscripts written by the hand of Bede. Three of these are still extant, in whole or in part. They are early, but the writing shows too much variation to permit of their being all from the same hand.[2]

In time, Bede's reputation grew mythical. He was supposed to have visited Rome in order to give the *Curia* the benefit of his scholarship. The University of Paris was convulsed by a dispute between Picard and English students, the Englishmen claiming priority on the ground that Bede had founded the University. Pope Martin V is alleged to have sent a legate to allay the quarrel. The legate is alleged to have allowed the English claim, agreeing that Bede, on his way to Rome, *had* stopped at Paris and founded the University there.[3] The

---

[1] See O. D. ROJDESTVENSKY in *Speculum*, iii, 314-21; E. A. LOWE, *English Historical Review*, xli, 244-6.

[2] See article by DR. MONTAGUE R. JAMES in *Bede: Essays in Commemoration, edited by A. Hamilton Thompson*, 1935, p. 235. Dr. James enumerates the following as extant in whole or in part:

(1) *The Gospels;* Durham, A. ii. 16: there is also a small slip in the Pepysian library, Magdalene College, Camb.

(2) *Epistles of Paul, glossed;* Trin. Coll., Camb., B. 10. 5: there is also a fragment in the British Museum, Cotton Vitellius C. viii.

(3) Cassiodorus *On the Psalter;* Durham, B. ii. 33.

Dr. James thinks (2) and (3) better claimants than (1).

[3] CÉSAR ÉGASSE DU BOULAY, *Historia Universitatis Parisiensis*, Parisiis, 1665, i, 113. Rashdall has described Du Boulay as 'perhaps the stupidest man who ever wrote a valuable book' (*Universities of Europe*, 1895, i, p. 271).

University of Cambridge also claimed Bede, and Fuller, though he obviously did not believe the claim, did not like to contradict it:

> Some report that Bede never went out of his cell, but lived and died therein. If so, the scholars of Cambridge will be very sorry, because thereby deprived of their honour, by Bede's living once in their University, whose house they still show, between St. John's College and the Round Church or St. Sepulchre's. Surely Bede was not fixed to his cell, as the cockle to his shell.[1]

Dante saw Bede in Heaven;[2] he also reproached the Cardinals for not studying their Bede as they should. When printing was introduced, the rapidity with which Bede's *History* was printed testifies to its continued popularity. At the Reformation Bede continued in favour with both sides. As an early translator of the Bible, he was applauded by the Wiclifites: and his knowledge of the Scriptures won him the praise of John Foxe, the martyrologist. Bede's characteristic apology for his writings, that at least they had kept him from doing worse things, is reproduced by Foxe:

> As touching the holiness and integrity of his life, it is not to be doubted: for how could it be, that he should attend to any vicious idleness, or had any leisure to the same, who, in reading and digesting so many volumes, consumed all his whole cogitations in writing upon the Scriptures? For so he testifieth of himself in the third book of Samuel, saying in these words: 'If my treatises and expositions', saith he, 'bring with them no other utility to the readers thereof; yet to myself they conduce not a little thus: that while all my study and cogitation was set upon them, in the meanwhile, of slippery enticements and vain cogitations of this world I had little mind.'

On the other hand, Bede, as a strenuous defender of the Roman allegiance and practice, was applauded by the Catholics. Thomas Stapleton, the Roman Catholic controversialist, translated the *Ecclesiastical History* into English, and dedicated

---

[1] FULLER, *Church History*, 1655, Cent. viii, p. 98.   [2] *Paradiso*, x, 131.
[3] *Acts and Monuments*, ed. Townsend and Cattley, i, 364-5.

it to Elizabeth, in the pathetic hope that it might convert her. Stapleton's translation, revised, is the one I have used in this lecture. It needs revision. Bede, for example, had recorded how Edwin of Northumbria provided for the needs of his subjects: where there were springs by the highway, he planted wooden stakes with metal cups attached to them, for the refreshing of wayfarers. In Stapleton the cups become great brazen basons to bathe in, and the stakes become quick-set bowers, planted around in the interests of propriety.[1]

To be simultaneously applauded by Foxe and Stapleton was a triumph, and is characteristic of Bede's wide appeal. We are driven back to the judgment of W. P. Ker: Bede's good sense is everywhere at home.

Bede is an ascetic, but with good sense: his asceticism was unlike that of the Egyptian hermit of whom St. Jerome tells us, who lived in an old cistern upon five rush-stalks a day.[2] We have seen that Bede's life of self-denial allowed him to keep a few treasures in his casket; albeit some pepper, some napkins, and some incense was all which the greatest scholar of his age thought fit to accumulate in a lifetime.

Self-denial and heroism are sacred things to Bede — whether in a King Oswald fighting for justice and righteousness, or in a soldier like Lilla throwing his body between his king and the sword of the enemy, or in monks like Cuthbert or Chad.

But it is characteristic of Bede that he, the historian of the earliest English monasticism and its great example, is also the earliest great advocate of the dissolution of monasteries. For those who entered monasteries in order to escape their civil or military duties (yet without submitting to the even more rigorous discipline incumbent upon the good monk) Bede, as we have seen, has complete contempt. 'The result of this', he wrote, 'the next age will see.'[3] The next age *did* see it, amid the

---

[1] ii, 16.

[2] RAND, *Founders of the Middle Ages*, p. 122. But *was* it rush-stalks? The text in MIGNE's *Patrologia*, xxiii. 5, runs *quinque caricis per singulos dies sustentabatur*. This would make it five dried figs per day—a meagre diet, to be sure, but, considering the rations of Egyptian hermits, too nutritious, one would think, to justify Jerome's expressions of extreme amazement. So I think it must have been rush-stalks.

[3] *Ecclesiastical History*, v, 23.

complete downfall of Northumbrian civilization. Bede's influence continued, a link between ancient and modern times. But it continued outside the limits of his beloved Northumbria, which lay in ruins.

Yet although Bede's main function was to connect Classical times with the Middle Ages, to help to bridge the gap between the end of the sixth century and the beginning of the twelfth, we must remember that what he passed on was not information, but the spirit of freshness in worship, in learning, and in teaching. 'Spending all my life in my monastery', he says, 'and observing the regular discipline and the daily singing of God's service in the church, the rest of my time I *was delighted* always to learn, to teach, or to write.' Bede placed the *opus Dei* first, as every true monk must; he would not allow either study or sickness to keep him from it. Alcuin, in a letter to the monks of Wearmouth, records the tradition that Bede believed that the angels were present at the canonical hours: 'Will they not say, Where is Bede? Why comes he not to the services with his brethren?' Only the residue of his time was given to learning and teaching, but he did that with gusto and originality. A few examples will suffice.

In the sixth century a certain Scythian monk at Rome, known as Dionysius Exiguus, in compiling his Easter Tables, had reckoned from the Incarnation.[1] The exact measure of Bede's originality here we shall never know: but Bede was certainly the first scholar and historian to make the reckoning by the year of our Lord the standard reckoning. Every time we date a letter we should render homage to the Venerable Bede.

His *Ecclesiastical History* was not only a pattern for all future historians; not only has it been praised by Mommsen for its accuracy, but in many ways it spread through Western Europe a new conception of history, and of other things. I may mention one detail. Bede wrote the *Ecclesiastical History of the English People* before there was any English nation in existence. He might have adopted the political unit and have written an Ecclesiastical History of Northumbria; he might have taken the geographical unit and have written an Ecclesiastical History

---

[1] POOLE, *Chronicles and Annals*, 1926, p. 22.

of the British Isles. He did neither. He preferred to consider all the Germanic-speaking inhabitants of the British Isles, despite their different origins, Angles, Saxons, and Jutes, as one people — English. It was not an individual conception of Bede's: the correspondence of Boniface and his fellow missionaries shows that they think of themselves, and of the folk they have left at home, not as Northumbrians, West Saxons, or Mercians, but as English. Yet it was Bede who gave worldwide currency to this conception. It is time we abandoned the fallacy that the Norman Conquest first hammered Englishmen into unity. Bede's *Ecclesiastical History of the English People* was one of the many forces which had made England into a people, long before Normans and Angevins formed the impossible idea of creating one empire out of England and so much of France as they could hold: an idea which led to the Hundred Years' War, that 'tissue of calamitous follies' which put back the clock in Western Europe for generations.

Yet Bede's title to our gratitude is not that he spread this or that idea, but that he made it his business 'to maintain a standard of learning, and to preserve the continuity of civilization'. The words are those which our President used, in his address last year,[1] to define the objects of this Academy, and of its members, individually or conjointly.

I suppose that it would be possible to demonstrate an apostolic succession, from teacher to pupil, from Bede in his cell at Jarrow to our President in his chair this evening.[2] Don't be alarmed; at this hour I am not going to attempt it. I have pointed out how Bede instructed Egbert, Egbert Alcuin. Alcuin was not so great a master as Bede, but he was master of a greater school. All Europe was his school, and his influence stretched to Fulda, to Tours, to Rheims, to many other places, till the streams came together in the University of Paris, and so flowed on to the University of Oxford.

Omitting intermediate stages, I will pass to three Oxford men of our own day who knew intimately their Dark Ages and their Bede. W. P. Ker, S. J. Crawford, and Charles

[1] J. W. MACKAIL, *Presidential Address*, July 1935, p. 9.
[2] Some earlier stages are given in the *History* of Ademar (Pertz, iv, 119).

Plummer all possessed that 'plain heroic magnitude of mind' which marked Bede himself. If you have followed this lecture carefully, you will have realized that anything of value in it I have learnt from those three men, through whom alone, if at all, I must claim to be in touch with the Venerable Bede.

S. J. Crawford, cut off before his time ('Farewell, too little and too lately known'), was a man whose scholarship Ker would have deeply admired. A colleague wrote Crawford's epitaph:

> For him books were no dead things; through their pages
>   He passed into a happy country, where
> He held communion with saints and sages,
>   Heroes and prophets, spirits wise and rare.
>
> He has left his books now; those great souls he knew
>   Called him from this small world of time and space:
> This is not death; he has gone to share the true,
>   The glorious life of that immortal race.[1]

Charles Plummer seemed the reincarnation of Bede, if ever one man seemed the reincarnation of another — in his vast learning, his humility, his piety, his care for the young. Elected a Fellow of Corpus at a time when celibacy was still imposed, Plummer never broke his monastic vow, remaining single during the fifty-eight years of his Fellowship. Gibbon spoke scornfully of the 'monks of Magdalen' and their unproductiveness. I wish he had lived to see the production of the monks of Corpus, and above all, Plummer's edition of Bede's *Historical Works*.

Plummer was born within a few miles of the spot where Bede was born, lived, and died; and Plummer was not altogether satisfied with the way in which collieries and furnaces had transformed what in Bede's day had been the wooded banks of the Tyne. I myself remember standing on the roof of the North Eastern Hotel at Newcastle, and thinking that, if Bede could have seen the circles of smoke with which I was surrounded, he would have had no doubt where he was, though he might have

[1] In Memoriam S. J. Crawford in *The Invisible Sun*, by V. DE S. PINTO.

wondered what he had done to be put there. When Plummer wrote, forty years ago, it was less common than it is in these days to doubt the value of such industrial over-development; and it is with the words of Charles Plummer, rather than any of my own, that I wish to close this lecture. 'Even rating these things at the very highest value that has ever been put upon them by the most zealous votary of material progress, we have not, it seems to me, amid all our discoveries, invented as yet anything better than the Christian life which Bede lived, and the Christian death which he died.'

II

BEOWULF AND THE 'HEROIC AGE' IN ENGLAND

THERE are certain places, the importance of which in certain ages we all recognize. We should like to know more of the Athens of Socrates or the Rome of Horace, of Assisi in the days of St. Francis, or of Florence in the days of Dante: we would give much to have a vision of that London in the suburbs of which Marlowe was stabbed, or of that earlier London down the streets of which Long Will stalked, 'loath to reverence lords and ladies', and where Chaucer, with no such scruples, saw his townsmen greet

> Those who in vineyards of Poictou withstood
> The glittering horror of the steel-topped wood.

But many people are slow to recognize Anglo-Saxon England, in the generations following the conversion of the English to Christianity, as one of these ages of wonder, periods without which the world would not be the world we know. Yet it is a period which it is vital for us to try and understand, if we are to follow either our national history or that of Western Europe as a whole.

Of this period the two great monuments are *Beowulf* and the *Ecclesiastical History* of Bede. Bede was a child when the conversion of England was completed on the Sussex coast, and his life accordingly falls in the first two generations of a completely Christian England. *Beowulf* is more difficult to date and to place exactly. But the combination of Christian elements with the manners of a still vividly remembered heathendom supports other pieces of evidence and places the poem (in the form in which we now have it) in the early ages of Christian England.

Elsewhere in the West the Seventh Century and the early Eighth formed the darkest period of the Dark Ages; but in the British Isles this age was one of learning and enlightenment.

53

Not only was it the age of the English saints — of Oswald and Cuthbert, Chad and Cedd, Etheldreda and Hilda, but it was also one of the eminent ages of English scholarship. In the great school of Canterbury, under Abbot Hadrian and Archbishop Theodore, men studied, Bede tells us, till they knew Latin and Greek as well as they knew their native English. I suspect the Venerable Bede of some exaggeration here. But we can say that never since that age have Britain and Ireland held quite the same supreme position in all matters of the mind which they then held throughout Western Europe.

Yet there exists in England a good deal of prejudice against this age of Bede and of *Beowulf*. It is a prejudice which has been largely aroused by the injudicious praise which has been squandered upon the period of Anglo-Saxon origins. Some Victorian writers loved to trace any virtues the English people might possess to their Germanic stock, without sufficiently allowing for what Mediterranean civilization had grafted on that stock. They have praised the Anglo-Saxon period for the wrong things, and in the wrong way.

John Richard Green began his *Short History of the English People* with an idyllic picture of the 'little body of farmer commonwealths in Sleswick'. The members of these commonwealths Green described as holding their village councils, just as their descendants, the men of later England, meet in Parliament at Westminster. Kings, according to Green, were unknown among them: it was not till the time of the migration to England that military necessity produced monarchical rule. 'Conquest', in the words of Green, 'begat the king.'

This picture of primitive, democratic, Utopian Anglo-Saxon society left too many things out of consideration: above all, it left out *Beowulf* and Bede. If anything is clear in Bede's *History*, it is that the king is no mere war-leader elected by a democratic commonwealth, but that the king, with the magnates and warriors who surround him, is essential to the state. In *Beowulf*, if anywhere, we find a picture of early Germanic society; and we find it to be about as unlike the 'farmer commonwealths' of Green's imagination as can possibly be. In *Beowulf* all is aristocratic, and everything centres in the king. So far from the English 'knowing nothing of kings in their own fatherland', we know the names of a whole dynasty who reigned over the English in Sleswick. And a long passage in *Beowulf* is devoted to the praise of the greatest king of this dynasty — Offa, the son of Wermund.

If our historians had studied *Beowulf* more carefully, their praise of our Anglo-Saxon origins might often have been more discriminating. On the other hand, writers like Sir Arthur Quiller-Couch or Mr. Hilaire Belloc are now insisting — and rightly — upon the importance of the Mediterranean coast lands as the regions from which all civilization has spread to the forests of the North. They have protested, and with reason, against 'our august mother's marriage lines' being found in Sleswick.

And so we have a very pretty quarrel. Advocates of Anglo-Saxon England, like the Rev. Stopford Brooke, have told us to 'look to the pit whence we are digged'. '*Beowulf*', they tell us, 'is sacred to us; our Genesis, the book of our origins.' On the other side Sir Arthur Quiller-Couch charges the Saxon hosts as vigorously as his namesake is reputed to have done at Mount Badon; he, too, claims to have antiquity on his side:

Always our literature has obeyed, however unconsciously, the precept *Antiquam exquirite matrem*, 'Seek back to the ancient mother'; always it has recreated itself, has kept itself pure and strong, by harking back to bathe in those native — yes, *native* — Mediterranean springs.

The quarrel has even received the official approval of a Government Report. 'Let those who wish be "Anglo-Saxons", and those who wish be "Mediterraneans".' But the quarrel is unnecessary, and the alternative an unreal one. No student of our origins has any business to study them in a partisan spirit. We have got to be both 'Anglo-Saxons' and 'Mediterraneans', and that simultaneously, when we study our beginnings. For, from the Seventh Century, the two elements have been combined. It is true that ever since that time there have been people ready to raise the cry of Alcuin: 'The house is a narrow one, and there is not room for both.' But it has been the business of the broader-minded people who laid the foundations of our civilization and our literature to maintain that the house is spacious, and that there *is* room in it for both.

This was the spirit of Bede: it was the spirit of the ecclesiastics of Whitby, who were summoned to investigate the case of Cædmon: they found a grossly ignorant neat-herd expounding the verities of the Christian religion in the language, metre and style of the Germanic heathen war-song. Instead of being scandalized, they gave him their blessing, and told him to get on with it. So it was with Bishop Aldhelm and King Alfred, who combined the task of spreading Latin education with the love of Anglo-Saxon verse. *Beowulf* is a monument of the same kind of compromise. Nor does the combination end in Anglo-Saxon times. There is nothing in English Fourteenth-Century literature quite so aristocratic and chivalrous, so full of the spirit of French courtesy and romance, as *Sir Gawayne and the Green Knight*; nothing which forecasts the future of English thought more strangely than *Piers Plowman*: these were the last great masterpieces written in the old alliterative verse.

The controversy between 'Mediterranean' and 'Anglo-Saxon' is, then, one which should never have arisen. The blame for it must rest largely upon the too exclusive claims made by Anglo-Saxon enthusiasts. But it also derives from a misunderstanding of the words 'Dark Ages' and 'Renaissance', a misunderstanding which we have inherited from the Seventeenth and Eighteenth Centuries. There is still alive a belief that all the period between the sack of Rome by the Goths and the 'revival of learning', nearly a thousand years later, is 'one long Gothick night'; that after this night the dawn first glimmers in the age of Chaucer: that Chaucer, with his love of Virgil and Ovid and the knowledge of Dante, Petrarch and Boccaccio, which he brought back from his Italian travels, marks for us the beginnings of the Renaissance: that then at last our Northern and our Mediterranean origins were blended in 'the language and literature whose destiny was fixed by the genius of Chaucer.'

But Chaucer does not mark the beginning of the blending of a barbarous native English with French, Italian or Latin influences. The first, and by far the most important classical revival in England, was this of the Seventh Century: we had another Renaissance when, in the Tenth Century, the learning of France, itself largely derived from England, helped onward the monastic revivals of Æthelwold and Dunstan: another when, in the later Twelfth and the Thirteenth Centuries, England shared in the creative impulse which had burst out first in the South of France: another in the Fourteenth Century with Chaucer: another when, in the late Fifteenth Century, Linacre and Grocyn brought a knowledge of Greek to England from Italy, as Hadrian and Theodore had done eight centuries before: another when Wyatt, like Chaucer, went to Italy and brought back new fashions.

All these periods are important. But the birth of our England dates from the Seventh Century. Then England was brought into touch with European civilization, and the Celtic lands beyond linked up once more with the Continent. Even earlier, some faint hints of Roman civilization had reached the Angles whilst they were still on the Continent. Discoveries in the peat-mosses of Sleswick enable us to form an idea of the armour of the forefathers of the chiefs who led the invading English to settle in Britain. They were no presidents of 'farmer commonwealths', clad in little else than the primitive integrity of their liberal principles. On the contrary, they were earls clad in magnificent armour, which had either been made within the Roman Empire or was at least modelled upon work which had been so made. And the Germanic language which these invaders used, already contained a few words of Latin and Greek origin for things which they had borrowed from the Roman civilization. The trader had been among them, if the missionary had not.

But these things were mere externals, and it was with the conversion of the English to Christianity, after they had been for some generations settled in England, that the real fusion of the 'Roman' and of the Germanic spirit began. And the 'Roman' element came in in two ways: the wave of Christianity and scholarship which had extended from Roman Britain to Ireland flowed back by way of Iona. And this wave was met by a direct stream of influence from Rome, begun by Augustine, and continued by a line of Romanizing missionaries, such as Wilfrid.

The struggle between the two types of Christianity, from Iona and from Rome, was quickly settled in favour of Rome, albeit the Celtic influence can be traced for generations. But Roman Christianity and native Teutonic ways proved in many respects difficult to blend.

For though our debt to 'Sleswick' has been exaggerated, it cannot be ignored. One example of the continuity of our race may be given. Owing to the marriage of the son of William the Conqueror with the daughter of the West Saxon house, we can trace all the links which enable us to say of our present king, as the West Saxons said of theirs, that 'his kin goes back to Cerdic'. Further (although we cannot in this case trace all the links) owing to the marriage of King Alfred of Wessex with a lady of the Mercian royal house, it comes to pass that King George VI is descended from that very King Offa who reigned over the English in Sleswick in the Fourth Century of our era, and who is praised in *Beowulf* as 'best of all mankind, as I have heard, betwixt the seas'. That the English brought with them the praises of this Continental Offa from the other side of the North Sea is a fact not to be neglected. If Hengest and Horsa did not bring over, as some would have us believe, a rough draft of the Declaration of Rights of 1688, and of the Act of 1894 for the establishment of Rural District Councils, they *did*, at any rate, bring with them some very vigorous institutions, one of which was a 'literature without letters', including songs and lays, celebrating their ancient gods and heroes. The story of Cædmon shows how widespread was the ability to remember and reproduce vernacular literature. At a feast, every one was expected to take his part, and even a neat-herd was overwhelmed with shame at the want of so general an accomplishment. So far as this poetry commemorated the ancient gods, it was, of course, utterly banned by the Church. The ancient heroes were also, though not equally, condemned: the legends concerning them were wrapped up with standards of morality and ideas of honour which were often at variance with those of Catholicism. Yet this poetry was so deeply loved by the Germanic tribesmen that a nominal conversion, or even a sincere conversion, to Christianity did not suffice to eradicate it. Its roots went very far back. For the antiquity of this literature we have the evidence of Tacitus. Writing in the greatest days of the Roman Empire, Tacitus records the feats of Arminius the liberator of Germany, and tells how Tiberius refused to compass his death by poison, saying that the Roman people took vengeance on its enemies by open arms, not by secret fraud. Songs about Arminius, Tacitus then goes on to say, are even in his day (a century later) current among the barbarian tribes. In these songs of the Germanic minstrels, we learn elsewhere from Tacitus, gods as well as heroes were celebrated: it was the only kind of annal or chronicle which the Germans possessed.

From time to time we get hints in different Latin or Greek writers concerning these poems: the most amusing is that of the bishop Sidonius Apollinaris. Sidonius, like some later ecclesiastics, combined his episcopal functions with the pursuit of literature. But at Clermont he had to live in the neighbourhood of the Burgundian tribesmen settled in the South of France, and *they* checked the flow of inspiration: 'How can I write Latin verse', he complains, 'when I live among the long-haired tribes; when I am having to bear up under the weight of Germanic words; when I am having to praise, albeit with a wry face, whatever the Burgundian chooses to sing: the Burgundian, with his hair smeared with rancid butter.'

So conversion to Christianity, and even the habit of dining with bishops, did not eradicate this love of native song. At a later date we learn that the monks of Lindisfarne could so little forget their ancient love of it that they brought minstrels into the Refectory. It was for this that Alcuin reproved them with the stern words which I have already quoted above. Here is the passage at length:

Let the word of God be read in the Refectory: there it behoves the lector to be heard, not the harper; the works of the Fathers rather than the songs of the Heathen. The house is a narrow one, and there is not room for both. For what is there in common between Ingeld and Christ? The King of Heaven does not wish mention of his name in common with those of pagan and lost kings. For the Eternal King is reigning in Heaven: the lost pagan is howling in Hell.

Ingeld (Hinieldus) is of course that tragic figure of the Germanic heroic world whose story is told at some length in *Beowulf*: the man who allowed himself to forget the old feud and to marry the daughter of the race which had slain his father; and whose life was wrecked in the clash of contending loyalties and obligations.

But this uncompromising view, that there was nothing in common between the loyalties which the old heroic lays inculcated and the loyalties demanded by the Christian creed, was not, as we have seen, held by the best Englishmen in the Seventh Century. Aldhelm, bishop of Sherborne, had been distressed by the way his half-civilized flock used to go back to their homes as soon as mass had been celebrated. Aldhelm was one of the great scholars of his age, and he composed, among other things, a learned Latin work on the metres of classical poetry, which he dedicated to the King of Northumbria. Yet this learned — not to say pedantic — courtier did not scorn to place himself, disguised as a minstrel, on the bridge which his home-going congregation had to pass on their way from church. His minstrelsy proved so popular that his flock got into the habit of stopping to listen; and then he gradually began to mingle words of Scripture among the more amusing matter. And this was no mere mixture of incongruous elements, but poetry which had vitality enough to last for centuries. King Alfred — a good judge — held that at no period had there been any equal to Aldhelm as a writer of English verse.

In the North of England, however, the palm was given to Cædmon. Everyone knows the story of the vision which turned the tongue-tied peasant into a great poet. So that, says Bede, no one ever equalled him in writing sacred verse, 'for he did not learn the art of poetry from men, or through man, but by the grace of God'. And so the pundits of Whitby Abbey, as we have seen, gave the solemn seal of official approval to this bold attempt at combining popular minstrelsy and Christian thought.

'Nothing', the late Sir Walter Raleigh has said, 'is more striking than the way the English people do not alter.' Nowadays, we often claim the love of compromise as a peculiarly English quality. Provided we can get a settlement of a dispute, we do not mind an appearance of somewhat illogical patch-work. 'The English', I read in to-day's *New York Times*, 'are not doctrinaires, driven ahead by their own logic. They will resist each logical inference as it arises, will deny that it is logical at all, or that, even if it is, it is binding upon free-born and individual-istic Britons.' If this characteristic be indeed peculiarly English, it is interesting to see it at work in the Seventh Century, simultaneously in the North and in the South of England, in settling the quarrel between the orthodox cleric and the minstrel at the crossroads.

Of course, in many other places and ages, the vernacular has been used for religious purposes. What is remarkable about the Old English religious poetry (and the Old Saxon which was imitated from it) is this: that the metre, tricks of style, even the very ethical standpoint of the old war-songs are all pressed into the service of the Christian religion with a magnificent reckless-ness:

Whither shall we go, if we betray thee, lordless, sad in mood, worthless, our virtue gone? In every land shall we be hated, despised among the folk, when the children of men, the valiant ones, make reckoning which of them ever best served his lord at the war, when on the field of battle hand and shield endured hardship in the struggle, smitten by the sword.

It is with these words that, in the Old English *Andreas*, the disciples of St. Andrew refuse to desert their master when bound on a rather desperate missionary journey to the land of the cannibals.

Now it seems clear that *Beowulf* was written under the influence of this vernacular Christian poetry. It may have been inspired by lost works of Cædmon and of Aldhelm. At any rate, there are striking points of verbal resemblance between *Beowulf* and the Christian poems of the school of Cædmon. And the whole spirit of *Beowulf* is Christian. It looks as if some man, by no means convinced that there is nothing 'in common between Ingeld and Christ', had set to work to write a poem which should bring in the great heroes of

Germanic minstrelsy, Ingeld and Froda, Hrothgar and Hrothulf, Sigemund and Heremod, Offa and Scyld. But the poet is careful to avoid anything incompatible with the Christian faith and morals. He goes further, and, after the manner of Aldhelm, 'works in words of Scripture among the more amusing matter'. It is an event of the greatest importance when book-learned men, like Aldhelm, or those Northumbrian clerics who interested themselves in Cædmon, begin to pay attention to the composition of verse in the vernacular.

England in the Seventh and Eighth Centuries has, then, a second claim upon our attention. It is not merely an age of learning, bridging over the gap between the close of the Classical age with Boethius in the Sixth Century and the period of medieval and modern scholarship which begins nearly two centuries later with the scholars of Charles the Great, Alcuin and the rest. But it is the period when in Britain (as also in Ireland) we can mark the beginnings of literature in the vernaculars. Those beginnings are still very remote from us. The metre and style of Old English poetry were destined to be superseded by fashions coming from the Provençal and French literature, which grew up in later days. But much of the spirit of the earlier literature has lived on to our own time.

In *Beowulf* the combination of Christian and heathen elements, though sometimes incongruous, is certainly better harmonized than in the passage from the *Andreas*, quoted above.[1] The scholars of a generation ago were chiefly interested in trying to strip off the Christian element in *Beowulf* — the work, as they believed, of monkish interpolators and revisers. Thus they hoped to be able to disentangle the original heathen lays from which they believed that *Beowulf* had been pieced together. Here and there a stalwart scholar can still be discovered engaged on this labour. But most students have long ago abandoned the attempt, and have come to agree that 'the Christian elements are, almost without exception, so deeply ingrained in the very fabric of the poem that they cannot be explained away as the work of a reviser or later interpolator.

[1] P. 61.

Whilst the episodes are all but free from these modern influences, the main story has been thoroughly imbued with the spirit of Christianity.'[1]

Nobody of course doubts that, before *Beowulf*, as we know it, was composed, there existed a number of short lays and traditions handed down by word of mouth, dealing with the stories told in *Beowulf*. For many of these stories are historic, and the short lay is the most likely medium through which a knowledge of these tales can have come down from the Fifth and early Sixth Centuries, when the events happened, to the Seventh and Eighth. But the assumption that *Beowulf* was composed simply by fitting together a number of these short lays, which had come down from heathen times, and adding various Christian interpolations, rests, in its turn, upon another assumption which has only to be stated to be seen to be very perilous. It is assumed that each of these heathen lays dealt with a limited portion of the story, but treated it in an elaborate way, and with the full 'epic breadth' which characterizes the elaborate long poem. It is assumed, in fact, that nothing was needed but a man with a talent for arrangement and interpolation, who could 'assemble the parts', fit one lay on to another, and so produce a complete epic. But an examination of existing short lays shows us that they are not of the kind which can be pieced together, so as forthwith to make an epic. Very often a short lay will hurry through a story as complicated as that of a long epic. Take, for example, the *Lay of Weyland* in the *Elder Edda*. In bulk, this is much shorter than the shortest of the twenty-four books of the *Iliad*, or of the *Odyssey*. But the story it tells is more complicated than the main story of the *Iliad* or of the *Odyssey*, and the length of time occupied by it is longer. It would be easier to summarize in one sentence the story of the Wrath of Achilles or the Return of Odysseus than the tale of Weyland.

The men who made the short lays made them for their own pleasure: they were not thinking of providing material convenient for the purpose of some epic poet who was to come after them. Therefore it should not be assumed, without

---

[1] KLAEBER, *Beowulf*, p. 1.

evidence, that these lost lays of heathen times were of such a character that an epic could easily be made by fitting them together. Half a dozen motor-bikes cannot be combined to make a Rolls-Royce car.

How the long epic, as opposed to the short lay, came to be written in England, is a question difficult to answer. It is likely enough that but for the example of the classical epic this would never have happened.

> There is too much education in *Beowulf*, and it may be that the larger kind of heroic poem was attained in England only through the example of Latin narrative. The English epic is possibly due to Virgil and Statius; possibly to Juvencus and other Christian poets, to the authors studied by Aldhelm and Bede.[1]

Not all are in agreement with the view here so cautiously expressed by Professor W. P. Ker. Yet it is difficult not to suspect the influence of the classical epic in *Beowulf*, when we notice how carefully the rules of the game are observed. The story begins *in medias res*, but the hero recounts his earlier adventures at a banquet: the poet is not satisfied with telling us that there was minstrelsy at the banquet: he must give us a summary of the lay sung. And such classical influence is not, on *a priori* grounds, at all unlikely. Enthusiasm for Virgil was a possible thing enough in Northumbria at this date: Alcuin, when a boy of eleven in the school of York, was 'a lover of Virgil more than of the Psalter'.

However that may be, there is a likeness sufficiently strong to challenge comparison, not merely between *Beowulf* and the *Æneid*, but between *Beowulf* and the *Iliad* or the *Odyssey*.

The inferiority of *Beowulf* is manifest first of all in the plot. The main story of *Beowulf* is a wild folk-tale. There are things equally wild in Homer: Odysseus blinds the Cyclops, and Achilles struggles with a river-god: but in Homer these things are kept in their right places and proportions. The folk-tale is a good servant, but a bad master: it has been allowed in *Beowulf* to usurp the place of honour, and to drive into episodes

---

[1] W. P. KER, *The Dark Ages*, p. 251.

and digressions the things which should be the main stuff of a
well-conducted epic. And then there is the difference of
language and of metre. Sir Arthur Quiller-Couch bids us
observe

> the difference of note, of accent, of mere music. And I have
> quoted you but a passage of the habitual Homer. To assure
> yourselves that he can rise even from this habitual height to
> express the extreme of majesty and of human anguish in
> poetry which betrays no false note, no strain upon the store
> of emotion man may own with self-respect and exhibit
> without derogation of dignity, turn to the last book of the
> *Iliad*, and read of Priam raising to his lips the hand that has
> murdered his son. I say confidently that no one unable to
> distinguish this, as poetry, from the very best of *Beowulf* is fit
> to engage upon business as a literary critic.[1]

A champion of *Beowulf* might reply that it is doing that
poem a great honour to pit it (even in a comparison to its dis-
advantage) against the greatest thing in all secular literature —
the twenty-fourth *Iliad*: perhaps the greatest thing even when
read in a translation: and what in the original, in language
compared with which, as Frederic Myers puts it, 'Virgil's seems
elaborate, and Dante's crabbed, and Shakespeare's barbarous.'

Yet Professor Chadwick has shown us how a study of *Beowulf*
can be made to throw new light upon the study of Homer. For
in both we have a picture of society in its Heroic Age. The
society of *Beowulf* is in many respects cruder and less developed,
just as the hall of Hrothgar is a less elaborate thing than the
hall of Odysseus. But there is a fundamental likeness in the
life depicted.

Now in Anglo-Saxon England this Heroic Age was brought
into contact with Christianity, and with all the civilization of
the Mediterranean which came to England with Christianity.
It is just this which makes the Seventh Century in England so
exciting an epoch. Christian gentleness, working upon the
passions of the Heroic Age, produces at once a type which is
the rough outline of what later becomes the medieval ideal of
the knight, or the modern ideal of the gentleman.

[1] *On the Art of Writing*, pp. 142-3 (Pocket edit.)

In the Heroic Age, elementary passions are still very near the surface. This causes the tension in the twenty-fourth *Iliad*. In spite of the command of Zeus, in spite of the laws of hospitality, there is always the possibility that the wrath of Achilles may overmaster him, and that he may slay Priam within his hut. And the history of Europe during the incursions of the Germanic barbarians tells of many a deed as griesly as that to which Achilles feared that he might, despite himself, be driven.

In the epoch of *Beowulf*, an Heroic Age more wild and primitive than that of Greece is brought into touch with Christendom, with the Sermon on the Mount, with Catholic theology and ideas of Heaven and Hell. We see the difference if we compare the wilder things — the folk-tale element — in *Beowulf* with the wilder things in Homer. Take for example the tale of Odysseus and the Cyclops — the No-Man trick. Odysseus is struggling with a monstrous and wicked foe, but he is not exactly thought of as struggling with the powers of darkness. Polyphemus, by devouring his guests, acts in a way which is hateful to Zeus and the other gods: yet the Cyclops is himself god-begotten and under divine protection, and the fact that Odysseus has maimed him is a wrong which Poseidon is slow to forgive.

But the gigantic foes whom Beowulf has to meet are identified with the foes of God. Grendel is constantly referred to in language which is meant to recall the powers of darkness with which Christian men felt themselves to be encompassed: 'inmate of Hell', 'adversary of God', 'offspring of Cain', 'enemy of mankind'. Consequently, the matter of the main story of *Beowulf*, monstrous as it is, is not so far removed from common medieval experience as it seems to us to be from our own. It was believed that Alcuin as a boy had been beset by devils because he neglected divine service in order to read Virgil. Grendel resembles the fiends of the pit who were always in ambush to waylay a righteous man. And so Beowulf, for all that he moves in the world of the primitive heathen Heroic Age of the Germans, nevertheless is almost a Christian knight. If Spenser had known *Beowulf*, he would have found a hero much nearer to his Red Cross Knight than Achilles or Odysseus. The

long sermon on humility which Hrothgar preaches to Beowulf
after his victory, is as appropriate as the penance in the House
of Holiness which the Red Cross Knight has to undergo (and,
the scoffer will here interject, hardly less painful).

Beowulf, then, has yet a third claim on our attention. Here we
find the character of the Christian hero, the medieval knight,
emerging from the turmoil of the Germanic Heroic Age. Not
but what many of Beowulf's virtues can be traced back to that
Heroic Age. For example, Beowulf's loyalty, when he refuses
to take the throne at the expense of his young cousin Heardred,
is a part of the Teutonic code of honour, though a part often
not put into practice. But the emphasis placed upon gentleness,
humility, and judgment to come is a thing in which we can
trace the influence of the new faith. In his dying speeches,
Beowulf rejoices that he has sought no cunning hatreds, nor
sworn oaths unrighteously: 'For all this may I have joy, though
sick with deadly wounds, that the Ruler of men may not charge
me with the slaughter of kinsfolk.' And he thanks the Lord of
all, the King of glory, that he has been able to win such treasure
for his people. And so the poem ends:

So did the people of the Geatas, his hearth-companions,
bewail the fall of their lord: they said that he was a mighty
king, the mildest and gentlest of men, most kind to his people,
and the most desirous of praise.

It was with reason that Professor Earle quoted the words
of Sir Ector de Maris over Lancelot dead as being 'like an
expansion of these closing lines of the *Beowulf*':

And now I dare say, said Sir Ector, thou, Sir Launcelot, there
thou liest, that thou were never matched of earthy knight's
hand; and thou were the courteoust knight that ever bare
shield; and thou were the truest friend to thy lover that ever
bestrad horse: and thou were the truest lover of a sinful man
that ever loved woman: and thou were the kindest man that
ever struck with sword: and thou were the goodliest person
that ever came among press of knights: and thou was the
meekest man and the gentlest that ever ate in hall among

ladies: and thou were the sternest knight to thy mortal foe that ever put spear in the rest.

And the stories told by Bede are enough to prove that the combination in Beowulf of valour with mildness and gentleness is no mere idealization. Seventh-Century England *did* produce men of that type, as can be proved from many of Bede's stories, such as that of Oswin, King of Deira.

Many different standards and ideals were brought into contact in England in the Seventh Century and the generations following: the civilization of Rome, the loyalties and the violence of the Germanic Heroic Age, the teaching of Christianity. We see these things combining, in different ways, in the historical record of Bede, in *Beowulf*, in the Old English poetry dealing with definitely Christian topics. The elements are, as yet, not perfectly fused: from their combination the civilization and ethics of modern Europe were to grow in the fullness of time.

NOTE

Towards the study of *Beowulf* as a work of art, Professor Tolkien has made a contribution of the utmost importance.[1] It has become a commonplace to criticize *Beowulf* because there is nothing much in the story—to assert that, despite its dignity of style, the plot is thin. I remember W. P. Ker, in a lecture delivered some forty-three years ago, saying how much of the merit of the Classical epic or Northern saga lies in the speeches which give us the standpoints of the opposite sides; but that the oratory of *Beowulf* is one sided. 'The dragon', said W. P., condescending to flippancy, 'is not eloquent, and the education of Grendel had been neglected.' Ker would have preferred a theme in which the clash of rival loyalties could have been developed, as it is in many an Icelandic saga, or in some of the stories alluded to in the episodes of *Beowulf*.

To this criticism Tolkien makes a reasoned and weighty

[1] *Beowulf, the monsters and the critics*, by J. R. R. TOLKIEN (*Sir Israel Gollancz memorial lecture, British Academy*, 1936).

reply. To Ker's verdict, 'The thing itself is cheap; the moral and the spirit of it can only be matched among the noblest authors', he answers,

> If there were a real discrepancy between theme and style, that style would not be felt as beautiful, but as incongruous or false . . . *Beowulf* is not a 'primitive' poem; it is a late one, using the materials (then still plentiful) preserved from a day already changing and passing, a time that has now for ever vanished, swallowed up in oblivion; using them for a new purpose, with a wider sweep of imagination, if with a less bitter and concentrated force.

There may have been poems, now lost, on Sigemund or Guthhere or Eormanric or Ingeld, which showed more 'bitter and concentrated force'; but, as Tolkien says,

> The author of *Beowulf* cannot be held responsible for the fact that we now have only his poem, and not others dealing primarily with Ingeld . . . The poem cannot be criticized or comprehended, if its original audience is imagined in like case to ourselves, possessing only *Beowulf* in splendid isolation.

The old stories were deliberately used to give a 'sense of perspective, of antiquity with a greater and yet darker antiquity behind . . . But in the centre we have an heroic figure of enlarged proportions'. *Beowulf*

> is a contrasted description of two moments in a great life, rising and setting; an elaboration of the ancient and intensely moving contrast between youth and age, first achievement and final death.

I

THE MAN AND THE 'SPIRIT OF THE AGE'

'The means by which Providence raises a nation to greatness are the virtues infused into great men.'   EDMUND BURKE

IT is two or three years since Sir Charles Oman protested against the thesis, set forth as he said by 'a whole school of historians', that 'history is a continuous logical process, a series of inevitable results following on a well-marshalled table of causes'.[1] Oman, on the other hand, commended Thomas Carlyle for his praise of the great individuals. (This does not, of course, involve an approval of Carlyle's selection of his heroes, or of his views as to those whom he does select.)

At almost the same time, our second veteran Oxford historian, Mr. H. A. L. Fisher, was saying very much the same thing:

Men wiser and more learned than I have discerned in history a plot, a rhythm, a predetermined pattern . . . I can see only one emergency following upon another . . . only one safe rule for the historian: that he should recognize in the development of human destinies the play of the contingent and the unforeseen.[2]

There will, of course, be no lack of those who will rush in where Oman and Fisher fear to tread: indeed a writer in the *Criterion* alludes to the very passage I have just quoted as showing 'the limitations of Mr. H. A. L. Fisher's *Weltanschauung*'. Yet we must remember that, over a long period of years, Oman and Fisher have watched history in process of being made; they have watched it, not only from the study, but from opposite sides of the House of Commons. It is their long experience which leads them to recognize the play of the unforeseen.

[1] *The Sixteenth Century*, 1936, pp. 62 *etc.*
[2] *A History of Europe*, 1935, *Preface*, p. vii.

70

Oman tells how in October, 1918, when the collapse of the German army was impending, he discussed the future with two well-informed foreign friends: 'Every prognostication which we made as to the future of Europe has gone more or less wrong.'

And in the history of Literature the same problem meets us. Are we to look primarily for our well-marshalled table of causes, or for the individual, producing something which had not been foreseen? Did Wordsworth make the 'Romantic Revolt', or did the 'Romantic Revolt' make Wordsworth? The problem, which came first, the hen or the egg, drove the ancient sage to suicide. Fortunately, twenty years ago, that great teacher of English, Sir Arthur Quiller-Couch, gave his answer to the problem:

> Gentlemen, I would I could persuade you to remember that you are English, and to go always for the thing, casting out of your vocabulary all such words as 'tendencies', 'influences', 'revivals', 'revolts'. 'Tendencies' did not write *The Canterbury Tales*; Geoffrey Chaucer wrote them. 'Influences' did not make *The Faerie Queene*; Edmund Spenser made it: as a man called Ben Jonson wrote *The Alchemist*, a man called Sheridan wrote *The Rivals*. . . .

So 'Q' quotes a typical passage from Dr. George Brandes:

> 'The strongest tendency even of works like Byron's *Don Juan* and Shelley's *Cenci* is in reality Naturalism. In other words, Naturalism is so powerful in England that it permeates Coleridge's Romantic supernaturalism, Wordsworth's Anglican orthodoxy, Shelley's atheistic spiritualism, Byron's revolutionary liberalism . . . Keats's poetry is the most fragrant flower of English Naturalism . . . It is my intention to trace in the poetry of England of the first decades of the [Nineteenth] century the course of the strong, deep, pregnant current in the intellectual life of the country which . . . produces a Naturalism dominating the whole of literature, which from Naturalism leads to Radicalism . . . Though the connection between these authors and schools is not self-evident, but only discernible to the understanding critical eye, yet the period has its unity, and the picture it presents,

---

[1] *Studies in Literature*, First Series, pp. 74 *etc.* (Pocket edit).

though a many-coloured restless one, is a coherent composition, the work of the great artist, history.'

Here Q bursts out, 'Is not that fine? Everything ending in "ion" permeating everything that ends in "ance", or "ity", or "ism", fighting it out like queer aquatic monsters in a tank, all subdued finally to a coherent com-pos-it-ion by a wave of the pen in the hand of that great personi-fi-cat-ion history! Gentlemen, tell yourselves that these foolish abstractions never did any of these foolish things. "The great artist, history!" Call up your courage and say with Betsey Prig that you "don't believe there is no sich a person".'

Two or three years later, W. P. Ker, beginning his Oxford lecture on Shelley, said in different words much the same thing as Q. The right way of thinking, he said, is Browning's at the beginning of *Sordello* — overcome and abashed at the thought that Shelley might possibly be there, among his audience. And, after quoting the passage from *Sordello*, he comments, 'How mean and poor in comparison with this reverence is the critic enumerating tendencies and playing with the spirit of the age.' Some years before, he had said, when discoursing to the Historical Society of the University of Glasgow on the Politics of Burns, 'The Spirit of the Age is a dangerous demon'.

And yet, W. P. calls Shelley himself to witness that we cannot ignore 'tendencies' and 'the spirit of the age'. Shelley is the first author quoted in the *New English Dictionary* for the phrase 'spirit of the age'. And Ker points out how, in the preface to the *Revolt of Islam*, Shelley had been the first to state clearly what is now a commonplace of literary history. 'I have avoided', Shelley says, 'the imitation of any contemporary style.' 'But', he adds:

there must be a resemblance, which does not depend upon their own will, between all the writers of any particular age. They cannot escape from subjection to a common influence which arises out of an infinite combination of circumstances belonging to the times in which they live, though each is in a degree the author of the very influence by which his being is thus pervaded ... And this is an influence which neither the meanest scribbler, nor the sublimest genius of any era, can escape; and which I have not attempted to escape.

And Ker goes on to quote from Keats, in *Sleep and Poetry*, concerning

> The shiftings of the mighty winds that blow
> Hither and thither all the changing thoughts
> Of man.

Keats and Shelley at the same time, but independently, were 'thinking of the spiritual life of the world as a succession of periods, each with its own imaginative and intellectual gifts and character. To both poets the idea of progress is immensely important'. And this, itself, 'is good evidence of the power of common fashions of thought'.[1]

'In my time', said that great and wise historian, Master John Froissart, 'I have seen two things: though they differ, yet they be true.' The importance to the historian of the individual mind of the man or men with whom he is at the moment dealing; the spirit of the age, and its influence upon that mind; both these things, though they differ, yet are they true, and we neglect at our peril either the one or the other.

But, if we ask which, at this present moment, we are most in danger of neglecting, there can, I think, be very little doubt as to the answer. The warning, given by Oman and Fisher and Ker and Q, is a timely and a necessary one.

The conditions of teaching in our schools and universities just now encourage and exaggerate the view which would attribute everything to 'influences' and to 'tendencies'. We have travelled far from the simple age when a Greek gentleman thought himself well educated if he knew Homer by heart. (And surely it was no small thing.) But nowadays we test a man's knowledge of his national poet by his ability to generalize, to abstract, to philosophize, to trace the evolution of this tendency or the decay of that: to discuss what has been said,

---

[1] W. P. KER, *The Art of Poetry*, 1923, pp. 30-33.

or can be said, about an author — in a way which might sometimes surprise the author himself if he came to life:

> I dreamt last night that Shakespeare's ghost
> Sat for a Civil Service post.
> The English paper of the year
> Contained a question on *King Lear*,
> Which Shakespeare answered very badly,
> Because he hadn't studied Bradley. [1]

Catchwords are mass-produced by students in thousands of
examination papers. 'The Growth of the Novel', 'The Romantic Revolt', 'The Renaissance', 'The Reformation', 'Feudalism',
and a hundred other terms are tossed to and fro, and much
time is misspent in teaching students to think in generalizations,
often with very little attempt to discover what is meant by
them. I remember a large University Board drafting an
examination paper for an Honours School in English literature.
A question was asked concerning the English literature of the
Renaissance. It was about to be passed, with a sigh of weariness,
when one of the Board asked: 'What exact period is in our mind,
when we speak, in this context, of English literature of the
Renaissance?' Various replies were hazarded, from which it
became clear that some members of the Board were thinking
of a period which had ended before the period of which others
were thinking had begun. It is things like this that make one
doubtful about the word Renaissance, as was the critic who
summed it up in the words of the Greek sceptic:

> Now concerning the Renaissance, whether it was, or was not,
> or is, or is not, I neither know, nor do not know, neither care,
> nor do not care.

And yet the necessities of teaching and lecturing compel us
to divide our history and literature into periods — Ancient,
Medieval, Modern, every one of which rigid divisions is, in fact,
a violation of the truth. And, having got these epochs, we
again divide them into 'The Rise', 'The Flourishing', and 'The
Decline' of different periods. For example, a publishing firm

[1] From *Lays of Learning* by GUY BOAS. (Reprinted from PUNCH by the
special permission of the Proprietors.)

wished to bring out a series of histories of English literature, dividing the various epochs between Saintsbury and Gosse. Now Dryden seems to mark the beginning of a period, and that period seems to end when the poets of 'The Romantic Revolt' begin a new epoch. And so it has become a commonplace in the history of English poetry to think of a period which begins around 1660, with Dryden and the Restoration of Charles II, and ends when Wordsworth begins to write towards the end of the Eighteenth Century. It has become customary to speak of that age, in a rough and ready way, as 'The Eighteenth Century'. That being the scheme for poetry, prose has got to conform. So the last chapter dealing with prose in Edmund Gosse's *History of Eighteenth Century Literature*, because it comes at the end of the period, is labelled 'Prose of the Decadence'. This chapter, 'Prose of the Decadence', is devoted to the prose of Goldsmith, Gibbon, Boswell, and Burke. (Johnson's prose mostly belongs to this period, but because of his verse he has been disposed of earlier.) That Goldsmith, Gibbon, Boswell, and Burke should mark the 'Decadence of Prose' seems odd. But the scheme of the book demanded it. And having so divided our period we must justify our divisions: and so Gosse tells us that the prose of the period was decadent because 'The anxieties of the American War, the hollow calm which preceded the French Revolution, the general interest in and apprehension regarding purely political questions, seem to have deadened the intellectual life of the country, or to have diverted it into the channels of action'. Impressive words. But were men more anxious about war and politics between 1760 and 1789, during the 'hollow calm', than they were after the calm had been broken? And why should men be 'diverted into channels of action' between 1760 and 1789, because the French Revolution and the Napoleonic wars were subsequently going to occur between 1789 and 1815? And why should all this, if it were so, make the prose of Burke's speeches on America 'decadent'?

But the mischief does not stop here. There is a further commonplace in our textbooks: that the reaction in England, which followed the Reign of Terror in France, produced an antipathy to ideas and aspirations, till new life came in with the Reform Bill. John Morley is very eloquent on this topic, and has imposed it as a dogma upon much literary criticism. I shall have, below, to quote a few, but far from the most scathing, of John Morley's denunciations.

And so we get the following result: the period which precedes the French Revolution is decadent, because the French Revolution has not yet arrived. The period which follows the French Revolution is reactionary and disillusioned, because the Reform Bill has not yet arrived. So that in the whole era, one of the greatest in our literature, from the accession of George III to the Reform Bill (1760-1832), people are only allowed to be other than decadent or disillusioned after the Fall of the Bastille (when the decadence ceases, which was due to there not yet having been a French Revolution), but before the Reign of Terror (when disillusionment sets in). Five happy years, at most, out of seventy-two — all the rest stricken by decadence or disillusionment. And it is curious how extremes meet. Carlyle himself exaggerates his respect for the great personalities, till it leads him back into the fallacy of the decadent age. For certain ages are, he imagines, dominated by persons whom he dislikes. Therefore the whole age becomes unheroic and sickly. Carlyle wonders at Dr. Johnson worshipping: 'That Church of St. Clement Danes, where Johnson still worshipped in the era of Voltaire, is to me a venerable place.' Yet the era of Voltaire and Johnson was also the era of John and Charles Wesley. And the age which follows pleases Carlyle no better: it is 'the sickliest of recorded ages, when British literature lay all puking and sprawling in Byronism'. Yet it was the age of Scott and Jane Austen, Shelley and Keats and Charles Lamb.

The dogma of the age of disillusionment following the Terror has led to the picture of Wordsworth, the progressive revolutionary, writing good poetry, but becoming a bad poet when he ceases to be a good revolutionary. It is in vain that Dr. Batho has shown how a study of dates refutes this political partisanship.

Generalizations are useful servants, but bad masters. We

allow ourselves to be hypnotized by a phrase like 'The Death of the Middle Ages', till our eyes are closed to the signs of vigour which any unembarrassed gaze would detect in this period of alleged decay. Our epochs are convenient formulas that we have ourselves invented, yet they become living organisms to us — as if they were animals or trees with periods of birth, youth, maturity, decay and death.

Nevertheless it is difficult to do without terms like 'The Middle Ages', 'The Renaissance', 'The Reformation'. But at this moment, we are much too prone to exaggerate these generalizations, to think too much in terms of an 'inevitable movement', and so to divide our people into progressives who are applauded because, whatever their faults, they were on the side of the 'inevitable movement', and reactionaries who are disapproved because, whatever their virtues, they opposed the 'inevitable movement'. And, with our eyes on the 'inevitable movement', we are apt to neglect the human personality, the hero, and to forget how often the so-called inevitability of the movement may be due to the unshakable courage, skill and faith of just one man. Which brings me back to Sir Charles Oman:

> The history of mankind is often accidental, even occasionally cataclysmic. It is not a logical stream of cause and effect, but a series of happenings, affected in the most inscrutable fashion by incalculable chances ... ranging from natural phenomena such as plagues or earthquakes to the appearance of outstanding human personalities who 'put on the clock' or occasionally 'put the clock back' ... There have been countless crises in history where the opportunity did not produce the man ... and when things paltered on without the solution which to us seems obvious, if only there had been some strong personality to provide it. And on the other hand, the man has sometimes made the opportunity, rather than found it waiting for him.[1]

Now one of the great virtues of a study of the Dark Ages is that, amid the general darkness, the acts of certain persons stand out. As Dean Armitage Robinson puts it, just because

[1] *The Sixteenth Century*, 1936, pp. 62-3.

the general level of enlightenment and goodness was not so high, 'the big man counted for more: he was bigger relatively than his equal of to-day'.

The conscience of one man in Rome was moved at the thought that innocent children throughout heathen lands were growing up without knowledge of Christ. So Gregory the Great sent Augustine on his mission: England was brought back into the community of European nations, and became, with Ireland, a city of refuge for what was left of learning amidst the European turmoil.

The conscience of a young Northumbrian warrior was moved, and so Benedict Biscop founded the monasteries of Monkwearmouth and Jarrow, and instructed from childhood the young Bede. From his tiny cell at Jarrow, Bede steadied the world. Yet it might seem that Christian civilization was bound to be overthrown by 'inevitable movements' from without, and by decay from within. The movement of Mohammedanism, starting from what Carlyle has called 'a minority of one', had arrived, within a century, 'in Spain on this hand, in Persia on that'. It swept on — apparently nothing could stand before it. Nevertheless, in Bede's lifetime it was checked — at Constantinople by Leo the Isaurian, at Poitiers by Charles Martel. The internal decay of Christendom seemed even more deadly: yet the seed sown in England had grown, and the individual conscience of Boniface led him to reject the easy life of a great ecclesiastic in a (comparatively) peaceful England, and to fling himself abroad in an effort to bring salvation to the heathen Frisians and Hessians. Everything that was noblest in England followed him, in person if possible, if not by prayers and gifts. A restoration of the Church took place throughout the Frankish realm, and later Alcuin could become 'the schoolmaster of Europe'. But Alcuin lived to lament the first onslaught of the Vikings upon English civilization. And was ever any movement so 'inevitable' as the destruction which fell upon England in the year 867? Northumbria fell; East Anglia fell; Mercia fell; Wessex fell. By 878, what was there left, safe from Danish inroad? The island of Athelney: 'twenty-four acres of dry land, rising some thirty or forty feet above the surrounding swamps'.[1] The island of Athelney, and the conscience of King Alfred. No situation can ever have seemed more hopeless. It is all expressed in the words which G. K. Chesterton depicts the Mother of God as saying to Alfred, when he seeks for her consolation:

> I tell you nought for your comfort,
> Yea, nought for your desire,
> Save that the sky grows darker yet
> And the sea rises higher.
>
> Night shall be thrice night over you
> And heaven an iron cope.
> Do you have joy without a cause,
> Yea, faith without a hope?[2]

All these men, Gregory and Boniface, Bede and Alfred, toiled amid disillusionment and disaster. It is remarkable how repeatedly, in the correspondence of Boniface, comes the phrase 'fightings and fears, within, without'. Yet he persevered, and, if we estimate a man's success by his accomplishing that which he sets out to do, Boniface is one of the most successful men of history. It was Alfred's faith which saved Western Christendom. He added to his translation of Boethius the words 'I say, as do all Christian men, that it is God's purpose which rules, and not Fate'. On this belief the Danes broke. Many historians have held that 'this is the turning point in the history, not only of England, but of Western Europe. "Wessex was saved; and in saving Wessex Alfred saved England; and in saving England he saved Western Europe from becoming a heathen Scandinavian power." '[3] It is important to remember concerning Alfred that

> Had he, like Burgred of Mercia, given up the struggle in despair, and gone as a pilgrim to Rome, no one in his own day would have thought the worse of him; and he might

---

[1] HODGKIN, *History of the Anglo-Saxons*, II, p. 567.
[2] *Ballad of the White Horse.*   [3] PLUMMER, *Alfred the Great*, p. 105.

have won that pale halo of medieval saintship, which, as it was, he did not gain. But England would have been lost to Christianity.[1]

'England would have been lost to Christianity.' Ultimately, England might have been reconverted. But the clock would have been put back for centuries.

It is in the period between Alfred and the Norman Conquest that the doctrine of the inevitable tendency, and the doctrine that any age preceding a period of violent change must itself be a period of 'hollow calm' or 'inertness' or 'decadence' works the greatest mischief.

The Normans won the Battle of Hastings. Therefore, it is argued, they must have deserved to win: it must have been all in the inevitable order of progress. The Normans must have been progressive; the Anglo-Saxons must have been decadent. Anglo-Saxon civilization is maligned, in order that the defeat of Hastings may be shown to be inevitable.

And so we get the traditional view of England immediately before the Norman Conquest, which still rules in our History Schools. One has only to turn to the standard works of Previté-Orton, Stenton, Trevelyan, to name only a few out of many. 'The higher culture to be found in Normandy', we are told, contrasted 'with the clownish inertness into which much harried, subjugated England had fallen ... In spite of Edward the Confessor's efforts, she had withdrawn into a Scandinavian seclusion, and had sunk far below the level of an earlier time.'[2] 'The continued decadence of Anglo-Saxon prose and poetry in this period had been all of a piece with the political failure.'[3] 'On turning from the history of England between 950 and 1050 to that of Normandy during the same period, one is conscious at once of passing from decadence to growth.'[4] Year after year our students learn this story of Anglo-Saxon decadence, till it becomes a religious dogma, which it is impious to question. And yet, what is the evidence? It all comes to the

[1] PLUMMER, *Alfred the Great*, p. 199.
[2] PREVITÉ-ORTON, *Outlines of Medieval History*, 1924, pp. 121, 123.
[3] TREVELYAN, *History of England*, p. 111.
[4] STENTON, *William the Conqueror*, p. 23.

fact that, in a succession of single combats at Hastings, William was repeatedly victorious over Saxon champions who opposed him. Which proves the strength of his muscle and nerve. But, because in the evening William was a victorious general and Harold a mutilated corpse, that does not prove that Saxon civilization for a century before had been decadent. Harold of England had to meet a simultaneous attack from Harold of Norway and William of Normandy. If William of Normandy had had the handicap — if Normandy had been attacked by the King of France at the moment William landed in an undisturbed England, who can be certain that he would have won?

Or, suppose the winds had blown differently. Suppose Harold's great fleet, manned by skilled seamen, had caught the Norman transports, with some three thousand horses or more embarked on their frail timbers. Would the energy of the Conqueror have prevailed, even in a dire crisis like that? Or would our modern historians be moralizing on the absurdity of trying to conquer an island by cavalry, and drawing interesting parallels between the inevitable failure of William in 1066 and another Armada throwing its horses overboard at a later date?

Appeal is made to every kind of special pleading, in order to prove the weakness and disunity of Anglo-Saxon civilization. For example, the difference of laws in different parts of the country is urged: 'A man of Warwickshire would realize that his limbs were valued at a higher or lower rate than those of his neighbour of Leicestershire.'[1] No doubt he would: yet similar local particularism did not prevent the France of Louis XIV, or Germany before 1918, from being mighty nations. Americans are still Americans, though you can get a drink or a divorce in one state that you cannot get in another. And, in fact, it was not till 1926 that the special legal peculiarities of Kentish law were abolished in England. The survival of local law is urged against Anglo-Saxon civilization in a way in which it would never be urged against that of any other country or age, because the historian is determined to make out a case for decadence and disunion.

[1] STENTON, *William the Conqueror*, p. 10.

We may take another example. The last members of the royal house of Wessex, we are told, are 'a feeble folk'. Really, the line in five generations produced six competent kings: Edward the Elder, Athelstan, Edmund I, Edred, Edgar and Edmund Ironside; with one clear failure, Ethelred the Unready. It further produced one bad boy (Edwig); one 'martyr' (Edward II); one saint (the Confessor); and it united England into one realm. There are indeed few dynasties which could show so good a record. But their 'physical weakness' is 'illustrated' by their 'ominous childlessness'.[1] Yet their descendants through the female line rule us to this day. The male line, I admit, ended with Edgar Atheling — who was the twenty-first in direct male descent from Cerdic, the founder of the dynasty — not such a bad show. This Anglo-Saxon decadence is emphasized in order that it may be contrasted with Norman 'growth' — although the direct male line of William the Conqueror expired with the death of his youngest son. But that is ignored — because 'English' at this period must signify decadence, and 'Norman' must signify growth.

Meantime, every achievement of the later Saxon period is either ignored or belittled. Students are seldom told that, in the generations before the Norman Conquest, English jewellery, metalwork, tapestry and carving were famous. Orthodox historians omit to mention that the illumination of the Winchester school is unrivalled. In building on a large scale England had certainly something to learn from Normandy — and learnt it, as the Confessor's great Abbey at Westminster proved. And Saxon architecture too had its merits; the expert speaks of 'the greater cosmopolitanism of Saxon architecture, as compared with the more competent, but equally more restricted and traditional architecture of the Normans'.[2]

Most important of all — during the whole of the Anglo-Saxon period, the conception of a united England had continued to grow. The Anglo-Saxon poem on the death of Edward the Confessor claims that the Confessor was supreme over the whole island 'even as the cold surges lap it round'.

[1] STENTON, *William the Conqueror*, p. 10.
[2] CLAPHAM, *English Romanesque Architecture*, p. 152.

No doubt the claim was fictitious. To what extent did the writ of any king run from Westminster through the Highlands of Scotland before 1745? But the fact that the claim should be made is important. And it is preserved in a written vernacular literature which precedes by generations that of other great Western European states. The records of this literature are intermittent, but there is no ground for believing that it ever became 'decadent'. (Philologists would give a good deal for a parallel Norman-French poem of 1066. Nothing of the kind exists.) Further, in the England preceding the Norman Conquest, there had been a notable growth in the feeling of English unity which made Englishmen, as early as the reign of Edward the Confessor, unwilling to make war upon each other. About 1050 we have three distinct statements (two in English and one in Latin) that it was felt to be wrong for Englishmen to fight each other — it was, the Latin says, 'abhorred as civil war'. Imagine Florentines refusing to fight Siennese, Normans to fight the men of Languedoc, the different kingdoms of Spain and dukedoms of Germany refusing to fight each other, because it would be 'civil war'. But that *was* the stage which England had certainly reached, fifteen or twenty years before the Norman Conquest. And yet we are asked by historians to contrast the inefficiency of Anglo-Saxon England with the fact that 'the Spanish kingdoms were trying their young strength in the first battles of the great crusade which fills their medieval history'. The great crusade does indeed fill their medieval history. From the date when the Moslems first burst into Spain (711) to the date when they were finally conquered (1492), 781 years were to elapse. It took so long, because the Christians of Spain spent much, if not most, of their energy in fighting each other — which, after the great Viking invasion, the Christians of England emphatically did not.[1] Alfred, within a dozen years of the Viking conquest, had turned back the tide of Viking heathendom. In the next century a Scandinavian poet could say of Alfred's grandson, 'Now is the highest deer forest subject to valiant Athelstan', and, a few generations later, Scandinavia itself had been

[1] Cf. Prescott, *Ferdinand and Isabella*, Introduction, p. 5 (ed. 1890).

83

converted to Christianity, largely by English missionaries. Why should there be this curious bias?

It comes, partly, from thinking too much in terms of periods, to which a rise, maturity, and decline must be attributed; partly from another form of the same fallacy, the refusal to give its due to the great personality.

Instead of giving proper credit to the almost superhuman energy of William the Conqueror, who violently superimposed his will upon the current of English life, and for ever modified that current (though he did not destroy it), we attribute the revolutionary change to allegorical abstractions — a dying Anglo-Saxon period and the energetic youth of an adolescent Norman period. Because of this abstraction of 'decadence', the whole period from the death of Alfred to the Norman Conquest is neglected as a 'decline and fall'. People are interested in Alfred and the Vikings, but after that they refuse to appreciate Anglo-Saxon matters. As they approach the Norman Conquest they can see only Norman accomplishment. They refuse to recognize Anglo-Saxon accomplishment; there they have eyes only for failure. The Anglo-Saxon period is about to end — so it must be decadent. The belief that progress could only have happened in the way it did happen makes it impossible to be fair to the century and a half before the Conquest. Because the Norman Conquest modified all subsequent English history, therefore people are unwilling to believe that England could have progressed by any other means. They seem to believe that, if there had been no Norman Conquest, we should still to-day be drinking mead out of ox-horns, and calling to each other 'drinc-hæl', 'wæs-hæl'. Yet there is a very simple refutation of that fallacy. From the landing of Saint Augustine in 597 to the eve of the Norman Conquest in 1066 is a space of 469 years. Augustine found Britain a sparsely inhabited land, with heathen Germanic tribes in the East, and the defeated remnants of the Romanized Britons in the West. The England which the Normans conquered was a civilized medieval land, superior in many ways, if inferior in others, to contemporary France. The Norman conquerors themselves testified to English superiority in many fields.

Edward the Confessor, with his coins, his seals, his charters, his palace and abbey at Westminster, is, if we compare him to the Ethelbert to whom Augustine came, almost a modern king.

Such had been the progress of 469 years.

Another 469 years takes us from the Norman Conquest to 1535 — the year when More's head fell on the scaffold. Now the change which had taken place between the end of the Saxon period and 1535 was enormous. Instead of the beautifully illuminated Anglo-Saxon manuscripts of the Eleventh Century we have the printed book — and this is only one symbol of the change. But vast as the change is from the England of Edward the Confessor to that of Henry Tudor — is it as vast as that from the heathen England of 597 to that of Edward the Confessor? We have no right to assume that a country which had progressed as England had progressed during the Saxon period would not have continued to progress.

Now, just as people are unjust to the later Saxon period so they are to the later Middle Ages. Our interest culminates in the Crusades: in St. Francis, St. Louis, Dante. After that, we are waiting for the Reformation.

So we hail Wiclif — the Morning Star of the Reformation. But to William Langland, less than justice has been done. He comes immediately before the great upheaval of Wiclif, and people do not know what to make of him. No great figure of English literature has been equally neglected. He has even been divided into four or five authors, and we have been told that *Piers Plowman* was 'the voice and vision, not of one lonely, despised wanderer, but of many men, who, though of diverse tempers and gifts, cherished the same enthusiasm for righteousness and hate for evil'.[1]

Here again, let us remember Sir Arthur Quiller-Couch: 'Tendencies did not write *The Canterbury Tales*; Geoffrey Chaucer wrote them.'

I hope to satisfy the reader that Tendencies did not write *Piers Plowman*: that a man called William Langland wrote it. Meanwhile I will ask him at least to keep an open mind.

[1] *Cambridge History of English Literature*, II, p. 42.

But the failure to appreciate William Langland is typical of the dislike for the generations immediately preceding the Reformation. 'Weak as is the Fourteenth Century, the Fifteenth is weaker still: more futile, more bloody, more immoral.' So a great historian has written, and his words have been endorsed by another great historian. Yet it is rather hasty to dismiss, as 'futile', the century which discovered, among other things, printing and America.

And, just as people do not quite know what to make of William Langland, coming just before the Wiclifite upheaval, so they do not know what to do with Erasmus and Thomas More, coming before the Lutheran upheaval. All three are men of enormous personalities. But to those who are thinking in terms of an abstraction, 'The Reformation', they do not fit well into the pattern.

The mind of the historian is dominated by a revolution which 'is fated to come'. If the individual conscience cannot lend itself to the scheme — then so much the worse for the individual conscience. So we are told:

> Henry VIII embodied an inevitable movement of politics, while Fisher and More stood only for individual conscience. That is the secret of Henry's success. He directed the storm of a revolution which was doomed to come, which was certain to break those who refused to bend, and which may be explained by natural causes, but cannot be judged by moral considerations ... Political movements are often as resistless as the tides of the ocean; they carry to fortune, and they bear to ruin, the just and the unjust with heedless impartiality.[1]

Against these words of one great historian, I would put those of another great historian, who, 'with a cautious conviction that happenings *might* have happened otherwise', says

> No word is so dangerous as the word inevitable.[2]

And what is meant by saying that More and Fisher stood 'only for individual conscience'? Why 'only'? It might be said, I suppose, of an early Christian martyr, that he stood only for

---

[1] POLLARD, *Henry VIII*, pp. 438, 437.   [2] OMAN, *The Sixteenth Century*, p. 3.

individual conscience, and that the hunger of the Colosseum lions 'may be explained by natural causes but cannot be judged by moral considerations'. But, after the lions have gone back to their dens, and the martyr's bones have been swept out of the arena, the effect of the martyr's martyrdom upon his fellow men remains, to be judged by moral considerations. And so, to quote Oman again:

> Martin Luther's *'Here stand I: I can do no otherwise: God help me!'* at Worms; or Thomas More's *'I pray God preserve me in my just opinion even to death'*, are the things that counted in history.[1]

I believe that we should think of things in terms of the intelligence and conscience of man, not of blind forces of nature, tides destroying 'with heedless impartiality'.

---

[1] OMAN, *The Sixteenth Century*, p. 138.

PIERS PLOWMAN: A COMPARATIVE STUDY

I. THE FIRST VERSION (THE 'A-TEXT')

'Your young men shall see visions.'

§I. POEMS OF CATHOLICISM: THE 'DIVINE COMEDY' AND 'PIERS PLOWMAN'

THE habit of regarding great poets as representatives of this '-ism' or that, is well illustrated by a dictum of John Morley:

> The greatest poets reflect . . . a perfect and positive faith, in which mankind has for some space found shelter . . . Perhaps not more than four high names would fill the list of the chosen: Dante, the poet of Catholicism; Shakespeare of Feudalism; Milton of Protestantism; Goethe of that new faith which is as yet without any universally recognized label, but whose heaven is an ever closer harmony between the consciousness of man and all the natural forces of the universe; whose liturgy is culture, and whose deity is a certain high composure of the human heart.[1]

We will not intrude upon John Morley's worship of His Deity, nor even stop to ask what exactly is meant by that 'perfect and positive' faith of Feudalism in which Shakespeare found shelter; but it is important to ask whether we should think of Dante as the poet of Catholicism?

Certainly we should. Dante stands to us for the preceding thousand years of Dark and Middle Ages; of course we learn from him much about the outlook of those ages. Carlyle says that, if all had gone right with Dante, if he 'had been Prior, Podesta, or whatever they call it of Florence', he might never have written the *Divine Comedy*: 'Florence would have had

---

[1] Essay on Byron, 1870, reprinted in *Critical Miscellanies*, p. 133.

another prosperous Lord Mayor; and ten dumb centuries continued voiceless.' But if Carlyle had stopped there, it would have been only a half-truth; he adds, 'and the ten other listening centuries (for there will be ten of them and more) would have had no *Divina Commedia* to hear!' Dante, as we know,[1] looked forward to the listening centuries, though he did not expect that as many as ten centuries would continue to listen to him. And he looked, as we also know, right across those ten 'dumb' centuries which he is supposed to represent, back to the poets of Rome. It was as the fellow of Virgil and Horace, of Ovid and Lucan, that he hoped to be remembered. We should think of him as 'the poet of Catholicism', certainly; but we may also think of him in the way Shelley does in the *Defence of Poetry*, as throwing a bridge over the stream of time, and uniting the modern and the ancient world. We may sometimes get more out of marking how the poets unite the ages, than by separating them into compartments: 'Dante the poet of Catholicism, Shakespeare of Feudalism'.

And, in the way it unites different ages, the *Divine Comedy* resembles our English *Piers Plowman*, whose poet has also been claimed as the poet of Catholicism.

In one of the best essays which have been written on *Piers Plowman*, Mr. Christopher Dawson described it as written by 'at once the most English of Catholic poets and the most Catholic of English poets'.[2] Some months after I had quoted this judgment, I was wondering exactly what interpretation I should myself put upon the word 'Catholic' in the phrase which I had repeated with warm agreement. By a curious coincidence, I found a letter from Mr. G. G. Coulton awaiting me, asking that very question: 'Did I mean Roman Catholic?' To some extent Mr. Dawson had answered the question him-self: for he had said that the spiritual successors of *Piers Plowman* are to be found among the Puritans and the rebels, with Fox and Bunyan and Whitfield and Blake. I would go further, and say that we find in *Piers Plowman* that determination to follow the search for 'Saint Truth' wherever it may lead, which has

---

[1] See above, p. 25.
[2] *The English Way*, 1933, p. 160.

marked some later searchers who, in the words of Canon Streeter, 'have cheerfully for truth's sake renounced, not merely the good things of this life, but the hope of a life to come'.[1] But no renunciation such as Canon Streeter had in mind can be found in *Piers Plowman*. The hope (and the fear) of the life to come is there everywhere present. In that, the poem belongs to its age, the age of the *Divine Comedy*. Yet, however Catholic the poem may be, the course of English history has been such that, as Mr. Dawson agrees, subsequent English writers most akin to the author of *Piers* have not been Catholics. And the disappointment of Gerard Manley Hopkins, when he came to read *Piers Plowman*, is enlightening.

Piers Plowman shows remarkably little trace of the influence of Wiclif or his followers, although they were active when the later versions of the poem were being written. Indeed it reflects the ideals of an England not yet rent by divisions which it is fashionable to-day to call ideological. English religious life had not yet been parcelled out between Roman Catholic and Protestant, Anglican and Nonconformist, or the English social outlook divided between Radical and Conservative. *Piers Plowman* combines things which have since been separated, and so, in its broad appeal, is the most thoroughly English of all our religious poems; any Englishman who will take the trouble to understand it can sympathize with it. *Piers Plowman* stands to win as the spirit of unity wins, for that is one of its great messages:

Cry we to all the commons · that they come into Unity,
And there abide and do battle · against Belial's children.[2]

§2. 'THE BRIDGE OVER THE STREAM OF TIME'

It is as true of *Piers Plowman*, as it is of the *Divine Comedy*, that it is a bridge uniting two worlds. Like the work of Chaucer or Dante, *Piers* stands near the beginning of modern vernacular

---

[1] *Reality*, 1935, p. 160. But the renunciation has not always been cheerful.
[2] B. xx, 77-8.

literature. Yet it has behind it a primitive vernacular tradition: a tradition of which Chaucer and Dante knew nothing. It is written in a metre which was already old when Cædmon composed in it his Hymn of Creation, the Venerable Bede his Death Song, and some unknown poet his Dream of the Rood; the rhythm has by the Fourteenth Century adapted itself to a somewhat altered language, but the underlying principle is the same. Nevertheless, *Piers Plowman* is not merely what Quiller-Couch has called it, 'the last dying spasm' of Anglo-Saxon literature. It is our first great modern poem: this mighty 'philosophical and religious' poem was planned, and in great part written, about 1362, when Chaucer, a young courtier in his early twenties, had as yet written none of the works which were to bring him fame. And *Piers Plowman* is the one poem in the old alliterative metre which has never quite passed out of the consciousness of the English nation. In every subsequent age, some English writer or scholar has known of it.

There was, of course, no deliberate archaism in the choice of this ancient metre; it was chosen because, in the West Midlands and farther north, it was still a natural measure for a long and ambitious poem. The Old English heroic poems were utterly forgotten by the Fourteenth Century, but the fact remains that together with this metre a certain tradition of heroism had been passed down through the ages. There could hardly be a more heroic theme than that of *Beowulf*: the story of the champion's mighty youth leads up to the tale of the ancient king who gives his life for his people in a struggle with an evil power, though the younger men, all save one, fear to face it. 'It is an heroic-elegiac poem; and in a sense all its first 3136 lines are the prelude to a dirge: one of the most moving ever written . . . If the funeral of Beowulf moved once like the echo of an ancient dirge, far off and hopeless, it is to us as a memory brought over the hills, an echo of an echo. There is not much poetry in the world like this.'[1] Beowulf, slaying the dragon and slain by the dragon, reminds us of the last fight of Thor. 'The winning side is Chaos and Unreason;

[1] J. R. R. Tolkien, *Beowulf, the monsters and the critics* (1936), pp. 33, 36.

but the gods, who are defeated, think that defeat is not refutation.'

'*Defeat is not refutation.*' Those words of W. P. Ker summarize much of the great literature of the world, but nowhere are they found more strongly than in poems in the old alliterative measure. It was in the same metre that, in the dark days of Ethelred the Unready, the unconquerable mind had expressed itself in *The Battle of Maldon*:

> Thought shall be the harder · heart the keener,
> Mood shall be the more · as our might lessens.

'There is nothing equally heroic before *Samson Agonistes*.'

In the generations following the even more disastrous rout of the Saxon hosts at Hastings, in those ages of defeat, when, students are taught to believe, English minstrelsy was dead, the English poets continued to sing of their heroes. The poems have been lost, but we know something about them from Latin chroniclers. The themes are those of English kings defending their realm against invaders from oversea: Alfred, Edmund Ironside, Offa; of outlaws, friends of the oppressed, defying the tyranny of the rich and powerful, tales of Hereward, Edric Wyld, or those lost stories of Robin Hood which the slothful parson in *Piers Plowman* knew better than his service books; of disinherited princes and princesses who at last come into their own; of wronged heroes and heroines vindicated at last. Above all, in these dark years, his people drew comfort from their memory of King Alfred, and of the valour and learning which he had gathered round him:

> At Seaford · sat many thanes,
> Many bishops · many book-learned;
> And Alfred also · England's shepherd,
> Darling of England . . . Comfort of England.

Thus an Englishman wrote in days when barons and book-learned bishops were Norman, not English. In the *Proverbs of Alfred* there is special emphasis on reticence, caution, and above all on patience:

2 . THE BRIDGE

Thus said Alfred:
If thou hast a woe · tell it not to the weakling,
Tell it to thy saddle-bow · and ride singing forth.

Not all these poems of the generations following the Norman Conquest were in alliterative verse, and when alliteration was used, it was often mingled with end-rhyme. But when English again became the language of the book-learned, and so was more frequently written down, we find pure alliterative verse to be the heroic measure beloved in the great houses of the West and North, just as the rhymed verse of Chaucer or Gower was preferred in the East and South, in the king's court and in London. In the latter half of the Fourteenth Century, three of the most heroic poems ever written in the English tongue were composed in this ancient measure.

In *Sir Gawayne and the Green Knight*, a north-western poet took up a romantic story, such as any minstrel might have told. But he told it in a different way. 'Whatever epic may mean, it implies some weight and solidity; Romance means nothing, if it does not convey some notion of mystery and fantasy.' The story of this alliterative *Gawayne*-poem is romantic, mysterious and fanciful enough; but it is told with a weight and solidity which reminds us of the great epics. The feelings, from week to week, and at last from day to day, of a man doomed to a death from which there seems no escape, are depicted with a restrained power which the greatest poets have never surpassed.

In the alliterative *Morte Arthur*, the heroic story of Arthur, which had been first given to an astonished Twelfth Century by Geoffrey of Monmouth, is retold. The result is a poem more truly 'epic' than anything surviving in English literature between *Beowulf* and *Paradise Lost*.

In *Piers Plowman* we have a poem which has in its subject a real affinity to *Paradise Lost* and *Paradise Regained*. However inferior *Piers* may be to Milton's epic as a work of art, the theme of both is to 'justify the ways of God to men'. I would not dare to call the author of *Piers* 'the greatest of English religious poets', but, with a qualifying 'perhaps', that has been said of him by an historian whose judgment is entitled to

93

respect. *Piers Plowman*, besides being a religious and even theological poem, is also in the heroic tradition. This comes out with overwhelming force in the last three *passus* of the poem. *Piers Plowman* bears something of the same relation to the alliterative *Morte Arthur* which *Paradise Lost* and *Paradise Regained* bear to that unwritten epic on the wars of Arthur over which Milton for many years pondered, but which he never even began.

The alliterative metre died out in early Tudor days; a fine poem on the Battle of Flodden is one of the latest examples. Yet the metre has natural affinities to the English tongue, and might yet be revived. Modern poets have taken an interest in it — not always according to knowledge. Gerard Manley Hopkins claimed that 'the old English verse seen in *Pierce Ploughman*' was in 'sprung rhythm'. But when he came to read *Piers Plowman*, he was disappointed with it. 'I am reading that famous poem, and am coming to the conclusion that it is not worth reading', he writes to Robert Bridges;[1] its verse, he thought, had fallen into 'a degraded and doggerel shape'.

Despite the antiquity of its metre, the anxious, inquiring spirit of *Piers Plowman* is strangely modern. We might call its poet the 'morning star of the Reformation' with more truth than Wiclif, whose outlook was in many ways very medieval. In that case, however, we must use the word 'Reformation' in no narrow-minded sectarian sense, but to include the Counter-Reformation as well as the Protestant Reformation; in fact to signify that renewal of the spirit which has to come from time to time to most forms of organized religion. (Few can boast, like the Carthusians, 'Never reformed, because never deformed'.)

So that there was reason when Fuller, in his *Worthies of Shropshire*, classed 'Robert Langland', as he called the author of *Piers*, among post-Reformation worthies: 'Forgive me Reader,' he says, 'though placing him (who lived one hundred and fifty years *before*) *since* the Reformation: for I conceive that the Morning Star belongs rather to the Day than to the Night.' And so Fuller concludes that 'this Robert, regulated in our

[1] 18 Oct. 1882, *Letters*, 1935, I, 156.

Book not according to the Age he was in, but the Judgement he was of, may by *Prolepsis* be termed a Protestant.'

Now Fuller, of course, was wrong in making the poet a proleptic Protestant. Yet we can see how he came to be wrong; he was impressed, like other Protestants, by the denunciation in *Piers Plowman* of the wealth of the Church, and above all by the prophecy that a king would come who would punish the religious orders for breaking their rule of poverty and penance, a king who would compel them to return to their first state, and who would incidentally give an incurable knock to the Abbot of Abingdon. (And even to-day, it is difficult not to think of *Piers Plowman*, as we pass Abingdon, where no stone remains above ground of that once so mighty church.) But protests like these are a feature of Catholic literature as early as Bede. Nothing could be further from the poet's ideal than the Dissolution of the Monasteries, as it actually took place. He is an enthusiast for the pure monastic life, and this very prophecy of the confiscation of monastic wealth is the sequel to a passage glorifying the religious orders and their schools. For a monastery, where learning is followed, no praise, the poet thinks, can be too high:

> For if Heaven be on this earth · and ease to any soul,
> It is in Cloister or in School · by many skills, I find.
> For in Cloister cometh no man · to chide nor to fight,
> But all is obedience there and books · to read and to learn.
> In School there is scorn · but if a clerk will learn,
> And great love and liking · for each of them loveth other.
> But *now* is Religion a rider ——[1]

and he goes on to draw, in scornful contrast to his ideal, the monk riding abroad 'as he a lord were', followed by his hounds, or asking a servant 'where he learnt manners', if that servant does not kneel when offering him his cup. The poet can say nothing worse of the Religious Orders than that some of them 'have no ruth, though it rain on their altars'. He would have despised the abbots and priors who, a century and a half after his day, made over their sanctuaries to be unroofed and

[1] B. x, 300 etc.; C. vi, 153 etc.

their libraries to be destroyed by the Tudor monarch, whilst they themselves received extravagant pensions for thus aiding and sharing the cupidity of the king and his court. He would have thought it no cause for rejoicing that the rain is falling where the High Altars of Glastonbury and Whitby stood, and over the desecrated burial places of Augustine at Canterbury and Alfred at Winchester.

The very exceptional popularity of *Piers Plowman* is shown by the large number of surviving manuscripts. And the evidence of the manuscripts seems to prove that this popularity began instantly: *Piers Plowman* spread widely in the short and imperfect form in which it was published about 1362. It circulated therefore first during the interval of peace which followed the treaty of Brétigny. Froissart has left an account of the horrors of the winter campaign of 1359-60, which led the hitherto victorious English king to agree to terms of peace. But Froissart's words are not more vivid than are the allusions in *Piers Plowman* to that winter which seemed as if it would last for ever. This first, imperfect issue of the poem was named by Skeat the A-text. Some fifteen years later the poem was completed and published (the B-text). This can be dated with some exactness from its allusions to the political difficulties which threatened England, whilst the reign of Edward III closed in disappointment and gloom, after the death of the Black Prince. Still deeper is the horror aroused in the mind of the poet by the wars which the Pope was waging against Christian folk. But the A-text had had a good start, and the B-text was never able to drive it quite out of circulation. Men had to copy what they could get. The final and most widespread version of all, the C-text, was a revision, published in or around 1394, at a time when, as the allusions show, the actions of Richard II were making him unpopular in London.

During the Fifteenth Century the poem continued to be often copied, and even into the Sixteenth. The Bodleian library possesses a manuscript (a combined A- and C-text) which was transcribed in his own hand by Sir Adrian Fortescue about 1532. Seven years later, Sir Adrian was attainted and executed by the government of Henry VIII, 'probably for no other crime than fidelity to the faith of his fathers'. It was eleven years after Sir Adrian's execution that *Piers Plowman* was printed.

The attacks upon the corrupt clergy ensured the popularity of *Piers* among the militant reformers, and this edition of 1550 was issued (from a good manuscript now lost) by one of them, Robert Crowley, printer and divine. He was a propagandist rather than an antiquary, and he sometimes grievously misread his original. He explains his author's alliterative metre: 'The nature of his metre is, to have three words at the least in every verse which begin with some one letter. This thing noted, the metre shall be very pleasant to read.' The sense, Crowley complains, 'is somewhat dark, but not so hard but that it may be understood of such as will not stick to break the shell of the nut for the kernel's sake'. Crowley's manuscript was a B-text; he notes one variant which shows that he had also seen a C-text; he did not pursue his textual investigations further. After toiling at the manuscripts at intervals during twenty-nine years, I sometimes think him wise.

The MSS. and Tudor reprints satisfied the curious till the revival of antiquarian studies in the early Nineteenth Century, when the C-text was first made available in a handsome volume, edited by the Rev. Thomas Whitaker, a famous Yorkshire antiquary.

§3. WILLIAM LANGLAND AND HIS FAME IN RECENT YEARS

Of the author, Crowley had not been able to learn much; only that his surname was Langland, and that he was born at Cleobury Mortimer in Shropshire. Crowley gives him the Christian name of Robert — a mistake which persisted into the Nineteenth Century. It arose from an error in certain manuscripts. The poet speaks of himself as 'I-robed in russet'. In two manuscripts still extant this has been miswritten as 'I, Robert in russet'. As this miswriting occurs in the first line of the *Do-well* section, which in the earliest versions is a distinct poem, although an avowed sequel, and as poems were constantly quoted by their first lines, this scribal error has caused much confusion.

There is really no doubt that the writer's Christian name was William. In all the texts, A, B, and C alike, the author speaks of himself as 'Will', and this cannot have been taken over mechanically in the later texts from the earlier one, for each of these texts has its distinct 'Will' passage, introduced in a distinct way. The suggestion that 'Will' was meant as a fictitious name of an imaginary dreamer is a mere anachronism, a modern conception, altogether alien to the age of *Piers Plowman*. *Piers Plowman* belongs to a definite type of 'Vision' writing, the technique of which demands that, when 'Will' or 'Ralph' or 'Dante' is introduced as the author's name, we should accept it as such. In all three texts, A, B, and C, and again in a different place in each of these texts, the author alludes to his tallness. As the poet grows older he tells us more and more about his life, till, in the latest version, we have a very clear picture; he is a cleric, and earns his living by singing for the souls of such as find him food; but he can only have been in minor orders, for he lives *with his wife* in Cornhill.

There is a further reason, besides contemporary custom, why we should take these allusions as referring to the poet himself. In the earliest version they are so vague as to be almost unintelligible; they only become clear in the light of what we are told more explicitly later. Now an allusion must allude to something: if the allusions in the first version were to a fictitious 'Will', that 'Will', to make the allusions intelligible, must have been depicted less obscurely. People could not be expected to wait fifteen years for the explanation. The theory of multiple authorship involves us in the assumption that the earliest text alludes to a 'Will' who did not exist in fact, and who at that date did not exist in fiction either. The vague references of the first version can only have been understandable if they referred to a figure already known in the circle for which the poem was written; later, when the poem had a wider public, that figure is outlined more explicitly.

We shall find the same thing constantly recurring. There

are many passages in the A-text which are puzzling, till the
B-text explains them by showing us what was all along in the
writer's mind.

One scrap of information which has escaped Crowley's
search is important. At the end of one manuscript[1] there is,
in a hand of the early Fifteenth Century, a short Latin Chronicle
of the events of the late Thirteenth and first half of the Fourteenth
Centuries. The events recorded show that this Chronicle was
compiled by some well-informed person specially interested
in the history of the South Welsh border. At the end, in a hand
closely resembling, if not identical with, the preceding
Chronicle entries, is a Latin note that 'the father of William
Langland, Stacy [*i.e.* Eustace] de Rokayle, was a gentleman,
and lived at Shipton-under-Wychwood, holding land of the
Lord Despenser in Oxfordshire, and the aforesaid William
wrote *Perys ploughman*'. Independent evidence proves that
Eustace de Rokayle *did* live at Shipton in Oxfordshire, and that
his family *were* adherents of the Despensers, the great lords of
the Welsh Border, patrons of the monasteries of Great Malvern
and Tewkesbury. To doubt the truth of this statement as to
William's parentage because he did not take his father's surname is again an anachronism; even two centuries later a son
often did not take his father's surname, and in *Piers Plowman*
itself the poet discusses the circumstances under which it is
unreasonable for a son to 'refuse his sire's surname'. William
may, of course, have been illegitimate, but the change in surname is in itself no reason to presume this.

This early Fifteenth Century note is very good evidence;
the script shows that it cannot be very much later than the
poet's death. If the note had connected him with some member
of the Langland family (which was well known in the West
Country), it *might* have been guesswork. But what is likely to
have led the writer of the note to say that William Langland was
a son of Eustace de Rokayle, save the fact that he *was*?

In the latest version of the poem, the poet tells us that his

[1] MS. D.4.1, now in Trinity College, Dublin. But there is nothing to connect
the note, or the Chronicle, with Ireland, as has been rashly assumed. Its
affinities are with the South Welsh Border.

father and his friends put him to school. Contrary to the usual idea, *Piers Plowman* is the work of a well-educated man, not however very learned. Dante and Chaucer, deeply learned as they were, make mistakes which seem strange to modern scholars; but Langland's mistakes are of a more elementary kind, and show that his knowledge of Latin was rather limited. But he has enough Latin to get along, and, it would seem, some French; he is poor, but of gentle birth, at least on his father's side, and of thoroughly aristocratic sympathies. In the A-text he shows Knighthood as one of his great ideals; he has particular dislike for the rising bourgeois class. Thirty years later his politics are unchanged; he complains that soap-sellers and their sons have been made knights for silver, whilst the nobly born, who, for the right of this realm and the king's worship, have ridden against our enemies, have had to pledge their lands. The Hundred Years' War is bringing social changes, and the poet sees, and deplores, what the modern historian would call the decay of feudalism and the rise of capitalism.

The poet's use of the alliterative measure is consistent with his aristocratic sympathies, for, as I have tried to emphasize, the great alliterative poems are knightly in tone: the delight of gentlemen, albeit country gentlemen, of the West and North. Yet one of the many features which characterize the A-, B-, and C-texts alike is that, whilst they are written in a provincial metre, and in a dialect which is not what we should expect in London, the local allusions in each text point emphatically to London. Like another Shropshire Lad of later days, the poet surveys that endless line of faces pacing down the London street, and his mind goes back to the hills of the Welsh Border: 'I too would be where I am not.' Except the references to Malvern Hills, there is nothing to connect the poem with any part of the country save London and the home counties; but in each text are many local allusions which would be natural only in a Londoner. All the signs fit an author born and educated amid the feudal life of the Welsh Marches, but passing a penurious and proud maturity among the citizens of London.

The little we know of his life harmonizes with the bitter

scorn of wealth which runs through the poem. But Langland's scorn is not the dislike of the proletarian for the classes above him. It is the scorn of the new poor for the new rich.

When the revival of Middle English studies came, a revival which will be for ever associated with the great names of Skeat and Furnivall, Skeat with his amazing industry managed, despite his many other tasks, to publish all three texts, A, B, and C, together with invaluable notes, between 1867 and 1884. This massive edition was beyond the purses and the industry of most readers. But Skeat's school-edition of the Prologue and the first seven of the twenty *passus* (or sections) of the B-text was much studied. And it was through this small edition that the poem has had its wide circulation. A fellow student of mine, after we had read it with W. P. Ker forty-five years ago, took it with him when, in the following year, he went lumbering in Canada. He kept it in his log cabin, and I remember Ker's amusement when his former pupil told him later how *Piers Plowman* had raised his prestige among the lumber-jacks.

Skeat's edition was published just in time for John Richard Green to give the poem its rightful place in his *Short History of the English People*. Green made a magnificent use of it, as a document illustrating English history; and he fixed the point of view from which it has almost always been regarded since.

To Green, Langland is 'the gaunt poet of the poor' who 'dwells on the poor man's life, on his hunger and toil, his rough revelry and despair, with the narrow intensity of a man who has no outlook beyond it. The narrowness, the misery, the monotony of the life he paints reflect themselves in his verse . . . The cumbrous allegory, the tedious platitudes, the rimed texts from Scripture which form the staple of Langland's work are only broken here and there by phrases of a shrewd common sense, by bitter outbursts, by pictures of a broad Hogarthian humour.'

'Narrowness' is the last quality that can reasonably be attributed to the author of *Piers Plowman*. But indeed there was very much more than anyone at that moment could be expected to see, in the great poem so suddenly restored to its place in the history of the English mind. The light thrown upon contemporary history, however important, was only incidental; the poem as a whole tells the story of the struggle of the human soul. What Green scornfully called 'the cumbrous allegory, the tedious platitudes', are the essence of the poem. *Piers Plowman* can be made to illustrate the history of England in the Fourteenth Century, as the *Divine Comedy* might be used to illustrate the history of Italy in the Thirteenth. But *Piers Plowman* is like the *Divine Comedy* in that it is a great poem, 'noble in plan', existing in its own right, apart from the excellent use which can be made of it to illustrate history.

'Noble in plan.' Fifteen years ago, Professor Grattan and I ventured to apply this term to our poem, generally considered formless and, in great part, unintelligible. The misunderstanding of *Piers Plowman*, as of much other medieval literature, is the price we have to pay for our modern contempt of Allegory. It is to be hoped that Mr. C. S. Lewis's epoch-making *Allegory of Love* will dissipate this contempt, and will have an influence far beyond those allegories with which it more immediately deals.

But there is a second cause which makes the understanding of *Piers* difficult. The wealth of the monasteries had degraded and corrupted the contemplative life, the essence of which is ascetic poverty. But by the subsequent dissolution of the monasteries the very idea of such a life has disappeared from English consciousness; the words 'Abbey' or 'Priory' came to mean the country houses of noblemen or gentlemen. Now the meaning of *Piers Plowman* is the quest for God, in three stages — *Do-well*, *Do-better*, and *Do-best* — each of which is revealed in and through Piers Plowman.[1] The first stage, the life of active labour in the world, *Do-well*, as typified by Piers Plowman when he first appears, is clear. But is not there something higher? And so to Langland the clerkly or monastic life of

[1] There is no excuse for any further misunderstanding of this point, since it has been so excellently set out in an article by Mr. NEVILL K. COGHILL (*Medium Ævum*, II, 108). No one who has not thoroughly mastered Mr. Coghill's article, and learnt what it has to teach, has now any business to write about *Piers Plowman*.

renunciation, charity, poverty and contemplation is *Do-better*. Yet there is a still higher ideal. The man who has renounced all may be called back into active life, to rule and direct others. The episcopal ideal is higher than the monastic or clerkly ideal: it is *Do-best*. All this needs explaining to-day; in the Fourteenth Century it was well understood.

Now in modern England we all profess enthusiastic admiration for *Do-well*. And some few persons might even be found who would spare a kind word for Archbishop *Do-best*. But the very ideal of the voluntary poverty of the recluse has largely dropped out of our lives. Despite the efforts of individuals, from Nicholas Ferrar onwards, to revive 'the silence of prayer and the solitude of contemplation', our sympathies have been narrow during the past four centuries. Tennyson, I doubt not, was a more spiritually minded man than the tough Sir Thomas Mallory. But to Mallory it is quite natural that Percivale, having seen the marvels of the Sangreal, should 'take a religious clothing'. Tennyson's Arthur does not conceal his distress because Percivale leaves human wrongs to right themselves, and 'cares but to pass into the silent life'. To Tennyson, the later Middle Ages are 'a time that hover'd between war and wantonness'. Yet abroad, it was the time of the great mystics and of the *Imitation of Christ*, in England of Langland and Walter Hilton and Dame Julian of Norwich. And the difficulty that we modern English feel in grasping the frame of mind which places complete self-abnegation and contemplation above the virtuous and energetic Active Life, is one of the obstacles which have stood in the way of an understanding of *Piers Plowman* as a whole. But the Middle Ages had no doubt that the Contemplative Mary had chosen her part better even than the Active Martha. Yet the Middle Ages at the same time recognized that only a few have the call to the Life Contemplative, and that, of those few, some are compelled by duty to mingle worldly cares with the life of the spirit, and so must perforce live the Mixed Life of both Activity and Contemplation.

In view of the preference which medieval writers give to Mary over Martha, we might expect the Mixed Life to be regarded, at best, as a mere makeshift compromise, for those who were unable to attain to the full Contemplative Life. And so it was sometimes considered; so that for long I felt a difficulty in Langland's placing of the Mixed Life above both the others, till it was pointed out that this has high authority. Thomas Aquinas tells us that though the Contemplative Life in itself is better than the Active Life, yet an Active Life which consists in teaching the virtues learnt in the Contemplative Life is more perfect than the purely Contemplative Life; therefore it was the life which Christ chose. So, in the *Meditations of the Life of Christ* (attributed wrongly to St. Bonaventura) we are told of the three stages: the first, Active, in which the mind is purged and strengthened by virtuous acts; the second, Contemplative, in which it is illuminated and instructed in true wisdom. Finally, imbued by these two earlier stages with virtue and wisdom, comes the third stage, the life of Prelates and Preachers, which is an Active Life, but an Active Life devoted to ruling and helping others.[1]

But, useful as is a comparison between Langland and the great European writers of Medieval Christendom, we are on even safer ground when we compare him with his exact English contemporary, Master Walter Hilton, canon of Thurgarton in Nottinghamshire. They were probably born, and they certainly died, about the same time (Hilton in 1396), Langland the greatest English religious poet, Hilton the greatest master of English prose, of the day. How much each may have read of the other's work we cannot say. But it was the same England which formed them. Langland, a poor clerk in Fourteenth-Century London, probably had access to few books; we are deceiving ourselves if we suppose that he had read all that an expert in medieval theology has read to-day. His knowledge must have been largely derived from what he heard in sermons,[2] or got from conversation with other men.

[1] The vital paper, in which Mr. H. W. WELLS compared with *Piers Plowman* these passages from Thomas Aquinas and the *Meditations*, will be found in the *Publications of the Modern Language Association of America*, XLV, 123-40 ('The Construction of *Piers Plowman*').

[2] The close connection between Piers and the contemporary sermon has been excellently shown by Prof. OWST, *Preaching in Medieval England*, p. 295, and *Literature and Pulpit in Medieval England*, pp. 6, 574, etc.

Chaucer depicts himself poring over his books, as dumb as any stone; Langland depicts himself as discussing his problems with any who (he hopes) can teach him. This probably represents a real difference in the way the two poets came by their learning.

Yet some books Langland knew. He makes one of his characters say

> There are books enow
> To tell men what Do-wel is · Do-better and Do-best both.

And one book of this kind was Hilton's *Book that is called Mixed Life*.

The three kinds of good life, as there defined by Walter Hilton, were common knowledge; Langland could not have missed them, and they are the three kinds of good life which in *Piers Plowman* are named Do-well, Do-better, and Do-best. The Active Life, says Hilton, is for those who labour 'as busily as they may, for help of themselves and of their fellow-Christians, for they can do nought else'; the Contemplative is for those who forsake all business of worldly goods, 'and make themselves poor and naked'; the Mixed Life belongs to Prelates and other men of Holy Church, who must sometimes use Active Life, and sometimes give themselves to prayers and meditations.

It follows that the Active Life is essentially for the laity, who have 'a good will', but no 'skill in devotion'; the Contemplative and Mixed Lives are mainly clerical. Yet some temporal men, who have received 'gifts of grace and of devotion', but who for the sake of their fellows are not free to leave utterly the business of the world, may follow this Mixed Life, as Prelates also do. Christ himself, says Hilton, chose the Mixed Life, to give such men an example, by his own working, that they should use this Mixed Life as he did.

There are some minor differences between Langland's view of the three good lives, and Hilton's. Langland represents Christ as living and teaching all three lives in turn. And Hilton does not, like Langland, definitely place the Mixed Life of the Prelate above the Contemplative Life of the man who has 'run into Religion'; to Hilton each is the best life for certain people, according to their circumstances.

Of course these ideas are not limited to Christendom. In Kipling's story of *The Miracle of Purun Bhagat*, we are told how the wise and good Prime Minister of a semi-independent Indian state, at the age of sixty, resigned his power, and took up the begging bowl of a holy man. Thereby, in the phrase of William Langland, he passed from *Do-well* to *Do-better*. But when the hill side upon which his hermitage is built begins to totter, and he resumes his old power of command to warn the villagers below, this return of the contemplative man to the Active Life, for the good of others, has analogies to Langland's *Do-best*. And, in many ages and many religions, will be found stages analogous to the Active, Contemplative, and Mixed Life, *Do-well*, *Do-better* and *Do-best*.

This idea of the three kinds of good life must be as old as Christianity itself is in England. In a passage to which Hilton refers in his *Book that is called Mixed Life*, Gregory the Great had pointed out that Christ lived the Mixed Life of Activity and of Contemplation.

We are told in a sermon attributed to St. Augustine: 'Peter appears in many places, that he may bear the figure of the Church.'[1] It would be perilous to assume that Langland knew that text; yet it makes a good motto for *Piers Plowman*. The Latin title of the poem, *Visio Willelmi de Petro Plowman*, never allowed the medieval reader to forget that Piers is Peter: Piers represents, in turn, each of the three ways of life which the Church teaches. Langland sees Christ also as living and teaching those three lives. Hence the identification of Piers with Christ: 'But it would be truer to say that Jesus lives Piers (for Piers is a way of Life) than that Jesus *is* Piers or that Piers *is* Jesus.'[2]

But before depicting these three ways of life, Langland asks us to consider a world in which most men are suffering from the want of them. The poem therefore begins with a picture

---

[1] AUGUSTINE, in Migne, v, 1940.
[2] COGHILL in *Medium Ævum*, II, 119.

of society, for the most part neglectful of Holy Church and her teaching. Langland was convinced that it is 'by evil that men know the good';[1] that it is the very mixture of evil and good in the world which teaches us what is right and wrong:

> Whereby wot men which is white · if all things black were,
> Or who were a good man · but if there were some shrew?
> And he that may all amend · have mercy on us all.

Only when men are convinced of the need of amendment does Piers 'puts forth his head', to teach the way. He vanishes, and after long search is found again, teaching a better way: *Do-better*. But again he is taken from our sight, and *Do-best* concludes with a passionate prayer that he may be found again. As Skeat said fifty years ago, in the másterly 'Introduction' with which he crowned his work on *Piers*, 'What other ending can there be? We are all still pilgrims upon earth. *That* is the truth which the author's mighty genius would impress upon us in his parting words.'[2]

For twenty years after Skeat's magnificent pioneer edition, itself the work of some twenty years, Skeat's labours were left unchallenged. Then Professor Manly suggested a revolutionary view. Reading the A-, the B-, and the C-texts each completely through for the first time during the convalescence from a serious illness, he came to the conclusion that the A-text was the work of two distinct men (A1 and A2); that B and C again were distinct authors. One John But had avowedly added a few lines to the end of an A-text. Hence the view that *Piers Plowman* was not written by one William Langland, but by five men.

The theory is creditable to Manly's acumen. He was the first to see, what a further study of the texts shows conclusively: that, in the form in which Skeat published them, A, B, and C could not be the work of one man. Skeat purified his texts from innumerable false readings — but he was pioneering, and could not remove them all. The texts as he printed them contain many verbal variants which are in-

---

[1] B. x, 435 etc.
[2] Clarendon Press edition, vol. II, 1886, p. lvi.

compatible with unity of authorship. But such verbal variants can be traced, with complete certainty, to the corruptions of scribes. When Skeat's work is finally revised in a definitive edition, it will appear that the critical texts of A, B, and C approximate to each other much more closely than they appear to do in Skeat's editions, as published between 1867 and 1886.

Apart from these verbal differences, there remain the psychological differences which Manly traced between his A1, A2, B, and C. But here, the psychological difference lay, I think, in Professor Manly himself. Everything in A1 he had read carefully many times before: he came to it therefore well prepared.[1] To the study of A2, B and C as complete poems, he came for the first time, for previously he had read only portions of these. Further, A1 deals entirely with the Active Life in the world, A2 and the B- and C-additions take us into regions much less material and concrete; but we have no more reason to think them therefore the work of a different writer, than we have to believe that the Dante who wrote the *Inferno* did not write the *Paradiso*. That the continuations are more difficult to follow than the first section of the A-text is true: but that is due to the fact that they deal with higher and more complex ways of life and deeper problems than those to which the simple-minded Ploughman is at first a sufficient guide.

Manly's theory had a most friendly reception from the scholarly public, because, with the exception of Skeat and Jusserand, that scholarly public was in just the same position as Manly himself was when he first formed his theory. Most of us were quite familiar with everything in A1. We had read it repeatedly, often in class in Skeat's school-edition, which is simply A1, with some (unessential) additions made by B. But we knew very little of A2, or the B-continuation (the bulkiest part of *Piers Plowman*) or the C-additions. Skeat himself had noted how people had misunderstood the poem, because the former part was better known than the latter. But his own cheap

---

[1] The B-text takes over the *Prologue and Passus i-viii* of the A-text, with only very trifling omissions. The man who knows Skeat's small edition of B, *Prologue and Passus i-vii*, therefore knows A1. But A2, the overwhelming bulk of B, and all C, will be to him unexplored territory.

edition of the opening *passus*, together with the rather prohibi-
tive price of his complete edition, had helped to increase this
misunderstanding.

The references found in all three versions of *Piers*, A, B and
C alike, to the poet's name 'Will', and to his tallness, are
exactly parallel to the references which the eagle, in the *House
of Fame*, makes to Chaucer's name 'Geoffrey', and to his portli-
ness: 'Thou art noyous for to carie.' 'We are not bound to
believe', says Jusserand,[1] 'that a real eagle carried to the
House of Fame, beyond the spheres, such a precious and
considerable load as was our friend Chaucer. But when the
same Chaucer describes himself as going home after having
made his "rekenynges", and reading books until his sight is
"dasewyd",[2] we should be quite wrong in displaying here any
of our elegant scepticism.' To suppose that such allusions are
meant to refer to fictitious authors, whom the poets imagine
writing their poems instead of themselves, is illegitimate. To
say that 'Long Will, the dreamer, is obviously as much a
creation of the muse as Piers the Plowman', is as if we should
say that the Geoffrey of the *House of Fame* is obviously as much
a creation of the muse as the eagle. As Mr. Christopher
Dawson says, 'Medieval authors, so far as I know, never
created a purely imaginary character of this type'. Those who
assume it have been challenged for nearly thirty years to
produce a precedent, and have not yet done so.

The second point made by Jusserand nearly thirty years
ago has also remained unanswered. The alleged differences
between the three texts, in those few cases where they can be
maintained, are no more than we find between the different
parts of the work of any great poet. The critics are, in fact,
demanding from every portion of *Piers Plowman* a machine-
made, standardized similarity, such as no great poet ever
shows. And Langland was a great poet.

The best proof of the unity of the poem, in its three texts,
will be found in an analysis of it.

---

[1] *Mod. Philol.*, VI (1909), p. 326.
[2] *House of Fame*, II, 145, 150.

§4. THE FIELD FULL OF FOLK, AND PIERS THE GUIDE (A-text: Part 1)

The poet tells how he wandered abroad 'wonders to hear':

> But on a May morning · on Malvern Hills
> Me befell a ferly · of fairy enchantment;
> I was weary of wandering · and went me to rest
> Under a broad bank · by a burn side,
> And as I lay and leaned · and looked on the waters,
> I slumbered in a sleeping · it sweyed so merry.

He dreams that he is in a wilderness, he knows not where (yet it may well be that we can identify the very spot on the Malvern Hills which suggested the scene of the vision). The dreamer looks up, East, on high to the sun, and sees a tower of wondrous workmanship; a deep vale beneath, a dungeon therein, with deep ditches and dark and dreadful of sight.

Between is a fair field full of folk — ploughmen working hard, wasters destroying the produce in gluttony: dandies and anchorites: merchants: honest minstrels and loafing japers: beggars, their bellies and their bags crammed full, fighting over their ale. Pilgrims were there, pledged to go to Rome (they had leave to lie all their life after): hermits with hooked staves, great tall lazy lubbers on the road to Walsingham, and their wenches after them: friars, preaching, and glossing the gospel for their own profit: a Pardoner using his Bull to reach after the rings and brooches of the ignorant, and sharing with the parish priest the silver which, but for them, the poor would have. The dreamer sees parsons, complaining to the Bishop that their parishes were poor since the pestilence time, and asking licence to take well-paid posts in London; he sees a hundred in silk hoods, sergeants that serve at the bar.

> Thou mightest better measure the mist · on Malvern Hills
> Than get a 'mum' from their mouth · till money be shewed.

The poet's mind hovers between London and his field in the wilderness: he sees barons and burgesses, bakers and butchers, tailors and fullers, masons and miners, cooks crying 'Hot pies, hot', taverners touting their wines, Gascon or Rhenish:

> All this I saw sleeping · and seven times more.

There are in this Prologue many striking parallels to the Prologue to the *Canterbury Tales*, which Chaucer was to write, a score of years later. But in the next *Passus* of *Piers Plowman*, the gulf between the two poets is revealed.

A lovely lady comes down from the cliff and greets the dreamer: 'Dost thou see how busy these folk are?'

> 'The most part of these people · that pass on this earth,
> Have they worship in this world · they wish for no better;
> Of other Heaven than here · hold they no tale.'

The dreamer is afraid of her face, fair though she be. He asks her concerning this world's treasure, which men are grasping so greedily, and the Tower and the Dungeon. She explains the two great realities, between which the crowd is bustling so heedlessly. In the Tower dwells Truth — the Creator — who formed us all, gave us five wits, and clothing, meat and drink to be used with measure. The Dungeon is the Castle of Care: there dwells Wrong, the Father of Falsehood, who tempted Adam and Eve, Cain and Judas.

> Those who trust in his treasure · are soonest betrayed.

The dreamer asks the Lady who she is. He ought to know, she replies; she is Holy Church who received him at the font, and taught him his faith. The dreamer falls on his knees before her: 'Teach me no more about treasure, but tell me how I may save my soul.' Holy Church replies:

> 'When all treasures are tried · Truth is the best.'

By Truth, we have seen, is meant the Creator. And God is Love. That the spirit of Truth is the spirit of Love is explained in the rest of this *passus*. The Father, who formed us all,

> Looked on us with love · and let his son die
> Meekly for our misdeeds · to amend us all.

And yet would he them no woe · that wrought him that pain,
But meekly with mouth · Mercy he besought
To have pity on that people · that pined him to death.

And men must follow that example. Chastity without Charity
will end in Hell. 'Now have I told thee what Truth is, that no
treasure is better', says Holy Church. 'I may no longer stay.'

But William, aware that a thing is known by its contraries,
having been told what Truth is, therefore asks to be taught to
know Falsehood. 'There he stands, on thy left', says the Lady;
'Falsehood and his many companions.' The dreamer turns,
and sees, not Falsehood as yet, but a gorgeous lady:

Crowned with a crown · the king hath none better;
All her five fingers · were fretted with rings,
Of the purest precious work · that prince ever wore.
In red scarlet robed · and ribboned with gold,
There is no queen alive · more cunningly arrayed.

Holy Church explains that this is Meed the Maiden. Lady
Meed will reappear in the *Faerie Queene* as 'Lady Munera'.
She is Gifts, Reward, this world's treasure. 'The Lady Meed
is nothing more or less than the power of the purse,' says Mr.
Christopher Dawson. Another *alias* (she has many) is 'The
Almighty Dollar'. Langland's outlook is conservative; he
believes in the old world of feudal obligations. He hates the
'cash-nexus'. Holy Church complains that Meed is as intimate
as herself in the Pope's palace:

And so should she not be · for Wrong was her sire.
I ought to be higher than she · for I came of a better.

By the trickery of Flattery, Guile and Liar, Meed is to be
married to Falsehood; and with a final warning against the
whole rabble, Lady Holy Church takes her leave of the
dreamer.

He sees Falsehood's retainers trooping in for the Bridal: to
house them a proud pavilion is pitched on a mountain side,
with ten thousand tents around it. The marriage contract is
read out, and the names of the witnesses: Piers the Pardoner;

Bet the Buckinghamshire beadle; Randolf, the reeve of Rutland; Munde the miller; all callings notorious for extortion. The deed is sealed in 'the Date of the Devil', instead of *anno Domini*.

But Theology protests. Holy Church had spoken of Meed as utterly bad, but Theology sees things differently: Meed is of noble birth, says Theology, she might kiss the king for cousin if she would; what is wrong is that she should be wedded to a bastard of Beelzebub; so let her be taken to London, 'where Law is handled'. Falsehood's followers consent, relying on their skill in ,bribery; they persuade Meed, and set out for London.

But Conscience hears of what is going on, and informs the king, who orders the arrest of Falsehood and his retinue. They learn of this and scatter: Falsehood flees to the Friars; Guile disguises himself as a 'prentice serving in a shop; Liar finds no welcome 'for his many tales', till

> Pardoners had pity · and pulled him into house,
> Washed him, and wiped him · and wound him in clothes,
> And sent him on Sundays · with seals to church,
> And he gave pardon for pence · by the pound about.

Leeches, spicers, minstrels, then entertain Liar in turn; Friars disguise him in a cope when he visits them (which is often).

Meed alone, though terrified, does not try to escape. She is arrested, but is given honourable confinement, with mirth and minstrelsy. She is at home to Justices and clerks at Westminster, distributing gold cups, ruby rings and promises of preferment. A confessor, 'coped as a friar', shrives her politely. She gives him a noble, but he suggests that she should make quite sure of salvation by paying for a stained glass window, and graving her name there. She promises that her name shall appear on every window and altar in his church.

The king comes from Council, and sends for Meed. He blames her courteously, for having wished to marry Falsehood. But he will forgive her if she will marry his knight Conscience, late returned from service abroad. (The French war has not long been over.) Meed, of course, will do whatever the king wishes; but Conscience indignantly refuses. 'Your father she felled', he says; he is addressing the son of Edward II. He adds, 'She has poisoned popes'; and he gives a terrible catalogue of her crimes. But Meed puts up a magnificent defence, for Langland can see both sides. She stuck by the king, she says, in Normandy, and would have won the war for him; hope of plunder would have emboldened his soldiers' hearts through that grim winter; it was Conscience who shamed him, and counselled him

> To leave his lordship · for a little silver,
> That is the richest realm · the rain-clouds float over.

Meed it is who makes a king beloved, and reckoned a man. She concludes the catalogue of her virtues,

> No wight, as I ween, without Meed might live.

The king almost inclines to her side, but Conscience, in a long reply, shows that there are two kinds of Meed. One, good Meed, is God's reward for good works: the other, evil Meed, will provoke God's vengeance; and Conscience ends with a prophecy that the reign of this evil Meed shall give place to that of Reason, Love, and Loyalty.

The king gets impatient, and orders Conscience to give Meed the kiss of reconciliation. Conscience refuses, unless Reason bid him. So he is sent to fetch Reason, whom the king welcomes courteously, and seats on the Bench between himself and his son (the son, no doubt, denoting the Black Prince). Peace, representing the ordinary peaceable citizen, comes to Parliament, and puts up a bill against Wrong, one of the king's purveyors, who has made his privilege of commandeering royal provisions into a cloak for all kind of ill-doing. Meed intervenes, and tries to buy off the plantiff by giving him a present of pure gold. Peace is willing to compound on this basis, but the king, now thoroughly roused, will not have it so. Reason puts Meed to shame, and the vision closes with a magnificent picture of a king from whose council Reason and Conscience are never to depart.

The sleeper awakes, but, ere he has walked a furlong,

drowsiness seizes him, he sits down and sees once again the Field full of Folk, and Conscience preaching. These pestilences, says Conscience, were for pure sin, and so was the South West wind which wrought such destruction on a Saturday at even (15 January 1362). Then the Deadly Sins come up and confess. Some of the sinners are very slightly sketched (Wrath does not appear at all), but the confessions of Envy and Covetousness are masterly. Glutton, on his way to shrift, is tempted to take some refreshment, and this gives occasion for a wonderful picture of the inside of a London alehouse. At last a thousand penitents throng together, weeping and wailing for their wicked deeds, crying for grace to seek Saint Truth.

They blunder over valleys and hills without a guide, till they meet with a palmer:

> A bowl and a bag · he bare by his side,
> A hundred of ampuls · on his hat placed,
> Signes of Sinai · and shells of Galicia,
> Many a cross on his cloak · and keys of Rome,
> And the vernicle before · that men should know
> And see by his signs · whom he had sought.

The palmer has been to Bethlehem and Babylon, India and Assisi; but when the pilgrims ask him the way to Saint Truth

> 'I saw never palmer · with pike nor with scrip
> Ask after him ere · till now in this place.'
> 'Peter!' quoth a ploughman · and put forth his head,
> 'I know him as kindly · as clerk doth his books.'

And thus Piers comes on the scene, saying that all these years, as an honest labourer, he has served Truth,

> Dyked and delved · and done what he hight,
> Within and without · watched his profit.

Piers refuses the hire which the pilgrims offer him, but directs them, by way of the Commandments, to the Tower of Truth, where the Seven Christian virtues are. 'This were a wicked way without a guide', the pilgrims complain; and Piers promises to go with them, when he has ploughed his half acre.

Meantime, he sets them all to work — work in which a knight among the pilgrims offers to share. But Piers tells him that it is not his duty to labour: the ploughman will do that for both: the knight's duty is to protect Holy Church and plough-man alike, and not to oppress his tenants.

Piers prepares for his pilgrimage by making his will; it is the testament of a humble, dutiful son of the Church, who has always paid his tithe, his debts, his dues to the poor. Then he proceeds to inspect what the pilgrims have done by way of cultivating the half acre. Some had been sitting and singing at the ale,

> And helped plough the half acre · with 'Hey! trolly-lolly!'

Then, says Piers, they shall have no grain at need,

> And though ye die for dole · the Devil have him that recks!

Intimidated by this, the slackers sham blind or lame; they will put up a prayer for Piers and his plough. Piers is not deceived. 'Ye are wasters,' he says. They must work honestly,

> Or ye shall eat barley-bread · and of the brook drink.

Those who are really blind and bed-ridden shall have as good as Piers himself, and Anchorites and Hermits who keep their Cells shall have his alms whilst he lives, and one meal a day only. A truculent waster offers to fight Piers, proffering his glove, and Piers calls on the knight to defend him. The knight warns Waster, but courteously, for he is own brother to Chaucer's 'very perfect gentle knight', and cannot speak villainy to any man. Such courtesy is lost on Waster.

> 'I was not wont to work,' quoth Waster, · 'now will I not begin',
> And set lightly by the law · and less by the knight,
> And counted Piers at a pea · and his plough both,
> And menaced him and his men · when they next met.

So Piers calls on Hunger to help him. Hunger seizes Waster by the maw:

> He buffeted the braggart · about the cheeks,
> That he looked like a lantern · all his life after,

till Piers intervenes to save him. Blind and bed-ridden are
cured by the thousand, and Hunger gives Piers good advice,
what to do when he has gone. But Hunger will not go till Piers
has given him his dinner:

> I have no penny, quoth Piers, pullets to buy,
> Neither geese nor swine · but two green cheeses,
> A few curds and cream · and an oaten cake,
> And a loaf of beans and bran · baked for my children . . .
> I have pot herbs, and parsley · and many col-plants,[1]
> And eke a cow and a calf · and a cart-mare,
> To draw afield my dung · while the drought lasteth.
> By this livelihood we may live · till Lammas time,
> By that, I hope to have · harvest in my croft,
> Then may I dight thy dinner · as thee dear liketh.

Thus Hunger was pacified till Harvest time, when new corn
came to market. But *then* he was fed with good ale, and put to
sleep; and no beggar would eat bread with beans in it, or drink
ale but of the best and the brownest. Landless labourers *then*
demanded dainty food, and cursed the king and his council
for making such laws to grieve workmen,

> But while Hunger was their master · would there none chide,
> Nor strive against the statute · so sternly he looked.

Langland has deep sympathy for the very poor, but no sympathy at all for anyone, knight, monk, or labourer, who expects
an easy time. His outlook is grimly ascetic; accustomed to
hardship, he suspects any men who ask for much in the way of
comfort.

The poet goes on to tell how Truth heard of Piers setting folk
to work, and bade him purchase a pardon from the Pope: all
Piers' helpers are to have a share in it.

The pardon seems a model of what pardons from the Pope
ought to be, as contrasted with pardons actually current in the
hands of vulgar pardoners who, like the one in the *Prologue*,
pronounce absolution from broken vows, in return for rings
and brooches. Piers' bull, on the contrary, offers pardon and

---

[1] Cabbages.

remission of purgatory only in exchange for actual good deeds done, and patient suffering of adversity.

A priest asks to see the pardon; with a hint at the ploughman's ignorance, he says he will construe it to him. Piers unfolds the pardon. The dreamer, standing behind them both, beholds the bull, and it consists only of two Latin lines from the Athanasian Creed:

> They that have done good shall go into life everlasting; and they that have done evil into everlasting fire.

'I can find no pardon', says the priest, 'it is but do-well and have-well; do-evil and have-evil.'

Then Piers, 'for pure teen', rends the pardon asunder.

Now this action of Piers has always been found the most difficult thing to understand in the whole poem. The 'rending' is omitted altogether in the C-text, perhaps because readers found it difficult. Many, like M. Jusserand, have felt that 'the passage is absolutely unintelligible and inconsistent, to the point of being a serious blemish'.[1] Yet the context, taken as a whole, gives us, Jusserand says, 'one of the grandest, if not the grandest scene in the poem, the most memorable, even for us to-day, the culminating point of the work'.[2] It had seemed as if Piers, with his pardon, was to be the solution, and it is Piers himself who destroys the pardon which we thought was to be 'the culminating point of the work'.

Yet there is an explanation of all this, if we give its due weight to the Latin text with which Piers accompanies his action:

> And Piers, for pure teen, pulled it asunder, And said,
> 'Though I walk through the Valley of the Shadow of Death, I will fear no evil, for Thou art with me'.[3]

As so often in *Piers Plowman*, we need the help of parallel passages, to show the working of the poet's mind. We must remember that, alike in both divisions of the A-text, in the B-additions, and in the C-additions, the poet makes his appeal to the *Psalter* with a constancy which we can hardly match elsewhere in great

[1] *Mod. Philol.*, vii, 321.   [2] Ibid., vi, 315.   [3] Psalm xxiii.

literature, save in Thomas à Kempis. The Psalmist's ideal of
righteous dealing has been particularly emphasized by quotations from Psalm xv, 'the gentleman's psalm' as it has been
called, defining the duties of the just man to his neighbour:
'Lord, who shall dwell in thy tabernacle?' The *Psalter* is, to
Langland, the manual of just action, of *Do-well*. It is, therefore,
quite natural that he makes his ploughman put his trust in
the text in which the Psalmist, in his character of the just man,
after telling how he has been led 'in the paths of righteousness',
continues, 'though I walk through the Valley of the Shadow of
Death, I will fear no evil'. These words express the same trust
which Socrates expressed when he told his judges 'that there
can no evil happen to the good man, either in life or after death'.

Piers' pardon had been a reward promised in exchange for
righteous deeds done. But the priest has denied that the
document is a pardon at all, and the voice of authority seems to
be on the side of the priest. So Piers abandons his charter. It is
disputed: so be it: he will trust no longer to parchment, to
bulls with seals, but to the Psalmist's assurance that death can
have no terrors for the just man. The action is like that of the
tradesman who, when pressing Charles James Fox for payment,
threw all his bills into the fire: 'now my debts are debts of
honour'.

Of course, more than one interpretation of the Psalmist's text
is possible, and indeed several may have been in the poet's mind
at one time. For medieval interpretation gloried in its multiple
meanings, literal, allegorical, moral and anagogical. Some
commentators had explained 'the Valley of the Shadow of
Death' as signifying the deceit of heretics — and there may be
in Piers' quotation an implied trust that he will be saved from
heresy. But the obvious interpretation is that of the 'Ordinary
Gloss', which had been current for six centuries in Langland's
day, and was to remain current long after his death. Whatever
other interpretations we may place upon the text, we are not
justified in ignoring the 'Ordinary Gloss', all the more so because
it gives here the common-sense explanation which would occur
to the average man. The 'Ordinary Gloss' explained the
Psalmist's words in the way I have suggested above, but with

more elaboration: 'Thou leadest me in the paths of righteousness' is taken by the 'Ordinary Gloss' to refer to the few very
just men who keep to the narrow *path*, as opposed to the broad
way. Such men need not fear the valley of the Shadow of Death,
the Gloss explains, *through faith that they will later be rewarded by
the presence of God*.[1]

But, whatever the comfort Piers may derive from this text,
there is no doubt that his words are uttered in great distress.
After he has torn his pardon up, 'for pure teen', he goes on:

> I shall cease from my sowing · and swink not so hard,
> Nor about my livelihood · so busy be no more.
> Of prayers and of penance · my plough shall be hereafter,
> And loathe what I loved · though livelihood fail me.
> The prophet ate his bread · in penance and weeping —

And just as the poet earlier in the poem had illustrated his ideal
of just dealing, from the psalm of righteous action, 'the gentleman's psalm', so now he makes his ploughman emphasize
this further ideal of penance and weeping by a Latin quotation
from a psalm of the penitent and vexed soul athirst for God,
'Like as the hart desireth the water-brooks' (XLII):

> My tears have been my meat, day and night.

And, in the next place, our once so provident and industrious
ploughman is made to appeal to the gospel text about taking
no thought for the morrow:

> The fowls in the firmament · who feeds them in winter?
> When the frost freezeth · food them behoveth,
> Have they no garner to go to · but God feeds them all.

He feels the insufficiency of those things which of old he has
loved, but which he will now despise. Piers, whose characteristic till now has been his conviction that he knows the way to
Saint Truth, and can guide the pilgrims thither, has undergone
a conversion. We cannot say that old age and experience have

---

[1] See articles by the writer in *Essays and Studies by members of the English
Association*, IX, 50 etc. (1924), and *London Medieval Studies*, I, 34 etc. (1937).
Parts of both these articles are incorporated in this essay.

taught him, as they taught Rochester at a much younger age, 'that all his life he has been in the wrong'. But they have taught him that all his life has been insufficient. For the first time his confident satisfaction fails him; he is aware of something lacking. Perhaps I may quote what Prof. Grattan and I wrote fifteen years ago:

> It is clear that his vexation is really directed against himself. Piers has suddenly realized that *Do-well*, the life of honest labour, which has hitherto been his earnest aim, is not enough. Implicit in the passage is the higher ideal which the poet was to depict later under the name of *Do-better*.[1]

A great modern Platonist, after a lifetime of search, said the same thing in a little book which he sent to the printer a fortnight before he died: 'Can a man follow the high quest of God steadily, while his mind is deeply engaged in secular interests?'[2] Piers' words put this eternal question in a more picturesque form than does Paul Elmer More.

The priest, naturally enough, regards Piers' words with supercilious surprise:

> 'What?' quoth the priest to Piers · 'Peter! as me thinketh
> Thou art lettered a little · who learned thee on book?'

Piers has changed, under our eyes and the priest's eyes, from the humble, unlettered, industrious ploughman into an indignant and eloquent preacher, full of biblical learning. The priest's surprise is justified, for within twenty-four lines our hitherto lowly ploughman has quoted four Latin texts. More than that, he assumes a tone of authority against the priest, such as a mere husbandman could never have shown. 'Lewd lorel' (ignorant son of perdition) is what Piers calls the priest. The contention between Piers and the priest grows so fierce that the dreamer wakes,

> Meatless and moneyless · on Malvern hills.

Many a time at midnight, when men should sleep, he ponders

[1] BUCHAN, *History of English Literature*, 1923, pp. 22-3.
[2] PAUL ELMER MORE, *Pages from an Oxford Diary*, XXVI, Princeton, 1937.

upon this controversy as to the merits, on the one side of *Do-well*, on the other of Indulgences and Bishop's Letters; and he sums up in favour of *Do-well*. The Pope has power to grant pardon, he loyally believes (God forbid else). Yet *Do-well* is better. Unless *Do-well* help, there is no safety,

Though thou be found in Fraternity · among the Four Orders.

And so the poem ends with a prayer that God may give us such grace that, at the Day of Doom, *Do-well* may report that we have done as he bade.

This first section of the A-text (A1) is, in itself, a great poem. But it is an introduction to an even greater whole, and when we have seen it in this light, we shall find it a much more powerful poem than it could ever have been in isolation. It has concluded with a forecast of the glorious sequel which is to follow.

John Richard Green was right when he said that Langland 'dwells on the poor man's life, on his hunger and toil, his rough revelry and his despair'. But he was wrong when he went on to say that Langland does this 'with the narrow intensity of a man who has no outlook beyond it'. That mistake is at the bottom of most subsequent mistakes about *Piers Plowman*. It is usual to regard the poem as a satire on social and political evils. The best manual of Middle English yet written classes *Piers Plowman* under 'Works dealing with contemporary conditions', and under the sub-heading 'Satire and Complaint'. The poem *does* deal with contemporary conditions; it *is* full of satire and complaint. But, if we forget that it is also very much more, we shall, during our reading of the rest of the poem, be constantly puzzled. For whilst, up to this point, we have found the A-text fulfilling our expectations, we shall find the rest of the A-text, and the B- and C-additions, failing to do so. We shall perceive 'profound and far reaching changes' between that part of the A-text which we have been considering, and the part which we are now to consider; and we shall assuredly feel in the B-continuation a 'vagueness and lack of definite organization and movement';[1] in fact, a failure to give us (except incidentally) what we are expecting. We may then be tempted to agree with

[1] *Cambridge History of English Literature*, ii, pp. 11, 12, 17, 18, 28, 31.

the view put forward with such infectious enthusiasm and eloquence thirty years ago: that the first part of the A-text is a great poem, remarkable for its picturesqueness, verve, faculty of visualization and structural excellence; but that the rest of the A-text is the work of a continuator, who had not the requisite ability and failed to understand his original; his ideal being no longer the honest labourer, but the righteous ecclesiastic. From this it is an easy step to the statement that the B-text is the work of yet another man, a man who 'had no skill in composition, no control of his materials or his thought', and the C-text merely the revision of an unimaginative and very pronounced pedant.

The B-text however forms by far the largest part of the poem; it is generally agreed that it shows the greatest range of power, and contains nearly all the supreme poetry that is in *Piers Plowman*. There is less political and social satire in B than in A, but what there is, like the bell-the-cat fable, or the dinner with the gluttonous doctor, is as good as anything in A. And so far from the B-poet not controlling or directing his own thought, or being at the mercy of chance associations of words and ideas, he is, in fact, very emphatically controlling his thought, but to an issue which is not what we have been traditionally led to expect.

The poet had, at the outset, defined the object of his poem, when he requested Holy Church to teach him how he might save his soul. But, it will be objected, if the poem aims at showing the way of salvation by the three good lives, *Do-well*, *Do-better*, and *Do-best*, each revealed in Piers, why spend so much time on Meed and the Sins, before we arrive at Piers at all? To Langland however, convinced (as has been pointed out above) that 'by evil, men know the good',[1] it would seem quite natural to begin thus. First we have 'a lively but unregenerate picture of the commune'; then later 'a profound and spiritual picture of the same world transformed by religion'.[2] The poet has begun by showing us evil in official life (the vision

[1] B. x, 435.
[2] See the most important and significant article by H. W. WELLS, *The Philosophy of Piers Plowman*, in *Publications of the Modern Language Association of America*, LIII, pp. 339-49 (June 1938).

of Meed) and in private life (the Vision of the Sins). Then Piers, the guide, has directed the penitents by the way of the Commandments, and has purchased a pardon. It has been observed by a very capable critic that, up to this point, Langland's answer to the question 'How may I save my soul?' is open to the objection that 'It is not what a man *is* that Langland considers to be wrong, but only what he *does*'; that 'Langland never stops to raise the question of the origin of the various sinful acts'.[1] The answer of Piers to the penitents had been to direct them on a path which is a dull and wooden allegory of the Commandments.

Langland knew that, thirteen hundred years before he was born, the same question had been asked which he puts to Holy Church, 'What shall I do that I may have eternal life?' and the same answer had been given which Piers gives when he directs the pilgrims: 'Keep the Commandments'. But when this answer had failed to satisfy, there followed in the Gospel the overwhelming further demand: 'Go and sell that thou hast, and give to the poor, and come and follow me'.

It is the enormous step from the first to the second which Piers makes, when he resolves that he will cease from sowing, that his plough henceforth shall be of prayer and penance, that tears shall be his meat day and night and that he will take no more thought for the morrow than the fowls of the air. This is the Contemplative Life as Walter Hilton defines it: when men forsake 'all business, charges, and government of worldly goods, and make themselves poor and naked to the bare need of the bodily kind', and so get cleanness of heart and come to contemplation, which 'may not be had without continual travail of spirit in devout prayers, fervent desires and ghostly meditations'.

It follows that, in his later developments, we shall find Piers no longer the honest labourer, but the religious devotee, likened to, and at times identified with, Christ himself. This is the right and inevitable development of the theme. Yet for thirty years we have been asked to regard it as evidence of misunderstanding and different authorship, that in the latter part of the A-text

[1] G. Hort, *Piers Plowman and Contemporary Religious Thought* (1937), p. 85.

which we are now about to consider, the 'model man is not the plain, honest, charitable labourer like Piers, but the dutiful ecclesiastic'. But we ought to have been prepared for these later developments by seeing Piers, the plain, honest, charitable labourer, transfigured into a Latin-quoting clerk, who praises the life of Contemplation and Poverty. We have seen that the scoffing priest notices the change: 'Thou art lettered a little, who learned thee on book?' Why should we overlook what the scoffing priest noticed?

Then the dreamer wakes, and Piers will not be found again till he appears as *Do-better*, the life of Contemplation, Poverty and Charity, culminating in the story of how Christ himself lived that life.

But William will have to pass through deep waters of difficulty and doubt, before he reaches that culmination.

§ 5.   THE SEARCH FOR 'DO-WELL', 'DO-BETTER'
AND 'DO-BEST' (A-text: Part 2)

The natural sequel is accordingly the search for the three lives, which has the title, 'The Do-well life, the Do-better life, and the Do-best life, according to Wit and Reason'. All the summer the poet roams about, seeking where *Do-well* dwells. 'Among us', answer two friars whom he meets: but this statement leaves him incredulous. He walks on, by a wood side,

> Bliss of the birds · made me abide,
> And under a linden on a lawn · leaned I a while,
> To learn the lays · that lovely fowls made.
> Bliss of the birds · brought me asleep.
> The marvellousest dreaming · dreamed I then.

A tall man, like himself, calls him by his own name. The man is 'Thought' — his own thought.

The interest now is not so much in what the characters do as in what they say, no longer in the misdeeds of Meed or Glutton, but in the instruction of Thought or Wit. Just so in parts of the *Pilgrim's Progress* the bustling allegory of action gives place to discourse between two characters. Thought describes *Do-well* as the honest life of a kindly, gentle and truthful man, who wins his livelihood by his labour or by his land.

Do-better does all this: but also he is lowly as a lamb, has distributed his wealth, has entered a Religious Order,. and has rendered the Bible. (*Do-better* therefore is a learned clerk, otherwise he could not translate. We must remember that this was written about 1362; as yet there is no hostility between the Religious Orders on the one hand, and those who wish for a vernacular Bible on the other. That was to come later.) *Do-better* preaches the duty of long-suffering toleration. (He is, in fact, the Charity which suffereth long.)

Do-best is above both and bears a bishop's crosier, with power to push adown the wicked.

Day after day Thought and the dreamer walk together, discussing *Do-well*, till they meet Wit: a sober man, of soft speech. We must get the modern meaning of the word quite out of our mind — 'Wit' is 'understanding': sometimes 'knowledge'. Thought introduces the poet to Wit under the name of Will:

> Where Do-well and Do-better · and Do-best be in land,
> Here is Will would wit · if Wit could him teach.

Wit counsels William to be content with *Do-well*, unless he has a call to a higher state.

> If clean conscience accord · that thyself dost well
> Wish thou never in this world · for to do better. [1]

Good married folk are the root of *Do-well* (as contrasted no doubt with *Do-better* and *Do-best*, both of them most clearly manifested in lives of clerical celibacy). From such good wedded folk all the rest spring, till we reach *Do-best*:

> Right as the rose · that red is and sweet
> Out of a ragged root · and a rough briar
> Springeth and spreadeth · that spicers desire,
> So Do-best out of Do-better · and Do-well doth spring. [2]

And so Wit sums up: *Do-well* is to dread; *Do-better* is to suffer; so comes about *Do-best*, who brings down pride and self-will.

[1] A. x 87-8.　　[2] Ibid., 119.

This, though vaguer, harmonizes with what has been said already of the three manners of life: *Do-well*, the secular life, dreading God; *Do-better*, the suffering life of self-abnegation; *Do-best*, the episcopal life of spiritual authority, correcting the obstinate.

Wit has a wife, Dame Study, who is a scold: 'Here comes a fellow', she says, 'who would make use of my wits to know the difference between *Do-well* and *Do-better*. Unless he does well he will never do better!' But the dreamer placates the lady, and she sends him for further information to her cousin Clergy. Clergy, of course, is not the Clergy as an order; he is 'Learning', and his wife is Dame Scripture, 'Writing'.

Clergy and Scripture give the seeker the same definition as Thought had done before: *Do-well* is the active life of all true workers. *Do-better* gives bread and clothes to beggars, comforts the sick and prisoners, 'obedient as brethren and sisters to each other' (the obedience of the cloistered brotherhoods and sisterhoods). *Do-best* is 'a bishop's peer',

> Prince over God's people · to preach or correct.

He has benefices, as he is worthy to have.

So there seems to be agreement among the authorities whom William has consulted: *Do-well* is the active life, *Do-better* the cloistered life of contemplation, poverty, patience and charity, *Do-best* the rule of God's church.

As to the first and last there is no difficulty: but we may be puzzled when *Do-better* seems to fluctuate between a life of Clerkly Contemplation, of Poverty, of Patience, and of Charity.[1] Yet there is no inconsistency. 'Sell all that thou hast and give to the poor' is the first step to the Contemplative Life. Contemplation goes with Poverty and Patience because it belongs, in Hilton's words, to those who 'make themselves poor and naked'.

But Mr. Wells is, I am sure, right, when he says that these three lives are mental states rather than vocational callings.[2] *Do-best* is not the bench of bishops; he is the righteous rule of God's Church of Unity. *Do-best* is typified by a good Pope

---

[1] Compare B. xv, 147 etc. See below, p. 155.
[2] *The Philosophy of Piers Plowman*, see above, p. 123.

or a good Bishop. But this does not mean that only Popes or Bishops can '*do-best*'. Chaucer's poor parson, when giving of his substance to his poor parishioners, would represent *Do-better*; when sharply snubbing the obstinate, he would represent *Do-best*. In the same way, though *Do-better* is, pre-eminently, Charity, nevertheless *Do-well* and *Do-best* are also charitable.

William is told that even *Do-better* (this cloistered life of Clerkly Contemplation, Poverty, Patience and Charity) *may* have great possessions: but *Do-better* holds them only in trust to distribute to the poor. In other words, a religious house is not *necessarily* corrupt because well-endowed. But there follows a contrast with the contemporary religious orders: the monk buying land and riding on a palfrey from town to town, dagger and sword at his side:

> This is the life of these lords · who should live with Do-better,
> And, wellaway, worse · if I should tell all.[1]

And so we come to a discussion of riches generally. Can the rich be saved? Who indeed will be saved? This question has been an undercurrent of the debate all along: and we have been told that some, like the descendants of Cain, were unpleasing to God from their birth. The age was oppressed, as every student knows, with this fundamental problem of predestination. So the seeker faces Clergy and Scripture with the complaint that for all his search for *Do-well* he is no farther. Long ere he was born, he was predestined — marked in the legend of life, or else unwritten for wicked. Solomon, the example of the wise and just ruler, and Aristotle, who wrought better?

> And all Holy Church · holds them in hell.

Yet 'was there never in this world two wiser of works'. On the other hand the thief on the cross was saved:

> On Good Friday, I find, · a felon was saved
> That had lived all his life · with lyings and thefts.
> And, since he knew on the cross · and to Christ shrove him,
> Sooner had he salvation · than Saint John the Baptist . . .
> A robber had remission · rather than they all.[2]

[1] A. XI, 214-5.   [2] Ibid., 271.

'What then is the good of learning?' William asks. So he de-
nounces Clergy [Learning] to his face. Clergy was never
commended by Christ: for men were told not to consider before-
hand what they would speak, but to speak out what was given
to them at the moment. The ignorant rather than the learned
are saved:

> None are sooner saved · more settled in conscience
> Than poor people, as ploughmen · and pastors of beasts;
> Shoemakers, sewers, · simple peasants
> Pierce with a *pater noster* · the palace of Heaven
> Without penance, at their parting · into high bliss.

And with these words the debate suddenly ends.

There seem to be three problems here: the general problem
of predestination; the salvation of the learned and righteous
heathen as typified by Aristotle; and arising out of this, the
problem of whether learning furthers a man's salvation at all:
whether the blind faith of an ignorant man repeating the *pater
noster* by rote is not perhaps better.

Here are difficulties enough propounded for Clergy to solve.
But instead of a solution, no answer is vouchsafed to the
questions raised. The A-text breaks off sharply. We have only
seven manuscripts which we can here call as evidence. Four of
them conclude in this way, with the seeker's defiance of the
authorities to whom he has been sent for instruction. The three
other manuscripts add a concluding *passus*, short, hurried, but,
in its opening fifty-five lines at least, very clearly authentic.
In this conclusion no attempt whatever is made to solve the
problems the dreamer has raised.

William's statement of his problems is excellent, and the concluding lines, just quoted, are beautiful; they contain much
which no one would deny, much indeed that has already been
admitted in the discussion: they are, in fact, founded on a
text of St. Augustine. In the B-text, when William is reproved
for those words, it is admitted that they are (partially) true:
'Thou saidest sooth concerning some.'[1]

It is recorded that Brother Giles, the companion of St.

---

[1] B. XII, 160.

Francis, once asked the greatest of Franciscan doctors, St. Bonaventura, if a poor ignorant fellow could be saved. 'Of course, if he love God', was the answer. 'Can he love God as much as a great scholar?' asked Giles. 'Any old woman', answered Bonaventura, 'can love God better than a doctor of theology.' Whereupon Giles called to the bystanders, 'Hear, all you people! Any old woman, who can neither read nor write, can love God better than Brother Bonaventura.'

But William's words go much further than this. He has been sent by Thought to Wit, and on to Clergy and Scripture, to learn of *Do-well*, *Do-better* and *Do-best*. *Do-better* and *Do-best* have both been explained in words implying the clerical life. I do not agree, as I have tried to show, that this change from the 'ploughman-ideal' to the 'clerkly-ideal' denotes any change of authorship. But that there *has* been such a change as Manly points out is undeniable. Yet now, suddenly, William turns on his instructors, and says that *Do-better* and *Do-best* are not better, but worse, than *Do-well*. And he denies the efficacy even of *Do-well*.

> Are none forsooth · sovereigns in Heaven
> As these that wrought wickedly · in world when they were. [1]

'Clergy was never commended by Christ.' Surely now we may expect from Clergy some *apologia pro vita sua*, and also *pro vita de Do-well*.

Another proof that the subject has got out of hand can be found in the title. The name of this section, as we have seen, is 'The Do-well life, the Do-better life, and the Do-best life, according to Wit and Reason.' So far as Wit is concerned the title is justified. But whatever may have been the original plan, Reason has not yet appeared upon the scene at all.

The obvious explanation is that the poet could not devise a satisfactory answer to the objections he had made William raise, and that nevertheless he did not wish to suppress his work. So he let it be copied in this abruptly broken form. It might of course be suggested that the poet died suddenly, leaving the work unfinished; but that would be to assume him to a peculiar

---

[1] A. XI, 284.

degree lucky in the moment of his death; for he had just made a passionate plea for a solution of problems which the greatest thinkers had found it most difficult to solve. Nor must we neglect the evidence of the three manuscripts of the A-text in which a sort of conclusion *is* appended. If, as we are nearly all agreed, this conclusion is at least in its opening the work of the author of the immediately preceding *passus*, it proves that the poet really was at a loss for an answer to be put into the mouth of Clergy or Scripture or Reason. So, after having allowed some copies to be issued unfinished, he appended to others the formal 'conclusion in which nothing is concluded'. In it Clergy doubts if the dreamer is worthy of further answer: Scripture is quite certain that he is not. So Clergy withdraws from the dreamer's company. This is important. Big stages in the vision have hitherto been marked by the dreamer awaking, and so losing sight of his allegorical characters. *Here Clergy definitely will have no more to do with him.* That has a meaning. Clergy enters his house, draws the door after him, and tells William to go and do well or do evil, whichever he likes. Scripture, upon William's submission, relents so far as to give him instructions for his further search. But in this travel he is met first by Hunger and then by Fever; the final lines, which are the work of one John But writing very many years later, in the reign of Richard II, tell us that William is dead. Exactly where the original writer stopped, and where John But began, it is difficult to determine. What is interesting is But's assertion that, in addition to 'that which is written here' — the A-text — William also' wrought 'other works both, of Piers the Plowman and much people also'. These 'other works' are presumably the later visions which are found in what Skeat christened the B-text or the C-text, where the vision of *Do-well* is concluded, and those of *Do-better* and *Do-best* added.

PIERS PLOWMAN: A COMPARATIVE STUDY

II. THE LATER VERSIONS (THE B- AND C-TEXTS)

'Your old men shall dream dreams.'

§6. THE POET CONTINUES THE DREAM OF HIS YOUTH (B. XI)

THE B-text, written about 1377-8, works over the whole of the poem as it had been written some fifteen years earlier. Very occasionally a passage is cancelled: much more frequently added or enlarged. These additions are amongst the most deservedly famous things in *Piers Plowman*. To the *Prologue* the poet adds, among other things, the fable of the rats who plotted to bell the cat. But the well-known old fable carries to Langland a very special moral. When they got their bell, no rat dared to adjust it:

> There was no rat in the rout, · for all the realm of France,
> Durst have bound the bell · about the cat's neck,
> Nor hung the collar on his head · all England to win.
> They held them unhardy · and their counsel feeble,
> And their labour lost · and all their long study.

This, so far, is the usual story: but we leave the usual story when a valiant mouse

> Strode forth sternly · and stood before them all.

The astute mouse demonstrates that it is good for the rats and mice to have a cat to keep them in order. 'Talk no more of the collar', he says, 'I did not subscribe, and if I had subscribed I wouldn't own up to it.' The troubles which face the nation now that the Black Prince is dead, and a child-king must follow, are weighing heavily on the poet's mind:

> Where the cat is a kitten · the court is ill kept.

The poet's frankness concerning the evils to be feared from the reign of the 'kitten' is noteworthy. He quotes the text 'Woe to the land where the king is a child'. The Fourteenth Century was, indeed, more free to speak its mind on this matter than the Sixteenth; and when Robert Crowley printed *Piers Plowman* in the reign of Edward VI he had to protect himself by explaining that the text meant not a child in years, but a child in wits — 'where the king is childish', in fact. As no one could deny the precocity of the poor boy-king Edward, Crowley felt safe.

Many other additions and alterations occur in B. It is no longer Conscience but Reason who preaches repentance to the sinners — a change for the better. (In the A-text the poet may for the moment have forgotten, when he made Conscience the preacher, that he had already depicted Conscience as a layman and a warrior.)

The Deadly Sins were expanded, and immensely improved in the process. Avarice is now questioned whether he had ever made restitution of his ill-gotten gains:

'Repentedst thou ever · or restitution madest?'
'Yes, once I was lodged · with a lot of merchants,
I rose when they rested · and rifled their mails.'
'That was no restitution · but a robber's theft.
Thou hadst been better worthy · be hanged therefore
Than for everything else · that thou hast here showed.'
'I weened rifling was restitution · for I learned never read on
book,
And I know no French in faith · but of the farthest end of
Norfolk.'[1]

But when the revision reaches the end of the A-text, the temporary conclusion in which the vision had been huddled up is cancelled, although one hint from it is used. In this final *passus* of the A-text, as we have seen, Scripture had scorned William for his bitter words concerning Learning, and later, relenting, had sent him on his journey, but without condescending to answer his difficulties, or in any way to continue the discussion. We find, in the B-text, Scripture's scorning reduced to two

[1] B. v, 232 etc.

lines: subsequently we shall find that she *does* continue the discussion on the subject of Salvation, and the problems which the dreamer had raised are then taken up and further discussed by other characters throughout two long *passus*.

Now, after the passage describing the dreamer's doubts and Scripture's scorning, which is taken over from the A-text, but before the B-continuation with Scripture continuing the discussion, the poet has inserted a very remarkable passage of about a hundred lines. This passage has been quoted and summarized as proof of the inconsequence of the author of the B-text, and of how he is at the mercy of any chance association of words and ideas.

Yet these lines have a very distinct meaning, coming where they do, between the bitter words with which the dreamer broke off his search for *Do-well* and *Do-better* about 1362, and the visions in which the search is resumed about 1377. The dreamer falls into a dream within the dream. Fortune shows him the mirror of Middle-Earth (the World). He is led away by Lust of the Flesh and Lust of the Eyes. These two fair damsels advise him to pursue other things than his search for *Do-well* and *Do-better*, and he follows their advice:

> Of Do-well nor Do-better · no daintee[1] me thought;
> I had no liking, believe me, · of them aught to know.
> Covetousness-of-Eyes · came oftener in my mind
> Than Do-well or Do-better · among my deeds all.

Pride advises him to 'account Clergy light' — and he has certainly done this at the end of the A-text. Other sins of passionate youth, Recklessness and Fauntelte (Childishness) misdirect him, in spite of the warnings of Age. In place of seeking for *Do-well* he is advised to make money, no matter how, and confess to some Friar — the very solution he had rejected so emphatically at the end of the former vision with the words:

> Though thou be found in the Fraternity · among the Four
> Orders
> And have Indulgence double-fold · save Do-well thee help
> · I would not give for thy pardon · one pie's heel.

[1] Importance.

But he *now* follows the bad advice — for a time —

Till I forgot Youth · and ran into Age.

But when attacked by Age and Poverty he finds the Friars disappointing. With this denunciation of the Friars ends what we may call 'The Vision of the abandoned Search'. Another character, Loyalty, is introduced. The dreamer wishes that he might avow among men this last vision, with its bitter conclusion regarding the Friars. 'Yes, tell it', says Loyalty, 'by Peter and Paul, and take them both to witness.' And with what Skeat calls the 'venerable' pun upon *fratres* 'friars', Loyalty quotes the text 'Hate not the brethren (*fratres*) in thy heart, but refute them publicly.' And Loyalty further gives the poet the rules which should govern such writing:

Thing that all the world wot · wherefore shouldst thou spare
To rehearse it in rhetoric · to reprove deadly sin?
But be nevermore the *first* · the default to blame;
Though thou see evil, say it not *first*, · be sorry it is not amended.
Nor thing that is private · publish thou it never.
Neither laud it for love · nor lakke¹ it for envy.

'He saith sooth', says Scripture. And then she resumes her preaching.

Now this vision, telling how the poet in his youth abandoned the search for *Do-well*, and how, as old age approached, he was urged to avow his vision among men, and to reprove deadly sin, but upon the condition that he should publish no private scandal, and show neither favour nor envy, can only be an apology for the fifteen years' interval between the abandonment of the A-text by the poet, about the age of thirty, and his resumption of his task, in the revised B-text, about the age of forty-five — his 'middle age', as it is called later. Of course the visionary's confessions need not be strictly autobiographical. We are not bound to believe that he, any more than Bunyan, led a life of wild dissipation. But we have sixteen manuscripts to show that the work was discontinued after 1362, and another sixteen to show that it was taken up again about 1377.

¹ Blame.

Either the vision means that, or it means nothing. Of course we may say, if we like, that it all means nothing — that the author of the B-text was 'incapable of organized or consecutive thinking', that he had 'no control of his materials or his thought', and that this very passage proves that B's writing 'defies analytical presentation'. But does it? Let us continue. The renewed preaching of Scripture is on the melancholy text that 'Many are called, but few chosen'. The poet's heart trembles, and he disputes with himself, in perplexity, whether he be chosen or not chosen, and remembers how Christ called all — Saracens and Schismatics. So the B-text plunges at once into those questions of predestination and the salvation of the righteous heathen to which the writer, when he broke off the A-text with Will's defiance of 'Clergy', could find no answer.

At this point, inevitably, Trajan comes into the vision. For Trajan is the stock example of the 'Saracen' who nevertheless attained Salvation. But this does not solve all the poet's difficulties; his anxiety had been for the learned men of old time, Aristotle and the rest: and it was not for his *learning* that Trajan was saved, as Trajan himself is made to say:

All the Clergy under Christ · might not catch me from Hell,
But only Love and Loyalty · and my lawful judgments. [1]

Then follows the praise of humility [2] and poverty. This is not as disconnected as may appear at first sight, for Trajan is the stock example also of humility. He is one of the three great examples of that virtue which Dante saw figured on the cliff of Purgatory in the circle of the Proud. He, the great emperor, accepted reproof from a poor widow. [3]

Then our dreamer goes on to contrast with this standard of patience and poverty the avarice and ignorance of priests. This *is* a digression, and he apologizes for it as such:

This looking on unlettred priests · hath made me leap from
poverty
Which I praise if patience be there · more perfect than riches. [4]

Yet even this apology may be a warning to us not too hastily to

[1] XI, 139, 140.   [2] Ibid., 233.   [3] *Purgatorio*, x, 73-93.   [4] XI, 309, 310.

declare the B-text inconsequent. A writer who thinks it necessary to apologize for so pardonable a digression can hardly be
one whose writing 'defies analytical presentation'.

But the dreamer is still in the same questioning and querulous
mood which possessed him when he denounced Clergy. We
have seen that this quarrel with Clergy broke off in the A-text
before the introduction of Reason, who, apparently, was to
have been one of the characters who would direct the seeker to
Do-well. Now, the poet once again sees his vision of the Middle-
Earth: this time it is Nature who shows it him, and all the
creatures upon it.

> I was fetched forth · by examples to know
> Through every creature and kind · to love my Creator.
> I saw the sun and the sea · and the sand beside it,
> And where birds and beasts · went beside their mates.
> Wild snakes in woods · and wonderful birds
> With feathers flecked · of no few colours,
> Man and his mate · I might both behold,
> Poverty and plenty · both peace and war.
> Bliss and bale · both I saw at once,
> And how men took Meed · and mercy refused.

It seems to the poet (and here we are reminded of Swift) that
Reason follows all creatures save man. Much of the thought
is a medieval commonplace. But the expression of it is full of
poetry.

> Reason I saw soothly · pursue all beasts
> In eating, in drinking · in engendring their young . . .
> Birds I beheld · that in bushes made nests,
> No man had the wit · to make the least.
> I wondered from whom · and where the magpie
> Learned to lay the sticks · where she lies and breeds;
> No wright as I ween · could work such a nest,
> For a mason to make · such a model were wondrous.
> And yet I marvelled · how many other birds
> Concealed so closely · and covered their eggs
> On marshes and moors · that men could not find them . . .

But what most moved me · and my mood changed
Was that Reason regarded · and ruled all beasts,
Save man and his mate.[1]

The dreamer rebukes Reason:

'I have wonder of thee' quoth I · 'that witty art holden,
Why thou followest not man and his mate · that no mischief
befall them.'

Reproving the dreamer for his carping fault-finding, Reason replies:

'My time is to abide . . .
God might amend in a minute · all that amiss standeth,
But he suffereth . . .'

The dreamer blushes for shame, and awakes, realizing the necessity for patience and humility:

'Now know I what Do-well is.'

As he looks up, he sees one gazing upon him: 'What is it, then?' says the stranger:

'Ywis, Sir', I said,
'To see much and suffer more · certes', said I, 'is Do-well.'

'If thou hadst done so', the stranger retorts, 'thou wouldst have received teaching from Clergy and Reason.' And as the stranger moves off the dreamer arises, follows, and asks his name. It is 'Imaginative'.[2]

§7. THE POET'S DOUBTS ARE ANSWERED (B. XII)

Of course, if we try to fit the discourse of Imaginative to the modern meaning of his name, it may seem to us unintelligible. But the medieval 'Imagination' calls to mind that which is not

---

[1] B. XI, 309-62.

[2] Why 'Imaginative' comes in just at this point has been shown by Dr. Otto Mensendieck, and in a short but most important paper by Prof. H. S. V. Jones, ' "Imaginatif" in *Piers Plowman*', *Journal of English and Germanic Philology*, XIII, 583-8. (1914). See also EDMUND GARDNER, *Imagination and Memory in the Psychology of Dante.*

present. The modern signification, the faculty which 'unites former images and ideas . . . *and thus creates brilliant and novel results,*[1] is not the governing medieval conception of Imagination. The medieval *Imaginatio* may mean 'memory'. ' "Ymaginatyf" means *ars commemorativa* according to Roger Bacon, and Bartholomew Anglicus in his *De Proprietatibus Rerum* speaks of it as the faculty of seeing things not present and bringing back what lies in the past'.[2] It is the special function of 'Imagination' to enable Reason to work. 'Imagination is the servant to Reason' — an essential servant, 'for without Imagination Reason may not know'. So the matter was stated by that 'noble and famous doctor', Richard of St, Victor. And this is precisely the function of Imaginative in *Piers Plowman*. The seeker has signally failed to understand through Reason. Now comes Imaginative, explaining where he is at fault,. and reconciling him to Reason. This is why it is Imaginative who reproaches the seeker for his pride,[3] by which he has lost the company of both Clergy and Reason. Had he listened instead of talking, Imaginative now reminds him, he might have learned what Clergy and Reason know; but now, for his pride and presumption, Clergy will not keep him company; yet Shame may bring him to his senses. And the seeker admits that 'there smiteth no thing so smartly, nor smelleth so sour, as Shame'. This confession of shame by the poet, about 1377, for what had been written about 1362, is difficult to understand unless A and B are identical. 'Ashamed he can only be if he, B, has done himself what he relates, and not if he simply repeats what he found in a manuscript written by somebody else.' To suggest that it is the imagined dramatic shame of an imaginary character, is as unconvincing as to suppose that the faults for which Beatrice reproves Dante in the *Purgatorio* are the imaginary faults of an imaginary dreamer.

Imaginative — Memory — tells the seeker:

[1] DARWIN, *Descent of Man*, Part I, Chap. III.
[2] MENSENDIECK, *J.E.G.Ph.*, IX, p. 405 (1910). It is not necessary to agree with all the explanations of Dr. Mensendieck in order to recognize how very substantially he has added to our understanding of *Piers Plowman*, both in this article and in his earlier monograph, *Charakterentwicklung und ethischtheologische Anschauungen des Verfassers von Piers the Plowman*, London, 1900.
[3] B. XI, 413.

I have followed thee in faith · these five and forty winters,
And many times have moved thee · to think on thine end,
How many years have fared away · and so few to come,
And of thy wild wantonness · when thou wast young
To amend it in thy middle age · lest might failed thee when
old. [1]

But the things in his past life of which Imaginative more particularly reminds the dreamer in the B-text are the bitter words
to Clergy uttered first in the A-text. Imaginative solves the
problems which had been raised in the reckless words in which
the seeker had denounced Clergy to his face:

Why I have told thee all this · — I took full good heed
How thou didst contradict Clergy · with crabbed words,
Saying 'unlearned more lightly · than lettered were saved'. [2]

And Imaginative goes on to prove the value of learning. [3] As
for the difficulty (which had been raised in the A-text) about
the penitent thief — he *was* saved, indeed, but not ranked with
the 'maidens, martyrs, confessors, and widows.' [4] Why one
thief repented and the other not, is one of those questions that
all the clerks under Christ cannot solve: [5]

And so I say of thee · that seekest the 'wherefore's
And didst reason with Reason · rebuking as it were. [6]

Some things are beyond the reach of any learning: Aristotle
the great clerk,

Whether he be saved or not saved · the sooth wot no Clergy,
Nor of Socrates nor of Solomon · no Scripture can tell.

Now we see why Clergy and Scripture had not been able to
give the dreamer the assurances for which he had craved.
Nevertheless, says Imaginative, we must pray for these Learned
Heathen,

That God of his grace · give their souls rest,
For lettered men were unlearned yet · but for lore of their
books.

---

[1] B. XII, 3 etc.   [2] Ibid., 156 etc.   [3] Ibid., 72 etc.   [4] Ibid., 204.
[5] Ibid., 216 etc.
[6] Note how the writer of the B-text takes equal responsibility for the cavils
raised in the A-text and those raised in the B-text.

The dreamer objects that 'all these clerks say that no heathen can be saved': but Imaginative denies this angrily. He quotes the instance of Trajan:

Trajan was a true knight · and took never Christendom,
And he is safe, so saith the book · and his soul in Heaven;
For there is fulling[1] of font · and fulling in bloodshedding,
And through fire is fulling · and that is firm belief.

Truth (the righteous, true man) *must* be approved by God:

But Truth that trespassed never · nor traversed against his
law,
But liveth as his law teacheth · and believeth there be no
better,
And if there were, he would amend, · and in such will dieth,
Would never true God · but Truth were allowed.

Then Imaginative abandons argument, and appeals to the same text to which Piers had appealed in the A-text, 'Though I walk through the Valley of the Shadow of Death I will fear no evil.' And he adds:

The gloss granteth upon that verse · a great meed to truth . . .

So 'the B-man', at any rate, had 'The Gloss' in mind, in quoting this text.[2]

After these words Imaginative vanishes, and the poet awakes and many a time has much thought of this vision. Just so, in the A-text, soon after Piers had uttered the same verse, the poet awoke, and many times at midnight pondered on his vision. But in the B-text the poet has given us the clue which was withheld in the A-text. The gloss upon the Psalm which, though never referred to, was implicit in the story in the A-text, is here explicitly mentioned.

Solvitur ambulando. If we read *Piers Plowman*, with no theories of single or multiple authorship, but trying simply to understand, we shall constantly find B explaining A. In the two passages we are specially considering, B cannot be another man *imitating* A, for the A-text has proved unintelligible until

[1] Baptism. [2] See above, p. 118 etc.

we turn back to it in the light of the gloss to which B refers. B knew what A meant; as nobody else has ever done.

It is a commonplace of Dante criticism, that Dánte must be interpreted by Dante. Throughout *Piers Plowman*, we need to interpret *Piers Plowman* by *Piers Plowman*.

The disappearance of Imaginative after his reference to the gloss marks an essential stage in the poem. The problems which had been raised by the poet in his dispute with Clergy and Scripture, and which they could not solve, had caused him temporarily to abandon the search for *Do-well*, *Do-better* and *Do-best*. They have now been solved by Imaginative, and from this point the search for *Do-well*, *Do-better* and *Do-best* is continued, *on the lines which had been definitely laid down earlier in the A-text*. Each stage is now in turn achieved. Far from being 'without a definite plan' the argument is well-planned, though the plan is often obscured because, both in the A-text and the B-text, the writer omits connecting links in his thought. But the thought is there.

Now that he has expressed his contrition for his treatment of Clergy, the first stage in the renewed search is that the seeker is allowed to meet Clergy again. But before we turn to this, we may note the close parallel between the two *passus* of *Piers Plowman* which we have been considering, and two passages in the *Divine Comedy*. The calling to mind of the poet's past misdeeds and the shame which the poet feels; this resembles the meeting of Dante and Beatrice.[1] But the things for which Dante is there reproached are not only spiritual difficulties. Dante's spiritual difficulties are solved when the poet reaches the Heaven of the Just: and he does not express the shame and penitence which William shows, for he had not uttered his grief publicly, as William had in the A-text. Dante asks the spirits of the Just to solve for him the problem which has long held him hungering, and for which he found no solution on earth.[2] Exactly as Imaginative knows William's difficulty without being told, so do the Just Rulers tell Dante 'Thou didst say, "a man is born upon the bank of the Indus . . . sinless in life or words . . . where is the justice which condemns him?" '[3] The

[1] *Purgatorio*, XXXI.　　[2] *Paradiso*, XIX, 25 etc.　　[3] Ibid., 70-8.

Just answer unhesitatingly that 'to this kingdom never rose one who did not believe in Christ'.[1] Yet in the next Canto Dante finds, among those who have given him that answer, not merely Trajan, but the Trojan Ripheus. The *Aeneid* calls Ripheus the justest man in Troy. Yet he perished with the rest: *Dis aliter visum*; 'God's ways are not our ways'. But Dante says of this just man that because he had placed all his love upon righteousness, God opened his eyes as to the redemption to come, and he believed.[2] So mortals must not judge — 'we who see God know not as yet all the elect'.[3]

I have already quoted Shelley's dictum that 'The poetry of Dante may be considered as the bridge thrown over the stream of time, which unites the modern and ancient world.' Shelley goes on to say that 'It is a difficult question to determine how far they [Dante and Milton] were conscious of the distinction which must have subsisted in their minds between their own creeds and that of the people. Dante at least appears to wish to mark the full extent of it, by placing Riphæus, whom Virgil calls *iustissimus unus*, in Paradise.'

It is interesting to note how, as the years passed, the aperture broadened through which Trajan emerged from his torments. Our first news comes from an anonymous monk of Whitby, a writer so primitive that he may possibly in his youth have met Cædmon face to face, for he wrote his *Life of Gregory* before Bede. The Englishman makes the Romans responsible for the authenticity of his story: 'certain of our people say that it is told at Rome'. He does not say that Gregory actually uttered any prayer for a heathen: Gregory only showed by his tears his desire for a mitigation of Trajan's pains: and this desire was granted, though grudgingly, on the understanding that the incident was not to be repeated.[4]

[1] *Paradiso*, XIX, 104.   [2] Ibid., XX, 121-4.   [3] Ibid., 133-5.
[4] For an account of the Trajan story in the Middle Ages, see GASTON PARIS, *La Légende de Trajan*, in the *Bibliothèque de l'Ecole des Hautes Etudes*, XXXV, 261-98. The starting-point of the whole legend, the life by the Whitby monk, was, however, necessarily unknown to Gaston Paris, as it had long been lost. Its rediscovery was announced by Paul Ewald in 1886, and it was edited by F. A. GASQUET in 1904 (*A Life of Pope St. Gregory the Great . . . now for the first time fully printed from MS. Gallen* 567). A very useful summary of the history of the legend will be found in the Preface to Sir ISRAEL GOLLANCZ'S *St. Erkenwald* (1922).

The Venerable Bede, though he knew and used this life of Gregory, was too cautious to use this anecdote concerning Trajan. But Paul the Deacon and John the Deacon did: John says 'it is told in the English churches': he is as careful to put the responsibility for the story upon the English church as his English authority had been to put it upon the Romans. John further points out that though Trajan was released from pain he was not necessarily admitted to Heaven. Later story (misunderstanding, perhaps, the concluding words in the account given by Paul the Deacon) made Gregory suffer lifelong sickness as punishment for having presumed to pray for a pagan. In one version Gregory might have escaped his 'seven pains' by allowing Trajan to remain in Hell;[1] but he was too much of a sportsman to agree to such a condition.

Yet in spite of these caveats, saving clauses, and punishments, it came to be believed that Trajan had been not merely relieved from his torments but admitted to Heaven; and similar stories concerning just heathen came to be localized elsewhere: in Vienna and in London. A Middle English alliterative poet records how St. Erkenwald, the Saxon bishop of London (675-93), saved from Hell the soul of a righteous nobleman who had lived in the days of ancient pagandom. The body of this London magistrate had been miraculously preserved undecayed, and was found when repairs were being done to St. Paul's; it was a second time united to the soul, and St. Erkenwald baptized it with his tears. The soul mounted to Heaven, and

All the bells of London town · burst forth at once.[2]

The poet is a contemporary of Langland, and the peculiarities of his vigorous style remind us of the author of *Sir Gawayne and the Green Knight*. The tale which he tells with such pathos is an almost exact replica of what the tale of Trajan and Gregory had become.

But this cannot have satisfied those who longed for the salvation of the righteous heathen: for such cases were necessarily too exceptional to form at all hopeful precedents.

[1] *Kaiserchronik*, herausg. VON H. F. MASSMANN, 1849, ll. 6069-81.
[2] *St. Erkenwald*, ed. GOLLANCZ, 1922.

Langland and Dante have each his way of getting over this difficulty. In *Piers Plowman* Imaginative is made to say that Trajan 'took never Christendom', although this is directly contrary to the later versions of the story, in which Gregory baptizes his reanimated body. And Langland contradicts the authorities in making Trajan's salvation depend solely upon his own virtues:

> *Not through prayer of a pope,* · but for his pure truth
> Was this Saracen saved, · as Saint Gregory beareth witness.

But Dante will not contradict current ideas as flatly as this: and he explains carefully how Trajan *was* saved: how he was first recalled to life by the prayers of Gregory, and in this second life believed, so that at the 'second death' his soul was worthy to come to Paradise. But in Ripheus Dante proceeds to depict another pagan. The Fourteenth-Century author of 'what is perhaps the most valuable commentary we possess on the *Divina Comedia*' calls our attention to the subtlety 'by which Dante makes us understand the depth of the Divine Grace, which sometimes extends to an infidel and a pagan, and inspires him with the true faith, by which he is saved. So that this story is, as it were, a reply to what has been said above about the just and virtuous man who is born on the banks of the Indus. The author introduces one pagan, Ripheus, whose salvation might least of all be expected, in that he lived many centuries before Christ, in Troy, where the pride of antiquity flourished, a Gentile and no Hebrew.'[1]

Ripheus 'more than a thousand years before baptizing' nevertheless died a Christian, just as much as did Trajan, who was miraculously brought back to life in order that he might so die. This throws a new light upon the apparently uncompromising assertion in the preceding canto, 'Never did any rise to this realm who did not believe in Christ.' Of Ripheus it might be said, as Langland says of Trajan, that he was saved not 'through prayer of a pope', but 'for his pure truth'.

Faith, Hope, and Charity, Dante says, stood as baptism for Ripheus. It follows that mortals must not judge. So we are

[1] BENVENUTO DA IMOLA, *Comentum*, Florentiae, v, 262-3.

told in *Piers Plowman*: 'there is baptism of font, and baptism in blood-shedding, and through fire is baptism'. Those three kinds of baptism were a medieval commonplace. Bede tells us how the executioner who was commanded to put St. Alban to death was converted on the spot and, refusing to obey, was himself beheaded: 'Of whom it is clear', says Bede, 'that though he was not baptized in the font, yet was he baptized in his own blood, and so made worthy to enter into the Kingdom of Heaven.' Again, a man might have accepted the faith, yet might die before baptism could be administered; catechumens who died whilst still under instruction, or the penitent thief himself, were examples of this baptism of the Holy Spirit. This is what Langland means by 'baptism through fire', which he explains as 'the divine fire, not burning but enlightening'.

Father Dunning tells us that 'It is the common teaching of the church that an act of perfect contrition or perfect charity will, in case of necessity, take the place of the Sacrament of Baptism'.[1] But, when Father Dunning seems to argue that this *was* the common belief in the Middle Ages, it is necessary to protest. If it had been, then clearly there would have been no problem to perplex either Dante or Langland. A really righteous heathen, obeying the dictates of conscience, would have attained to this substitute for baptism, and so would have been saved.

That this was *not* the general belief in the Middle Ages is proved by any amount of evidence, for example by the story of Trajan. For, since Trajan had lived righteously, there would have been no need of his resuscitation to receive sacramental baptism, and the whole story of what Dante calls Gregory's 'great victory' would be unintelligible.

The words of Dante concerning the righteous heathen whom he meets in the First Circle of Hell are indisputable:

> They did not sin: and though they have merit, *it suffices not, for they had not baptism.*

'For such defects, and for no other fault are we lost (*perduti*)',

[1] T. P. DUNNING, *Piers Plowman*, 198.

Virgil continues; at which words 'great sadness' takes Dante's heart. The virtues of those pattern wives and mothers, Lucretia, Marcia and Cornelia are *not* accepted in place of baptism. The perfect contrition of Lucrece for a crime of which she was innocent does not save her: she is in Limbo. It is inconceivable that Dante would have depicted his virtuous heroines and sage philosophers in Hell, if there had been any common teaching in his day that an act of perfect contrition or charity would take the place of the Sacrament of Baptism, and admit them to Heaven.

Equally indisputable are Langland's words:

> 'All these clerks,' said I then · 'that on Christ believe,
> Say in their sermons · that neither Saracens nor Jews
> Nor no creature of Christ's likeness · without Christendom
> will be saved.[1]

William Langland must have known what was being preached in the London of his own day.

It was some three or four years before Langland wrote his B-continuation that Dame Julian of Norwich had her revelation. And Dame Julian's words are equally uncompromising:

> One point of our Faith is that many creatures shall be damned: as angels that fell out of Heaven for pride, which be now fiends; and man in earth that dieth out of the Faith of Holy Church, that is to say they that be heathen men.

How then, Dame Julian asks, can it come to pass that 'all manner of things should be well, as our Lord showed me'? Dame Julian leaves it an unsolved problem. 'Our Lord shall save his word in all thing, and he shall make all well that is not well. How it shall be done there is no creature beneath Christ that wotteth it.' Dame Julian, then, knew nothing of the comforting doctrine that any act of perfect contrition or perfect charity will, in case of necessity, take the place of the Sacrament of Baptism.

There had certainly been some learned men who took a hopeful view of the prospects of the virtuous pagans. The

[1] B. XII, 275-7.

'comfortable saying' of the Fourteenth-Century Franciscan commentator, Nicholas de Lyra, encouraged Thomas More in the Sixteenth Century to hope for the salvation of the just heathen.[1] And it has always seemed to me that the view Dante held, when he depicted Ripheus in Heaven, is different from that which necessitated the general condemnation of the righteous heathen at the beginning of the *Inferno*. It means, as Benvenuto da Imola, the old commentator, saw, that 'the Divine grace sometimes extends to an infidel and a pagan'. And if 'sometimes', we naturally ask, why not always in the case of the just heathen? I may of course be wrong, but I have always supposed the passage to mean this: that Ripheus is a test case, and that his salvation involves that of others. It is in this way that Shelley seems to have read his Dante: and the intuition of one poet in interpreting another is not lightly to be set aside.

As to Langland there can be no doubt. He himself interprets the baptism of the Spirit, the *baptismus flaminis*, in the way that a broad-minded Christian would interpret it in the present day. But we have his own word that 'All these clerks say in their sermons' that the heathen without Christendom will not be saved, and the stern indignation which Imaginative shows at this narrow-mindedness proves how bitterly Langland felt about such bigotry.

So that, whatever may have been the case with Dante, there is no doubt that Langland 'was conscious of the distinction between his creed and that of the people'. It is this consciousness which makes him abandon his work in despair, and which costs him so many years of struggle and self-reproach. He believes, for a long time at any rate, that he has against him the opinion of all learned men. He lives to express contrition for the unseemly violence with which, in his youth, he had told of his dismay at this. But for all that, age only confirms him in his confidence that

> Would never true God · but Truth were allowed.

Langland, then, like Dante, 'throws a bridge over the

---

[1] I have given details of this in my Life of Thomas More, pp. 129, 179.

stream of time'. And we ought to be grateful to him for having told us what it cost him to build that bridge. Not often has the struggle of a poet's soul during a long series of years been told as it is in these first two *passus* of the B-continuation. To regard them as a succession of disjointed passages with no connected meaning at all, is the price we have to pay if we start with the assumption that the B-continuation cannot have been the work of the writer of the A-text — an assumption opposed to much conclusive evidence, and supported by none. The *reductio ad absurdum* of this assumption is to be found in the analysis of these two *passus* given in the *Cambridge History of English Literature* — an analysis which reduces its maker (in spite of his very real love of and admiration for this B-continuation) to the despairing admission that 'such writing as this defies analytical presentation'. We may grant that the analysis in the *Cambridge History* is incoherent indeed; but this is because his theory will not allow the analyser to understand the meaning of the text which he is analysing.

For these two *passus* stand to the rest of the B-continuation in something of the same relationship in which the *Prelude* stands to the *Excursion*. The poet pauses, to take a review of his own mind. Imaginative — Memory — must recall his old self, and solve his old doubts. Then he proceeds with his 'great philosophical poem, containing views of Man, Nature, and Society', with its three divisions — *Do-well* (Honest Labour), *Do-better* (Contemplative Charity), *Do-best* (Righteous Rule of the United Church). His subject is Wordworth's:

> Of the individual Mind that keeps her own
> Inviolate retirement, subject there
> To Conscience only, and the law supreme
> Of that Intelligence which governs all.

§8. 'DO-WELL' IS FOUND IN 'THE ACTIVE MAN' (B. XIII, XIV)

And so, the poet's doubts having been solved, the search for *Do-well*, *Do-better*, and *Do-best*, is resumed. Conscience invites William to dinner to meet Clergy, who had withdrawn from

William's company when he showed impatience, and who has had nothing to do with him since. It sounds an unpromising opening, but turns out to be one of the liveliest passages in the whole poem. William's patience will now be tried, for there are two other guests, a doctor who is a famous preacher,[1] and Patience, a poor pilgrim, begging his meat. William and Patience are put at a side table, whilst Conscience and Clergy entertain the doctor. But William cannot get on with his food:

> For this doctor on the high dais · drank wine so fast,
> He ate many sundry meats · mortrews and puddings
> Tripe and wild boar's flesh · and eggs fried in grease.
> Then said I to myself · (that Patience heard it)
> It's not four days since this fellow · before the Dean of Paul's
> Preached of the penances · that Paul the apostle suffered
> In famine and cold · with flaps of scourges.

But, says the poet, reverting again to the pun on *fratres* (brethren or friars), these friars don't tell how Paul was in danger *in falsis fratribus*, 'among false friars':

> And I wished verily · with will full eager
> That the dishes and platters · before this same doctor
> Were molten lead in his maw · and Mahoun amidst.

Patience tries to keep William from reproaching the doctor for his gluttony, and Conscience has to change the subject by asking the doctor to define *Do-well* and *Do-better*. The doctor, 'ruddy as a rose, rubbed his cheeks', and proceeded to lay down the law on every subject from the nature of *Do-well* to the prospects of international peace. 'All the wit in this world', says the doctor,

> 'Cannot conform a peace · between the pope and his enemies,
> Nor between two Christian kings · can no wight peace make
> Profitable to either people.' · And he put the table from him.

---

[1] For an attempted identification of this doctor, see M. E. MARCETT, *Uhtred de Boldon, Friar William Jordan and 'Piers Plowman'*, New York, 1938.

The dinner party breaks up, and Conscience sets out on a pilgrimage with Patience. They meet Hawkyn the Active Man, a minstrel, a purveyor of honest entertainment. In the very first page of the A-text, in the vision of the Field of Folk, the author had gone out of his way to commend honest minstrelsy (as contrasted with the entertainments given by japers and janglers, Judas' children). The poet now repeats the same doctrine here. Besides being a minstrel, Hawkyn is also a maker of wafers — he has in fact many callings:

> 'I am a minstrel' quoth that man · 'my name is *Activa-Vita*,
> All idleness I hate · for from "Active" is my name.'

But Active gets little thanks for his labour,

>   save a benison on the Sunday,
> When the priest prayeth the people · their *paternoster* to say
> For Piers the Plowman · and his profitable servants.
> And that am I, Active · that idleness hate.
> For all true travaillers · and tillers of the earth,
> From Michaelmas to Michaelmas · I find them with wafers.

Active Hawkyn is the servant of Piers: he bakes the food which the ploughman provides. He is the hard-working, Christian man, the Active Life. Why, it may be said, repeat the picture of the Active Life, which has already been depicted in Piers? I do not think that here we have mere repetition. As Walter Hilton explains, all men must *begin* with the Active Life. Piers had represented that almost perfect Active Life which is preparatory to the higher life. He had vanished from our gaze in the act of passing from Active to Contemplative, from *Do-well* to *Do-better*. Hawkyn is the inferior type of Active Man as Hilton defines him — ignorant, rough, untaught, with no savour of devotion, yet with a fear of God, and good will to his fellow-Christians. It will be made clear to Hawkyn that there *is* a higher life than his — even the most ignorant needs to have a firm conviction of that. But he will not be able to follow that life in its fullness: he will disappear, and from that point Piers Plowman will reappear, to teach us no longer the Active Life of the ploughman, but the life of supreme charity of which Christ gave the example in dying for men.

Hawkyn's coat is not brushed — and on further inspection we find that the stains on his coat are the Seven Deadly Sins, which are again enumerated at length. This enumeration has been instanced as an example of the helplessness of the poet of the B-continuation. 'He cannot control himself or his conceptions; and consequently he represents poor *Activa-Vita* as guilty of every one of the sins in its most wicked and vilest forms.'[1] Nothing could show better than does this criticism the difficulty which the modern mind finds in following medieval allegory. *Literally*, Hawkyn is a minstrel, a wafer seller, a hard-working, industrious, cheerful soul, whose only fault is that his coat is untidy: and for this, as he says, he is the less to blame, since he has but one coat, and sleeps in it of nights. *Allegorically*, Hawkyn stands for the whole body of sinning, penitent laity; and collectively, at one time or another, that body *is* guilty of every one of the sins, in thought, word and deed, of which the burden is intolerable. The poet is not 'helpless': it is we who are unfamiliar with his method. 'The art of reading allegory', says Mr. C. S. Lewis, 'is as dead as the art of writing it, and more urgently in need of revival if we wish to do justice to the Middle Ages.'[2]

Neither is it unnecessary repetition when, after Hawkyn has been urged to brush his coat clean, Patience proves to him that his active life of honest labour is not the highest life. True, in the earlier passage Piers, the type of honest labour, had found that there was a higher ideal. But in the A-text this had been expressed so rapidly and allusively that its meaning has been generally missed. In the light of this later passage in the B-text, the obscure earlier draft in the A-text, which has puzzled Langland's readers, becomes perfectly clear. The same lines are repeated almost verbally:

We should not be too busy · about our livelihood.

The same gospel texts are quoted: 'Take no thought for the morrow'; 'God feedeth the fowls of the air'. Patience proves laboriously to Hawkyn that Charity, the life of patient poverty,

---

[1] *Cambridge History of English Literature*, II, 26.
[2] *The Allegory of Love*, p. 116.

is better even than the righteous earning and just spending of money: in other words, that *Do-better* is more pleasing to God than *Do-well*.[1] This again is one of the many passages where what is implicit in the A-text only becomes clear when the B-text shows us what was in the poet's mind all the time.

This praise of patient poverty contains some of the grandest passages in the poem. Langland prays for the involuntary poverty of the wretched:

> But poor people, thy prisoners · Lord, in the pit of mischief
> Comfort those creatures · that much care suffer
> Through dearth, through drought · all their days here,
> Woe in winter times · for wanting of clothes
> And in summer time seldom · sup to the full;
> Comfort thy careful · Christ in thy Kingdom,
> For how thou comfortest all creatures · clerks bear witness.[2]

Poverty was embraced by Christ, and

> In that sect our Saviour · saved all mankind.[3]

And the poet praises the voluntary poverty of him who forsakes land and lordship and bodily pleasure, 'and for God's love leaves it all, and liveth as a beggar':

> And as a maid for man's love · her mother forsaketh
> Her father and all her friends · and followeth her mate,
> Much is such a maid to be loved · by him that her taketh;
> So fareth it by every person · that possessions forsaketh,
> And putteth himself to be patient · and poverty weddeth,
> Which is sib to God himself · and so to his Saints.[4]

Just as Piers, earlier, had shown acute distress when he realized that Active Life was not enough, so is it now with Hawkyn, who

> Swooned and sobbed · and sighed full oft
> That ever he had land or lordship · less or more,
> Or mastery over any man · more than himself . . .
> And wept and wailed · and therewith I awaked.

Precisely in this way the earlier vision had concluded, fifteen

[1] B. XIV, 100-1.   [2] Ibid., 174 etc.   [3] Ibid., 258.   [4] Ibid., 264-6, 270-2.

years before, by the 'teen' of Piers' dispute, which awoke the poet 'meatless and moneyless on Malvern Hills'. 'Land or lordship' may seem inappropriate to a minstrel or a seller of wafers; but Hawkyn, Active Life, stands for all, from the lowest to the highest, who are too 'fleshly and boisterous', too much cumbered with the world, to undertake the life of Contemplation, Poverty and Charity. Piers had been qualified, Hawkyn is *not*.

So Hawkyn passes out of the story, sobbing; and Piers, the Active Life which is fitted to become Contemplative, is once more the Protagonist.

§9. 'DO-BETTER' IS FOUND IN CONTEMPLATION, POVERTY, AND THE CHARITY OF CHRIST (B. XV-XVIII).

Accordingly the poet devotes the next four *passus* to the search for Charity: the first section (*Passus* XV) 'finishes *Do-well* and begins *Do-better*'. After his waking the poet still has no knowledge:

> My wit waxed and waned · till I was a fool,
> And few men liked · my way of life.
> Loath was I to reverence · lords or ladies,
> Persons in pellure · with pendants of silver;
> To sergeants and such · I said not once
> God save you, Sirs! · nor saluted once;
> That folk held me a fool · and in that folly I raved,
> Till Reason had ruth on me · and rocked me asleep.[1]

In his new vision the poet confesses to his thirst for knowledge; he would fain know

> All the sciences under sun · and all the subtle crafts.

He is reproved for his presumption:

> Thou art imperfect · and one of Pride's knights.
> For such a lust and liking · Lucifer fell from Heaven.

[1] B. xv, 3-11.

But, above all, William wants to know where Charity can be found:

> I have lived in *land*, said I, · my name is *Long Will*,[1]
> And I found never full charity · before nor behind.
> Men are merciful · to mendicants and to poor,
> And will lend where they believe · loyally to be paid;
> But the charity that Paul praiseth best —

this complete self-abnegation, which seeks not her own, the charity which is *Do-better*, where is it to be found?

Critics have asked what is the relevance of the poet introducing his name just here. It should be obvious. Long Will is the seeker after *Do-well* and *Do-better*, and now, having found *Do-well*, the Active Life, he begins the next stage — the search for *Do-better* — Perfect Charity. It is very much in the same way that Dante introduces his name into the *Divine Comedy* at the critical moment. Through Hell, up the mount of Purgatory to the Earthly Paradise, Dante has been led by Virgil; but suddenly Virgil leaves him, and Beatrice, who is henceforth to be his guide, calls him by his name 'Dante':

> Turning myself at sound of my own name
> Which of necessity is here recorded,

Dante sees that it is Beatrice who is speaking to him, and the next stage in his progress begins. So with Long Will. He is told that without the help of Piers Plowman he will never find Charity, and the search for Charity under the person of Piers Plowman, *who now reappears*, is continued till it culminates in the supreme example of Charity — Jesus.

At the mention of Piers Plowman the dreamer swoons 'all for pure joy', and sees a vision of the Tree of Charity and its fruits, expounded by Piers. The souls of the patriarchs, as they fall from this tree, are seized by the Fiend, and carried to Limbo. Piers hastens in pursuit, to rescue them, and it is said that for these fruits Jesus will, in the fullness of time, struggle with the

---

[1] B. xv, 148: 'Long Will' because of his tallness, to which he has already referred in the A-text. But there is also probably an anagram, Will Long land. Such anagrams were very much in the style of the time. Gower signs his *Vox Clamantis* in a similar way.

Fiend. So the birth of Jesus is told, and his life, in outline, till the betrayal by Judas on Maundy Thursday:

> Then went forth that wicked man · and with the Jews met,
> And told them a token · how to know Jesus,
> Which token to this day · too much is used,
> That is kissing and fair countenance · and unkind will. [1]

On the Friday is to be the jousting — and the poet awakes, and searches eastward and westward for Piers. He meets Abraham (who is Faith) and then Hope. The visions of Faith and Hope lead up to that of Charity, who is the Good Samaritan, who is Jesus, who, in the armour of Piers — human nature — is to joust in Jerusalem with the Foul Fiend and False Judgement and Death. [2]

It shows again how unintelligible allegory is to the modern mind, that students for thirty years have been invited to note (as an example of the inability of 'the author of the B-text' to control his thought) that then *instead of the jousting, we have an account of the Crucifixion*. [3] To compare the Crucifixion to the struggle of a young champion is a medieval commonplace; it comes repeatedly in the Towneley Play of the Crucifixion: 'Ye must joust in tournament', say the mocking soldiers to Christ. Long before the days of Langland, or of Miracle Plays either, in the *Dream of the Rood*, the story of the Crucifixion had been portrayed as the struggle of a young warrior. The double idea runs through the whole of Langland's dream of Christ's passion, very much as it does through the Anglo-Saxon *Dream*. Wretched, ill-clad, 'wet-shod', the poet wanders till he falls asleep, and dreams of Palm Sunday, and the music of the organ, and the hymn 'All Glory, Laud, and Honour'. He sees Christ ride into Jerusalem, like a knight, looking eagerly to be dubbed and win his gilt spurs. But Christ is mocked, crowned with thorns, crucified, till he cries 'It is-finished' and swoons

> Piteously and pale · as a prisoner that dieth
> The lord of life and of light · then laid his eyes together.

---

[1] B. xvi, 146.   [2] B. xvi, 162-3; xviii, 27-8.
[3] *Cambridge History of English Literature*, ii, 27.

There follows the story of the blind knight Longinus (Longeus) who 'with a keen spear y-ground' 'bare Him through the heart'. Thereupon the blind knight's eyes are miraculously opened, and he yields himself, as a defeated champion, to the dead Christ. Then the scene of the vision changes to the Gate of Hell, and the struggle with the Foul Fiend in person.

It is no longer Pilate who is watching the combat of Jesus with Death, like the judge at a tournament. It is no longer the 'much people' who are mocking with the words

If thou be Christ and King's son · come down from the rood.

It is now the Four Daughters of God who are watching: Mercy and Peace expound the mystery to Truth and Righteousness, how God, that began all, became man

> to see the sorrow of dying
> The which unknitteth all care · and commences rest . . .
> God adventured himself · and took Adam's nature . . .
> Both in Heaven and in Earth · and now to Hell he thinketh,
> To wit what all woe is · that wots of all joy.[1]

Then a great light shines and a voice rings out,

> Here cometh with crown · that King is of glory.

The fiends hold a council in dismay: 'such a light it was fetched Lazarus': till one of them exclaims[2]

> Now I see where a soul · cometh hitherward sailing
> With glory and with great light · God it is, I wot well.

Again the light bids unlock:

> Dukes of this dim place · anon undo these gates
> That Christ may come in · the King's Son of Heaven.
> And with that breath Hell brake · and Belial's bars.

Christ faces Lucifer:

> Now beginneth thy guile · 'gainst thee to turn; . . .
> Thou art doctor of death · drink what thou madest!
> For I, that am lord of life, · love is my drink,
> And for that drink today · I died upon earth.
> I fought so, me thirsteth yet · for man's soul's sake.[3]

[1] B. XVIII, 212-223.   [2] 304 etc.   [3] 359 etc.

Christ's thirst will not be quenched till the final day of judgment in the Vale of Jehoshaphat, when he will

> Drink right ripe wine · the Rising of the Dead,
> And then shall I come as a King · crowned with angels,
> And have out of Hell · all men's souls . . .
> To be merciful to man · then my nature it asketh
> For we be bretheren of blood · but not in baptism all.[1]

The horror of that 'Day of Wrath! O day of mourning!' hung heavily over the Middle Ages. Luther, in his childhood, 'shivered whenever he looked at the stained glass window in the parish church, and saw the frowning face of Jesus, who, seated on a rainbow and with a flaming sword in his hand, was coming to judge him, he knew not when'.[2] But Langland depicts Christ at the Day of Doom coming, not in anger, but in mercy. Langland goes much further than Thomas of Celano does when, in his great hymn, he appeals passionately to the proven mercy of the Judge — *tantus labor non sit cassus*. Langland makes Christ in Hell promise mercy at that last day:

> My Righteousness and Right · shall rule all Hell,
> And give mercy to mankind · before me in Heaven.
> I were an unkind king · save I my kind help.[3]

The great words which Langland puts into the mouth of Christ, as he harrows Hell, seem to promise that, at his Second Coming, he will bring universal salvation to all.[4] Then he leads forth his faithful from Hell, binding Lucifer in chains, whilst the other fiends flee and hide themselves in corners. The Four Daughters of God are left:

> Then piped Peace · of poesy a note;
> 'After sharp showers · most sheen is the sun,
> Is no weather warmer · than after watery clouds' . . .
> Till the day dawned · these damsels danced.

And the poet wakes to the sound of the Easter bells:

---

[1] B. xviii, 368 etc. [2] LINDSAY, *History of the Reformation*, I, 194 (1909).
[3] B. xviii, 394 etc. [4] HORT, op. cit., pp. 122, 125, 127.

And called Kit my wife · and Calote my daughter,
'Arise and reverence · God's resurrection
And creep to the cross on knees · and kiss it for a jewel,
For God's blessed body · it bare for our behoof.
It afeareth the Fiend · for such is the might,
May no griesly ghost · glide where it shadoweth'.[1]

§10. 'DO-BEST': THE RIGHTEOUS RULE OF
THE ONE CHURCH—NOT YET FOUND ON EARTH
(B. XIX, XX)

The next *passus* is said to 'finish *Do-better* and begin *Do-best*'.
It opens with Jesus still depicted as *Do-better*. The poet writes
his dream down, but falls asleep that same Easter Day, and
sees — is it Jesus the jouster whom the Jews did to death, or is
it Piers the Plowman?

Conscience answers, falling on his knees, that it is Christ,
the Conqueror, in the colours and coat armour of Piers (i.e.
Christ's human nature). Knight, King and Conqueror may
be one person:

To be called a knight is fair · for men shall kneel to him;
To be called a king is fairer · for he may knights make;
But to be conqueror called · that cometh of special grace.

Conscience goes on to describe the epiphanies of Christ, from
his birth at Bethlehem heralded by angels and then acknowledged by the three kings, in whom was all the wit of the world.
In his youth Jesus turned water into wine, for the sake of his
mother Mary, and so began *Do-well*. But when, later, he made
the lame to leap, and gave light to the blind,

He comforted the careful · and caught a greater name,
The which was *Do-better* · where that he went.

Jews for envy put him to death, but Conscience tells how he
rose again, and appeared to Mary Magdalen, and to the
apostles, and how he overcame the unbelief of St. Thomas.
The story of Christ appearing to and blessing St. Thomas

[1] B. XVIII, 405 etc.

shows Langland able to do what Milton scarcely can — able to
expand the words of Christ, yet leaving us with no sense of
inadequacy:

'Thomas, for thou trowest thus · and truly believest it,
Blessed mayest thou be · and shalt be for ever.
And blessed may they all be · in body and in soul,
That never shall see me in sight · as thou dost now,
And loyally believe all this · I love them and bless them.'

When this deed was done, Christ passed to *Do-best*, delegating
his power to Piers. The Holy Ghost falls upon Piers and his
fellows at Pentecost. Piers is now no longer the Human Nature
of Christ, but St. Peter, and his story becomes the story of the
Church. Piers' plough, his harrow and his seed have now all
an allegorical meaning. Out of the cross Piers builds a great
barn, to harbour his corn,

And called that house Unity · Holychurch in English.

But Pride musters a great host to destroy the work of Piers,
and colours everything so cunningly that all is confused. We
have here the same complaint which inspired the story of Lady
Meed, a complaint against the growth of what we may roughly
call capitalism. To the conservative Langland it appears that
the power of the purse is destroying the old values, the old
world of feudal loyalties and obligations, till a Christian's duty
is no longer clear:

That Conscience shall not · know by contrition
Nor by confession · who is Christian or heathen;
Nor no manner merchant · that with money dealeth,
Whether he win rightly · wrongly, or with usury.
With such colours and cunning · cometh Pride armed,
With the Lord that liveth after · the Lust of the body.

Conscience calls all Christians into the House of Unity;
they dig a ditch around it, and it stands like a peel. Only the
rabble whom the poet had earlier depicted as the friends of
Lady Meed remain outside: liars and usurers, thieves, flatterers,
those who have wittingly and wilfully held with Falsehood

And for silver were forsworn · soothly they wist it.

The parallels in thought between the poet's early story of
Meed in the A-text and this final section of the B-text are
indeed so close that it becomes difficult to understand how,
after careful study, anyone can believe that they are the work
of different authors. There is no copying, such as we might
expect from an imitator: it is the poet gathering up the different
threads, and weaving them together as his poem reaches its
conclusion.

All Christian creatures (except this rabble) repent:

> And then welled water · for wicked works,
> Eagerly running · out of men's eyes.
> Cleanness of the commons · and clerks' pure living
> Made Unity Holychurch · in holiness to stand.
> 'I care not,' quoth Conscience, · 'though Pride come now,
> The Lord of Lust shall be letted · all this Lent, I hope.'

Conscience calls all the Christians within Unity to their
communion, but he insists that they must first pay their debts
and follow the cardinal virtues. A brewer prefers to sell his
bad ale; and an ignorant vicar says that he knows nothing
of cardinal virtues; the only cardinals *he* knows come from
the Pope, and the country is the curseder for them. This vicar,
despite his 'lewedness', becomes the mouthpiece of the poet.
Perhaps Langland has emphasized the ignorance of his vicar
because he hardly dares to put such scathing words into a more
reputable mouth. (Very similarly, at the beginning of the B-
text, he had put his political creed into the mouth of a 'lean
lunatic'.)

> Therefore, quoth this vicar · by very God I would
> That no cardinal come · among the common people;
> But in their holiness · hold them still
> At Avignon among the Jews —
>   'With the holy thou shalt be holy' . . .
> Imperfect is that Pope · that all people should help,
> Who hires soldiers to slay · such as he should save . . .
> God amend the Pope · that plunders Holy Church,
> And claims to the King · to be keeper of Christians,
> And counts not though Christians · be killed and robbed.

The poet awakes again, heavy of cheer, knowing not where he will find a meal. Need meets him, and reminds him of the yet greater need which Christ suffered:

> Who said in his sorrow · on the rood itself,
> 'Both fox and fowl · may fly to hole and creep
> And fish with their fins · float to rest;
> I must needs abide · where need hath taken me,
> And suffer sorrows full sour · that shall to joy turn.'
> So be not abashed · to beg and be needy,
> Since he that wrought all the world . was willingly needy,
> None ever so needy · nor poorer died.

Again the dreamer falls asleep, and sees Antichrist, in man's form, destroying Truth:

> In each country where he came · he cut away Truth.
> Friars followed that Fiend · for he gave them copes,
> And Religious reverenced him · and rang their bells,
> And all the Convent came forth · to welcome that tyrant,
> And all his, as well as him · save only fools,
> Which fools were liefer · to die than to live
> Longer, since loyalty · was so rebuked.

Conscience summons the 'fools' who will not give in, to take refuge once again in Unity Holychurch, and there abide and do battle against Belial's children. Kind [i.e. Nature] hears the cry of Conscience for help, and sends the visitation of pestilence to teach men to lead better lives:

> Kind heard Conscience · and came out of the planets,
> And sent forth his foragers · fevers and fluxes,
> So that a legion · lost their lives quickly.
> There was 'Harrow and help · here cometh Kind,
> With Death that is dreadful · to undo us all.'
> The Lord that lived after Lust · then aloud cried
> After Comfort, a knight · to come and bear his banner:
> 'Alarm, Alarm,' quoth that knight · 'each life keep his own'.

The dread fight goes on. Old Age bears the banner before Death, 'by right he it claimed':

Death came driving after · and all to dust pashed
Kings and knights · Kaisers and Popes . . .
Many a lovely lady · beloved of knights
Swooned and died · for sorrow of Death's dints.

But as soon as the pestilence ceases, the powers of evil set on
again:

Lechery laid on · with a laughing cheer,
And with secret speech · and subtle words,
And armed him in idleness · and in high bearing.
He bare a bow in his hands · and many bloody arrows,
Were feathered with fair behest · and many a false troth.

As the fight goes on, Age and Death draw near to the poet
himself, and he cries out to Nature, asking what he is to do.
'Wend unto Unity, and hold thee there, and learn some
craft,' is the answer:

'Counsel me, Kind,' quoth I · 'what craft is best to learn?'
'Learn to love,' quoth Kind, · 'and leave off all other.'
'How shall I come to money so, · to clothe me and feed?'
'If thou love loyally,' quoth he · 'lack shalt thou never
Meat nor worldly weed, · while thy life lasteth.'

The poet takes refuge in Unity Holychurch, and the rest of
the siege is told, as it were, from the inside. The danger to
Unity comes from those who should have been the defenders.
Conscience cries that he fails 'through imperfect priests and
prelates of Holy Church'. Friars hear the cry, and offer to
help. After some parleying, Conscience accepts their help,
upon conditions. That such conditions should be needed is a
satire upon the mendicant orders, but even this conditional
admission of the friars is the ruin of the defence. The wounded
cry for help, 'Is there a surgeon in this siege?' Friar Flatterer
answers the call, and goes among the garrison till he lulls them
all asleep. Then Pride and the other Sins make their final
assault. There are cries for Contrition, who should keep the
gate. But the answer comes:

'He lieth and dreameth · and so do many others.
The Friar with his physic · this folk hath enchanted,
And plastered them so easily · they dread no sin.'
'By Christ,' quoth Conscience then, · 'I will become a
    pilgrim,
And walk as wide · as the world lasteth.
To seek Piers the Plowman · who Pride can destroy,
And give Friars their maintenance · who flatter for need,
And contradict me, Conscience.
                        Now Nature avenge me,
And send me hap and health · till I have Piers the Plowman.
Then he groaned after grace · till I 'gan awake'.

§II. SOME PARALLELS IN ENGLISH POETRY

To discuss whether or no Langland left *Piers Plowman* unfinished is superfluous. 'What other ending can there be?' as
Skeat has asked. How, in the days of the Great Schism,
could the poet tell the story of Unity Holychurch save with a
broken and a contrite heart? But we equally fail to follow
Langland's thought if, like John Richard Green and many
after him, we speak of the poet's 'terrible despair'. On the
contrary, as Dr. Coulton has truly said, Langland in his
conclusion 'is invulnerable in his faith, since the breakdown
of outer bulwarks drives him only to more direct communion
with the mystic message which speaks straight to his own heart,
and which he can no more disbelieve than he can disbelieve
in his own existence'. The ending of *Piers Plowman* reminds
Dr. Coulton of the text, 'The kingdom of God cometh not with
observation: the kingdom of God is within you.'

And, in this, *Piers Plowman* resembles other great English
poems with which we might compare it. They end, not with
the victory of the cause, but with the individual human soul
refusing to accept defeat. The *Faerie Queene* begins happily
enough with the knights who, helped by Arthur, are to be the
victorious patrons of the different virtues. And we know
how the poet had hoped to draw all the threads together to a
triumphant conclusion. Likewise, it may well be that the young

Langland, when he began his great poem, contemplated a triumphant close. But events took a turn different from that which Langland or Spenser would have wished, and this is reflected in the later books of the *Faerie Queene*. We find that the victories of Artegall and Calidore end in frustration; Mutability rules all things, and the poet sees no hope save that which is 'firmely stayd, upon the pillours of Eternity'. Closer still, because less accidental, is the parallel with the conclusion of *Paradise Lost*. Michael tells Adam of Christ's victory and triumph, and we might expect him to end, as we might expect Langland to end, with the glory of the risen Christ, and the further prophecy of his Second Coming to judge the world. And at that point Michael does indeed pause 'as at the world's great period', just as Langland, after his vision of Christ prophesying his Second Coming, marks a pause by waking from his vision with the words, 'Arise and reverence God's resurrection'. But each poet deliberately reverts to the back-slidings of the Church, depicted by the medieval Catholic and the Seventeenth Century Protestant with a startling similarity. And after this picture of the world, 'under her own weight groaning', we are left with nothing save the unconquerable mind of the individual man — Conscience, Adam, Eve, William Langland, John Milton. And so each poem ends with the beginning of a pilgrimage: Conscience seeking for Piers as wide as the world lasteth; Adam and Eve, hand in hand, with the world all before them, where to choose.

And likewise *The Prelude* ends, not with any triumph, but with the vision of this age, too weak to tread the ways of truth, falling back to old idolatry. But,

> Though men return to servitude as fast
> As the tide ebbs, to ignominy and shame
> By nations sink together, we shall still
> Find solace . . .
> 　　　　　　　. . . what we have loved,
> Others will love, and we may teach them how;
> Instruct them how the mind of man becomes
> A thousand times more beautiful than the earth

On which he dwells, above this Frame of things
(Which, 'mid all revolution in the hopes
And fears of men, doth still remain unchanged)
In beauty exalted, as it is itself
Of substance and of fabric more divine.

So wrote the Wordsworth of 1805-6, a man of thirty-five. And so it remained with one vital change only. The later Wordsworth altered 'and we may teach them how' into

and we will teach them how.

It was Lord Grey of Fallodon who said, 'When you read Wordsworth you feel that you will never give in.'

§12. THE C-TEXT

The poet may have been in middle age, about forty-five, when he finished his poem, amid the troubles of the English nation and of the Catholic Church.

Twenty years later, more or less, a revised version of the poem was written. Whoever made this revision had access to the poem in a very accurate form, uncorrupted by scribal changes. The B-text of the poem, on the other hand, as it has come down to us, is not exactly as the poet left it. After we have compared all the sixteen manuscripts of the B-text, we are forced to the conclusion that the original from which they are all alike derived was not the author's autograph, but had already undergone some considerable verbal changes at the hand of scribes. Yet from these verbal changes the copy used as the basis of the C-text was free, so that we have the paradoxical result that the correct B-reading is sometimes to be found in the C-manuscripts, whilst it cannot be found in any B-manuscript which is still extant.

There is accordingly not as much difference between the real B-text and the real C-text as there appears to be in those texts as printed in Skeat's great edition. Some of the apparent changes in C are only the correct B-text shining through, as it were, into the C-text, after that correct reading has been lost from all extant manuscripts of the B-text. Nevertheless, a large number of alterations, omissions and additions *were* made in this revision. Some of these C-text additions seem to be made simply for the sake of alteration. Would the original poet, it has been asked, have treated his work in this way?

And certainly it would be strange, if we imagine William Langland revising his poem with a view to a definitive edition. But no such thing was possible in the Fourteenth Century. To-day, the alterations which a man makes in his book are meant to be followed in all future editions. But in Langland's England, once a book had been put into circulation, it was beyond the power of the author to stop the further multiplication of the earlier copies. When the C-text was made, *Piers Plowman* had been in process of being copied for thirty years. It may be that some friend asked Langland for a copy, and the poet, who was much too poor to order one from the scriveners, set to work to copy out his own work. As he wrote he made alterations, sometimes for the better, sometimes otherwise. He had probably no idea of superseding his earlier work; he was just letting his fancy play on the copy he was writing.

Certainly, meddlesome scribes have interfered with the C-text, as they have with the A- and B-texts. I have sometimes thought that the poet may have died, leaving his work of addition unfinished, and that some friend may have taken great liberties in issuing the C-text. The last two *passus*, however, (*Do-best*) were not revised at all for the C-text, either by the poet or by anyone else. Such differences as there are between B and C in these two final *passus* are purely scribal.

But there are some autobiographical passages in the C-text which seem to bring us into very close touch with the poet. He wakes in Cornhill, in the cot where he lives with his wife Kit; he is clothed like an idler, but little loved by the idlers of London whom he satirizes. So Reason asks the poet how *he* can justify *his* way of life? Cannot he find some useful work?

Certes, I said, · so me God help,
I am too weak to work · with sickle or with scythe,
And too long, believe me, · low for to stoop
To work as a workman · any while to dure.

'How can you excuse yourself from labour?' says Reason.

> When I was young, quoth I, · many years hence,
> My father and my friends · found me to school,
> Till I wist witterly · what Holy Writ meant . . .
> And yet found I never, in faith · since my friends died,
> Life that me liked · save in these long clothes.

So, he says, he lives in London and on London both; his tools
are

> My *pater noster* and my primer · *placebo* and *dirige*
> And my psalter sometime · and my seven psalms;
> Thus I sing for the souls · of such as me help.

It is the life of a poor Chantry-clerk: and he picks up a meal
from time to time at the house of one or other of his patrons:

> So rebuke me in no wise, · Reason, I thee pray;
> In my conscience I know · what Christ wills me to do.
> Prayers of a perfect man · and penance discreet
> Is the liefest labour · that Our Lord pleaseth.

'Yes', retorts Conscience, 'but begging in cities doesn't seem
to me the life of a perfect man.'

> That is sooth, I said, · and so I confess
> That I have lost labour · and life misspent.
> And yet I hope, as he · that oft hath chaffered,
> And aye hath lost and lost · and at the last him happed
> He bought such a bargain · he was ever the better,
> And set his loss at a leaf · at the last end,
> Such a winning he won · through words of grace;
> So hope I to have · of him that is almighty
> A gobbet of his grace · and begin a time
> That all times of my time · to profit shall turn.

William Langland must by now have been over sixty, and
it is difficult not to hear in these words the authentic voice of
the aged scholar. He has spent his life in the search for St.
Truth: he has achieved neither wealth, nor honour, nor depth

of learning. But he will not give in. He passes out of our sight,

> Still nursing the unconquerable hope,
> Still clutching the inviolable shade.

NOTE

The controversy as to the authorship of the different versions of *Piers Plowman* was opened by Prof. Manly in *Modern Philology* (Jan. 1906).

The Seven Deadly Sins are enumerated four times in *Piers Plowman*, but never does the writer enumerate all at his first attempt. They are enumerated twice in the A-text (*Passus ii* and *v*), and in both cases 'Wrath' is omitted. In the B-continuation the writer again twice enumerates the Sins. In B, xiii, he omits Gluttony; in B, xiv, Gluttony and Envy.

One would think that, if anything, this goes to prove that A is B. The natural comment is that of M. Jusserand: 'Such peculiarities are indeed so peculiar as to be, in a way, the author's mark — his seal and signature.'

But no. We were asked to assume that in the A-text these omissions were due to mutilation of the author's manuscript, whilst in the B-text they were due to the writer's incapacity for consecutive thinking: A was a 'careful artist', B 'perfectly helpless'; they must be different men.

The omission of 'Wrath' was not the only fault in the account of the Deadly Sins in the A-text. 'Sloth', in A, promises, quite appropriately, to be regular at church service. Then, surprisingly, Sloth promises further to repay all ill-gotten gains. Prof. Manly's theory was that two leaves had been lost from the archetypal manuscript from which all our extant manuscripts of the A-text are derived: one had contained the (lost) confession of 'Wrath'; the corresponding lost leaf, later in the quire, was supposed to have contained a more appropriate ending to the confession of 'Sloth' and the beginning of the confession of a later character, Robert the Robber, to whom the promise of repayment would therefore belong.

This was an acute and ingenious conjecture.

B, when he worked over the A-text for his B-revision, remedied these crudities which he found in the A-text. (This might seem odd in a 'perfectly helpless' writer.) But B did it in a way which shows that no suspicion crossed his mind that two leaves were missing, exactly where Prof. Manly had postulated their absence. Therefore, it was argued, he cannot have been A, for A must have known this.

This was the argument which, thirty years ago, took the whole world of English studies by storm. For years it was considered a proof of invincible ignorance not to accept it, either in the original form put forward with much ability by Prof. Manly, or in the modified (and, I think, inferior) form adopted by Dr. Henry Bradley.

But when we turn to the B-text, we find the conjecture to be quite unnecessary. B supplies the missing Confession of 'Wrath'. He also prefixes to 'Sloth's' vow a confession in which 'Sloth' laments that, from negligence, he has withheld the wages of his servants, and forgotten to restore what he has borrowed. Upon such a confession, the vow of restitution follows naturally, and indeed inevitably.

We must never forget that 'Sloth' is much more than mere laziness. 'Sloth' is 'Accidie', *akedia*, heedlessness of every kind. Misappropriation of cash proceeds often, in the first instance, from Accidie, Neglect, as well as from deliberate and intentional theft (Avarice or Covetousness).

We saw above[1] (with reference to the gloss upon the text, 'Though I walk through the Valley of the Shadow of Death') that an explanation, which is necessary to the understanding of the passage in the A-text, only becomes explicit in the B-text. The A-text proved unintelligible, until we turned back to it in the light of what the B-text told us.

The difficulty about 'Sloth's' ill-gotten gains is another example of the same thing. There is no need for any elaborate theories and conjectures about missing leaves. The B-text gives us a perfectly coherent Confession of 'Sloth'. What is explicit in the B-text was presumably in the mind of the writer of the

---

[1] Pp. 118 etc., 141 etc.

A-text, though he did not explain it clearly, either in the 'Sloth' passage or in the 'Valley of the Shadow of Death' passage. But, however difficult in A, both passages are clear enough in B. B knew what A meant; as nobody else has ever done.

So far from affording an argument for different authorship, both these passages are strong arguments in favour of B being A, so long as we accept the texts which have come down to us. If we start by assuming that B is not A, and if we rearrange the text of A to suit some theory of missing or shifted leaves, they can then be converted into an argument to reinforce our original assumption.

It has not been sufficiently realized how the argument that B is a different man from A begins by taking for granted the very thesis which it claims to prove.

The method of arguing from a working hypothesis is, of course, legitimate. But the hypothesis that A and B are different men does not work. It involves us (admittedly) in large conjectural emendations in order to make A intelligible, and (admittedly) it leaves B unintelligible. Yet *Piers Plowman* is no more unintelligible than the *Divine Comedy*. It is evidence of the working of 'the spirit of the age' that Langland's purpose can be expressed in the words in which Dante expressed his purpose to Can Grande: 'To remove those who are living in this life' [the Field of Folk] 'from the state of wretchedness' [Lady Meed and the Seven Sins] 'and to lead them to the state of blessedness' [through the quest for *Do-well*, *Do-better*, and *Do-best*].

VI

MARTYRS OF THE REFORMATION: MORE AND TYNDALE

§1. THOMAS MORE

FROM his own day to ours, Sir Thomas More has always appeared to the practical Anglo-Saxon mind as a paradoxical figure. When we learn, in our schooldays, of the great statesman and lawyer who would rather be decapitated than tell a lie, we are moved by feelings of respect, tempered by astonishment; like the little American girl when she read the story of the boy who stood on the burning deck, we are inclined to say, 'I think he was very good; but he wasn't very smart.'

A boy grows into a man, and a man on rare occasions into an eminent historian, into a Froude, or an Acton, or a Creighton. The respect for More remains; and though the grounds for the perplexity may have shifted, the perplexity remains also. To our great historians More is an incomprehensible riddle.

From those who adhere to the faith for which More died, he has generally received a tribute of complete and understanding sympathy. Elsewhere, however (and sometimes even among those of his own faith), More is regarded as a daring innovator, who somehow or other became one more example of 'the lost leader', one more example of the Triumphs of the World:

> 'Behold,' she cries, 'so many rages lull'd,
> So many fiery spirits quite cool'd down.'

As to the cause of this change, historians are not agreed. Some great writers put it down to the bad influence of Henry VIII. More, they say, allowed his sentiments to be moulded by the official theology of the court, till under that sinister influence he was changed from a 'liberal' into a 'pseudo-liberal'. Creighton and Acton had their little quarrels, but upon this estimate of More they are in complete agreement. Froude also agrees, except that his respect for Henry VIII will not allow of that monarch retaining the part of More's misleader, a role which in Froude's pages has to be undertaken by the Roman Catholic Church: it was that which turned the 'genial philosopher' into the 'merciless bigot'.

Thirty years ago, the great English biographer and organizer of English biography, Sidney Lee, expressed the traditional English view of More:

> None who read the *Utopia* can deny that its author drank deep of the finest spirit of his age ... There is hardly a scheme of social or political reform that has been enunciated in later epochs of which there is no definite adumbration in More's pages. But he who passes hastily from the speculations of More's *Utopia* to the record of More's subsequent life and writings will experience a strange shock. Nowhere else is he likely to be faced by so sharp a contrast between precept and practice, between enlightened and vivifying theory in the study, and adherence in the work-a-day world to the unintelligent routine of bigotry and obscurantism. By the precept and theory of his *Utopia* More cherished and added power to the new light. By his practical conduct in life he sought to extinguish the illuminating forces to which his writing offered fuel.
>
> The facts of the situation are not open to question ... Sir Thomas More's career propounds a riddle which it is easier to enunciate than to solve.[1]

Yet one thing is clear. There is no sixteenth-century Englishman as to whom there exists more intimate information. If we wish to solve the 'riddle of his career', there is no one whose motives we can learn to appreciate so fully. More's son-in-law, William Roper, 'knowing at this day no one man living, that of him and of his doings understood so much as myself', wrote, in Queen Mary's reign, his deeply understanding notes on More's life. Nicholas Harpsfield, in the same reign, wrote a careful official biography. An even more elaborate biography

[1] *Great Englishmen of the Sixteenth Century*, 1904, pp. 32, 33, 61.

by More's nephew, William Rastell, has been lost, but some priceless fragments remain. Had it not been for Rastell, much of More's written work might have been lost also. The reminiscences of the young people who had lived with More in the Great House at Chelsea were collected by yet a fourth biographer, Thomas Stapleton. The family tradition did not finally work itself out till a fifth biographer and a sixth (Cresacre More, More's great-grandson) had told the story.

Even more important are More's own writings. In *Utopia* More expressed the hopes and fears for the world felt by the scholarly circle surrounding Erasmus and himself. More's defence of the things for which he most cared is extant in his voluminous controversial and devotional writings. And, in his letters, we can trace his thoughts (especially during his last months of imprisonment) in a way which is possible with only very few of the great men of history.

Yet, abundant as this material is, much of it has only been made easily accessible during the past few years, and much of it is not easily accessible even now. The misunderstanding of More is chiefly due to neglect of what he has himself written, and also in some degree to neglect of what his biographers tell us.

Let us take a single paragraph from Roper's *Life*, and see what we can get from a study of it.

As an example of the 'fruitful communication' which he 'had ofttimes with his familiar friends', Roper records a conversation in which More told him of the three great wishes of his life:

So on a time, walking with me along the Thames' side at Chelsea, in talking of other things he said unto me: 'Now would to our Lord, son Roper, upon condition that three things were well established in Christendom, I were put in a sack, and here presently cast into the Thames.'

'What great things be those, Sir,' quoth I, 'that should move you so to wish?'

'Wouldst thou know what they be, son Roper?' quoth he.

'Yea, marry, with good will, sir, if it please you,' quoth I. 'In faith, son, they be these,' said he. 'The first is, that where the most part of Christian princes be at mortal war, they were all at an universal peace. The second, that where the Church of Christ is at this present sore afflicted with many errors and heresies, it were settled in a perfect uniformity of religion. The third, that where the king's matter of his marriage is now come in question, it were to the glory of God and quietness of all parties brought to a good conclusion.' Whereby, as I could gather, he judged that otherwise it would be a disturbance to a great part of Christendom.[1]

We can date this conversation pretty exactly — it must have been after the King's marriage had come in question, but before the peace of Cambrai, in which More took a big part and by which England secured the only long-continued cessation from foreign warfare which this country enjoyed during the troubled reign of Henry VIII. More, when he spoke these words, was a man of fifty, and was shortly to become Lord Chancellor. He could look back on a life of public service. The son of a Lincoln's Inn lawyer, he was taught the ways of the great whilst still a boy, by service in the household of Cardinal Morton. He was subsequently himself trained as a lawyer at Lincoln's Inn, after a short spell of education at Oxford. This was a combination which, though it may seem natural enough to us to-day, was rare in More's time — but it is typical of More's two great interests. Oxford, with its theological training, led to the secular priesthood or the cloister — a calling which throughout his life had a great attraction for More. Lincoln's Inn and the Law led to the political career which, after a period of hesitation between the Church and the Law, was to be More's vocation. Like some great modern statesmen, More came to political life after an apprenticeship in the service of his city. For nearly eight years he had been one of the two Under-Sheriffs of London. The post was then a very important one, for the Sheriffs had to perform

[1] *The Lyfe of Sir Thomas Moore*, by William Roper, ed. by E. V. Hitchcock, 1935, pp. 24, 25.

legal duties for which, being men of business rather than lawyers, they had not usually any special qualifications, and their permanent legal officials consequently carried a considerable responsibility. Then More left the service of the city for that of Henry, and for nearly a dozen years had been rising in political life, when this conversation with his son-in-law took place.

The passion for universal peace was one which More shared with his scholar friends, and above all with Colet and Erasmus. During the twenty years of Henry's reign England had been plunged into one futile campaign after another, till the vast accumulated wealth of Henry VII had been wasted, and the resources of the country so exhausted as to make for a time any further war impossible. No danger had been averted and no advantage gained; historians have been puzzled to find the justification or even the explanation of Henry's wars, or, as Sir Walter Ralegh described them, 'his vain enterprises abroad, wherein it is thought that he consumed more treasure than all our victorious kings did in their several conquests'. It is true that there was comparatively little fighting, and that such fighting as there was proved quite inconclusive. Continuous war in the sixteenth century had become too expensive for the resources of any government, and Henry had but few subjects compared with his rivals, Francis I or Charles V. Historians often speak as if, therefore, Henry's wars were negligible. That is not so. Taxation and the depreciation of the coinage caused terrible suffering. We are the poorer to this day for the confiscation of art treasures, treasures which the monasteries of England had created and housed during eight centuries, but which were destroyed in the vain attempt to refill Henry's exhausted treasury.

All these useless wars More detested. Yet his ideal was anything but a policy of selfish isolation for England. It is because he cares for Europe, not because he ignores Europe, that More is a lover of peace. European scholars were hoping for a Reformation by reason and argument, not by violence. If this was to be brought about, it could only be in an atmosphere of European peace. The scholars were an international body, very closely knit together. Their greatest danger lay in the rising passions of nationalism. We may take Erasmus as their great example. To Erasmus, Europe was one great State. For Holland, as the country of his birth, he had a certain love, combined with a feeling that it was rather a provincial backwater, remote from the real centres of civilization. His feeling towards his country was very much what an Englishman long resident in London, where he has grown eminent, might cherish towards a remote district of agriculturists and fishermen in which he happened to have been born and bred. Erasmus has a sentimental combination of affection and dislike for Holland, but Europe is the country which demands his allegiance.

More's feelings are much more complicated: he is a thoroughly loyal Englishman. But we can never understand More if we allow ourselves to forget the Great Turk. The threat to the whole of Christian civilization from the marauding bands of Asia was a very real thing to him. That Christian princes should be struggling one against another whilst Belgrade and Rhodes were falling, and whilst all the chivalry of Hungary perished on the field of Mohacz, till the Turk reached the gates of Vienna, seemed to More to be treachery to the common cause. There were Lutheran pacifists in More's day, who held that the Turk was a divinely appointed scourge, and that Christians should allow themselves to be enslaved and butchered without offering resistance to the Moslems, who had at least the merit of not being Papists. More disagrees, and (in language which has found an echo in later ages) he complains that these pacifists are so pugnacious. Whilst they argue that no man should withstand the Turk, but let him win all, says More, they arise up 'in great plumps' to fight against their fellow-Christians, and destroy many a good religious house. More feels that war between Christians is detestable. The wars of Christendom are, to him, civil wars. He has both an English and a European patriotism.

This balance and combination of loyalties brings More very closely into touch with problems of to-day. To More, the whole question cannot be entirely settled by allegiance to a king, or loyalty to the country in which a man happens to have been

M

born. Yet he would have been the last to deny the binding power of these obligations.

Few in these days will censure More for his longing for peace among the states of Europe; there will in some quarters be less sympathy for his second aspiration, that whereas the Church is afflicted with many errors and heresies, it were settled in perfect uniformity. More was very frank as to his hatred of heretics. The accusation that he was himself a bitter persecutor can be refuted; but the fact remains that he believed it necessary to prohibit 'the sowing of seditious heresies'; and he believed that, in extreme cases, it was right to punish with terrible death those who defied this prohibition.

Seditious heresies. Emphasis must be laid upon the adjective. To those who were in any kind of doubt or spiritual trouble, More was always the gentlest of counsellors. His son-in-law, Roper, had in his youth a violent bout of Lutheranism. More and he lived together in the same house, and argued together constantly, but Roper records that he never knew More lose his temper; never knew him 'in a fume'. People in spiritual difficulties, troubled with 'vehement and grievous tentations of desperation', would come to More for advice. At the time when More was Chancellor, and at the height of his controversy with the Lutherans, a distinguished Lutheran scholar, Simon Grinæus, needed to come to England to consult manuscripts of Plato and commentaries thereon, in the College libraries of Oxford. More entertained him hospitably, and gave him every possible assistance, only insisting on a promise that his guest would not spread his heresies during his stay in England. Grinæus acknowledged More's kindness by dedicating his work, when published, to More's son John. Rather naïvely, Grinæus emphasizes the enormous personal trouble More took, accompanying him everywhere, and, when that was not possible, sending as escort his secretary, a young scholar, John Harris. Grinæus would have been pained had he known that, in fact, More had very little belief in the value of any heretic's promise. We knew from John Harris himself that he was instructed to see that Grinæus issued no Lutheran propaganda. If Grinæus had done so, More would have bundled him out of the kingdom unceremoniously. But, so long as he behaved properly, More showed him untiring generosity and kindness. And also, amid all the cares of office, More spent many hours in a vain attempt to bring Grinæus back into the fold, first by discussion in his home, and later by correspondence. Nor was this merely the freemasonry of scholarship. More would have been even gentler with a poor and ignorant heretic than with a learned one. 'Little rigour and much mercy should be showed', he said, 'where simpleness appeared, and not high heart or malice.' More argued eloquently that the whole Bible might be suffered to be spread abroad in English among the laity. His sense of discipline was too strong to allow him to press this claim against the opinion of the bishops; but under episcopal supervision, at any rate, translations of the Bible in whole and in part should be issued, he thought, and even issued, where necessary, gratis. But it must be an authorized translation, made by the most responsible scholars. At a time when civil war might break out over the interpretation of a biblical text, More denied the right of Tyndale, or any individual, to issue his translation of the Bible on his own authority. The public and deliberate defiance of authority in matters of religion was, to More, sedition; and, like other forms of sedition, might, in extreme cases, merit the death penalty.

The trial of heresy was a matter for the bishops. But the responsibility of the Church, More held, ended with the excommunication of the heretic. It was the State which, 'from fear of outrages and mischiefs to follow', had decreed that the seditious heretic, when the Church had excommunicated him, should suffer a terrible death.

Unless we realize More's haunting fear of religious violence, we shall never understand how he came to defend the persecution to the death of 'seditious heretics'. The most noteworthy thing about More is his political foresight. He realized, as few other men did, how chaos and religious wars would follow, if the unity of the Medieval Church were shattered. 'The world once ruffled and fallen in a wildness', he asked, 'how long would it be, and what heaps of heavy mischiefs would there fall, ere the way were found to set the world in order and peace again?' That those who disturbed the unity of Christendom by deliberate defiance of ecclesiastical authority should suffer for it, seemed to More as natural as that a rebel should suffer for deliberate defiance of civil authority. And so, in his *Dialogue against heresies* he gives 'his opinion concerning the burning of heretics, and that it is lawful, necessary, and well done'. In a later treatise he examined the case of the heretics (seven in all) who had suffered death in recent times — (actually within the past eighteen years). He maintained that they had had no wrong, under the law. (There were at least five other cases during those eighteen years of which More seems to have been unaware.) But, further, More went so far as to say that, if the bishops had 'taken as good heed in time as they should have done', there would have been more burnt by a great many in the preceding seven years, though perhaps fewer in the end. Nothing can justify his words — we can only understand them if we realize his horror at the impending destruction of everything he loved. 'For heretics, as they be', he says, 'the clergy doth denounce them; and, as they be well worthy, the temporalty doth burn them; and after the fire of Smithfield hell doth receive them, where the wretches burn for ever.' Not that Reformers were more merciful to each other. Lutherans burnt Anabaptists. Latimer refers to the burning of fourteen Anabaptists with no disapproval. 'We should not have disapproved of it, if we had lived then, unless we had been Anabaptists ourselves,' says Froude, very truly. If we ask why Latimer is forgiven for his intolerance, and More blamed, the answer is to hand. More, it is asserted, had shown a dozen years before, in *Utopia*, that he knew better.

More has suffered the fate of many pioneers, in that he has been interpreted in the light of those who have followed him. *Utopia* has been followed by a long series of 'Ideal Commonwealths', often written in direct imitation. Francis Bacon in the *New Atlantis*, and William Morris in *News from Nowhere*, have drawn pictures of the world as they would like to see it. So *Utopia* has been christened an 'ideal commonwealth'. Now the citizens of Utopia are depicted as not insisting on any dogma except in the existence of God and the immortality of the soul.

Therefore, it has been argued, More believed the vague deism of the Utopians more 'ideal' than the Catholic faith of his own day. And it is certainly the case with the romance of William Morris, that it represents the writer's ideal — the world as he would have it, if he could shatter it to bits and remould it nearer to the heart's desire. But if we want to understand *Utopia* or *News from Nowhere*, we must think of the first as published in 1516, and the second as published in 1890.

More's education was Medieval; and the Middle Ages recognized many kinds of law: canon law and common law, the law of God and the law of nature. In 1516 one of the most debated questions of the day was whether, apart from revelation, nature and philosophy taught that the soul was immortal. Three years before, this question had led to an important decision of the Lateran Council. By that decision teachers of philosophy were put in their place. They were instructed to point out the difference between the merely philosophical and the Christian view as to the immortality of the soul.

More's contribution to the discussion is to depict a Commonwealth based entirely upon the law of nature and on philosophy, the Commonwealth of Utopia. But the views of the Commonwealth, as to what *unaided philosophy* can teach regarding the immortality of the soul, are actually stricter than those of many Christians, and a marginal note is added drawing marked attention to this. So far is the Utopian Commonwealth from having any doubts about immortality, that the man who does not accept the immortality of the soul is not allowed to rank as a citizen, or even as a man. The Utopians cannot believe that a man who holds that the soul perishes with the body can be anything but a potential criminal, restrained from felony only by his cowardice, 'and thus he is of all sorts despised, as of an unprofitable and of a base and vile nature'. And then comes the sentence upon which are based the many laudations of the toleration of Utopia: 'Howbeit, they put him to no punishment.' No punishment, indeed! It is a mere mistranslation, as More's critics might have seen, if they would have referred back to the Latin original.

In Utopia, as in ancient Sparta, where all life was lived in common, to be sent to Coventry was a living death. What More really wrote was that the unbeliever is not put to any bodily punishment. The Utopians do not threaten him with violence, to make him dissemble his disbelief. He may, in private, with learned men, even argue in defence of it. On the same principle More, whilst silencing Simon Grinæus publicly, was willing to spend long hours in trying to convert him privately. So the Utopian disbeliever in immortality is not allowed to counter the public odium by defending himself *publicly* in argument. And nobody, in Utopia, is allowed to argue vehemently or violently about religion. If he does so, he is punished with bondage. If still recalcitrant, the bondsman is punished with death.

An inhabitant of Utopia has little liberty, as little as a warrior in the Spartan State, or an inmate of a monastery, although the Utopian has an easier life than either. Utopia is indeed modelled on the Spartan and the monastic disciplines, with the austerities of both alleviated. That God exists, and that in an after-state vice is punished and virtue rewarded, are the only Utopian religious dogmas. But there is a Utopian State religion — a kind of greatest common measure of all the different religions prevalent among the Utopians. In their dark churches an elaborate ritual is practised with music, vestments, incense, and candles. The Utopian priests are inviolate. And the Utopians believe that miracles happen among them very often. It is odd that, a year before Luther began his attack by fastening the Ninety-five theses to the church door at Wittenberg, More should have singled out so many things which the Protestants were later to impugn. More makes them part of the State religion of Utopia — a religion based upon reason, and containing nothing to which any reasonable man can object, More thinks.

More is very careful to point out that the Catholic Church has many practices to which a man would not be led by his unaided reason. From his early manhood to the day before his death, More from time to time wore a hair shirt, and followed other ascetic practices. Reason, the Utopians hold, would not lead a man to such austerities, 'unless any goodlier opinion be inspired into man from Heaven'. There are celibate ascetics in Utopia; the Utopians would ridicule them if they based their austerities on reason; but as they base them on religion, the Utopians honour them.

But what comes out most emphatically in Utopia is the prophetic fear which More, the moderate reformer, felt of the violent reformer. Any man who, in Utopia, *attacks* any established religion, even though it be idolatrous and super-stitious, in the interests of his own purer and more spiritual religious outlook, is liable to be punished with bondage, and, if still recalcitrant, with death. *It is one of the weak points of Utopia, that any kind of reformation is impossible.* More has guarded his citizens so strenuously against violence, that they seem to have nothing before them but a monotonous eternity of the benevolent despotism of their patriarchal constitution. No man may use contentious rebuking or inveighing against any of the recognized religions of Utopia upon pain, first of bondage, and, if that fails, of death. But contentious rebuking and in-veighing were the stock-in-trade of the Protestant Reformer. As More said of the Reformers, 'In railing standeth all their revel'. A Protestant Reformer in Utopia, who publicly derided miracles, vestments, music, incense, candles, the inviolability of the priesthood, and salvation by works, would soon have sighed for the (comparative) toleration of England in the days of Chancellor More.

More's third wish, as he walked along the Thames, side by side with Roper, was for a settlement, to the satisfaction of all parties, of the question of Henry's marriage with Catherine of Aragon, because otherwise he saw that it would be a dis-turbance to a great part of Christendom. Many reasons com-bined to make More long for this good conclusion: firstly, his sympathy and friendship with Catherine. He had hailed her with enthusiasm when, some twenty-seven years before, he watched her entering London as Prince Arthur's bride. 'There is nothing wanting in her', he had said, 'which the most beautiful girl should have.' Since that time she had been his gracious hostess many and many a year: she and Henry had so enjoyed More's company that they had asked him, when the day's routine was done and after the Council had supped, to be merry with them. This happened so frequently that not once in a month could More get leave to go home to his wife and children.

But, apart from the personal question, the separation of Henry from Catherine meant a quarrel between England and the Emperor Charles; yet, on the friendship between those two, in More's view, rested all hopes of permanent European peace and stability. But the threat to European unity was more deadly even than that. If the Emperor opposed the divorce, and the Pope would not grant it, then Henry had his own solution. So far as England was concerned, Henry would be King, Emperor, and Pope all in one; he would be Supreme Head of the English Church, and his Archbishop of Canterbury should declare him to be still a bachelor.

Wolsey's failure to achieve any solution on less drastic lines led to his fall, and More was commanded to fill Wolsey's place as Chancellor. More tried to avoid the dangerous honour. Already the King had consulted him on the 'divorce' question, and he had been unable to accept the royal view. But when Henry had promised More that in prosecuting the matter of the divorce he would use only those whose consciences were persuaded, while those who thought otherwise he would use in other business, More had no excuse for refusing office. The judicial side of his office he transacted with a dispatch and incorruptibility which, together with his reputation as a jester, made him one of the most popular figures of sixteenth-century tradition.

Otherwise his short Chancellorship was a succession of disappointments and humiliations. The business of the divorce went on, and with it the King's claim to be Supreme Head of the Church of England. Finally, on 15 May, 1532, came the event which, if there be any one such event, must mark the beginning of modern England. The clergy of England made their submission to the King. It is here that we should make, if we make it anywhere, the division between Medieval life and our Modern life. The fact that this division cuts into the middle of a dynasty and of a reign is all to the good, because it emphasizes the fact that you can mark no deep gulf between Medieval and Modern history. The deepest is here. Within ten years all the Abbeys in England had been dissolved, and were in rapid process of conversion into gentlemen's country mansions. The epoch which had begun with the landing of St. Augustine and his monks in 597 had come to its close. In the Refectory of (shall we say) Northanger Abbey, in 1530, St. Augustine, the Venerable Bede, Thomas Becket, and Thomas More might all have felt at home. Nothing except some differences in the pronunciation of their Latin would have prevented them from understanding each other perfectly. Ten years after More's death, Northanger Abbey has just been adapted out of the old monastic remains by Master Tilney, of the Court of Augmentations. Imagine Jane Austen paying him a visit. She would soon have got used to the archaic fashions and archaic English of her host, and, as he showed her with pride the remodelled kitchens, where every invention had been adopted to facilitate the labour of the cooks, she would have remarked to him that 'his endowments of that spot alone might at any time have placed him high among the benefactors of the convent'.

On 15 May the clergy made their submission. On 16 May More resigned the Chancellorship. His public career, then, had fallen entirely within what we may call the Monastic or Medieval Period of English History. Mommsen has remarked that, when an age is passing away, Destiny seems to allot to it one last great figure, so that it may not pass without honour and dignity. More is the last great hero of Medieval England.

For a time, More was permitted to live quietly in his Chelsea home, carrying on his controversy with the heretics. But his refusal to be present at the coronation of Anne Boleyn embittered the quarrel, and an attempt was made to involve him in the matter of the 'Holy Maid of Kent'. His proved innocence saved him, but on 13 April, 1534, he was summoned before the royal commissioners at Lambeth. Roper tells us that he would not allow his wife and children to follow him, as they usually did, to the riverside, 'but pulled the wicket after him, and shut them all from him, and with a heavy heart, as by his countenance it appeared, with me and our four servants there took his boat toward Lambeth. Wherein sitting still sadly a while, at the last he suddenly rounded me in the ear, and said: "Son Roper, I thank our Lord the field is won." ' More was quite willing to swear the oath recognizing Elizabeth as heir to the throne, for that was a matter on which he considered himself bound by the decision of Parliament. But, in the form in which the oath was tendered, he could not take it without renouncing the spiritual authority of the Pope, and that he would not do, though he tried to avoid offence by not stating exactly his reasons for refusing the oath. More was not, as is frequently stated, put to death for this refusal to take the oath. Refusal was not treason, but only 'misprision of treason', and the penalty was not death, but confiscation of all goods and imprisonment during the king's pleasure.

Like some other inmates of Tudor prisons, More found opportunity for much writing. But he no longer carried on controversy with the heretics. This was not from any motive of caution; indeed, he might have continued to dispute with the Lutherans without using any argument to which Henry would have objected. But More's writings in the Tower are for the most part devotional. The exception is his *Dialogue of Comfort*, in which he returns to that favourite form of debate which he had used with success in the first book of *Utopia*, and in the *Dialogue concerning Heresies*. But in the *Dialogue of Comfort* More is no longer defending this dogma or that; he is defending the right of the individual soul to hold any dogma at all against the command of the civil power.

The *Dialogue of Comfort* takes the form of a discussion between two Hungarian noblemen, as to how they ought to act in face of the Turkish conquest. There is no word of reflection upon Henry or his advisers; but clearly much of what is said is applicable to the case of More and his fellow sufferers. The *Dialogue of Comfort* is one of the most delightful of More's books. Whilst his own personal case grew more perilous, he saw more cause for optimism as to the future of Christendom. The Lutherans were coming to recognize that they must make common cause with their fellow-Christians, at least in resisting the Turk; and there was even talk of further reunion. So More, in the words which he puts into the mouth of the old Hungarian gentleman, sees causes for hope:

The first is, that in some communications had of late together, hath appeared good likelihood of some good agreement to grow together in one accord of our faith.

The second, that in the mean while till this may come to pass, contentions, despicions (i.e. disputations) with uncharitable behaviour is prohibited and forboden, in effect, upon all parts . . .

The third is, that all Germany, for all their diverse opinions, yet as they agree together in profession of Christ's name, so agree they now together in preparation of a common power, in defence of Christendom against our common enemy the Turk; and I trust . . . that as God hath caused them to agree together in the defence of his name, so shall he graciously bring them to agree together in the truth of his faith. Therefore will I let God work, and leave off contention.[1]

It is unjust to remember the bitter words which More uses in his controversies with the heretics, unless we also remember the words in which he says farewell to controversy. He sees that reunion, if it is to come, will come through the common defence of those things upon which all Christians are agreed: 'Therefore will I let God work'.

So he turned to the devotional writing which occupied his last days, enduring, with contented good humour, the imprisonment which was the legal penalty of his refusing to take the oath.

Further legislation was passed, making it high treason maliciously to attempt to deprive Henry of his titles, one of which was Supreme Head of the Church of England. But More continued to take refuge in silence. He was nevertheless placed upon his trial. He claimed the liberty of silence. He said to his judges:

Ye must understand that, in things touching conscience,

[1] *Works*, 1557, p. 1153.

every true and good subject is more bound to have respect to his said conscience and to his soul than to any other thing in all the world beside; namely [i.e. particularly] when his conscience is in such sort as mine is, that is to say, where the person giveth no occasion of slander, of tumult and sedition against his prince, as it is with me; for I assure you that I have not hitherto to this hour disclosed and opened my conscience and mind to any person living in all the world.

But the Solicitor-General, Rich, was prepared to swear that More, in conversation with him in the Tower, had said that Parliament could not make the King Supreme Head of the Church. More denied this, and there is no doubt that Rich was lying. But More was found guilty, and sentenced to death. After the verdict had been given he felt it his duty to speak out, stating that England 'might not make a particular law, disagreeable with the general law of Christ's Universal Catholic Church, no more than the City of London might make a law against an Act of Parliament to bind the whole realm'. After some friendly words to his judges, he was taken back to the Tower. On the way, his daughter Margaret, 'pressing in among the midst of the throng and company of the guard, that with halberds and bills went round about him, hastily ran to him, and there openly in the sight of them all, took him about the neck and kissed him'. On the fifth day after, he was executed on Tower Hill. A depressed Winchester man, obsessed by 'very vehement and grievous tentations of desperation', had in old days found comfort from his advice. As More passed to execution, 'he thrust through the throng and with a loud voice said, "Mr. More, do you know me? I pray you for our Lord's sake help me: I am as ill troubled as ever I was." Saint Thomas answered, "I remember thee full well. Go thy ways in peace, and pray for me: and I will not fail to pray for thee." ' He made (according to Henry's wish) only a brief speech from the scaffold, stating that he suffered 'in and for the faith of the Holy Catholic Church', and that he died 'the faithful servant of the King, and, in the first place, of God'.

More's case is different from that of the 'seditious heretics' whose punishment he had justified, in that he had avoided any act or word which could be construed as giving occasion of slander or of tumult. (Lord Acton has indeed blamed him for the length to which he carried his submission.)

The outstanding fact about More is, that his regard for an oath was such that he cheerfully faced perpetual imprisonment rather than swear an oath which he thought false. He remained firm, though he knew that nothing less than his death would satisfy Henry. Indeed, he feared the Government might resort to torture, which was mercifully spared him. His death was compassed by deliberate perjury.

More's claims to distinction are very various. He was a member of that earliest group of Greek students, with whom English classical scholarship begins. He was High Steward of Oxford and Cambridge, an educational pioneer, particularly enthusiastic about the education of women. As a writer of English prose, his position is specially important. It was not till long after his day that anyone could rival his mastery of many different types of English: dramatic dialogue and rhetorical monologue, narrative and argument combined in a style at once scholarly and colloquial. More's *History of Richard III* remained a pattern of historical writing unequalled for a century. His death as a martyr 'for the faith of the Catholic Church' was also a statesman's protest against the claim of the civil power to dictate religious belief, and should make him the hero of all who care for religous liberty. For over twenty years he exercised important judicial functions of different kinds, and it was his promptitude and incorruptibility as a judge that most impressed his countrymen. It is as 'the best friend that the poor e'er had' that his fellow Londoners remembered him, in the old play of *Sir Thomas More*. Swift had learnt from *Utopia* many of the things which make *Gulliver's Travels* remarkable, and he repaid his teacher by giving him the magnificent testimonial of being the person 'of the greatest virtue this kingdom ever produced'.

§2. WILLIAM TYNDALE[1]

On 6 October next, four centuries will have passed since William Tyndale was strangled, and his body burnt, at Vilvorde near Brussels. A little more than a dozen years later, Roger Ascham, travelling through Brabant as secretary to the English ambassador to Charles V, saw at the town's end the 'notable solemn place of execution, where worthy William Tyndale was unworthily put to death'. To-day, the vast, sinister group of towers and dungeons, where Tyndale spent the last sixteen months of his devoted life, and upon which Ascham gazed, has vanished from the earth. William Tyndale, the man whose choice of words has, for four hundred years, exercised supreme influence upon English prose, has indeed little surviving in brick or stone with which his memory can be linked. A pilgrim to-day, wishing to honour his memory by following the course of his travels, might see, as he visited the Rhineland towns, not a few buildings which Tyndale saw in the early sixteenth century; but he would find few which he could certainly associate with the memory of the martyr. He would, perhaps, be brought nearest to his hero as he stood in front of the great Cathedral of Antwerp, and gazed up at the masonry which Tyndale saw fresh from the workmen's hands. If our pilgrim then penetrated the maze of narrow streets just north of the Cathedral, he might pass the place where the House of the English Merchants stood — the hospitable home which sheltered Tyndale for a year, and which would have continued to shelter him, had not his innocent trustfulness allowed him to be enticed from its protection, to imprisonment and a martyr's death.

A martyr's death has ensured that, throughout all later English history, William Tyndale has received the honour due to him as a saintly hero. But, despite his fame, it is only gradually, and not fully even yet, that his importance to the history of English literature and his influence upon the English language is coming to be understood. 'Many have come in his wake who dared not have shown him the way', and followers

---

[1] From *The Times Literary Supplement*, 3 Oct., 1936.

have obscured the fame of the pioneer. The followers often did this quite deliberately, albeit with no evil intent. In 1525 unauthorized translation of the Bible into English was still forbidden, and Tyndale's adversaries asserted that he had deliberately made his version false, in order that his heresies might seem the Word of God. Later, when translation had been sanctioned, editors found it necessary, for a time, to conceal their debt to Tyndale. If the cause for which Tyndale had given his life were to triumph, it became important that his name should not be connected with versions which, while professedly by others, were mainly his. And so, at last, his name became separated from his work. Tyndale, whose care was much for the cause, and little for himself, would have been the last to complain. But the result has been great confusion in the history of the English language and of English prose. The very excellent scholars who were responsible for fixing the text of the Authorized Version of the English Bible in the reign of James I are constantly spoken of as 'the translators', and their virtues have been sung by a succession of professors of English. These revisers of the Authorized Version had indeed many virtues, but above all they had that great and rare virtue of not meddling with what was too good to be improved. They were the last of a long series of revisers who had based their work on Tyndale, with comparatively little modification: for indeed, where one reviser had altered Tyndale's wording, his successor had often returned to the original. And Tyndale had fixed the pattern upon which they had all alike worked.

It seems certain that the Bible as we now read it in the Authorized Version has had, and will continue to have, more influence upon the English language and upon English prose style than any other book. All the more important therefore is it to realize that we owe it, not to the seventeenth but to the sixteenth century, to Tyndale, and to a less extent to his followers, especially to Coverdale. And these writers were not themselves innovators in style or language. They wrote the 'clean English' which had come down to them from an earlier day. So that the tradition of our English language and of English style is an older one than we usually think.

Saintsbury, in his eloquent praise of the Authorized Version of 1611, has written: 'All the elements, all the circumstances of a translation as perfect as can be accomplished in any circumstances and with any elements, were then present, and the workers were worthy of the work. The plays of Shakespeare and the English Bible are, and ever will be, the twin monuments not merely of their own period, but of the perfection of English, the complete expressions of the literary capacities of the language, at the time when it had lost none of its pristine vigour.' But in the text book from which very many students have learnt what they ought to think about English literature, Saintsbury tells them that Tyndale is 'more noteworthy for his hapless fate and for a vigorous controversial pen, than for distinct literary merit'.

And yet Tyndale is the man to whom, above all other men, the literary merit of the English Bible is due, because he impressed upon his translation his own character of simplicity, strength and truth. And, Mr. A. W. Pollard has said, the Authorized Version of 1611, alike in language, rhythm and cadence, is fully ninety per cent Tyndale's. As to the New Testament, this is indisputably true; and when we come to consider influences, it is the New Testament which has principally counted, and will count.

If the reputation of Tyndale has been overshadowed by that of the Authorized Version coming after him, it has also been overshadowed by that of John Wiclif before him. Sometimes Wiclif and Tyndale are even classed together, and we are told that the earlier English versions had supplied the 'translators' of the Authorized Version with 'excellent quarries of suitable English terms, if not very accomplished models of style'. Wiclif is one of the great figures of English history, but the two translations of the Bible made under his inspiration are poor in style; and (a consideration of supreme importance in considering literary history) they were never printed till modern times. Despite the large number of manuscripts still surviving, their influence in the sixteenth century must have been very limited. Their influence on Tyndale is negligible. He must have known of the existence of a Wiclifite version, but of his own translation he says: 'I had no man to counter-feit [imitate], neither was helped with English of any that had interpreted the same, or such like thing in the Scripture beforetime.' From Tyndale, such words are conclusive. But that does not mean that Tyndale had no tradition of literary English prose preceding him. There was such a tradition, stretching back for centuries. Thomas More referred to it when, in his controversy with Tyndale, he said that people would do well to read neither Tyndale's works nor his, but to 'occupy their minds better' with 'such English books as may nourish and increase devotion'; he instanced three. One belonged to the fourteenth century, one to the fifteenth, and one to the sixteenth, but they were all alike accessible in a large number of printed editions. They were the favourite literature of the age. When we think of the Lady Margaret, and her benefactions to learning and to Cambridge, it is well also to remember her services to English prose. The Lady Margaret (and she was a very great lady: according to our ideas to-day, she would have had the title of Queen) believed, in common with her ancestor King Alfred, her grandson King Henry VIII, and her more remote descendant King James I, that it was part of her duty to provide proper prose reading for English-men. It was probably the assiduity of Wynkyn de Worde in printing works of devotion for her, that gained for him, in the early days of Henry VIII, the title of 'Printer unto the most excellent Princess, my lady, the King's Granddame'. It had been at her request that he had printed Fisher's funeral sermon on Henry VII, and as her printer he published Fisher's treatise on the Seven Penitential Psalms — a best-seller, strange as it may seem, running through five editions in three years. Cambridge was thus, owing to the labours of Fisher and Lady Margaret and others, becoming something of a nursing mother of English prose. And to Cambridge Tyndale migrated, after having graduated and taken his M.A. at Oxford. The influence of Erasmus had not died out, and during the years which Tyndale spent at Cambridge, the influence of Luther began to make itself felt. It was natural that, when Tyndale left Cambridge and returned to his native Gloucestershire, he became involved in controversy with the old-fashioned country clergy, who knew little of Erasmus, and, as yet, perhaps less of Luther. He was chaplain to a local magnate, Sir John Walsh. It is a testimony to Tyndale's sense of humour that we have a record of how little his arguments impressed his employer's wife. She was, 'as Master Tyndale did report her', a stout woman. 'Well', said she, 'there was such a doctor, he may dispend two hundred pound by the year, another one hundred pound, and another three hundred pound; and what think ye, were it reason that we should believe you before them, so great, learned and beneficed men?' It was at this time that (remembering the words which Erasmus had used earlier) Tyndale said to one of his opponents: 'If God spare my life, ere many years I will cause a boy that driveth the plough shall know more of the scripture than thou dost.' Meantime Cuthbert Tunstall, one of the circle of Erasmus and More, had become Bishop of London, and Tyndale hoped that Tunstall might give him a chaplaincy, and that he might be able to translate the New Testament in Tunstall's palace. In this he was disappointed, but he got a chaplaincy in the house of a London alderman, Humphrey Monmouth. Some years later Monmouth, under examination, declared that Tyndale 'lived like a good priest, as methought. He studied most part of the day and of the night at his book; and he would eat but sodden meat by his good will, and drink but small single beer'. But Tyndale found his task of translating and printing Scripture an impossible one to pursue in London: 'there was no place to do it in all England', he said later. Everyone knows the story of how he went abroad, and began to print at Cologne in 1525; how he was compelled to fly with his turbulent companion Roy, and with the sheets so far as they had been printed, up the Rhine to Worms, where he found another printer, and began the work over again. They are now the rarest of rare books. The imperfect Cologne edition is represented by a fragment in the British Museum; the Worms edition by a copy without title-page in the Baptist College at Bristol, and a fragment in the library of St. Paul's Cathedral.

It is not fanciful to see in the style of Tyndale's translation

the fhyppe/with Zebede their father /mendinge there nett?/
and called them. And they with out taryinge left the fhyppe
and there father and folowed hym.

¶ And Jefus wēt about all galile/teachynge in there fynago=
ges/ans preachynge the gofpell of the kyngdom/and healyn=
ge all manner of fycknes / and all maner difeafes amonge the
people. And hys fame fpred a broade through out all firia.
And they brought vnto hym all ficke people/that were taken
with dyvers difeafes and grypyng?/and them that were pof=
feffed with devyll?/and thofe which were lunaticke/and tho=
fe that had the palfy: And he healed thē. And there folowed
him a greate noūbre of people/from galile/ and from the ten
cetes/and from ierufalem / and from_ury/and from the re=
gions that lye beyend iordan.

The fyfth Chapter.

Then he fawe the people, he

Went vp vnto a mountaine/and wen he was fett/
hys difciples cam vnto him / and he opened his
mouth/and taught them fayinge: Bleffed are the
powre in fpirte: for thers is the kyngdom of heven. Bleffed
are they that mourne: for they fhalbe comforted. Bleffed are
the micke: for they fhall inheret * the erthe. Bleffed are they
which huger and thurft for righte wefnes: for they fhalbe fyl=
led. Bleffed are the mercyfull: for they fhall obteyne mercy.
Bleffed are the pure in hert: for they fhall fe god. Blef=
fed are the maynteyners of peace: for they fhalbe called
the chyldren of god. Bleffed are they which fuffre perfecucion
for rightewefnes fake : for thers is the kyngdom of heven.
Bleffed are ye whē men fhall revyle you/and perfecute you/
and fhal falfly faye all manner of evle fayng? agaynft you
for my fake. Reioyce ād be gladde/for greate is youre rewar=
de in heven. For fo perfecuted they the prophett? which were
before youre dayes.

⊇

Erth.
The worlde thi? kethe too poffeffe the erthe/and to defend there aw? ne/when they vfe violence ⁊ power: but chrift teache? th that the world mufte be poffeffed with mekenes on ly/and with oute power and viole? nce.

All thefe dedes here rehearfed as to norifhe peace/ to fhewe mercy/ to fuffre pfecucio/ and fo forth/ma? ke not a man ha? ppye and bleffed/ nether deferve t? he rewarde of he? ven : but declare and teftifie that we are happy and bleffede and that we fhall have gr? eate, pmocio i he? ven. and certyfy? eth vs i oure her? tes that we are goddes fonnes/ ⁊ that the holy go? oft is in vs. for all good thynges are geven to vs frely of god for chriftes blouddes fake ād his merittes

---

of the New Testament a reflection of Tyndale's own character: that 'plain heroic magnitude of mind' which distinguishes him pre-eminently among the earliest English Reformers of the sixteenth century. From the time when he spoke his words to the Gloucestershire priest, to the last words that he uttered at the stake at Vilvorde, he had one object only: to make from the original Hebrew and Greek an absolutely honest translation of the scriptures into English, a translation as simple and straightforward as might be; and to make such a translation available to all his countrymen. 'I call God to record', he wrote a few years before his death, 'against the day we shall appear before our Lord Jesus, to give a reckoning of our doings, that I never altered one syllable of God's word against my conscience, nor would this day, if all that is in the earth, whether it be pleasure, honour or riches, might be given me.' And Tyndale's earnestness and simplicity of character were his protection against the temptations of that over-ornate writing which was the besetting stylistic sin of the age in which he wrote. In the words of Westcott, 'it was Tyndale's influence that decided that our Bible should be popular and not literary, speaking in a simple dialect; and that so, by its simplicity, it should be endowed with permanence'. It was consistent with Tyndale's character that he should continue the straightforward tradition of prose which had marked the greatest English works of devotion since the fourteenth century and earlier, free from the 'ink-horn' terms and the circumlocutions which mar much Tudor and much Stuart prose.

Many of the orthodox, like Thomas More, were willing to allow an English translation of the Bible, under episcopal control. The principal criticisms brought against Tyndale's translations were three: firstly, that no individual ought to have undertaken such translation upon his own responsibility; secondly, that Tyndale had inserted prefaces and marginal notes, enforcing his heretical interpretations; thirdly, that by his choice of words, such as *love* for *charity*, *elder* for *priest*, *congregation* for *church*, he had given to his translation a subtle non-ecclesiastical bias. It is the peculiar merit of Tyndale as a translator that he did not seek to avoid this last criticism by the use of paraphrase and pleonasm. There is always, in translation, a temptation to use two words for one of the original, because we feel that neither of our words, alone, gives the full force of the original. Tyndale might have met his critics by coupling synonyms together: 'the greatest of these is love or charity'. He would thereby have ruined the simplicity of his translation — but most of his readers would have approved of such 'augmentation' of his English style. Never to use one word where two would do was the ambition of many contemporary writers. It is worth noting that when, finally, the Bibles were placed in the churches, the King's loving subjects were given permission, not simply to read them, but 'to have and use the commodity of the reading of the said Bibles'. Tyndale kept his translation free from such 'indenture English'.

Cuthbert Tunstall first sought to check the spread of Tyndale's Bibles by burning them; he then called in Thomas More to expose their errors in public controversy. More's criticism of Tyndale's style is interesting — especially his animadversion upon Tyndale's failure to distinguish between *Nay* and *No*, *Yea* and *Yes*:

I would not here note by the way [More says] that Tyndale here translateth 'No' for 'Nay', for it is but a trifle, and mistaking of the English word; saving that ye should see that he which, in two so plain English words, and so common, as is 'Nay' and 'No', cannot tell when he should take the one and when the other, is not for translating into English, a man very meet.

For the use of those two words in answering to a question is this: 'Nay'[1] answereth the question framed by the affirmative. As, for ensample, if a man should ask Tyndale himself, 'Is an heretic meet to translate Holy Scripture into English?' Lo, to this question, if he will answer true English, he must answer 'Nay' and not 'No'. But, an if the question be asked him thus, lo, 'Is not an heretic meet to translate Holy Scripture into English?' To this question, lo, if he will answer true English, he must answer 'No' and not 'Nay'.

[1] 'No' in 1557 edition.

And a like difference is there between these two adverbs, 'Yea' and 'Yes'. For if the question be framed unto Tyndale by the affirmative in this fashion, 'If an heretic falsely translate the New Testament into English, to make his false heresies seem the Word of God, be his books worthy to be burned?' To this question, asked in this wise, if he will answer true English, he must answer 'Yea', and not 'Yes'. But now, if the question be asked him thus, lo, by the negative, 'If an heretic falsely translate the New Testament into English, to make his false heresies seem the word of God, be not his books well worthy to be burned?' To this question, in this fashion framed, if he will answer true English, he may not answer, 'Yea', but he must answer 'Yes', and say, 'Yes, marry be they, both the translation and the translator, and all that will hold with them'.

And this thing, lo, though it be no great matter, yet I have thought good to give Tyndale warning of, because I would have him write true one way or other, that, though I cannot make him by no means to write true matter, I would have him yet at the leastwise write true English.[1]

Tyndale was not, as I have said, without a sense of humour, and he could be as tolerant of the stupidity of that 'stout woman' Mistress Walsh as More was of that equally stout woman, Dame Alice. Nevertheless it is easy to understand how More's inability to resist a joke, even on the most serious and terrible matters, must have appeared to Tyndale to be maddening frivolity, and to have marked him as a dishonest man. And, despite More's jeers at Tyndale's English, there is no very great difference between the style of More and the style of Tyndale, as translators. In some points Tyndale has an advantage: he always observes the distinction between *ye*, nominative, and *you*, accusative — 'ye have not chosen me, but I have chosen you' — a distinction which More systematically neglects. From Tyndale it has been retained in our Authorized Version.

Tyndale did not enliven his controversy with humorous episodes as freely as did More: yet we can see Tyndale's earnest

[1] *Works*, 1557, p. 448.

humour in such passages as the dialogue between the multitude and Little Flock. In the end the multitude turn on Little Flock:

'Thou art a strong heretic, and worthy to be burnt.' And then he is excommunicate out of the church. If Little Flock fear not that bug, then they go straight unto the King: 'An it like your Grace, perilous people and seditious, even enough to destroy your realm, if ye see not to them betimes. They be so obstinate and tough that they will not be converted, and rebellious against God and the ordinances of his Holy Church. And how much more shall they so be against your Grace, if they increase and grow to a multitude! They will pervert all, and surely make new laws, and either subdue your Grace unto them, or rise against you.' And then goeth a part of Little Flock to pot, and the rest scatter. Thus hath it ever been, and shall ever be, let no man therefore deceive himself.

Tyndale did not deceive himself. Yet before the end came he had published not only the New Testament, but the Pentateuch and the Book of Jonah. When, lured from the House of the English Merchants, he was imprisoned in Vilvorde Castle, his one thought was still for his task. The only autograph letter of Tyndale's which survives is written to the governor of the Castle, begging for warmer clothing against the winter, for a lamp in the evening (for it is wearisome to sit alone in the dark), but above all for his Hebrew Bible, Hebrew grammar and Hebrew dictionary. And, in return, he writes, may you obtain your dearest wish, provided always it be consistent with the safety of your soul. 'If they shall burn me', he had written some eight years before, 'they shall do none other thing than I look for.' He was fortunate in meeting his death abroad, for the laws of the Empire had a degree of mercy, in that they caused the less noxious type of heretic to be strangled before being burnt.

The most complete refutation of the charge that Tyndale's translation was tendentious — intended 'to make his false heresies seem the Word of God' — lies in the fact that, five years before his death, Tyndale had offered that, if the King would suffer only a bare text of the Scripture to be put forth among his people, 'be it of the translation of what person soever shall please his Majesty', he himself would write no more: 'I shall most humbly submit myself at the feet of his Royal Majesty, offering my body to suffer what pain or torture, yea, what death his Grace will, so that this be obtained.' Two years later (1533) Tyndale's young fellow-Reformer Frith had made the same offer under tragic circumstances. Unlike many of the Reformers, Tyndale had not claimed the apostolic freedom 'to lead about a sister, a wife'. He remained a celibate priest: but, as time passed, his young friend, John Frith, became to him as a son. In Frith, Tyndale found consolation for the many disappointments he had suffered, at the hands of magnates like Tunstall who had failed to help him, and of turbulent fellow-Reformers, like William Roy and George Joy, who had compromised him and quarrelled with him.

It might almost be said of Frith and Tyndale that they had but one soul between them. And they had qualities for which they are not always given credit. Despite all their obstinate determination, Frith and Tyndale had a fundamental reasonableness. It has been said of Tyndale that

> There may be found in his books phrases and theories that are ungenerous and narrow-minded, but on some of the greatest questions, Tyndale has spoken, not like a fanatic, but like a citizen of Utopia.[1]

Two examples, from Tyndale, may suffice:

> To kneel before the cross unto the Word of God which the cross preacheth, is not evil ... But the abuse of the thing is evil, and to have a false faith, as to bear a piece of the cross about a man, thinking that so long as that is about him, spirits shall not come at him, his enemies shall do him no bodily harm.

> To speak of pilgrimages, I say that a Christian man, so that he leave nothing undone at home that he is bound to do, is free to go whither he will ... whether lively preaching,

[1] W. P. KER, in CRAIK's *English Prose*, I, 184.

ceremony, relic or image stir up his heart to God, and preach the Word of God, and the example of our Saviour Jesus, more in one place than another; that he thither go I am content . . . But to believe that God will be sought more in one place than in another or that God will hear them more in one place than in another, . . . is a false faith, and idolatry or image-service.

It would be interesting to make a book of selections from the writings of Thomas More, Tyndale, and Frith, with the object of showing how much, during all their embittered controversy, there was in common between them.

But, bitter as were the controversies not only of orthodox against Reformers, but even of Reformers among themselves, no shadow of misunderstanding ever arose between Tyndale and Frith. When Frith came to England on his final mission, Tyndale would gladly have accompanied him; but he knew that his presence would only have been an added danger and that his duties lay elsewhere. He wrote to Frith:

Finally, if there were in me any gift that could help at hand, and aid you if need required, I promise you I would not be far off, and commit the end to God: *my soul is not faint though my body be weary.* But God hath made me evil favoured in this world, and without grace in the sight of men, speechless and rude, dull and slow-witted. Your part shall be to supply that lacketh in me; . . . Abundance of love maketh me exceed in babbling.

But Frith was captured. Even in the Tower, Frith managed to carry on controversy with More. It was under difficulties: 'I may not have such books as are necessary for me; neither get pen, ink, nor paper but only secretly; so that I am in continual fear both of the Lieutenant and of my keeper, lest they should espy any such thing by me . . . Whensoever I hear the keys ring at the doors, straight all must be conveyed out of the way; and then if any notable thing had been in my mind, it was clean lost.'

From the Tower, knowing that for himself only a martyr's

death remained, though Tyndale was still free, Frith made a noble defence of Tyndale, quoting his protest that he had never altered one syllable of God's word against his conscience. 'Judge, Christian reader,' says Frith, 'whether these words be not spoken of a faithful, clear, innocent heart.' And he repeated Tyndale's passionate plea for the free circulation of *any* translation of the Bible. For, said Frith,

> the Word of God boileth in my body like a fervent fire, and will needs have issue, and breaketh out when occasion is given. But this hath been offered you, is offered, and shall be offered: Grant that the Word of God, I mean the text of Scripture, may go abroad in our English tongue, as other nations have it in their tongues, and my brother William Tyndale and I have done, and will promise you to write no more.

Tyndale had written to Frith urging caution: but when the news of Frith's capture reached him, he knew that for Frith there could be but one way. A recantation could only mean a life of misery and remorse which would lead, as in the case of Bilney, to a recantation of the recantation, and to death in the end — but the dishonoured death of a relapsed heretic, not the martyrdom of an enthusiast pitied even by those who condemned him. So Tyndale wrote to Frith:

> Fear not threatening, therefore, neither be overcome of sweet words; with which twain the hypocrites shall assail you. Neither let the persuasions of worldly wisdom bear rule in your heart; no, though they be your friends that counsel. Let Bilney be a warning to you. Let not their vizor beguile your eyes. Let not your body faint. He that endureth to the end shall be saved. If the pain be above your strength, remember 'Whatsoever ye shall ask in My name, I will give it you'. And pray to your Father in that name, and He will cease your pain, or shorten it. The Lord of Peace, of Hope, and of Faith, be with you. Amen.
>
> William Tyndale.

Frith for his part never hesitated for a moment. Not only did he refuse to recant: it is even said that he refused an offer of escape, devised, perhaps, by Cranmer, unwilling to condemn, and unable to acquit.

'Behold, and see, if there be any sorrow like unto my sorrow.' The Roman fortitude of the older Reformer, encouraging his young friend, whom he loved more than his own life, must not blind us to the agony which lies beneath his firm words.

Tyndale is among the most heroic of English figures. The traditional portrait depicts him, as he says he was, 'without grace in the sight of men'. The woodcut of the martyrdom of Tyndale in Foxe's *Acts and Monuments* may have idealized the figure of the Reformer. But it depicts the man as he truly was, 'an athlete of God'.

Before Tyndale's death at Vilvorde, the translation of the whole Bible by Miles Coverdale had already been printed. But Coverdale modestly admitted that this translation was only a temporary stop-gap, till the complete translation of Tyndale might be available. Such hopes were frustrated by Tyndale's death: but a composite Bible was printed abroad — the New Testament and the Pentateuch in Tyndale's version, Joshua to 2 Chronicles possibly from Tyndale's manuscript, the rest of the Old Testament and the Apocrypha from Coverdale. To avoid offence, the whole was described as 'truly and purely translated by Thomas Matthew', the advantage being, that as no one knew, or yet knows, who Thomas Matthew was, it was difficult to disprove his truth and purity. We do, however, know who the editor was. It was Rogers, who was the first to suffer in the Marian persecution. From this Bible the later revisions are descended.

Tyndale's last words had been, 'Lord, open the King of England's eyes'. 'Whether Henry's eyes were ever open to anything but what he considered his own interests may be doubted,' says Mr. A. W. Pollard, the most charitable of scholars. Let us give Henry the benefit of the doubt. The fact remains that within five years the royal eyes were to gaze upon the translation of Tyndale and Coverdale, disguised under the discreet anonymity of 'divers excellent learned men', and the King was to order a copy to be placed in every church within his realm.

2 . WILLIAM TYNDALE

It is perhaps worth while for those of us who are concerned with the writing of English to remember that the men to whom we owe the tradition of our English prose, if they did not end their lives on the scaffold or at the stake, for the most part came perilously near doing so. This applies to most of our great fifteenth-century writers, and with the turmoil of the early sixteenth century danger assuredly did not decrease. But none of them had a life of such utter disappointment and struggle as had William Tyndale — persecuted in one city, fleeing to another. The lives of More and Fisher, till within some three years of their deaths, had been peculiarly happy and successful, whilst Latimer and Ridley, Cranmer and Coverdale, had their moments of triumph. Coverdale indeed was spared to complete the work which Tyndale had begun — and perhaps it is fortunate that whilst the Gospels and the first books of the Old Testament were translated by the sternly simple Tyndale, the prophets and the Apocrypha were rendered by the somewhat more ornate hand of Coverdale. And it is in the magnificent periods of Miles Coverdale, rendering the words of the Book of Wisdom, that we may best think of Tyndale, and of his fellow-sufferer Frith; for apart from Frith, Tyndale would not have wished to be remembered:

We fools thought their life very madness, and their end to be without honour. But lo, how they are counted among the children of God, and their portion is among the saints . . .

But the righteous shall live for evermore, their reward also is with the Lord, and their remembrance with the Highest. Therefore shall they receive a glorious kingdom, and a beautiful crown of the Lord's hand; for with his right hand shall he cover them, and with his own arm shall he defend them.

VII

SHAKESPEARE AND THE PLAY OF
MORE[1]

SOME SEQUENCES OF THOUGHT IN SHAKESPEARE AND IN THE 'THREE PAGES' OF 'SIR THOMAS MORE'

THIS lecture does not propose to apply psycho-analysis to poetry. It merely essays a common-place (and, I hope, common-sense) application of a simple method, the possibilities of which have not, I think, been fully appreciated.

No one can have observed the workings of his own mind (or that of any of his fellow mortals) without being struck by the power of association. Some of these associations are common to a large number of us. The delight a dog will show when his owner fetches the whip is not an individual trait, but is common to many good dogs with clear consciences, who associate the whip with a walk rather than with castigation. Yet dogs also show associations which are exceptional, or even individual, due to a memory of something they may have experienced keenly. And in a man also we may be able to observe associations due to links of thought which are peculiar — sometimes so peculiar that a group of them marks 'the singularity of his essential being, his utter unlikeness to any other creature in the world'. And this singularity is not found only in the men of genius; it is often shared by humbler folk, like Kipps:

> He had ceased from rowing, and rested on his oars, and suddenly he was touched by the wonder of life: the strangeness that is a presence stood again by his side. . . .
> 'Queer old Artie!'

[1] Delivered (in part) as the Ludwig Mond Lecture in the University of Manchester, 1937. Printed (in part) in the *Modern Language Review*, vol. XXVI, pp. 251 etc.

'Ain't I? I don't suppose there ever was a chap quite like me before.' . . .

We can feel the 'essential being' of Wordsworth in the *Lines written above Tintern Abbey*, where he tells us what he owes to the 'forms of beauty' seen five years before on the banks of the Wye.

> Nor less, I trust,
> To them I may have owed another gift,
> Of aspect more sublime; that blessed mood,
> In which the burthen of the mystery,
> In which the heavy and the weary weight
> Of all this unintelligible world
> Is lightened: — that serene and blessed mood,
> In which the affections gently lead us on,
> Until, the breath of this corporeal frame,
> And even the motion of our human blood
> Almost suspended, we are *laid asleep*
> *In body, and become a living soul:*
> *While with an eye made quiet by the power*
> *Of harmony, and the deep power of joy,*
> *We see into the life of things —*

In *The Prelude* (Book II) we have a parallel passage:

> From Nature and her overflowing soul
> I had receiv'd so much that all my thoughts
> Were steep'd in feeling; . . . for in all things now
> I saw one life, and felt that it was joy.
> One song they sang, and it was audible,
> *Most audible then when the fleshly ear,*
> O'ercome by grosser prelude of that strain,
> *Forgot its functions, and slept undisturbed —*

At this very height of his description of the 'blessed mood' the poet feels doubt. In *Tintern Abbey*:

> — If this
> Be but a vain belief, —

In *The Prelude*:

> — If this be error, and another faith
> Find easier access to the pious mind, —

Yet the poet continues to tell how he has turned in spirit to these 'forms of beauty':

>   — If this
> Be but a vain belief, yet, oh! how oft,
> In darkness, and amid the many shapes
> Of joyless daylight; when the fretful stir
> Unprofitable, and the fever of the world,
> Have hung upon the beatings of my heart,
> How oft, in spirit, have I turned to thee,
> O sylvan Wye!

So in *The Prelude*:

> — If this be error . . .
> Yet were I grossly destitute of all
> Those human sentiments which make this earth
> So dear, if I should fail, with grateful voice
> To speak of you, Ye Mountains and Ye Lakes
> And sounding Cataracts! Ye Mists and Winds
> That dwell among the hills where I was born.
>   . . . if in this time
> Of dereliction and dismay, I yet
> Despair not. . . .

The sequence of thought is the same. The 'blessed mood' which the poet has felt; the sudden doubt 'if this be error'; yet must he speak of the comfort he has received, amid the 'fretful stir unprofitable', the 'dereliction and dismay'.

Now many have felt this 'blessed mood'; many have felt the shadow of doubt in the midst of their joy; all have found comfort in distress from memories such as those of which Wordsworth speaks. Yet, widespread as these feelings are, if we did not know anything of the authorship of the lines from *Tintern Abbey* and from *The Prelude*, I do not think it could be reasonably maintained that two minds had conceived them in entire independence of each other, or of some common source. And nevertheless, note how very small is the actual verbal repetition, almost limited to simple words like 'sleep', 'joy', 'life', 'if this be (error), yet'. The poet's power of language is shown by the way in which he clothes the same thought in words generally, though not always, different.

Of course, this argument of the individual mind shown by certain sequences of thought may be pressed dangerously. We must allow for chance. An American scholar has recently pointed out a resemblance between *Beowulf* and a story written in the second half of the eleventh century at the court of Kashmir[1]. There is a real likeness: though I think that it is one which could be accounted for by supposing that certain elements common wherever the human race is interested in stories, have happened to come together, and, alike in western Europe and in India have, independently of each other, made a very similar, yet fortuitous, combination. But the most striking thing, which the American scholar had not noted, is that in both stories the same moral is drawn, that 'Fate favours the brave'. Now this can only be an accident; it is part of the literary form in which the deeds of Beowulf and the Indian story are respectively dressed, and even if we allow the *stories* to have some ultimate connection, this literary form is independent, beyond possibility of dispute. But if the resemblances had been between two poems where a theory of literary connection was possible, say between *Beowulf* and some Latin poem of the Dark Ages, this verbal parallel, combined with the indisputable likeness of the story, would have seemed to many too strong to be dismissed as purely fortuitous. Yet fortuitous it must be.

Nevertheless, a point can be reached beyond which it becomes absurd to speak of fortuitous combinations.

It is for that reason that, in dealing with such a problem as the authorship of the three pages, sometimes attributed to Shakespeare, in the manuscript of the play of *Sir Thomas More*, it is vital to consider the different parallels with Shakespeare,

---

[1] *Eine mittelalterlich-indische Parallele zum Beowulf*, by A. H. KRAPPE, in the *Germanisch-Romanische Monatsschrift*, XV, 1927, pp. 54-8.

not merely in isolation, but as a series in succession. The evidence is cumulative. We must constantly ask ourselves: is it reasonable to dismiss this also as an accident, in view of the other parallels which we have already observed?

The veteran Shakespeare-scholars who have dismissed the claim that the 'three pages' are the work of Shakespeare, scholars like Sir Sidney Lee and Professor Alois Brandl, seem hardly to have allowed sufficiently for this cumulation. Brandl comes forward as the Devil's Advocate (a part which, as he genially admits, can never be a popular one). 'A hundred unreliable arguments', he says, 'do not together make one reliable one.'[1] But surely we must discriminate. If our arguments are so unreliable as not to be arguments at all, then clearly Brandl is right; the sum of a hundred noughts is still nought. But if our arguments *are* arguments, even though each taken singly may be unreliable, nevertheless, *if they are independent of each other*, they may together make a reliable group.

An anecdote may illustrate the point. A Jew, obviously in a state of some distress, was met by his Rabbi, who enquired the cause. 'I was called as a witness', was the reply, 'and I was fined £10.' 'No, no, Abe. You mean you were called as a defendant, and were fined £10.' 'No, I was called as a witness; the Judge said, "What is your name?" And I said (as you know) "Abraham Isaac Jacob Solomon". And the Judge said, "Are you a Jew?" And I said, "Now, don't be a silly ass." And I was fined £10.'[2]

Yet no one of these names is conclusive. Think of Abraham Lincoln, Izaak Walton, Jacob Tonson, Solomon Grundy. But most of us would agree that the *combination* suggests Jewish origin with sufficient certainty to render the retort upon the Judge eminently justifiable.

In practice, we constantly act on the principle that several

[1] 'Hundert unverlässliche Argumente geben miteinander noch nicht ein verlässliches' (ALOIS BRANDL, quoted in *Die Literatur*, Stuttgart, XXVII, Jan. 1925, p. 221).

[2] The person to whom this is alleged to have happened did not bear the actual names given above, which I selected to illustrate my point. I make this avowal to protect myself (and Mr. Jonathan Cape) in case there should be a gentleman bearing exactly these names, and he should accuse me of having taken his name in vain.

unreliable arguments together make a reliable one. You have to meet in a crowd a Mr. Harris, hitherto unknown to you, but who, you are informed, has red hair, wears a monocle and walks with a limp. You would address with some confidence a stranger possessing those characteristics; and if he responded to the name of Harris, you would accept the identification, without brooding over the fact that there are nearly a thousand Harrises in the London Telephone Directory alone. *You have not got mathematical, logical, certainty: you have that approximation to certainty which satisfies us in the actual affairs of life.*

And in one sense our problem is easier than this. For the crowd amid which we have to identify our man is not great. Shakespeare and the author of the three pages belong to a *small* group — the writers for the stage from about 1590 to 1600: a group of only a few dozen at most. When we come to weigh similarities of handwriting and spelling, this consideration will become very important.

Yet, I repeat, opponents of Shakespearean authorship have hardly grasped the nature of the problem. Fifteen years ago, five of us combined to write a book in which were put forward many scores of arguments, no one in itself absolutely conclusive, and some highly inconclusive. Next day, a journalist called to ask the opinion of an eminent Shakespeare scholar, now dead — one to whom every student owes a debt. 'My verdict', said that scholar, 'is, *not proven.*' But this was not so much to give a verdict, as to refuse to consider a verdict. For though there might have been in our book some arguments which so experienced a man thought he could reject at sight, the question whether the combination could be rejected was a problem which could only be decided after all the elements of that combination had been subjected to an exhaustive scrutiny, extending over weeks and months.

But now, after fifteen years, it is not too early to ask for a verdict. And to some students, the problem is not less interesting than a cross-word puzzle or a detective novel.

The main outlines of the problem are these. The play of *Sir Thomas More* is extant in manuscript in six different handwritings. It also bears the annotations of the licenser of plays,

Edmund Tilney. The three pages are written in a hand which Dr. Greg named D, in his monumental edition of the play. They form the only passage written in that hand. The character of his corrections shows that D is no copyist, but the author of the lines he writes. These lines had been cursorily attributed to Shakespeare, on grounds of style, in 1871; but there was no elaborate investigation till Sir Edward Maunde Thompson took up the problem *solely from the point of view of the handwriting* in 1916. With a boldness which is astonishing, when we remember that all he had of Shakespeare's hand was six signatures and the words *By me*, Sir Edward almost staked his reputation as a palaeographer upon his conviction that the two hands were the same. The confidence of this challenge has concentrated attention upon the palaeographical problems of the play, which have been the subject of several books and many articles. The literary problems have received comparatively little attention. I contributed a paper on them to the joint volume *Shakespeare's Hand in the Play of Sir Thomas More* (1923), and one or two friends have since given me some valuable hints which I shall use later in this lecture.

Above all, Professor Caroline Spurgeon has written a paper on *Imagery in the Sir Thomas More Fragment*,[1] part of which covers much the same ground as my earlier paper, but in a different way. It affords most valuable and welcome confirmation. I propose to approach the problem yet again, and again from a somewhat different angle, and in doing so I shall have occasion repeatedly to express my indebtedness to Professor Spurgeon.

What I wish to emphasize is the extreme complexity of the combinations common to the 'three pages' of *Sir Thomas More* and to Shakespeare. Sir E. K. Chambers, after dealing at length with the palaeographical problem of *Sir Thomas More*, and saying that it is not imperative on literary grounds either to ascribe or deny the play to Shakespeare, adds:

> Professor R. W. Chambers has shown that the combination of sympathy for the psychology of the mob, with a strong sense of order and degree, as maintainers of the social system against anarchy, is consonant with the political temper, not

[1] *Review of English Studies*, VI, 257-70.

only of the early Cade scenes, but also of *Julius Caesar, Troilus and Cressida* and *Coriolanus*.[1]

Now this seems to me to state only a small (albeit important) portion of the problem. Shakespeare combined his respect for order and 'degree' with a deep respect for all human personality irrespective of degree. His leading characters are drawn from the great ones of the earth, but these great ones are not more lovable than his servants or his clowns. Often they are much less so: for if we want common sense and balance we must turn from Timon to Timon's steward. Shakespeare 'has no respect for "the plainer and simpler kind of people" as politicians, but he has a great respect and regard for their hearts.'[2] For all his passionate love of authority and order, he was, as Bagehot has said, '*sympathisingly* cognizant with the talk of the illogical classes'.[3] And it is certain that in the 'three pages' the combination of these things is found: passionate abhorrence of mob rule, good-natured ridicule of mob logic, and a belief in the essential goodness of humble folk; it is, if possible, more emphatic and undeniable in the 'three pages' than in Shakespeare's acknowledged work. And there is something striking about it (just as there is about a very different combination, the *saeva indignatio* of Swift's Irish pamphlets, the combination of hatred of the oppressor with contempt for the oppressed). But this combination in the 'three pages' is worked out in detail through a number of other combinations, and these combinations in their turn are equally characteristic of Shakespeare. The argument that the author of the 'three pages' is Shakespeare lies, not in any one of these, but in the whole combination of combinations. Of the underlying combination, respect for authority or 'degree', joined to a belief that the poor and humble are 'sound and sweet at heart', I shall say no more, only asking that it be kept in mind.[4] My concern now is with the minor combinations.

[1] *William Shakespeare*, I, p. 509.
[2] BRADLEY, *Shakespearean Tragedy*, p. 326.
[3] In quoting this, I do not mean to agree that labourers are more illogical than professors.
[4] I tried to illustrate it at length in our joint volume on *Shakespeare's Hand in the Play of Sir Thomas More*, 1923, pp. 142-87.

The play of Sir Thomas More was written some time during the last dozen years of the reign of Elizabeth. The manuscript is in the British Musem. The play was never printed till it was edited by Alexander Dyce in 1844. It was then in very much better condition; Dyce could read much that is now illegible. It is the work of a group of playwrights, and is testimony to the remarkable freedom of the Elizabethan drama and the breadth of mind of a London audience. London was much more Protestant than most of England. The war with Spain was raging, and Queen Elizabeth had been excommunicated and deposed by the Pope. Seminary priests from abroad were constantly being hanged with torture at Tyburn. Yet these playwrights expected to be allowed to produce a play making a hero of Sir Thomas More, the greatest of all those who had been put to death on the charge of denying the Royal Supremacy. The people before whom the play was to be acted were mainly Protestants, the dramatists themselves were, so far as we know, Protestants. The bulk of the play is extant in the handwriting of Anthony Munday, who was a violent Protestant propagandist. The dramatists walked very warily, and were careful not to state in so many words why their hero was going to execution. By this discretion they hoped to get the play past the censor.

But they came to grief on another point. Early in the reign of Henry VIII, on 1 May, 1517, prentices had risen in a rather ugly anti-alien riot. According to tradition, this riot was quelled by the personal intervention of Thomas More. The first part of the play tells with great gusto how the citizens revolted on 'Evil May Day' against the insults of the favoured aliens, and how they were recalled to their allegiance by an eloquent speech of More.

But in the days of Elizabeth there was a large population of foreign refugees in London, and there was very strong anti-alien feeling. It was on this that trouble arose with the licenser of plays. What seems to have worried him was not that the play was written in honour of the greatest of all the martyrs for Rome. He was obviously prepared to allow *that*. He went through the play making slight alterations, then, concluding that it would not do, he turned back to the front page, and told the play-wrights that they must omit the whole of the riot scenes.

The fact that the bulk of the play is in the handwriting of Anthony Munday does not mean that it was all, or mainly, composed by him. It was he who made the fair copy, and he may have been part author: but it is hardly credible that so violent a Protestant partisan was the leading spirit in composing a play so sympathetic to the martyr for Rome. And there is a tell-tale mistake which shows that in one place at least he is only acting as a (not very intelligent) scribe. There are additions made by five different hands. Dr. W. W. Greg, in the edition which he brought out for the Malone Society in 1911, christened these hands by the non-committal names A, B, C, D, E. The problem is to get more interesting names, if we can. All serious study of the play must start from Dr. Greg's great edition. After further investigation, Dr. Greg agrees that A is probably Chettle, B possibly Heywood, E certainly Dekker. C has been identified with Kyd, but this identification Greg decisively rejects. A, B, D and E are the authors of the parts in their hands. But C is found transcribing B; he need not be the author of any of the lines in his hand; yet he plays an important part, revising stage directions, and fitting the additions into their places. He edits D's three pages slightly. One short passage in C's handwriting may well have been copied from something written by D: it is very good, and very Shakespearean in tone.[1] But to discuss this would complicate the argument; it is safer to credit D only with what is in his hand.

I propose, then, to examine in detail, passage by passage, the three pages in hand D. I intentionally modernize spelling and punctuation, and expand contractions. We are all familiar with Shakespeare in the modern spelling, whilst the play of *Sir Thomas More* has never been reprinted, save in the old spelling. This creates a subtle, quite unjustified, feeling of difference. I number the lines for convenience of reference, counting them as they are found in the manuscript.

---

[1] *See* E. K. CHAMBERS, *William Shakespeare*, 1, 514.

Enter Lincoln, Doll, Clown, George Betts, Williamson, others,
and a Sergeant at Arms. [1]

LINCOLN   Peace, hear me. He that will not see a
red herring at a Harry groat, butter at
elevenpence a pound, meal at nine
shillings a bushel, and beef at four nobles
a stone, list to me.

GEO. BETTS   It will come to that pass, if strangers be
suffered. Mark him.

LINCOLN   Our country is a great eating country,   5
argo they eat more in our country than
they do in their own.

CLOWN BETTS   By a half-penny loaf a day. Troy weight.

LINCOLN   They bring in strange roots, which is
merely to the undoing of poor prentices,
for what's a sorry parsnip to a good heart?

WILLIAMSON   Trash, trash; they breed sore eyes, and   10
'tis enough to infect the City with the
palsy.

LINCOLN   Nay, it has infected it with the palsy, for
these bastards of dung, as you know they
grow in dung, have infected us, and it is
our infection will make the City shake,
which partly comes through the eating of
parsnips.   15

CLOWN BETTS   True, and pumpions together.

Here the Sergeant interrupts the clamour.

SERGEANT   What say you to the mercy of the king, do
you refuse it?

LINCOLN   You would have us upon th'hip, would
you? No, marry do we not; we accept of
the king's mercy but we will show no
mercy upon the strangers.

[1] The stage direction, and many of the names of the speakers, sometimes
contracted, were added in the hand of C. The writer of the text (D) allotted the
speeches in this passage to Lincoln and the Sergeant, and marked the remaining
speeches by the word *other* (*oth.*, *o.*).

Now, any reader must be struck by the general resemblance of these lines to the Jack Cade scenes in *Henry VI, Part II*, and in particular by the use of *argo* for *ergo* in both scenes.

A difficulty as to the pronunciation of *er*, which has given us *clerk* and *Clarke*, *Derby* pronounced *Darby*, existed in Elizabethan days. This led to the mispronunciation which pedants called *Plateasmus*.[1]

Now it is a common Elizabethan joke to make the pedant, or some person of low degree, chop logic with *ergo*. This happens in Shakespeare five times, in Ben Jonson, Heywood, Dekker, Lodge, Greene, Sharpham and elsewhere. Therefore, in view of this common mispronunciation, against which school-boys were warned, it would seem to be an obvious elaboration of the jest to go farther, and make the man of low degree mis-pronounce his *ergo* as *argo*. Nevertheless, I only know of three examples. I have searched, or had search made, in all the extant plays between 1580 and 1610, and *argo* is reported only the three times we know: in this mob scene of D's addition to *Sir Thomas More*; in the Jack Cade scene in *Henry VI, Part II* (IV, ii) and (improved to *argal*) in *Hamlet* (V, i, 12, etc.). It is just possible (though extremely unlikely) that an example *may* have escaped the vigilance of Miss Mary McGregor, to whose help in this search I express my indebtedness. Anyway, we can say that this elaborated *argo*-jest, unlike the simple *ergo*-jest, is not a commonplace.

But the occurrence of this word in itself is nothing, compared with the context in which we find it. Jack Cade and his men chop their logic, and all the time the author is poking fun at them, with that 'good nature with which he seems always to make sport with the passions and follies of a mob, as with an irrational animal'. 'There's Smith the weaver,' says Holland. '*Argo*, their thread of life is spun,' says Bevis; and then Jack Cade enters with his questionable economics: 'There shall be in England seven half-penny loaves sold for a penny; the three hooped pot shall have ten hoops; and I will make it felony to drink small beer.'

[1] See the *Brevissima Institutio*, a portion of LYLY's *Latin Grammar* (in existence as early as 1569). One of the instances of *Plateasmus* supplied is *argo* for *ergo*. The passage is quoted by Prof. H. M. AYRES in *Speculum*, I, pp. 440-3.

The argument for identity of authorship does not lie in the fact that *argo* is unknown in extant Elizabethan drama outside Shakespeare and D's 'three pages'; it does not even lie in the occurrence in both scenes of both *argo* and the *halfpenny loaf* (striking as this is, for how many times elsewhere in Elizabethan drama is mention made of halfpenny loaves?). Nevertheless, the fact that the *argo* and the *halfpenny loaf* occur in both passages is not the point. The point is that the thought is the same: we have the same type of false argument, mingled with false economics, and discussion of the diet of the poor. The *argo* and the *halfpenny loaf* are merely, as it were, signposts which attract our attention. We look, and we find that the thought is being led in the same direction. It is that which matters, although, but for the signposts, we might have overlooked the similarity of the thought.

Professor Schücking has suggested Heywood rather than Shakespeare as the possible author of D's 'three pages'. The argument is definitely refuted by the fact that we know Heywood's handwriting, and it is *not* that of D. Yet it is worth while examining Schücking's argument, because nothing could show more strongly the special character of the relationship of these lines with Shakespeare, than a comparison of the relationship which Schücking tries to establish with Heywood.

Schücking points to no sequences of thought common to Heywood and D's 'three pages'; all we get is the occasional occurrence of a phrase or idea in common, and it is to this that Schücking trusts. Such common phraseology may sometimes have subsidiary value, but it forms no *foundation* for attributing to one author the different writings in which it occurs.

It is necessary to repeat again and again that it is not in the single phrase or idea that individuality shows itself, but in the *combination of ideas*, till we get a complex so marked that its reproduction can hardly be the result of mere accident. 'Our country is a great eating country,' says the agitator in *Sir Thomas More*. Schücking adduces, as a parallel between *Sir Thomas More* and Heywood, Heywood's allusion to the English love of 'the large excess of a full table'.[1] But that England is a

[1] *English Traveller*, I, i; *Works*, 1874, IV, 12.

country of large appetites is mentioned by the agitator in *Sir Thomas More* as a fact generally known and admitted, on which he can base his argument. How can the fact that a writer knows of a thing which everybody knows, be an argument that he is one particular man, whether Heywood or anybody else? It certainly cannot make for Heywood against Shakespeare, for in *Macbeth* also we have allusion to 'English epicures' (i.e. gluttons). It proves nothing either way, in favour of either Shakespeare or Heywood. This charge of gluttony is a frequent one. It may be that in the Sixteenth and early Seventeenth Centuries Englishmen were more prone to admit gluttony as a national fault than either before or since. If this be so, then such references go to prove that the play of *Sir Thomas More* and Thomas Heywood and William Shakespeare all belong to the Sixteenth or early Seventeenth Century. But we knew that already. What *is* Shakespearean is not 'Our country is a great eating country', but the combination of ideas which we find common to D's 'three pages' and to the Jack Cade scenes.

When we come to a comparison of the speeches of More in the 'three pages' and of Ulysses in *Troilus and Cressida*, we shall find that not only are the same ideas combined, but (what is even more remarkable) they are developed in exactly the same order. In the scenes of riot this is not always so, nor is that fact surprising. 'Then are we in order when we are most out of order,' says Jack Cade. 'You ... whose discipline is riot,' says More to the mob. That the *order* of the rioters is *disorder*, that their *discipline* is *riot*, is a striking way of expressing a thought, a way not very likely, one would imagine, to have occurred independently to many writers. Anyhow, there it is, and therefore we must not be surprised if, whilst we find the same elements in the mob oratory of D's 'three pages' and of the Jack Cade scenes, the elements are not invariably combined in the same order; the sequence is, as it should be, sometimes inconsequent. One principle, however, is followed both by D and by Shakespeare. The agitator, Lincoln or Cade, comes on the stage haranguing his followers and commanding silence. Cade *always* enters talking. It needed no Shakespeare to invent *that*, but it marks a certain similarity in the treatment of Lincoln and

Cade. Call it (*a*). In both scenes we have (*b*) the enumeration of things which go to make up the painful budgets of the poor, with false economics based on the *halfpenny loaf*, and (*c*) the logic-chopping with *argo*. Of very special importance is (*d*) the statement of the grievance of the rioters. In the play of *Sir Thomas More*, as D's collaborators had written it, the London citizens are represented as patient, law-abiding, loyal, honest and reasonable, but goaded to madness by wrongs such as no free men could endure. They have as sound reasons for rioting as men could have. But in D's 'three pages' we have the typical Shakespearean attitude to the mob. We begin with a grievance which, however quaintly expressed, has an element of truth: 'They bring in strange roots, which is merely to the undoing of poor prentices, for what's a sorry parsnip to a good heart?' says Lincoln, as D depicts him. 'Is not this a lamentable thing', says Jack Cade, 'that parchment, being scribbled o'er, should undo a man? . . . For I did but seal once to a thing, and I was never mine own man since.' It is impossible not to have sympathy with these complaints, but they are merely the prelude to (*e*) absurd statements about the corruption spread by such innovations. Parsnips, says Lincoln, have infected the City with the palsy, and this infection will make it shake, 'which partly comes through the eating of parsnips'. (Note the moderation of 'partly'.) It is in a very similar vein that Jack Cade addresses Lord Say:

> Thou hast most traitorously corrupted the youth of the realm in erecting a grammar-school: and whereas, before, our forefathers had no other books but the score and the tally, thou hast caused printing to be used; and, contrary to the king, his crown and dignity, thou hast built a paper-mill. It will be proved to thy face that thou hast men about thee that usually talk of a noun and a verb, and such abominable words as no Christian ear can endure to hear.[1]

These absurdities, depicted by the dramatist with fun and merry good humour, are, by a terrible combination, coupled with (*f*) merciless savagery: 'We will show no mercy upon the strangers,' says Lincoln; Cade hangs the Clerk of Chatham because he has

---

[1] *2 Henry VI*, IV. VII. 30 etc.

confessed that he can write his name. Finally we have (*g*) the instability of the rioters: in the 'three pages' Lincoln simultaneously accepts the king's mercy, but will show no mercy upon the strangers; Cade's followers alternately decide to accept the king's mercy and to go on rioting. The folly of the mob is emphasized in each case by comment: 'You are the simplest things that ever stood in such a question,' says the Sergeant to the mob in *More*; 'Was ever feather so lightly blown to and fro as this multitude?' says Cade.

Within this framework we have a number of other things common to D's 'three pages' and plays of Shakespeare other than *Henry VI, Part II*. These, in isolation, would not be arguments, but coming within this scheme common to the Cade scenes and 'the 147 lines' they have subsidiary force.

'You would have us upon the hip,' says Lincoln to the sergeant. Long ago Dyce noticed that this wrestling metaphor, though by no means confined to Shakespeare, is one of which he is specially fond. (Dyce merely made this remark in passing, with no thought of arguing for any Shakespearean authorship here.)

More striking is the imagery by which parsnips are spoken of as 'bastards of dung'. The term 'bastard' is common enough, as applied to some flower or plant which only half belongs to the family — an inferior or less proper kind, which has only a partial resemblance to its legitimate kinsfolk. Bastard Pimpernel is also called False Pimpernel; Bastard Saffron, also called Mock Saffron, is so named because used as a substitute for saffron. But that common use is inapplicable here: the parsnips are parsnips right enough. Why, then, 'bastards'? Professor Spurgeon[1] has pointed to the explanation by a comparison of *A Winter's Tale*, where Shakespeare applies 'bastard' to flowers, strange varieties:

> Carnations and streak'd gillyvors,
> Which some call nature's bastards. *W.T.* iv, iv, 82

So D applies the word 'bastard' to the parsnip, a strange root. But probably there is more in it than that; for a stranger is one

[1] *Review of English Studies*, VI, 259.

thing, a bastard another. The objection which Perdita has to the gillyvors finds its explanation in the gardening books of the time, which tell of the practice of putting vermilion or cinnabar, azure or verdigris between the rind and the small heads growing about the root, to modify the colour. And so Perdita does not care to get slips of these flowers because

> There is an art, which in their piedness shares
> With great creating Nature.

They are artificial, therefore illegitimate, therefore bastards. Lincoln, like Perdita, would say that, compared with the products of honest mother earth, such growths are artificial, bastard. It is an odd use of the word. For normally the wild or inferior variety is regarded as the bastard, and the more fully developed type as the legitimate. But here it is the cultivated kind which is called bastard, as against the wild growths which are regarded as Nature's legitimate children.

This is one of the cases (there are others, and they are most significant) where Shakespeare and D's 'three pages' throw light upon one another.

And it is only one out of a number of minor parallels between the opening of D's mob scene and Shakespeare. Parsnips breed sore eyes, says a rioter, and *sore eyes* give the *palsy* and are a cause of *infection*. This may seem difficult, but, as Professor Spurgeon has shown, it is Shakespearean. 'In Thersites' repulsive list of diseases (*T. and C.* v, i, 23) *cold palsies, raw eyes* go together; Biron tells Rosaline that the king and the two other lords are *infected*, "*they have the* plague, *and caught it of your eyes*"; and Anne cries to Gloucester (*R. III*, i, ii, 149), "Out of my sight! thou dost infect my eyes".'

But these fleeting parallels, even the striking similarity of thought which leads to an identical use of the figure 'bastard' in the 'three pages' and in *The Winter's Tale*, have, it seems to me, only subsidiary value. What seems to mark the individual mind is the complex of parallels, (*a*) the entry of the mob leader, *talking amid clamour*, (*b*) the false economics of the *halfpenny loaf*, (*c*) the logic-chopping with *argo*, (*d*) the *undoing* of the poor by parsnips (or writing, as the case may be), (*e*) the *infection*[1] spreading therefrom, (*f*) the murderous outburst, and (*g*)the instability of the mob. These parallels make the few lines in *More* read like a summary of the Jack Cade scenes in *Henry VI*. Those who hold that such a series can be the result of mere accident should find a parallel to such accident. So far, no one has even taken the first step, which is to find another example in Elizabethan drama of *argo*. The combination produces an effect of mingled humour and horror, quite unlike anything else in Elizabethan drama outside Shakespeare and this *More*-scene. It is instructive to contrast the treatment of rebellion and mutiny in *Jack Straw*, or Heywood's *Edward IV*, or Webster's *Appius and Virginia*, or his (and Dekker's) *Sir Thomas Wyat*, or the other mob scenes in *Sir Thomas More*.[2]

The Sergeant ridicules the rioters' wish to have things both ways: to accept the King's mercy, but to show no mercy upon the strangers:

SERGEANT	You are the simplest things that ever stood in such a question.	21
LINCOLN	How say you now! Prentices simple! Down with him!	
ALL	Prentices simple! Prentices simple!	

Enter the Lord Mayor, Surrey, Shrewsbury, [Palmer, Cholmeley, More] 25

MAYOR	Hold! In the King's name, hold!	
SURREY	Friends, Masters, Countrymen —	
MAYOR	Peace, ho! Peace! I charge you keep the peace.	
SHREW.	My Masters, Countrymen —	
SHERWIN	The noble earl of Shrewsbury, let's hear him.	30

With this compare *Julius Caesar*:

BRUTUS   My Countrymen —

[1] The word used in 'the 147 lines' and in the *Contention* is 'infect'; in *Henry VI* 'corrupt'. But no importance attaches to the choice of synonym.
[2] See *The Crowd in Elizabethan Drama*, by A. M. McGREGOR (a Univ. of London M.A. Thesis, 1927).

SEC. CIT.   Peace, Silence! Brutus speaks.
FIRST CIT.   Peace ho!
BRUTUS   Good Countrymen, let me depart alone . . .

Or

ANTONY   You gentle Romans —
ALL   Peace ho! Let us hear him . . .
ANTONY   Friends, Romans, Countrymen, . . .

The question which those who do not accept the Shakespearean authorship of D's 'three pages' have got to face is whether this
parallel to *Julius Caesar*, *in combination* with the parallel to the
Cade scenes, can fairly be put down to mere accident. It must
be noted that Professor Schücking, the most redoubtable of
those who deny the Shakespearean authorship, is convinced
that the likeness here cannot be mere accident. He attributes
it to D imitating *Julius Caesar*.

Now whether these likenesses can best be accounted for by
postulating such imitation, or by postulating the working of the
same brain, is a problem which may be deferred till we can
consider them all together.

What I have in mind at present is the sceptic who denies both
explanations; who holds that such likenesses are not beyond the
possibilities of 'the long arm of coincidence'. If we grant that
to our sceptic, we must ask him to proceed with a study of the
mob-scene:

GEO. BETTS We'll hear the Earl of Surrey.   31
LINCOLN   The Earl of Shrewsbury.
BETTS   We'll hear both.
ALL   Both! Both! Both! Both!
LINCOLN   Peace, I say, Peace! Are you men of wisdom,   35
             or what are you?
SURREY   What you will have them, but not men of
             wisdom.
ALL   We'll not hear my Lord of Surrey!
             No, No, No, No, No!
             Shrewsbury! Shr[ewsbury]!

MORE	Whiles they are o'er the bank of their obedi-ence,	
	Thus will they bear down all things.	40
LINCOLN	Sheriff More speaks! Shall we hear Sheriff More speak?	
DOLL	Let's hear him! A keeps a plentiful shrievaltry, and a made my brother Arthur Watchins Sergeant Safe's yeoman. Let's hear Sheriff More.	
ALL	Sheriff More! More! More! Sheriff More!	45
MORE	Even by the rule you have among yourselves, Command still audience.	
ALL	Surrey! Surrey!	
ALL	More! More!	
LINCOLN ⎫ BETTS ⎭	Peace! Peace! Silence! Peace!	50
MORE	You that have voice and credit with the number, Command them to a stillness.	
LINCOLN	A plague on them! They will not hold their peace. The Devil cannot rule them!	
MORE	Then what a rough and riotous charge have you, To lead those that the Devil cannot rule. Good masters, hear me speak.	55
DOLL	Aye, by the mass will we, More. Thou art a good housekeeper, and I thank thy good worship for my brother Arthur Watchins.	
ALL	Peace! Peace!	60

Mob scenes like this are found in *Henry VI, Part II*, in *Julius Caesar*, and later in *Coriolanus*, but in no other English dramatist writing within the limits of time within which the play of *Sir Thomas More* must have been written. Typically Shakespearean is Doll's plea that More should be allowed to speak, because he has given a post to her brother. But as we proceed with More's speech, we find in it parallels as close as those in the outcries of the mob:

ALL   Peace! Peace!   60

MORE Look: what you do offend you cry upon;
That is the peace; not [one]¹ of you here present
(Had there such fellows lived when you were
babes,
That could have topped the peace, as now you
would) —
The peace wherein you have till now grown up   65
Had been ta'en from you, and the bloody times
Could not have brought you to the state of men.
Alas, poor things! What is it you have got,
Although we grant you get the thing you seek?

BETTS Marry, the removing of the strangers, which can-   70
not choose but much advantage the poor handi-
crafts of the City.

MORE Grant them removed, and grant that this your
noise
Hath chid down all the majesty of England;
Imagine that you see the wretched strangers
Their babies at their backs, and their poor luggage,   75
Plodding to the ports and coasts for transportation,
And that you sit as kings in your desires,
Authority quite silenced by your brawl,
And you in ruff of your opinions clothed,
What had you got? I'll tell you. You had taught   80
How insolence and strong hand should prevail,
How order should be quelled — and by this pattern
Not one of you should live an aged man;
For other ruffians, as their fancies wrought,
With self same hand, self reasons and self right   85
Would shark on you; and men like ravenous fishes
Would feed on one another.

Here More pauses, and Doll interrupts:

DOLL Before God, that's as true as the Gospel.

We may therefore also pause, to compare More's speech, so far
as it has gone, with the great speech on 'Degree' by Ulysses in

¹ The manuscript is torn: but 'one' was obviously the word.

Troilus and Cressida. Both start from disrespect to authority:
the Earl of Surrey has been shouted down; Agamemnon has
been flouted. To both orators this suggests the same picture of a
flood surging over its banks:

> ULYSSES Take but degree away, untune that string,
> And hark, what discord follows! Each thing
> meets
> In mere oppugnancy: the bounded waters
> Should lift their bosoms higher than the shores,
> And make a sop of all this solid globe.

> MORE. Whiles they are o'er the bank of their obedience
> Thus will they bear down all things.

From this, both speakers pass to a further stage which assuredly
is not an obvious one; their words go beyond the ordinary Tudor
fear of civil war and anarchy. If authority is despised, degree
neglected, then the helpless, the babes or the aged, will be done
to death even by those nearest to them. Most people would say
that this is not a necessary or a logical consequence; that it is
the exaggerated language of a man obsessed by fear of anarchy.
If Degree be but taken away, says Ulysses, imbecility, that is
helpless childhood or age, must suffer:

> Strength should be lord of imbecility,
> *And the rude son should strike his father dead.*

Similarly More assures the mob:

> Had there such fellows lived when you were babes
> That could have topped the peace ... the bloody times
> Could not have brought you to the state of men. ...
> By this pattern
> *Not one of you should live an aged man.*

(Yet, after all, the rioters are depicted elsewhere as very decent
folk.) From parricide or infanticide both speakers pass to the
picture of self-devouring monsters:

ULYSSES And appetite, an universal wolf,
  So doubly seconded with will and power,
  Must make perforce an universal prey
  And last eat up himself.

MORE   and men, like ravenous fishes,
  Would feed on one another.

Agamemnon, whom Ulysses is addressing, is still the Grecian general, although his authority has been defied. The rioters, whom More is addressing, are perfectly loyal. Most people would hold that there is no need to trouble yet with any such thoughts as these of ravenous fishes and universal wolves eating up themselves. Shakespeare would not.

Shakespeare, as Raleigh says, 'extols government with a fervour that suggests a real and ever-present fear of the breaking of the flood-gates'. But my point is that this fervour, in itself highly characteristic, is expressed both in *Sir Thomas More* and in *Troilus and Cressida* by a quite individual succession of thoughts: (*a*) Degree neglected, (*b*) the flood surging over its banks, (*c*) the doing to death of the aged or the babes, (*d*) cannibal monsters. It is this linking of the thought that matters. The wording is not the same, nor have we any reason to demand that it should be the same. For if so striking a sequence of thought were uttered in the same words, we should have a mere repetition, such as we do not find, and ought not to expect to find, in the 'myriad-minded' Shakespeare.

Common Elizabethan phrases have too often been claimed as proofs of two authors being the same man, when they only show that two authors used a common language. Still, verbal echoes are not to be neglected, least of all when they are connected with a real image in the writer's mind.

It has been pointed out how frequent in Shakespeare, as illustrating insubordination or rebellion in men, is the image of waters breaking their bounds and overbearing everything. The comparison of Laertes, overbearing the officers of Claudius, to 'the ocean overpeering of his list' will occur to the reader. But both in *Coriolanus* and in D's 'three pages' this parallel in thought is closely associated with a verbal echo.

Cominius leads Coriolanus away with the words

> Will you hence
> Before the tag return? Whose rage doth rend
> Like interrupted waters, and o'erbear
> What they are used to bear.

Menenius remains to intercede for 'the consul Coriolanus':

BRUTUS He consul!
CITIZENS *No, No, No, No, No.*

In the 'three pages' Surrey provokes the mob by a jeer entirely in the manner of Coriolanus himself. The mob shout him down:

ALL We'll not hear my lord of Surrey:
No, No, No, No, No.

MORE Whiles they are o'er the bank of their obedience
Thus will they bear down all things.

Professor Spurgeon[1] has pointed out how 'the majesty of England' (l. 74) has a Shakespearean ring, recalling 'the majesty of buried Denmark', 'the beauteous majesty of Denmark (*Hamlet*, I, i, 48; IV, v, 21)'; how the rather peculiar use of *self* is Shakespearean[2]; and how the phrase 'ravenous fishes' (l. 86) also occurs in a Shakespearean passage (*Henry VIII*, I, ii, 79). In this speech (l. 86) and in *Hamlet* (I, i, 98) come the two earliest instances of the rare use of 'to shark' as a verb. All this has subsidiary value. But the striking thing is that in *King Lear*, just as in D's 'three pages', we pass from the idea of a state of things in which life is made impossible for the aged, to the idea of men devouring each other like cannibal sea-monsters. Albany says to Goneril:

> A father, and a gracious *aged man*
> ... have you madded. ...
> If that the Heavens do not their visible spirits
> Send quickly down to tame these vile offences
> It will come,

---

[1] Loc. cit., p. 262.   [2] P. 265

227

Humanity must perforce *prey on itself*
Like *monsters of the deep.*[1]

Note the entire difference of the language in which the same thought is expressed.

Finally, as a contrast to the leisurely way in which both More and Ulysses develop their argument, from Degree neglected, through the imagery of the waters, the argument of the injustice to helpless youth or age, and the imagery of cannibal monsters, observe how Coriolanus, in his wrath, leaps from the idea of Degree neglected to the very half line ('would feed on one another') with which More concludes a long passage. Coriolanus exclaims:

> You cry against the noble Senate, who,
> Under the gods, keep you in awe, which else
> *Would feed on one another.*

That is to say, whilst in D's 'three pages' and in *Troilus*, we have the full sequence (*a*) (*b*) (*c*) (*d*), we have in *Coriolanus* and *Hamlet* the sequence (*a*) rebellion, (*b*) flood; in *Lear* the sequence (*c*) outrage to the aged, (*d*) cannibal sea-monsters; and again in *Coriolanus* the sequence (*a*) rebellion, (*d*) cannibalism. Are these parallels still to be dismissed as mere accident?

Let us continue, then, from the point where More's speech is interrupted by Doll and Lincoln:

LINCOLN Nay, this is a sound fellow, I tell you; let's mark
      him.

MORE   Let me set up before your thoughts, good friends,   90
      One supposition, which if you will mark,
      You shall perceive how horrible a shape
      Your innovation bears; first 'tis a sin
      Which oft th' apostle did forwarn us of,
      Urging obedience to authority.
      And 'twere no error if I told you all
      You were in arms 'gainst God.   95

---

[1] *King Lear*, IV, ii, 49. This was pointed out to me by Dr. Perrett and Professor Sisson independently; and it has also been noted by Professor Spurgeon (p. 265).

ALL   Marry, God forbid that.

MORE   Nay, certainly you are.
        For to the king God hath his office lent
        Of dread, of justice, power and command;
        Hath bid him rule, and will'd you to obey.   100
        And to add ampler majesty to this
        God hath not only lent the king his figure,
        His throne and sword, but given him his own
        name,
        Calls him a god on earth. What do you then
        Rising 'gainst him that God himself installs   105
        But rise 'gainst God? What do you to your souls
        In doing this, O desperate as you are?
        Wash your foul minds with tears, and those
        same hands
         That you like rebels lift against the peace
        Lift up for peace, and your unreverent knees 110
        Make them your feet.

Now, in the first place, compare Menenius' speech in *Coriolanus*:

                 You may as well
    Strike at the Heaven with your staves as lift them
    Against the Roman state; whose course will on
    The way it takes, cracking ten thousand curbs
    Of more strong link asunder than can ever
    Appear in your impediment. For the dearth
    The gods, not the patricians, make it, and
    Your knees to them, not arms, must help.

In both passages the comparison of the State with the Divine Power (an obvious comparison) is followed by the admonition that subjects should use not *hands* or *arms* in rebellion, but *knees* in prayer. Two minds, it may be said, might have hit upon that antithesis independently. True. But how many more times have we to postulate such coincidences?

Now turn to *Richard II*, and we shall find further parallels spread over the last two acts, where Shakespeare is thinking intensely on the prerogative of the king. More speaks of *God*, adding ampler *majesty* to the *king* by lending him his *figure* (ll. 101, 102). The Bishop of Carlisle in *Richard II* speaks of the *king* as '*the figure of God's majesty*' (IV, i, 125). Such is the king's majesty, says More, that the rebels should 'make their knees their feet' (l. 111). This is surely an unusual phrase. The writer has a picture in his mind — the suppliants approaching the king by coming towards him on their knees — literally walking on their knees.

Now in the next act of *Richard II* we have the continuation, from a different point of view, of this question of the king's prerogative, and whether conspiracy against the king's majesty may be pardoned. 'For ever will I *walk* upon my *knees*,' says the Duchess, kneeling before the king — and when at last she has prevailed upon him to grant pardon to Aumerle, she exclaims '*A god on earth* thou art'. Now contrast with these sequences the 'curious parallels' which Schücking finds between D's 'three pages' and Heywood. '*Wash* your *foul minds* with *tears*,' says More to the mob (l. 108). Schücking justly finds 'a very close parallel' in the words of Mistress Frankford:[1] 'But when my *tears* have *washed* my *black soul* white.' But how can such a parallel prove anything for Heywood against Shakespeare, when we find that this very phrase is actually paralleled in Shakespeare quite as closely as it is in Heywood:

> Claudio . . . who . . . speaking of her *foulness*
> *Washed* it with *tears*. (*Much Ado* iv. i. 155)

But, in fact, such parallels *in isolation* prove nothing either for Heywood or for Shakespeare. Yet further, Schücking points out that the phrase *a god on earth* occurs in two plays of Heywood. And, in yet another play of Heywood, we have the line: 'I wish that I could *march upon my knees*.' These parallels seem to Schücking to be noteworthy, and I think they are. But the similarity between these phrases, as they occur in 'the three pages' and in the scattered plays of Heywood, is one which, as we shall see, involves no real connection of *thought*, such as we have found repeatedly between D and Shakespeare.

The parallels between D's 'three pages' and the later acts of

---

[1] *A Woman Killed with Kindness*, v, iii; *Works*, 1874, II, 151.

Richard II all have their root in the same thought of *revolt against the king's authority*. Touch that string, and from the mind of D, and from the mind of Shakespeare, issue, together with the same political doctrine, the same images and sometimes the same phrases.

Even at the cost of some repetition it is worth while going in detail over the two passages, to note how closely the same sequence is maintained in the 'three pages' and in *Richard II*:

(*a*) The rebels, says More, 'whiles they are o'er the bank of their obedience', will 'bear down all things'. We have found the same image used to illustrate the same thing, rebellion against authority, in *Troilus*, *Hamlet* and *Coriolanus*. So in *Richard II*:

> Like an unseasonable stormy day
> Which makes the silver rivers drown their shores,
> As if the world were all dissolved in tears,
> So high above his limits swells the rage
> Of Bolingbroke, covering your fearful land. . . .

(*b*) Against this flood, More and the Bishop of Carlisle respectively make head by argument. 'To add ampler majesty', says More, 'God hath lent the king his figure.' The Bishop of Carlisle exclaims:

> Shall the figure of God's majesty . . .
> Be judged by subject and inferior breath?

(*c*) Then comes the most striking thing — the extension, in the words of both speakers, More and the Bishop, of the evil from generation to generation. The idea of 'Degree' is linked in the mind of Shakespeare with the idea of father and son, childhood and old age. Modern revolutionaries have loved to commemorate a day or a year. *To Shakespeare revolution is never a matter of a day or a year*, but the breaking of a tie which binds the generations each to each. 'Take but degree away', says Ulysses, 'and the rude son should strike his father dead.' 'Had there such fellows lived when you were babes', More assures the rioters, they would not be alive; 'and by this pattern not one of you should live an

aged man' (ll. 63-7; 82-3). The Bishop of Carlisle prophesies
that, if Richard II is deposed, England will see

> future ages groan for this foul act. . . .
> And in this seat of peace tumultuous wars
> Shall kin with kin, and kind with kind confound. . . .
> Prevent it, resist it, let it not be so,
> Lest child, child's children, cry against you 'woe!'

The next thought is naturally whether such a crime, working
evil from generation to generation, can be forgiven.

(d) God has ordained the king 'a god on earth', says More
(l. 104), and there is nothing for rebels to do save pray for
forgiveness by

(e) making their knees their feet (l. 111). With a terrible
irony, Shakespeare in *Richard II* has left the question of forgiveness to be settled by the 'foul traitor' Bolingbroke himself.
Bolingbroke has become king; and, whilst he himself is plotting
the murder of Richard, he learns that Aumerle has plotted his
own death. When the duchess vows (e) for ever to walk upon
her knees, this is in *prayer to the king to forgive the treason* of Aumerle;
and she exclaims (d) 'A god on earth thou art', when by exer-
cising his prerogative of mercy to one guilty of treason against
him, Bolingbroke has proved himself a king.

Every one of these five parallels between D's 'three pages'
and *Richard II* has its root in the same thought in both plays —
revolt against the king's authority.

But there is nothing whatever of that community of thought
in the parallels which Schücking quotes from Heywood. They
are all merely repetition of similar phraseology. Jupiter says of
gold: 'Thou art a god on earth, and can'st all things.'[1] The
Fair Maid of the West says to the King of Fez, when he has
generously reunited her to her lover,

> Oh, were you of our faith, I'd swear great Mullisheg
> To be a god on earth.[2]

---

[1] *The Golden Age, Works*, 1874, III, 67.
[2] *The Fair Maid of the West*, I, v, 2, *Works*, 1874, II, 331.

When the Crusaders approach Jerusalem, Tancred devoutly exclaims:

> I cast my heart as low as to this earth,
> And wish that I could march upon my knees
> In true submission, and right holy zeal.[1]

The reference is to the posture of pilgrims approaching a holy place. It may be observed to-day, at Assisi, on the anniversary of the Portiuncula indulgence, when pilgrims will fall in prayer at the great west door, and move on their knees all the way up the vast nave, till they reach the tiny church which Francis repaired.

But the point is that, in D's 'three pages' and in *Richard II*, this attitude, appropriate to *worshippers* approaching a Holy of Holies, is spoken of as the right attitude for petitioners of an earthly monarch. It is justified, in that the petitioner is suing for a life which has been forfeited by treason, to a king who is 'a god on earth'. Shakespeare had in mind a picture of suppliants moving forward on their knees. The same picture comes in *Troilus and Cressida* (v. iii. 10), 'pursue we him on knees'. The same picture is clearly in the mind of D. When both in the 'three pages' and in *Richard II* the king implored is spoken of as 'a god on earth', there is the peculiar appropriateness that such humility of approach befits a god rather than a man. In Heywood there is no such connection of thought.

Yet I do not deny that the Heywood parallels are interesting, and, as Schücking claims, worthy of attention. Schücking of course admits that these parallels, and the few others which he quotes, 'by no means suffice to prove that the insurrection scene was written by Heywood'. But if such a superficial and isolated use of similar phrases is to be considered worth quoting, then I submit that the quite astonishing combinations common to Shakespeare and D's 'three pages' might well be considered conclusive.

Almost every reader of Heywood has been struck by his likeness to Shakespeare, since Charles Lamb christened Heywood 'a sort of prose Shakespeare'. The play of *Sir Thomas More*

[1] *The Four Prentices of London, Works*, 1874, II, 230.

concerns itself with what was peculiarly Heywood's field — the celebration of worthies connected with the City. If D be Shakespeare, we might expect him to remind us a little of Heywood and a great deal of Shakespeare. Which is exactly what he does. He is not Heywood, for, as I have said, Heywood's hand is known,[1] and is quite certainly not that of D.

After the admonition for the rebels to make their knees their feet, D makes More proceed

to kneel to be forgiven   111
Is safer wars than ever you can make
Whose discipline is riot. In! In! To your obedience;
Why even your wars
Cannot proceed but by obedience.
What rebel captain,
As mutinies are incident, by his name   115
Can still the rout? Who will obey a traitor?
Or how can well that proclamation sound
When there is no addition but a rebel
To qualify a rebel? You'll put down strangers,
Kill them, cut their throats, possess their houses,   120
And lead the majesty of law in liom
To slip him like a hound. Say now the king
(As he is clement, if th'offender mourn)
Should so much come too short of your great trespass
As but to banish you — whither would you go?   125
What country, by the nature of your error
Should give you harbour? Go you to France or Flanders,
To any German prince, to Spain or Portugal,
Nay, anywhere that not adheres to England,
Why, you must needs be strangers. Would you   130
be pleased

---

[1] Heywood's hand has been identified by Dr. Tannenbaum with that of the B addition to *Sir Thomas More*, and the identification is recognized by Greg as possible (*Times Literary Supplement*, XXVI, 1927, p. 871).

To find a nation of such barbarous temper
That, breaking out in hideous violence,
Would not afford you an abode on earth,
Whet their detested knives against your throats,
Spurn you like dogs, and like as if that God   135
Owed not nor made not you, nor that the elements
Were not all appropriate to your comforts,
But chartered unto them — what would you think
To be thus used? This is the strangers' case,
And this you mountainish[1] inhumanity.   140

ALL   Faith, a says true. Let us do as we may be done by.
We'll be ruled by you, Master More, if you'll
stand our friend to procure our pardon.

MORE   Submit you to these noble gentlemen,
Entreat their mediation to the king,   145
Give up yourself to form, obey the magistrate,
And there's no doubt, but mercy may be found
If you so seek it.

Yet Schücking objects that the likenesses which I quoted in
1923 between 'the 147 lines' and Shakespeare are 'superficial.'
'The decisive test as to the imagery employed is', he says, 'whether
it bears the particularly Shakespearean mark.' I agree. That
mark he justly defines as 'the acuteness of the observation', 'the
persuasive power of Shakespeare's almost paradoxical combination of things, the surprising riches of his associations'. Again,
I agree. It is just from these associations that I am arguing.
'Lines', Schücking says, 'like those from *Coriolanus*, I. i. 168:

> You dissentious rogues
> That, rubbing the poor itch of your opinion,
> Make yourselves scabs;

are therefore unmistakably Shakespearean; they would betray
his hand wherever they were to be found. Are there lines of this
sort in the "insurrection scene"? Certainly not.'

But it is useless to assert that there are no such lines, when it is
notorious, and has been for over sixty years, that there *are*.

[1] MS. momtanish.

Coriolanus's 'itch of your opinion' was compared by Richard Simpson in 1871 to More's 'ruff of your opinions':

> And that you sit as kings in your desires,
> Authority quite silenced by your brawl,
> And you in ruff of your opinions clothed.

And more recently in Professor Spurgeon's detailed study of the imagery, she shows how, of the twelve images[1] to be found in the 'three pages' *every one* can be paralleled in Shakespeare's known plays'.

For 'clothed in opinions', Professor Spurgeon compares Gratiano's 'dress'd in an opinion of wisdom' (*Merchant of Venice*, I. i. 91). 'Ruff' of course means 'pride' or 'excitement'. 'But', she says, 'the word naturally suggested its other meaning of an article of clothing, and so the verb clinches it into a metaphor, giving a double meaning to the noun ... This method of swift evolution, by way of association and suggestion, is a marked feature of Shakespeare's style in metaphor, and especially of his middle and later style, from 1594 onwards, and it is one in which he differs from most, if not all, of his contemporaries.' And not merely the style but the whole picture is Shakespearean. The mob, clothed in their opinions like robes of state, sit, pleased at having attained their ends. This is closely parallel to the address to 'the fond many' in *Henry IV, Part II* (I. iii. 94): 'And being now trimmed in thine own desires'.[2]

How *can* it then seriously be asserted that 'rubbing the poor itch of your opinion' is in Shakespeare's manner, but 'in ruff of your opinions clothed' is not? That this latter phrase is peculiarly Shakespearean is shown by the essay which Mr. E. E. Kellett, quite independently of the *More*-problem, published in 1923, *On a Feature of Shakespeare's Style*.[3] This feature is the way in which the use of a word suggests to Shakespeare a further thought based upon another sense of the same word:

[1] Other phrases might also, I think, have been counted as images: 'have on the hip', 'make your knees your feet', 'god on earth'; and these are equally Shakespearean.

[2] See Professor Spurgeon's article in *Review of English Studies*, VI, 262-4. The whole article should be consulted.

[3] In *Suggestions: Literary Essays*, Cambridge, 1923.

> The heavens, as troubled with man's *act*,
> Threaten his bloody *stage*.[1]

Mr. Kellett gave examples of this from Shakespeare, literally by the dozen. And the transition in this *More*-passage from 'ruff' (excitement) to 'clothed' is another example of the same (half-unconscious) verbal play as

> I am ambitious of a motley *coat* . . .
> It is my only *suit*.[2]

> All the *soil* of the achievement goes
> With me into the *earth*.[3]

> his *silver* hairs
> Will *purchase* us a good opinion.[4]

> having both the *key*
> Of officer and office, set all hearts i'the state
> To what *tune* pleased his ear.[5]

I don't deny that 'rubbing the poor itch of your opinion, make yourselves scabs' is in Shakespeare's manner. But to 'sit in ruff of your opinions clothed' is even more emphatically in Shakespeare's manner, because the double use of 'ruff' is a typical example of what has been proved to be a marked feature of Shakespeare's style. If then the *Coriolanus* passage 'betrays Shakespeare's hand', much more does the *More* passage do so.

Professor Spurgeon, like Mr. Kellett, undertook her examination of Shakespeare's images quite independently of *Sir Thomas More*. It was only when she had completed her investigations, after some years, that she applied them to this problem. And it is not merely that she found all the images in *More* paralleled in Shakespeare's known works, but also 'that they fall under the usual headings in the usual proportions found in Shakespeare, that the greater number of them express ideas and applications of those ideas peculiarly characteristic of Shakespeare and repeatedly found in his work, that they are moreover expressed

---

[1] *Macbeth*, II. iv. 6.   [2] *As You Like It*, II. vii. 43.
[3] *2 Henry IV*, IV. v. 190.   [4] *Julius Caesar*, II. I. 144
[5] *Tempest*, I. ii. 83.

in language in every case reminiscent of Shakespeare'. 'I confess', she writes, 'the result has astonished me.'

No doubt, certain of these likenesses in imagery and association, if considered individually, are commonplace, and might be found, not only in Shakespeare, but in any Elizabethan dramatist. But my argument is, that we must take them as a whole. Whether, when they are so taken, the total effect is that of a superficial likeness, is the question which the reader has to decide.

More particularly Schücking thinks my parallel of the greyhound and the puppet government 'superficial'. Titus Lartius summons the officers of the conquered Corioli 'to know his mind': the London rioters wish to impose *their* mind upon the king's officers. This is described in *Coriolanus* as

> Holding Corioli in the name of Rome
> Even like a fawning greyhound in the leash
> *To let him slip at will.*

in D's 'three pages' it is described as to

> lead the majesty of law in liom
> *To slip him like a hound.*

The officers of Corioli, the officers of Henry VIII, are to do only what their master (Titus Lartius or the London mob, as the case may be) allows. Surely, the parallel is exact; and it is emphasized by the image which Professor Spurgeon quotes from *The Taming of the Shrew* (v. ii. 52):

> O sir, Lucentio slipped me like his greyhound,
> Which runs himself, and catches for his master.

But I think enough has been said to show that there is some connection between the 'three pages' and Shakespeare. And indeed Schücking does not deny that there *is*.

If so, are we to attribute it to unity of authorship, or to D imitating Shakespeare, or to Shakespeare imitating D? We cannot date exactly D's addition, yet of the three plays most closely linked to it, one, *Troilus and Cressida*, is probably later, and another, *Coriolanus*, is pretty certainly later. It is surely a striking fact that the Shakespearean echoes in D range from plays as early as *Henry VI, Part II* (say 1590-91) to *The Winter's Tale* (say 1610-11). Many of these plays were not published at all till the Folio, and where they were, as in the case of the Jack Cade scenes, some of the striking parallels (such as the *argo*) do not appear in the Quarto *Contention*. Not till the Folio was published in 1623 is it easy to imagine how any man save Shakespeare can have had all these echoes ringing in his head together.

A theory of imitation would compel us to suppose, on any reasonable system of chronology, that D imitated Shakespeare's earlier plays, and that Shakespeare, when writing some of his later plays, imitated D. It is simpler to suppose D and Shakespeare the same person.

Besides, the assumption of imitation leaves unexplained the remarkable similarity between the handwriting and spelling of D and the handwriting and spelling of Shakespeare. An explanation which explains only one portion of the phenomena cannot be acceptable as against an explanation which accounts adequately for all.

We must therefore take into account the palaeographical evidence, the more so because it helps to illustrate in another way the literary argument. For, in the palaeographical as in the literary evidence, the point lies in the *combination*. In his final and authoritative summing up of the evidence Dr. Greg tells us that 'Of *e*, *h*, and *p* two clearly marked varieties occur in Shakespeare's signatures, and the same occur in D, while of *a* and *k* three varieties can be distinguished.' 'Such multiple agreement acquires considerable significance, even though the individual forms may be common.'[1]

But the individual forms are not all common. Of the three *a*'s found in Shakespeare's signatures and in D, one is extraordinarily uncommon. Sir Edward Maunde Thompson drew attention to it in 1916: and seven years later, in 1923, he said that both he and Mr. J. P. Gilson of the British Museum had been looking out for a parallel, but had, as yet, found none. That was fifteen years ago. Since then almost everybody interested

[1] *Times Literary Supplement*, XXVI, 1927, p. 871.

has been on the look-out for this particular kind of 'spurred a':
but with no success. I thought I had found a parallel in the hand
of George Chapman, and I wrote to the *Times Literary Supplement* to point it out, because I did not think it right that we should
continue to claim as a unique feature what I believed I had
found occurring elsewhere.[1] But the more skilled eyes of Sir
Edward Maunde Thompson and of Dr. W. W. Greg could see
that, though it was the closest parallel so far found, 'the parallel,
though striking, is not perfect',[2] and further examination shows
that this is the case. 'I think, therefore', says Dr. Greg, 'that
in its full peculiarity the resemblance between Shakespeare's
signature and D in this instance remains unchallenged and
unparalleled.'

But suppose that an exact parallel should turn up to-morrow
from some unknown source. How great must be the rarity of a
phenomenon of which only one example is found in fifteen
years, when we consider the number of people engaged upon
examining Elizabethan MSS., many of them on the look-out
for this peculiarity.

Think, for instance, of the amount of writing that may pass
under your eyes in an hour's work at the Record Office. Professor Sisson tells me that during six years he spent something
like three thousand hours reading MSS. at the Record Office
and the British Museum, and that he always kept an eye open
for this particular form of 'the spurred a'. He has not found a
single example. Then think of the number of other people who
have also been on the look-out for 'the spurred a' since Sir
Edward Maunde Thompson and Mr. Gilson began the search
about twenty-two years ago. After some nine years, Sir Edward
wrote that the quest seemed to have prospect of a career *ad
infinitum*. It is a testimony to the acumen of Sir Edward as a
palaeographer that he pitched upon a feature which all further
search has proved to be so highly exceptional.

But, further, it is not merely this odd form of 'the spurred a'
but the combination of 'the spurred a' with two other *a*'s,
which constitutes the peculiar link between D and Shakespeare.

[1] *Times Literary Supplement*, XXIV, 1925, p. 557.
[2] Dr. Greg, ibid., XXVI, 1927, p. 908. Compare Sir E. M. Thompson, ibid.,
XXIV, 1925, p. 600.

FROM THE PLAY OF *SIR THOMAS MORE*

(British Museum, Harleian MS. 7368), ll. 96-121 of the
three pages attributed to Shakespeare

And the combination of this with three forms of *k*, and with two forms of *e*, *h*, and *p* has to be added.

Then there is the long fine upstroke to certain initial letters. This is common; the argument lies in a *combination* of this upstroke with a downstroke, found once in a signature of Shakespeare's will and rather frequently in D, the pen touching the paper in descent, before the upstroke was begun, and so making a loop which, in its most characteristic form, resembles an 'elongated needle eye'. How far this feature is exceptional has been disputed; Sir Edward suggested 'a personal peculiarity'; Dr. Greg more cautiously says, 'The resemblance here is very striking, and must be allowed due weight, though it would be an exaggeration to regard it as constituting by itself a proof of identity.'

Then there is again the combination in both hands of the English script with an Italian long *f*. The fact that this is not as common in D as Sir Edward thought does not alter the undoubted fact that it *is* there. It is the only non-English letter in Shakespeare's signatures, and, except for an Italian *r*, the only non-English letter in D's 'three pages'.[1]

So we have the combination, in Shakespeare's hand and in D, of seven distinct combinations, one at least of which is, so far as is known at present, unparalleled.

Some people speak as if all this could be put aside if it could once be shown that Sir Edward Maunde Thompson had ever made a mistake. What Sir Edward did was to call the attention of palaeographers to a number of facts which, could they *all* have been shown to be unique, would have proved the Shakespearean authorship of the 'three pages' without any necessity of considering the literary parallels at all. Dr. Greg has shown that, of the characteristics claimed by Sir Edward as individual to D and to Shakespeare, two must be abandoned, and the other two are not quite as strong as Sir Edward thought, but still stand. We must never forget the handicap which Sir Edward Maunde Thompson voluntarily incurred by his self-denying ordinance in making his study strictly palaeographical, eschewing any literary

---

[1] Dr. Tannenbaum was the first to note the Italian *r*, but denies it and the *f* to hand D.

considerations whatsoever. He treated the 'three pages' exactly as he might have treated some quite colourless document: one that a hundred thousand Elizabethan Englishmen might have written. On purely palaeographical grounds, he claimed it as a holograph MS. of Shakespeare. But we are entitled to remember that, in fact, it is a dramatic fragment. There were only a few dozen people then writing for the stage, and the number of these can be much reduced by subtracting those whose handwritings are known, and are quite incompatible with that of D. In view of the very limited numbers among whom the choice must rest, the large numbers of exceptional features common to D's hand and Shakespeare's establish, if not a certainty, still a probability of identity. It has been objected that these peculiarities, common to Shakespeare and to D, might be tricks of writing taught in a certain school or town. And certainly if we were trying to identify, with Shakespeare's hand, a scrap of writing which might be the work of any Elizabethan who could write, this caution would be necessary. But we are dealing only with people writing for the stage about 1590 to 1600. And, if we can say 'This dramatic fragment was written by someone taught to write in the same school or town as Shakespeare', we shall in effect, have said 'by Shakespeare', unless we are prepared to invent the hypothesis of an Elizabethan dramatist, other than Shakespeare, educated at Stratford on Avon, but leaving no trace of his connection with that town, except his tell-tale handwriting.

Of course there are also differences between the two hands; and there are features which occur in one of them, but not in the other. But in the nature of the case this must be so. For D made his addition to *Sir Thomas More* ten, fifteen, or twenty years before the date when Shakespeare made the signatures, and we cannot suppose that such scanty evidence as the signatures provide gives us complete information, even of what the writer's hand was like at the date of writing. Shakespeare's signatures vary very much from each other. Indeed, as Dr. Greg has emphasized, if we had not documentary evidence to show these signatures to be those of one man, we should (judging by the mere formation of the letters) find less reason to suppose them to be written by the same hand than there is, granting them to be written by one hand, to suppose that the hand of the signatures also wrote the three pages. And the evidence compels us to grant that the six signatures are all six indisputably Shakespeare's. This is curiously parallel to the literary problem. On the one hand, Shakespeare's respect for authority, his hatred of mob rule, and on the other his belief in the real goodness of heart of humble folk, have led critics to the most diverse judgments upon his political views, according as they emphasized the one side or the other. In the 'three pages' we can see these two views combined in a way which no one can deny. Now in just the same way, a study of the handwriting of the 'three pages' helps us to see how the writer of the 'Record Office' signature could have been the writer of the 'British Museum' signature. The two signatures, regarded in isolation, look remarkably different, though we *know* that they are both Shakespeare's. The hand of D is compatible with them both.

It is difficult to see how the most cautious can dispute the verdict of Dr. Greg that, on the purely palaeographical evidence, the balance of probability inclines in favour of the identification of the hand of Shakespeare's signatures with that of D.

Now throw into the scales the evidence of the spelling. And here again the fact needs to be emphasized — a fact which people are amazingly slow to see — that it is a question of *combinations*. Professor Dover Wilson has had to reiterate that the argument 'depends rather upon the agreement of a large number of forms than upon the rarity of any one of them'. [1]

Nevertheless, some very rare spellings are common to D and to Shakespeare. In the 1600 Quarto of *Henry IV, Part II* (First issue), the name of Mr. Justice Silence is spelt *Scilens* some eighteen times. Yet it is an extraordinarily rare spelling. The spelling *silens*, although not common, is occasionally found; for example it occurs in Addition II to *Sir Thomas More*.[2] The spelling *scilence* is also found. A young Danish scholar, Miss Grethe Hjort, drew attention to an example,[3] and further examples have also been brought to the notice of Professor

[1] *London Mercury*, XI, 187.   [2] Ed. Greg, p. 69, l. 10.
[3] *London Mercury*, XI, 80. Miss Hjort is now a naturalized Englishwoman, and, as Greta Hort, is known for her excellent work on *Piers Plowman*. See p. 124 above.

Dover Wilson.[1] Which shows that people are on the look-out. But no one has reported a *scilens*. Professor Sisson tells me that he has kept a constant look-out, so far without effect; and so have many other people. Especially has this been the case since Sir John Squire gave notoriety to the argument by his story of the poor man who made millions by noticing a scrap of paper on which was written *The rest is scilens*. And it is not only workers at MSS., but any readers of early printed books, accurately reprinted, who may be in the quest for *scilens*.

Scilence, then, and *silens* are both exceptional spellings, but have been found. But the combination of them both, *scilens*, is so far only found in the Quarto of *Henry IV, Part II* and in the 'three pages'. Now, when we find a spelling so extraordinarily rare occurring eighteen times in one play as the name of a character, it seems only reasonable to attribute that spelling to the author. For the spelling of the name of a character would be less likely to be altered than ordinary words. This I think is clear from the survival of fluctuation in the spelling of names: *White, Whyte*. And a compositor is extraordinarily unlikely to have used repeatedly so exceptional a spelling, unless he found it in his copy. This is not mere theory. Dr. Greg, after a comparison of Harington's fragmentary MS. of his translation of *Orlando Furioso* with the book printed from it,[2] allows that it confirms the belief 'that a number of Shakespeare's actual spellings are preserved in the printed editions of his plays, and consequently that unusual spellings there found may legitimately be used to support his authorship of other writing in which they occur'. Printers, of course, *did* normalize: they favoured certain usual spellings, and for this reason the argument is all the stronger that certain unusual spellings in the Quartos are due to Shakespeare's practice.

Of all these unusual spellings *scilens* is the most striking. Those who believe it to be by mere coincidence that it also is found in D's 'three pages', and, so far, *nowhere else*, must possess

---

[1] One in the MS. of *The Second Maiden's Tragedy* (see *London Mercury*, XI, 187). Professor Dover Wilson writes to me that Mr. Dugdale Sykes has pointed out to him two *scilences*, in *Richard II or Thomas of Woodstock*, Malone Society Reprint, l. 1460, and in *The Two Merry Milk Maids*, 1620, p. 3 verso.

[2] *An Elizabethan Printer and his Copy*, by W. W. Greg, in *The Library*, Fourth Series, IV, 1924, pp. 102-18.

a more robust faith than I. And it is merely the most spectacular of a very large number of parallels pointed out by Professor Dover Wilson between the exceptional spellings of the Quartos and of the 'three pages'.

But if, on the score of handwriting taken by itself, there is a balance, on the whole, in favour of identification, then the occurrence of these peculiarities of spelling must surely incline the balance of handwriting *plus* spelling *heavily* in favour of identification.

What then must be our judgment regarding the parallels between the thought of D and of Shakespeare, in view of the conclusion (which I think we cannot evade) that, on the score of handwriting *plus* spelling alone, the balance inclines heavily in favour of D being Shakespeare?

Perhaps the real basis of the objection to the Shakespearean authorship lies in a rooted feeling that the discovery, at this time of day, of three pages in Shakespeare's autograph, is too good to be true. Many people feel, very rightly, that they must not allow themselves to be fooled by their hopes, and instinctively take sides against the bias of their inclinations.

Most young students probably make their first acquaintance with the problem in the pages of the *Cambridge History of English Literature*.[1] There they are told that the three pages cannot be by Shakespeare, because Shakespeare

> was far from being a believer in the divinity of kings. He treats the theory with mordant irony in *Richard II*, placing it on the lips of the hapless king, and proving its insufficiency by the remorseless logic of subsequent events.

But this is to put ourselves at the mercy of a phrase. What do we mean by 'the divinity of kings'?. The theory which Shakespeare 'places on the lips of the hapless king' is the theory that miracles will happen, that stones will prove armed soldiers, and angels will intervene, before Heaven will allow England's native king to fall. The Bishop of Carlisle at once reproves the king for thus neglecting 'the means that Heaven yields'; and the 'logic of subsequent events' justifies him. But when

[1] v, 248-9.

Bolingbroke seizes the throne, the same Bishop of Carlisle intervenes, and foretells the woe which will follow such rebellion against the legitimate king; and again the logic of subsequent events justifies the Bishop. We are dealing with drama, and the speeches of More and of the Bishop of Carlisle need not represent exactly the views of the dramatist, though their passionate fervour rather suggests that they do. But, anyway, the speeches, so far from being incompatible, are identical in standpoint, and, as we have seen, are often remarkably similar in phrase.

To this similarity of phrase between D and Shakespeare let us return.

Professor Schücking is the most determined of all the opponents of the Shakespearean authorship. Yet he feels that some of the literary parallels are too close to be attributed to accident. It is indeed to him that the credit belongs of having noted, before any of us, the close parallels between D's 'three pages' and *Julius Caesar*. He attributed this to D having imitated *Julius Caesar*. And that theory was plausible, until it was discovered that there were so many other parallels between D and Shakespeare, to which such an explanation is quite inapplicable on account of their date.

In the earlier parallels Schücking sees signs of D imitating Shakespeare; in the later parallels, especially those from *Coriolanus*, he sees only accident. But in *Coriolanus* these parallels are numerous.

The mere fact that the phrase 'would prey on one another' comes in D's 'three pages' and also in *Coriolanus* proves nothing. What matters is that, in each case, it occupies the same position as the conclusion to the same train of thought. Schücking suggests that both Shakespeare and the writer of the 'three pages' *may* be basing their thought upon some current association of ideas now lost, some commonplace which

> may have existed in the thinking of many contemporaries in those unruly times, and been usually couched in the same words, although by chance other examples of it are now wanting.[1]

[1] *Review of English Studies*, I, 42.

In any single case this is remotely conceivable. What is not reasonable is the number of these remotely conceivable hypotheses which we are implored to make, rather than draw the obvious conclusion that Shakespeare wrote the 'three pages'.

As a proof that the parallels are due, not to Shakespeare's authorship but to another man not quite perfectly imitating Shakespeare, Schücking quotes from the 'three pages' sixteen words and phrases which do not occur in Shakespeare. Now as to phrases we cannot argue, because we have no statistics of the number of unparalleled phrases which might reasonably be expected in any passage of Shakespeare. It would certainly be great: it is obvious that every page of Shakespeare must contain phrases not found elsewhere in Shakespeare. Schücking tells us that 'it were no error, if' occurs in the 'three pages', but does not occur in Shakespeare's works. Why should it? Putting aside phrases, eight *words* are left which occur in the 'three pages', but do not occur in Shakespeare. As to words, we are, thanks to Schmidt's *Lexicon*, in a position to get reliable statistics. Professor Sisson was good enough to make a rapid calculation for me of the number of words not occurring elsewhere in Shakespeare that we might expect to find *in any passage of his works*. He spent much of a week-end and gave the following figures. There are approximately 110,000 lines in Shakespeare, and in Schmidt's *Lexicon* are from 5000 to 6000 words only occurring once: such words occur, then, on an average, once in every 20 lines, and in the 147 lines of the 'three pages' we should consequently expect to find seven or eight. There was no collusion. Professor Sisson, when he made this calculation, did not know that eight was the number of words occurring in the 'three pages' but not occurring in Shakespeare, in virtue of which Schücking disputes the Shakespearean authorship.[1]

[1] Exact figures cannot be reached without agreement on many principles; for example, how far we should count proper names, or words involving them, and what to do with compounds. Among the eight 'words' which I counted in Schücking's list are 'Harry groat', 'Troy weight'; perhaps these should not have been counted as 'words'. The proportion of *hapax legomena* in different passages of Shakespeare varies greatly. I took down *Hamlet*, opened it at the long speech of the Ghost, and found a dozen words, not used elsewhere by Shakespeare, in fifty lines.

Dr. Tannenbaum admits that my parallels between Shake-speare and 'the 147 lines' are 'illuminating'. But he says these arguments are 'completely counterbalanced by Professor L. L. Schücking's keenly analytical Essay'. Now it is essential to Tannenbaum's views that the 'three pages' must have been written *before* 12 May, 1593. And it is essential to Schücking's case that they must have been written after *Julius Caesar*. For Schücking agrees that the likenesses to *Julius Caesar* go beyond mere accident, and therefore it is vital to his argument that they must be due to D copying Shakespeare. A chronology which would make a borrowing from *Julius Caesar* possible before May 1593 is incompatible with everything we know about the date of that play.

This is a very good example of the mutual antagonism of the objections raised against the Shakespearean authorship of the 'three pages'. To a quite remarkable extent, they cancel out. Yet tribute ought to be paid to the acumen of both Schücking and Tannenbaum. The first discovery of a quite undeniable link between the 'three pages' and Shakespeare was made by Schücking; and Dr. Tannenbaum, though he does not accept the identification of the Shakespeare signatures and D's hand, has nevertheless called attention to likenesses between them which had escaped even the acute scrutiny of Sir Edward Maunde Thompson. Others will rate these discoveries of Dr. Tannenbaum more highly than he does himself. And his services in other ways, such as the identification of Hand A in *Sir Thomas More* with that of Chettle, are very noteworthy.

It seems to me that this feeling of 'too good to be true' has resulted in a bias (an honourable bias, but a bias neverthe-less) against the belief that D is Shakespeare. Otherwise, one would think, people must have seen that the resemblances of thought and wording are not of the kind which can fairly be accounted for by borrowing. In *Richard II* the king is called 'the figure of God's majesty'. A borrower might well have transferred this phrase to More's speech. Instead we find a new phrase:

> And to add ampler majesty to this
> God hath not only lent the king his figure . . .

This is not like the work of a plagiarist. It is the same thought transfused by the poet's imagination. If we take the resemblances enumerated above we do, indeed, find many exact verbal echoes. But they are swamped in a much larger parallelism of thought. The resemblances are like those which we find between one of Shakespeare's plays and another.

This rhythm of thought produces, time after time, in the 'three pages' and in Shakespeare, sequences running to four, five, six, or seven elements. The fact that the phrases 'a god on earth' and 'march upon my knees' occur in different plays of Heywood, isolated, and in no sequence, does not render less remarkable the fact that, alike in *Richard II* and the 'three pages' from the idea of seditious violence springs that of water overflowing its *shores* (*banks*), of the sufferings of the *children* (*babes*), of people on their *knees* pleading forgiveness for sin against a *majesty* which bears the *figure* of *God*, and is indeed a *god on earth*.

More's speech, denouncing rebellion against the majesty to which God has lent his figure, forms part of a play in which More dies rather than obey that majesty against his conscience: the most passionate glorification of Tudor monarchy in all Elizabethan drama is the prelude to scenes celebrating the unbending mind which resisted Tudor despotism to the death. It was a London crowded with refugees, and full of anti-alien prejudice, which produced this noble plea for toleration and 'the majesty of Law': 'Imagine that you see the wretched strangers plodding to the ports and coasts for transportation . . . What had you got? . . . By this pattern . . . men like ravenous fishes would feed on one another.'

I would suggest one final test. Let anyone, remembering where we stand to-day, in this year 1939, read again carefully ll. 119-40 (pp. 234-5, above), and then ask himself:

Are not these the authentic words of him whom Carlyle called the 'loving, just and equal brother of all'?[1]

---

[1] After writing this, I received from Professor Dover Wilson a letter containing his comment on these lines. It is so relevant that, by his permission, I have printed it in a Note at the end of this book (p. 407).

VIII

THE ELIZABETHAN AND THE JACOBEAN SHAKESPEARE[1]

UNDER Elizabeth Shakespeare wrote his merriest comedies: under James his greatest tragedies. It has therefore been widely assumed that under Elizabeth Shakespeare was happy, under James unhappy. A further assumption extends, to England as a whole, these assumed moods of Shakespeare.

Both assumptions are precarious. Miss Sybil Thorndike once told an assembly of medical psychologists that, during the two years when she was acting exceptionally gruesome plays, she enjoyed exceptionally peaceful sleep. 'I got it off my chest,' she said. John Dryden also knew much about drama, and he regarded Comedy and Tragedy, not as the expression of national temper, but as a reaction against it. Comedy, he said, is pleasing to the 'sullen' English, who come to the theatre to be diverted; Tragedy to the 'gay' French, who come to make themselves more serious.[2]

But no doubts of this kind troubled my mind when I learned, as a boy, out of Stopford Brooke's excellent *Literature Primer*, all about the feelings with which Shakespeare, in 1601, passed from his happy Second Elizabethan Period, that of Comedy, to the 'stern time' of his Third, or Tragic, or Jacobean Period. 'Suddenly all his life seems to have grown dark ... Essex perished on the scaffold ... He may himself, as some have

---

[1] This lecture and the following are expanded from, 'The Jacobean Shakespeare and *Measure for Measure*', read as the Annual Shakespeare Lecture of the British Academy on 21 April, 1937. I am much indebted to three friends, J. E. Neale, C. J. Sisson, and Norman Baynes, who have read the proof of this lecture, as enlarged for publication; though, of course, I take sole responsibility for all it contains. I am particularly indebted, as all students of Shakespeare should be, to *The Mythical Sorrows of Shakespeare* (Prof. Sisson's Shakespeare Lecture of the Academy for 1934). But I have derived even greater advantages from personal conversations with Sisson, spread over a period of many years' friendship.

[2] *Essay of Dramatic Poesy*, in Ker's *Essays of John Dryden*, i, 72. Neander (Dryden) is speaking.

thought, have been concerned[1] in the rising of Essex . . . Added
to this we may conjecture . . . that he had unwisely loved . . .'
[In or after 1601, at the age of thirty-seven, mark; not before.]
. . . 'Disgust . . . Darkness of spirit . . . "The time was out of
joint" . . .' and continued to be so till 1608-9, when Shakespeare
left London, was reconciled to his wife, and began his Fourth
Period and his plays of forgiveness.

Stopford Brooke was not the first to think of this Essex story.
It dates back to the eighteenth century, when Edward Capell
based, upon the assertion that Shakespeare had a 'considerable
share in the confidence of the earls of Essex and Southampton',
the inference that 'it can hardly be supposed that he could be
a mute spectator of controversies in which they were so much
interested'.[2] But it is Stopford Brooke who, at first, second, or
third hand, has for sixty years presented the story in convenient summary to the schoolboys and schoolgirls of England.
And let no pessimist assert that our educational system has
been without results. Howbeit, there *is* no evidence that
Shakespeare was ever in the confidence of Essex, still less
therefore that he conspired with him. There *is* no evidence
that Shakespeare quarrelled with his wife, still less therefore
that he was reconciled to her. If critics say that to quarrel with
your wife is common form, I reply that it is not common form
to wait to be reconciled till, at the age of forty-five, you write
your dramas of reconciliation.

Nevertheless, the view has now become traditional among
Shakespeare scholars in England, that Shakespeare entered
upon his Jacobean period disillusioned, that with the fall of
Essex both he and England had suffered a 'spiritual fall'.
This view has of late been restated by Professor Dover Wilson,
with his habitual eloquence and charm. To Dover Wilson,
Shakespeare's eleven years between the defeat of the Armada
and the fall of Essex are 'halcyon days of happy ease, illimitable
hope and untarnished honour'. Then, with the execution of
Essex, 'England awoke with a start to the grim realities of life'.[3]

[1] In or before 1896, Stopford Brooke altered 'concerned' to 'slightly involved .
But the mischief was done.
[2] *Introduction* to Shakespeare, 1768, etc.
[3] *The Essential Shakespeare*, p. 36.

That the fall of Essex shook Englishmen with grief and amazement is undeniable: but we must not speak as if Englishmen, in the eleven years between the Armada and the fall of Essex, had known nothing of grim reality. From 1588 to 1599 persons noteworthy in politics, warfare, poetry, and drama had been dying, and those had been lucky who achieved, like Burleigh, a happy, or, like Sir Richard Grenville, a heroic end. The 'unique quality of happiness' which Professor Wilson and so many others see in these eleven post-Armada years is not exemplified by the deaths of Hawkins or of Drake, of Greene or of Peele, of Kyd or of Marlowe, of Spenser, thought to have died 'for grief, in great want',[1] or of Southwell, 'ten times tortured so extremely that the least of them was worse than ten executions'.[2]

And William Shakespeare also had had his share of trouble. Coming of a bourgeois family, with hopes of achieving gentility, he had restored the family fortunes, and was just about to realize his ambition when, in 1596, he suffered the cruellest blow which I can imagine falling upon any man. His only son died.

It may be that, in *King John*, the reply of Constance to the empty words of comfort uttered by the celibate Cardinal,

He talks to me that never had a son,[3]

reflect the bitterness which Shakespeare felt at some wellmeant, clumsy condolence; it may be that her lament over the 'vacant garments' of Arthur was suggested by the vacant garments of Hamnet Shakespeare. Yet these words may have been written when Shakespeare's son was still alive and well. What we do know is, that in the three or four years following his loss, Shakespeare wrote his happiest work: he created Falstaff, Prince Hal, King Henry V, Beatrice and Benedick, Rosalind and Orlando. Then came Viola, Sir Toby Belch and Lady Belch. From which we may argue (if we will) that Shakespeare was no reed shaken by the wind, no victim of disillusionment,

---

[1] FULLER, *Worthies of England.*
[2] JANELLE, *Robert Southwell*, p. 80.
[3] III. iv. 91.

likely to be thrown by personal misfortune into 'a dominant
mood of gloom and dejection', but a man of the type of Walter
Scott — Walter Scott who 'out of the very pit of financial
disaster, stood up undismayed to fight his last battle'.[1]

And for England, as for Shakespeare, these later Elizabethan
days had been glorious, but yet no 'halcyon days of happy
ease'. It was at no cheap price that in 1588 and the following
years (just as in 1914 and the following years) the freedom of
England was preserved. 'For every battle of the warrior is
with confused noise, and garments rolled in blood.' The State
Papers for the months following the defeat of the Armada
afford much dreary reading. The sailors who had saved
England were perishing from malnutrition. Over and over
again we read, 'It would grieve any man's heart to see them that
have served so valiantly to die so miserably', or 'It is a most
pitiful sight to see the men die in the streets of Margate', or
other like words. There is bitter recrimination among the
leaders, who are too exhausted, too near to their own stupendous
victory, to see, as we do, its epoch-making finality. Then,
year after year, the war dragged on. The dramatists are
reflecting Elizabethan conditions when they show peaceful
workmen[2] unwilling to be pressed for military service — from
which, if they return at all, it is likely to be as cripples and
beggars. It was not only Falstaff who 'misused the king's
press damnably'. When John Donne meets a captain, he is not
reminded of the glories of service against Spain, but sees him

Bright parcel-gilt, with forty dead men's pay.[3]

The later books of the *Faerie Queene* and the *View of the Present
State of Ireland* do not reflect either 'illimitable hope' or 'a
unique quality of happiness'. The hard-won victories of
Artegall and Calidore come to naught. Mutability bears sway
over all things: 'which makes me loath this state of life so tickle,
and love of things so vaine to cast away'.

[1] ROBIN FLOWER in *The Times*, Friday, 22 Dec. 1933, p. 11.
[2] e.g. Strumbo in *Locrine*; Ralph in *The Shoemaker's Holiday*; Bullcalf and
Mouldy in 2 *Henry IV*.
[3] Satire I. MS. Harl. 5110 dates this as not later than 1593. Yet Donne's
sermons have been instanced, to show that 'disillusionment' was Jacobean.

And, amid the mingled triumphs and disappointments of foreign war, there was no solution to the peculiar domestic problem of the Tudor Age — the absence of an undoubted heir to the throne. During most of the sixteenth century it remained true, in the phrase of Thomas More, that the ship of state had but one anchor.[1] In 1509 More had prophesied for Henry and Catherine of Aragon a son, a grandson, and a great-grandson. More is a saint, but in this he proved no prophet. At any moment the one anchor might give, and the land be plunged in civil war. This problem of the succession had caused the fall of the noblest in England: of More and Fisher; of Lady Jane Grey and Mary Queen of Scots; of the poet Surrey and his son the fourth Duke of Norfolk; of the families of Stafford and of Pole. If we would understand Shakespeare's feelings at the accession of James, we should remember that the Elizabethan horror of civil war had been the inspiration of his first great work.

Two years ago, by going to the shores of the Pacific, I had the exceptional good luck to see the three parts of *Henry VI* and *Richard III* acted as one series, when all Shakespeare's history plays were produced, 'in their great processional pageant of tragedy' by the Pasadena Community Play House. To see this was to realize that Shakespeare began his career with a tetralogy based on recent history, grim, archaic, crude, yet nevertheless such as, for scope, power, patriotism, and sense of doom, had probably had no parallel since Aeschylus wrote the trilogy of which the *Persians* is the surviving fragment. One idea runs through the whole — the sufferings of England from its self-centred 'Machiavellian' nobles, beginning with Cardinal Beaufort, and culminating in the tremendous Richard Crookback. Those who rejoice in modern catchwords might describe it as 'A study of ego-centric Narcissism'. 'I am myself alone', is the dominant note. Whether or no this tetralogy incorporates the work of earlier dramatists, it is in Shakespeare's Richard that its unity of purpose, the effect of the whole, comes out. Whatever portions may, or may not, have been the work of others, 'Shakespeare has taken them over, and he must be

---

[1] *Epigrammata*, p. 188 of *Lucubrationes*, Basle, 1563.

responsible for them'.[1] Shakespeare followed up this great success by a second tetralogy, *Richard II, 1 Henry IV, 2 Henry IV,* and *Henry V.* This is a much more finished work, but the tragic tension is a good deal relaxed, and markedly so, as I have noted, in those plays which must have been written in the years after the death of Shakespeare's son. Nevertheless, the mass effect of these eight plays, and of *King John,* is one of deep tragedy. 'Life', says Mr. Masefield, 'was never so brooded on since man learned to think, as in this cycle of tragedies.' But there is love there too — love of England. When these historical tragedies were finished, Shakespeare 'had done more than any English writer to make England sacred in the imaginations of her sons'.[2]

Therefore, if we are to understand the spirit of Shakespeare under King James, we must not forget his Elizabethan History Plays. Critics constantly speak as if Shakespeare, before that seventeenth-century gloom which they regard as coming upon him after the fall of Essex, could give us nothing more bitter than *Romeo and Juliet.* During the Elizabethan period he is supposed to be filled with the 'Tudor gaiety of spirit'.[3] Only at the beginning of the seventeenth century does he become 'subject to a dominant mood of gloom and dejection'.[4] Then, we are told, 'the rose-red vision gave place to the grey', and Shakespeare, suffering from 'the ferment of doubt and the bitterness of disillusion',[5] satirizes 'theories about the moral government of the universe which, for the time being at least, he does not share'.[6] To a critic who demands what Heminge and Condell would have thought if, when they asked Shakespeare for a new comedy, he had answered that he could not possibly comply with their wishes, he being then in his tragic period, Professor Walter Raleigh makes reply:

> What they would have thought may admit a wide conjecture; what they got is less doubtful. If they asked for a comedy

---

[1] LASCELLES ABERCROMBIE, *A Plea for the Liberty of Interpreting,* 1930, p. 18. (Annual Shakespeare Lecture of the British Academy.) Abercrombie is speaking of possible passages of Kyd in *Hamlet;* but the argument is the same.
[2] JOHN MASEFIELD, *William Shakespeare,* pp. 116, 123.
[3] A. W. POLLARD and DOVER WILSON, *William Shakespeare,* in GARVIN's *Great Tudors,* p. 593; cf. *The Essential Shakespeare,* p. 18.
[4] *The Essential Shakespeare,* p. 115.
[5] E. K. CHAMBERS, *Shakespeare: a Survey,* p. 210.   [6] The same, p. 216.

when he was writing his great tragedies, they got *Measure for Measure* or *Troilus and Cressida*; if they asked for a tragedy when he was writing his happiest works of wit and lyric fantasy, they got *Romeo and Juliet*.[1]

Raleigh's answer is a telling one, and contains deep truth — but not the whole truth. It neglects the historical tragedies, and other things. It is true that Shakespeare wrote *Romeo and Juliet* in the same 'First Period' in which he produced *A Midsummer-Night's Dream*. But it is also true that the Folio attributes to Shakespeare *King John*, *Richard II*, the three parts of *Henry VI*, *Richard III*, and *Titus Andronicus*, which, whatever we may think of them as works of art, make a grim group of seven plays, belonging to the same 'First Period' as *Romeo and Juliet*.

We all know the formula of Shakespeare's four periods — how first he was 'in the workshop', botching the plays of his predecessors: how then, 'in the world', he produced his great Comedies and mature Histories: how then he spoke 'out of the depths', in his great Tragedies: and then 'on the heights', in his final Romances. Now this classification was useful in the original tentative form in which it was put forward by Edward Dowden sixty years ago. There is a fundamental common sense about it, as there is in much which that great critic wrote. But it is capable of exaggeration, till it becomes a hard and misleading dogma. Shakespeare's early plays have been much too lightheartedly taken from him, and distributed among Greene, Peele, Nash, Lodge, Kyd, and Marlowe, as if they were the creation of a workshop, not of an individual. Even when attributed to him, this early work is not taken seriously enough — as if it did not matter what a prentice did 'in the workshop'. Then come the mature Comedies and Histories. Then a spiritual crisis is imagined, about 1601, to separate the Comedies from the great Jacobean Tragedies, *Othello*, *King Lear*, *Macbeth*, and the rest, and a second crisis, about 1608, to separate the Tragedies from the Romances, *Cymbeline*, *The Winter's Tale*, *The Tempest*.

[1] *Shakespeare*, p. 131.

Mr. Peter Alexander has done much to combat this exaggeration by showing how very unsatisfactory are the grounds upon which the three parts of *Henry VI* have been often rejected from the canon of Shakespeare's works. But people have been slow to realize what must be the repercussions of Mr. Alexander's arguments upon the current view of Shakespeare's mood in his Jacobean days. In that current view, as we have seen, we are asked to contrast the 'self-laceration, weariness, discord, cynicism, and disgust' of Shakespeare when, in or after 1603, he is writing his great tragedies, with the juvenile gaiety of the Elizabethan Shakespeare. But there is much besides gaiety in the Elizabethan Shakespeare. If we put aside Aaron the Moor and the many other villainous characters in *Titus Andronicus*, we are left with the fact that, in the great tetralogy of *Henry VI* and *Richard III*, very few of the leading characters are other than evil. It is the tragedy of the two Dukes of Gloucester. Humphrey, the good duke, fulfils his duty as Protector to his young nephew, and is done to death, almost without a struggle, by the ferocious lords who surround him — the Cardinal, Suffolk, York. Richard, the bad duke, betrays the young nephews to whom he is Protector, and perishes also. Cardinal Beaufort, Suffolk, the 'she-wolf of France', are, like Richard Crookback, altogether evil, and the world to which they belong seems evil also: at least as evil as the world of Shakespeare's Jacobean tragedies, where Iago, Regan, Goneril, Edmund, seem rather to stand out as unnatural exceptions.

The ties between these Elizabethan historical tragedies, and Shakespeare's Jacobean masterpieces, are many. The dying Cardinal Beaufort has visions of his victim which anticipate the self-betrayal of Lady Macbeth:

> Died he not in his bed? Where should he die?
> Can I make men live, whether they will or no?
> O, torture me no more! I will confess . . .
> He hath no eyes, the dust hath blinded them.
> Comb down his hair; look, look! it stands upright,
> Like lime-twigs set to catch my winged soul.[1]

[1] *2 Henry VI*, III. iii. 9.

Richard III is very different from Macbeth; yet they echo each other:

> I am in
> So far in blood that sin will pluck on sin . . .[1]

> I am in blood
> Stepp'd in so far that, should I wade no more,
> Returning were as tedious as go o'er . . .[2]

> I shall despair. There is no creature loves me;
> And if I die, no soul will pity me:
> Nay, wherefore should they, since that I myself
> Find in myself no pity to myself? . . .[3]

> I have lived long enough: my way of life
> Is fall'n into the sear, the yellow leaf,
> And that which should accompany old age,
> As honour, love, obedience, troops of friends,
> I must not look to have . . .[4]

Most terrible, in this first historical tetralogy of *1, 2, 3 Henry VI* and *Richard III*, is the ineffectiveness of the good characters, till the time when Henry of Richmond steps in, almost like a divine avenger, to bring the ghastly series of murders to a close. Henry VI is a saint: he dies with a prayer for his murderer,

> O, God forgive my sins, and pardon thee.

Yet his feeble saintliness is as much responsible for the horrors of these plays as is the villainy of the villains — and Henry has to suffer the martyrdom of knowing that it is so. The man who depicted Henry VI had not yet risen to the height of his power; but he had assuredly been already 'in the depths'. Father Martindale says that 'the greatest mystery of all is not Evil as such: it is the terrible inadequacy of the Good'.[5] And Shakespeare seems to see things so, in his earliest historical tragedies. And, however that may be, Shakespeare's sense of the evil of the world is continuous — from Richard Crookback

---

[1] *Richard III*, IV. ii. 64.   [2] *Macbeth*, III. iv. 136.
[3] *Richard III*, v. iii. 200, etc.   [4] *Macbeth*, v. iii. 22, etc.
[5] *The Terminal*, No. 7, 1937.

and King John, through Iago, to Antonio and Sebastian in *The Tempest*.

As he grows older his experience deepens, he is aware of evil in a more poignant fashion, there is less rhetoric, keener feeling. But this applies to good as well as to evil. It is mis-leading to emphasize the deepening apprehension of evil, if we forget that together with the evil, the Jacobean Shakespeare comes to depict a courage, patience, faith, and love, which the evil cannot touch.[1] When Lear enters, with the body of Cordelia in his arms, we are reminded of his own words, that upon such sacrifices the gods themselves throw incense. It is the same with the last words of Desdemona. The victory of love over a horror worse than death has never been so depicted as in her attempt to shield the husband who, she knows not why, has murdered her:

EMILIA   O, who hath done this deed?
DESDEMONA Nobody; I myself. Farewell:
            Commend me to my kind lord: O, farewell!

Othello, 'most painful of all tragedies', leaves us pondering (said A. C. Bradley) on '*love, and man's unconquerable mind*'. We think of the song of the ancient poet: 'Many waters cannot quench love, neither can the floods drown it: if a man would give all the substance of his house for love, it would utterly be contemned.' Or, in the words of the fourteenth-century mystic,

    Love is stalwart as the Death, Love is hard as Hell.

But we feel nothing of this when the Crookback, giving a scornful glance at, or a scornful touch to, the grey beard of the lovable, loving, feeble, foolish king whom he has murdered, meditates on

    this word 'love' which greybeards call divine.

Shakespeare had written that Love 'bears it out even to the edge of doom'. But not till his Jacobean days does he show, in the persons of Cordelia and Edgar and Desdemona, a love

---

[1] Compare BRADLEY's *Shakespearean Tragedy*, pp. 84, 147-8, 174, 198, 242, 322-6.

which alters not when it alteration finds, nor bends with the remover to remove. For Juliet had to face no such alteration in Romeo, and the charming picture of the faithfulness of Julia to the faithless Proteus is not pressed to the edge of doom. It was left for the Jacobean Shakespeare about 1604 to depict a love that is never shaken by any tempest which Evil can bring. How then can we say that this Jacobean Shakespeare was 'disillusioned', 'cynical', and 'quite obviously believed in nothing'?

Secondly, Shakespeare's power as an artist grows. We begin with the crude 'Senecan' horrors of his Elizabethan tragedies, with scenes like that of Queen Margaret, giving to the Duke of York, before she stabs him, the napkin which she has stained with the blood of his son, that he may dry his cheeks withal. Uncertain as the chronology of Shakespeare's plays must be, 'the most striking thing about it is the continual advance it shows in the scope and subtlety and elaboration of dramatic art'.[1] Shakespeare's career 'is only intelligible as the career of an artist'.[2] Obviously the career of an artist is the career of a man. As Carlyle said, 'How could a man delineate so many suffering heroic hearts if his own heroic heart had never suffered?' But this does not justify reckless biographical interpretations. To take one example. To Shakespeare, disillusionment always follows regicide, alike with Richard III, with Bolingbroke, with Brutus, with Claudius. But this reaches its height in the words of Macbeth:

> Life's but a walking shadow, a poor player
> That struts and frets his hour upon the stage
> And then is heard no more; it is a tale
> Told by an idiot, full of sound and fury,
> Signifying nothing.

'How strange that this judgment on life, the despair of a man who had knowingly made mortal war on his own soul, should be frequently quoted as Shakespeare's own judgment, and should even be adduced, in serious criticism, as proof of his

---

[1] LASCELLES ABERCROMBIE, *Liberty of Interpreting*, 1930, p. 11.
[2] The same, p. 12.

pessimism.' So Bradley wrote, thirty-four years ago.[1] Yet still to-day, because Shakespeare's power to depict the disillusion-ment of regicide grows, critics say that he himself is growing weary and disillusioned. What is growing, is the power of Shakespeare's art. Beyond that, it is perilous to dogmatize.

And, thirdly, with this growth in the subtlety of Shakespeare's dramatic art, there goes, naturally, an increase of his power to depict his characters changing. The characters of the earliest plays are static: but Lear and Gloster, Desdemona and Othello are not the same when they die as they were when we first met them. What Mr. Dover Wilson says of Lear is true of them all: 'Never is Lear greater, . . . more his real self, than in the final moment.'[2] And this development is the most significant of all.

Those who talk about the Jacobean Shakespeare, in a mood of gloom and dejection, satirizing theories about the moral government of the Universe, could by similar methods find such a Shakespeare among the horrors of the Elizabethan historical tragedies — *Henry VI*, *Richard III*, *Richard II*, *King John*. Yet from pessimism the History Plays are saved by their faith in England, their sympathy for the sufferings of

This land of such dear souls, this dear, dear land.

Over and over again it has been said, that the hero of the History Plays is England. We hear of the passion roused by the death of Talbot on the stage. But there is more in the Fourth Act of *1 Henry VI* than the heroism of the Talbots, father and son. The meaning lies in their betrayal by the mutual jealousies of the two commanders, York and Somerset. This comes out with striking effect when the play is acted. The stage direction says, 'Enter York with Trumpet, and many Soldiers'. The 'many soldiers' must have taxed the resources of Shakespeare's theatre. And York is the greatest of all English warriors, save only Talbot. Nevertheless York will not go to the help of Talbot, because Somerset has not sent him aid. In vain does

---

[1] *Shakespearean Tragedy*, 1904, 1905, p. 359.
[2] *The Essential Shakespeare*, p. 126.

Sir William Lucy pray for help, going from one of the rival commanders to the other:

> LUCY O, send some succour to the distressed lord!
> YORK He dies, we lose; I break my warlike word;
> We mourn, France smiles; we lose, they daily get;
> All 'long of this vile traitor Somerset.
> LUCY Then God take mercy on brave Talbot's soul.

Somerset is to blame. But York would rather have a defeat for which he can blame Somerset, than step in to remedy Somerset's deficiencies. So he marches away, with his many soldiers, abandoning Talbot to his fate, and leaving Lucy alone to comment

> Thus, while the vulture of sedition
> Feeds in the bosom of such great commanders,
> Sleeping neglection doth betray to loss
> The conquest of our scarce cold conqueror,
> That ever living man of memory,
> Henry the Fifth.

The succession of Talbot scenes is a deadly indictment of defeatism. Such scenes might well draw 'the tears of ten thousand spectators at least, at several times'.

In Shakespeare's great scheme, as finally set out, England's disasters begin when, in spite of the warning of the wise and good Bishop of Carlisle, Richard II is deposed:

> O, if you raise this house against this house,
> It will the woefullest division prove
> That ever fell upon this cursed earth.
> Prevent it, resist it, let it not be so,
> Lest child, child's children, cry against you 'woe!'

'Disorder, horror, fear and mutiny' reign, and England becomes 'the field of Golgotha, and Dead Men's skulls'. As the son enters, dragging in the body of the father he has slain, and the father carrying the son he has killed, every country-born London prentice must have felt, 'There, but for the grace of God, go I.'

From London by the king was I press'd forth;
My father, being the Earl of Warwick's man,
Came on the part of York, press'd by his master;

At last the series of eight plays ends with Richmond's mighty speech, promising to unite the White Rose and the Red:

Smile Heaven upon this fair conjunction
That long have frown'd upon their enmity!
What traitor hears me, and says not 'Amen'?
England hath long been mad, and scarr'd herself;
The brother blindly shed the brother's blood,
The father rashly slaughter'd his own son
The son, compell'd, been butcher to the sire:
All this divided York and Lancaster,
Divided in their dire division,
O, now, let Richmond and Elizabeth,
The true succeeders of each royal house,
By God's fair ordinance conjoin together!
And let their heirs (God, if thy will be so)
Enrich the time to come with smooth-fac'd peace
With smiling plenty and fair prosperous days!
Abate the edge of traitors, gracious Lord,
That would reduce these bloody days again,
And make poor England weep in streams of blood!
Let them not live to taste this land's increase
That would with treason wound this fair land's peace!
Now civil wounds are stopp'd, peace lives again;
That she may long live here, God say Amen!

The spectators in an Elizabethan theatre almost surrounded the stage; they were brought into the very play, and a deep 'Amen' must have risen from them all.

Is it conceivable that the man who wrote this was all the time hoping that the descendants of 'the true succeeders of each royal house' would be disinherited in favour of Essex, who was not of 'this house' at all, who had no dynastic or other claim whatsoever? Mr. Dover Wilson writes, 'Essex ... was her [Elizabeth's] cousin ... All he had to do was to secure her "voice" before she died, and the crown was his.'[1] Essex *was* Elizabeth's cousin (twice removed); but on the Boleyn, not the Tudor, side. The fact that Henry VIII had married the great-granddaughter of a Lord Mayor of London did not convey a claim to the throne to all descendants of that city magnate.

The dynastic problem which threatened England was that Henry VIII had had two sisters, Margaret and Mary, and that, with previous parliamentary sanction to will the crown, Henry had willed that the younger, Suffolk, branch should succeed rather than the elder, Stuart, branch. The question was, should this be set aside? There were further complications. Could James, not being an Englishman, succeed? Queen Elizabeth could, by her support, have strengthened one or other of the rival claims. But Essex was not in the running. The picture of Shakespeare writing his plays to show Essex how a king should behave, and believing that if Essex 'wisely became friends with the old Queen, the crown would fall into his lap',[2] has no support. Elizabeth was a great queen, incapable of a folly grosser than that of Lear, sharing out to his daughters his kingdom in return for flattery. Also the Lords and Commons of England would have seen to it that the rightful dynasty was not disinherited. And Shakespeare was the last man to believe that

> This royal throne of kings, this scepter'd isle,
> This happy breed of men, this little world,
> This blessed plot, this earth, this realm, this England,
> This nurse, this teeming womb of royal kings,

could be bestowed at will

> Like to a tenement or pelting farm[3]

upon a handsome but sulky young favourite, as a reward for wisely becoming friends with the old Queen.

We know that, on the eve of Essex's rebellion, Shakespeare's company was trapped, by some of Essex's followers, into acting

---

[1] *The Essential Shakespeare*, p. 96.
[2] The same, p. 102.   [3] *Richard II*, II. i.

the deposition of Richard II. We know that this insult was deeply and justly resented by Elizabeth. Yet we know that the Queen bore Shakespeare and his company no malice for it, and that they acted before her a fortnight later, on the eve of the execution of Essex. This does not to my mind support the theory that Shakespeare and his company had for years been acting their plays in order 'to hold the mirror up to Essex'; the Government had a good spy service, and would have discovered the plots which modern criticism has hatched, if they had existed in Tudor days. And the reference in *Henry V*, in which Shakespeare says that *if* Essex returned victorious from Ireland, it would nevertheless not entitle him to so warm a welcome as the victor of Agincourt justly received, does not, to me, convey any sinister intention against the line of 'the true succeeders of each royal house', the line which, in the person of James I, would continue to unite the claims which had been divided between York and Lancaster.

In September 1599, Essex, realizing that his Irish expedition was becoming a disastrous failure, most disloyally held a secret conference with his enemy Tyrone. It may possibly be, that at this conference the Irish leader helped to lure Essex to his doom by the treasonable suggestion that Essex might sometime become King of England, helped by Tyrone as Viceroy of Ireland. It may be that 'the tempter's voice reached a mind not unfitted to hear it', for Essex was rapidly ceasing to think, speak, or act like a sane man. But that Shakespeare had for years been dangling the prospect of the crown before the eyes of an Essex not yet either ruined or mad, is a fantasy of modern scholarship for which, thank God, there is no shadow of foundation.

It all depends upon the assumption that at the beginning of the seventeenth century Shakespeare was suffering sorrow and disillusionment, and that it is the business of the critic to find some cause for this alleged disillusionment. And we may agree that if, for years before the tragic outbreak of Essex in February 1601, Shakespeare had been encouraging him to hope for the crown, then Shakespeare would have had cause enough for remorse. But what ground have we for the fundamental assumption that Shakespeare was in a mood of dejection between 1601 and 1608, and more particularly about the year 1603?

The evidence given is that he was then devoting himself to tragedy. About 1603, we are told, we have the creation of Iago, who, 'if we put aside Richard Crookback as a crude juvenile effort', is 'Shakespeare's earliest creation of a character wholly evil', whilst 'at the same time Iago's victim is blameless'.[1]

But why, in attempting to distinguish the mood of the juvenile, as contrasted with that of the mature Shakespeare, should we 'put aside' whatever in the juvenile Shakespeare does not harmonize with our picture, on the ground that it is 'crude and juvenile'? Crude or not, the picture of Richard is enormously powerful, particularly if *Richard III* is acted in rapid succession upon *1, 2, 3 Henry VI*. Whether we adhere to the older view, that Shakespeare, in *Henry VI*, was working over the plays of other men, or accept the recent arguments in favour of a completely Shakespearean authorship, we cannot ignore Cardinal Beaufort, the Duke of Suffolk, Margaret of Anjou — all of them wholly evil — and their innocent victim, Duke Humphrey. Nor can we ignore King John and the innocent Arthur: nor Aaron the Moor. Shakespeare served his apprenticeship to tragedy amid an atmosphere of 'Senecan' horrors, and of 'Machiavellian' villainies[2] bringing innocents to destruction. That is the normal type of his early tragedy. *Romeo and Juliet*, with its 'star-cross'd' lovers and no villain, is the exception. These facts will bear repetition.

But, it will be replied, Othello and Desdemona arouse our sympathy, and Iago our horror, to an extent without precedent in Shakespeare's Elizabethan tragedies. True — but that only shows how Shakespeare's power as a dramatist has grown: how he is now able to do supremely what he and some of his fellow dramatists had all along been striving to do, since he wrote, or (if you prefer it) since he recast and revised *Titus Andronicus*.

[1] *The Essential Shakespeare*, p. 120.
[2] *See* MARIO PRAZ, *Machiavelli and the Elizabethans* (Annual Italian Lecture of the British Academy, 1928).

In *Hamlet, Othello, Lear, Macbeth*, we have a series of works of art — the greatest which England has ever produced. Are we to say that we owe them to a dominant mood in their author of gloom and dejection; of self-laceration, weariness, discord, cynicism, and disgust?

Great art is produced by a great people in its great age. On what grounds are we to believe that 'the accession of James I ushered in a period of cynicism and gloom, self-indulgence and crime', or that 'a shadow lay across the land, the shadow of the tomb, and the air seemed thick with the breath of corruption'?[1]

We cannot account for Shakespearean tragedy in terms of the 'Elizabethan catastrophe' of Essex, and the Jacobean 'spiritual fall'. There would have been an Elizabethan catastrophe, if Essex had been able to persuade the Londoners to back him in a civil war. Essex may, as Professor Dover Wilson puts it, have fallen like Lucifer from Heaven; but, if so, every Londoner was an Abdiel: and Shakespeare lived in London. The city which refused to arm in support of Essex in February 1601, was in arms on 25 March 1603, in support of its 'master, liege lord, and king', James. It was the triumph of legitimacy and common sense. And in this English triumph Shakespeare shared, or else the History Plays signify nothing. I do not mean that the History Plays are political pamphlets. I do not believe that we can so interpret great drama, any more than I believe that the *Philoctetes* was written by Sophocles as a pro-Alcibiades manifesto. But Shakespeare was what Ben Jonson called him: *Shakespeare nostras*, 'our English Shakespeare'. The History Plays express that horror of civil war which was the creed of good Englishmen. The plays advocate one policy only: that of all right-minded Englishmen — order, 'degree', legitimacy, unity. The plays are the final stage of a national saga which had been in formation for eighty years, since Thomas More began it with his *History of Richard III*. These History Plays are often quite wrong in their facts. Burgundian prejudice led to libels on Joan the Maid; Yorkist calumny and Tudor politics led to the misrepresentation of Suffolk. All this untruth, and much more, finds its echo in

---

[1] *The Essential Shakespeare*, pp. 36, 113, 114.

Henry VI. But where the History Plays are triumphantly and gloriously right, is in the interpretation of the spirit of England, as it had grown up during the sixteenth century. When Shakespeare had lived to see this policy of legitimacy and unity carried to a happy conclusion by the union of the kingdoms under the legitimate heir, his work as a writer of historical plays was done. He turned, in his supreme tragedies, from the problems of the fate of England to those of human fate. If the hero of his Elizabethan tragedies is England, that of his Jacobean tragedies is mankind. Sir Edmund Chambers has remarked, with insight, that in Shakespeare's great Jacobean plays — *Othello, Macbeth, King Lear* — 'the issue has shifted from the relations of man and man to the relations of man and his creator'.[1] But why are we asked to believe that supreme world-tragedy, one of the rarest types of art, is produced by an age of gloom and dejection, and by a mood, in the poet, of weariness and disgust?[2]

On the contrary, the time was ripe for the greatest decade which English literature had seen, or was to see. The establishment of the succession on 25 March 1603, meant the reaping of the full fruits of the victory of 1588, and the beginning of a brief period of peace and stability, in which were accomplished a number of the greatest things in all English history, chief among which we must count the great tragedies of Shakespeare. When James addressed his first parliament in 1604, he thanked England for the welcome given him, and said that he had brought with him two gifts which he trusted that they would receive in place of many words: one was peace with foreign nations, the other was union with Scotland.[3]

One of the captains who routed the Armada had written, in the first brunt of his disappointment after the battle, to Walsingham, 'our parsimony at home hath bereaved us of the famousest victory that ever our nation had at sea'.[4] Whether the nation was to be bereaved of the fruits of this 'famousest

---

[1] *Shakespeare: a Survey*, p. 219. Of course I do not agree when Sir Edmund goes on to describe these plays as 'a definite arraignment of the scheme of things'.
[2] *The Essential Shakespeare*, pp. 115, 117.
[3] GARDINER, *History of England*, 1883, i, 165-6.
[4] *Calendar of State Papers, Domestic*, Elizabeth, ccxiv. 43 (8 Aug. 1588).

victory' had been the question for fourteen years. Civil war and foreign intervention would have ruined all. And now there was peace, 'just and honourable',[1] at home and abroad. The peculiar trouble of the Tudor Age, the uncertainty of the succession, had vanished; the peculiar trouble of the Stuart Age, the constitutional dispute, had still to assume any acute form.

There is abundant evidence that it was in no spirit of cynicism and gloom that the new reign began. Francis Bacon said that England was 'as a man that awaketh out of a fearful dream'.[2] If we turn to the recently published Calendar of the *Hatfield House Manuscripts* (1603-4) what we see is a great nation passing in safety through a serious dynastic crisis by its own steadiness, and its determination to tolerate no civil strife. Englishmen in 1603 were overjoyed to find that they had got safely past the danger which two generations had dreaded. Over and over again in the Hatfield Papers we read words such as, 'The like joy, both in London and all parts of England, was never known'. Sir George Carew writes from Coventry:

> All men are exceedingly satisfied and praise God, who of His goodness hath so miraculously provided for us, contrary to the opinions of the wisest, who for many years past trembled to think of her Majesty's decease, as if instantly upon it the kingdom would have been torn in sunder.

From York, Burghley writes to his brother Cecil:

> The contentment of the people is unspeakable, seeing all things proceed so quietly, whereas they expected in the interim their houses should have been spoiled and sacked.[3]

Such quotations could be multiplied. Foreign nations were equally surprised. Especially noteworthy is the report of the French ambassador to his great king, Henri IV, admiring the steadiness of Englishmen at the crisis.[4] The report, so far as I know, has never been printed or translated. It deserves to be.

---

[1] GARDINER, op. cit., i, 214.
[2] *Works*, ed. SPEDDING, vi, 1858, pp. 276-7.
[3] *See* vol. xv, ed. M. S. GIUSEPPI, *passim*, especially pp. 8, 11, 25-6.
[4] *Brit. Mus. Add. MSS.* 30639.

It records the satisfaction of the English at having again a king, after having been so long governed by women. For, amazing as it may seem to us, who habitually contrast Gloriana in her prime with James in his decline, the change from the Elizabeth of 1603 to the James of 1603 seemed, at first, a change for the better. Lord Burghley wrote to his brother Cecil that James 'won the hearts of all men with familiarity and gracious courtesy'.[1] 'Instead of a lady whom time had surprised, we have now an active king', said Sir Walter Ralegh. And he used these words at a time when it was vital to convince his auditors that he was speaking with sincerity.[2]

Yet we are asked to imagine Shakespeare still moping over the fall of Essex, because Shakespeare was the friend of Southampton, who had been the fellow-conspirator of Essex. But, by Elizabeth's noble clemency, a clemency which it would be difficult to parallel in previous English history, Southampton had escaped with his life, and now James had released him and restored his honours. His friends were wild with delight. John Davies of Hereford wrote:

Now wisest men with mirth do seem stark mad,
And cannot choose — their hearts are all so glad.
Then let's be merry in our God and King,
That made us merry, being ill bestad.
Southampton, up thy cap to Heaven fling . . .
For he is come that grace to all doth bring.

Samuel Daniel addressed Southampton:

The world had never taken so full note
    Of what thou art, hadst thou not been undone:
And only thy affliction hath begot
    More fame than thy best fortunes could have won; . . .
Only the best-compos'd and worthiest hearts
God sets to act the hard'st and constant'st parts.

Why should Shakespeare mope?

Because, we are told, James's favourite, Robert Carr, was 'introducing a strain into public life, which reminds us of the

[1] *Hatfield MSS.* xv. 28.   [2] *See* GARDINER, op. cit., i, 129.

poison and debauchery of the decadent Italian renaissance'.[1]

But at the period we are considering, Robert Carr was pressing his fortunes abroad. Shakespeare cannot have known if he was alive or dead. Carr's sinister and deplorable rise to power synchronizes with Shakespeare's change from Tragedy to his 'optimistic' Romances. If Carr had any influence upon Shakespeare's dramas, it can only have been to lift him out of his tragic 'depths' on to his romantic 'heights'. Which is absurd. Q.E.D.

Obviously, many of the hopes raised by James were doomed to disappointment. But, as James lost popularity, Prince Henry won it. People fancied a likeness between him and his great namesake the

> thunderbolt of war,
> Harry the fifth, to whom in face you are
> So like, as fate would have you so in worth,
> Illustrious prince.[2]

There can seldom have been a brother and sister who possessed such power of winning hearts as Prince Henry and his sister, Princess Elizabeth. Their England cannot have been a very depressing place. The revisers of the Bible, in 1611, rejoice that the 'supposed and surmised' disasters did not follow upon the death of 'Queen Elizabeth of most happy memory', and that now the Government is established in King James and his 'hopeful seed'. *We* know that Prince Henry was doomed to a premature death, Princess Elizabeth to a life of disasters gallantly endured, Prince Charles to the scaffold. To us, the happy opening of the reign of James is overcast with a gloom which Shakespeare could not see in 1603. We cannot really enter into the minds of men of a past age, 'unless we can think away everything that has happened since, and call up a mist over the face of time'.[3]

Yet two of the most honoured Shakespeare scholars combine to tell us that, with Shakespeare's *Hamlet*, and Elizabeth's death in 1603,

[1] *The Essential Shakespeare*, p. 114.   [2] BEN JONSON, *Prince Henry's Barriers*.
[3] P. S. ALLEN, *The Age of Erasmus*, p. 224.

the majestical roof and brave o'erhanging canopy of the Renaissance universe become the baseless fabric of a dream, and we find ourselves in the world of Ben Jonsoh and John Webster, of Robert Carr and George Villiers, of Strafford and Cromwell.[1]

In *The Critic*, Tilburina tells her father, the Governor of Tilbury Fort, that she sees the Spanish fleet. Her father, 'a plain matter-of-fact man' replies:

> The Spanish fleet thou canst not see — because
> — It is not yet in sight!

Of the dangers which beset historical and literary judgment, one of the most subtle is the Tilburina complex — the habit of seeing things which are not yet in sight, and which sometimes, like the Armada from Tilbury, never will be.

Oliver Cromwell is not yet in sight.

In 1603 the future Lord Protector was a baby. The only Oliver Cromwell who yet mattered was his uncle and god-father, the Huntingdon squire. And we meet him, sure enough, in the *Hatfield Papers*, hastening North to offer his loyal congratulations to James, whom later he will entertain in Huntingdonshire. Imagine that, as he trots northward, Uncle Oliver meets three weird Professors, who tell him that his godson will harry James's son to his death, and rule England in his stead. He would probably reply: 'If I thought the little brat would do any such thing, I would strangle him in his cradle with mine own hands. But ye lie in your throats, as deep as to the lungs, like the Professors that ye are.'

But though men could not foresee all the future, some things they could foresee. The could foresee that, by the union of 1603 — to quote Bacon again —

> This kingdom of England, having Scotland united, and shipping maintained, is one of the greatest monarchies that hath been in the world.[2]

Bacon, with marvellous foresight, compares it, not to anything

---

[1] A. W. POLLARD and J. DOVER WILSON in GARVIN'S *Great Tudors*, p. 594.
[2] Spedding, *Life and Letters of Bacon*, 1868, iii, 307, etc.

big, but to the grain of mustard seed, 'smallest among grains', which will 'grow and spread'. Bacon looked upon that 'most happy and glorious event', the uniting in itself of the island of Britain, 'as a full period of all instability and peregrinations'.[1] And though Ben Jonson might join in poking fun at the Scots, he too knew what it meant:

> Here are kingdoms mixed
> And nations joined, a strength of empire fixed
> Conterminate with heaven; the golden vein
> Of Saturn's age is here broke out again.

There are times when a man whose personality may be un-attractive is nevertheless able to give a nation gifts which the noblest and the greatest have failed to do. Ever since the tenth century, it had been the aim of English statesmen to unite the whole island of Britain in a federation. Where Edward I had failed, James succeeded. The dream of six centuries, and the words of the Anglo-Saxon Chronicle, came true in 1603.

In 1604 the Commons drew up, for their new monarch, a statement of the rights of Englishmen. What other nation, at this date, could have produced such a document? To talk of the 'spiritual fall' of such an England is absurd. The historian, knowing all, may see the beginning of the deadly quarrel between King and Commons. But it would be an anachronism to dream of Shakespeare seeing things so. At that happy moment, it was possible to combine an insistence on English liberties worthy of a Roundhead with a loyalty 'conservative and monarchical to the core'.

Next year (1605) Francis Bacon dedicated to James his *Advancement of Learning*: the first step in that *Great Instauration* of knowledge which was to enlarge the boundary of human empire, to the effecting of all things possible. When, in all human history, has a statesman presented to his king a gift so optimistic and so significant?

Next year (1606) the settlers sailed for Virginia, and the continuous history begins of the English-speaking peoples putting a girdle round about the earth. We may think of

---

[1] *Advancement of Learning*, Bk. II, ii, 8.

Southampton, the Virginia Company, 'The Sea Adventure', *The Tempest*, among other things.

Next year (1607) the revisers set to work on the Authorized Version of the Bible.

What a Quinquennium! The Bible, Shakespeare, our free institutions, our search for knowledge. These are the things which must hold together all who speak the English tongue. Think of Bacon's 'grain of mustard seed'.

And we have evidence that Shakespeare, like Bacon, looked forward with optimism. *Macbeth* touches topics of much interest to King James. Macbeth sees in a glass the long succession of Scottish kings, Banquo's seed. If Shakespeare had wished to do no more than compliment James, he would have called pointed attention to *one* final figure, James, King of both realms. Yet he does not. Macbeth exclaims

> *Some* I see
> That two fold balls and treble sceptres carry.

'*Some* that carry', not '*one* who carries'. England, after generations of weary waiting, has not only a king. England has *heirs*.

And we have lived to see the eleventh in direct descent from James Stuart crowned king over that Kingdom which James united, and over much more. Shakespeare and Bacon, not such great saints as Thomas More, have proved better prophets. The grain of mustard seed has grown.

Why should we believe that Shakespeare faced the new reign with less courage than Bacon, or Ben Jonson, or Samuel Daniel, who, just after James's accession, bids us look upon

> the wonderful architecture of this state of England ... being continually in all ages furnished with spirits fit to maintain the majesty of her own greatness.

Of course Jacobean England had its troubles. Shortly after Elizabeth died, a serious outbreak of plague raged; and the theatres were closed. But on 9 April 1604 they were reopened; and when, on All Saints' Day of that year Shakespeare and his fellows, who had been sworn grooms of His Majesty's chamber, acted *Othello* at court, I see no reason to believe that Shakespeare was in 'a dominant mood of gloom and dejection' on account of Essex. Still less do I desire to draw the Dark Lady from her well-earned retirement, to revive, exactly at this juncture, her superannuated love affair, and again to lacerate William's heart. Nor am I willing, with Sir Edmund Chambers, to reject both these causes, and nevertheless to make Shakespeare suffer from a 'ferment of doubt and bitterness of disillusion',[1] whilst admitting inability to find any justification for this alleged ferment and bitterness.

I submit that the fantasy of Shakespeare regarding Essex as his future king, and consequently plunged in cynicism when James comes to the throne, carries with it a mischievous corollary. It comes between Shakespeare's mind and our own, and so prevents our proper attention to Shakespeare's earliest Jacobean plays. Critics look for irony and cynicism: and they find cynicism by interpreting everything ironically.

All's Well that Ends Well has been conjectured to have been Shakespeare's first bow to James's new court[2] in 1603; *Measure for Measure* is known[3] to have been acted at court on St. Stephen's Night, 1604, that is to say eight weeks after *Othello*. Now both *All's Well* and *Measure for Measure* end in a reconciliation. That, of course, is the head and front of Shakespeare's offending. The man ought to have known that he is now in his period of disillusionment, cynicism, and gloom, and that he will not be in his forgiveness-period for five years yet. So the critics fasten upon *All's Well* and *Measure for Measure* like a stern schoolmaster, seizing two small boys who are to be flogged for being caught out of bounds. Accordingly we are told that

> In *All's Well that Ends Well* — supremely cynical title — ... the self-torturing mood of the play, the bitter mood of 'I'll show you a happy ending', is only too apparent.[4]

But what about Shakespeare's audience? How did he convey to them his bitter intention of making a supremely cynical

[1] *Shakespeare: a Survey*, p. 210.
[2] *The Essential Shakespeare*, p. 107.
[3] After generations of discussion, this has been proved by A. E. STAMP, *The Disputed Revels Accounts*, 1930.
[4] *The Times Literary Supplement*, No. 1030, 31 Oct. 1921, p. 650.

happy ending? How will they understand it? I have been told that Sarah Bernhardt once declared that, when she felt her powers failing, she would commit real suicide on the stage. Is Shakespeare committing dramatic suicide? Had he no more loyalty to the fortunes of his company than he is supposed to have had to the Tudor succession, the heirs of 'Richmond and Elizabeth'? Or is he sending his audience away satisfied, and believing that they really have seen a happy ending, just as the divine Sarah hoped that her dying spasms would be mistaken for a piece of consummate acting?

Again, we are told that in *Measure for Measure*

the lowest depths of Jacobean negation are touched. Cynicism has taken on a kind of diabolic vigilance; with the exception of the kindly, timid Provost, there is no character who is not suspect, and those whose claims to goodness or decency seem most vigorous are precisely those in whom meanness, self-regard, and hypocrisy root deepest.[1]

Yet Shakespeare's fellows, Heminge and Condell, who talked, acted, and rehearsed with him, and then, at the end of the reign of James, looked back upon their friendship, seem to know nothing about this cynical Jacobean negation. To them, Shakespeare is a 'worthy friend and fellow' 'who, as he was a happy imitator of nature, was a most gentle expresser of it'.

Let us, then, look a little closely at *Measure for Measure*.

---

[1] U. M. ELLIS-FERMOR, *The Jacobean Drama*, p. 260.

MEASURE FOR MEASURE

In *Measure for Measure* Shakespeare took as his source an old play, *Promos and Cassandra*, written by George Whetstone a quarter of a century before. Now, just as certainly as *Hamlet* was a story of revenge, so was *Promos and Cassandra* a story of forgiveness. In this play Cassandra (like Isabel) pleads for her brother, who (like Claudio) had been condemned to death for unchastity. The judge, Promos (like Angelo) will grant pardon only if Cassandra yield to his passion. Cassandra at last does so. That is the essential difference between the old plot, and Shakespeare's play. Nevertheless, Promos orders Cassandra's brother to be beheaded, and the head to be presented to her. Cassandra complains to the King; the King gives judgment that Promos first marry Cassandra, then lose *his* head. But, this marriage solemnized, Cassandra, now tied in the greatest bonds of affection to her husband, suddenly becomes an earnest suitor for his life. In the end it appears that the kindly gaoler has in fact released the brother, and presented Cassandra with a felon's head instead. So, to renown the virtues of Cassandra, the King pardons both brother and judge, and all ends well.[1]

The story shows the violence of much Elizabethan drama. John Addington Symonds says, in *Shakespeare's Predecessors*, that the sympathies of a London audience were like 'the chords of a warrior's harp, strung with twisted iron and bull's sinews, vibrating mightily, but needing a stout stroke to make them thrill'. The playwrights 'glutted their audience with horrors, cudgelled their horny fibres into sensitiveness'.

Now mark how Shakespeare treats this barbarous story. According to Professor Dover Wilson, at the time when he wrote *Measure for Measure* Shakespeare 'quite obviously

---

[1] WHETSTONE retold the tale in prose (*Heptameron of Civill Discourses*, 1582). It is derived from the *Hecatommithi* of Cinthio (1565), who also wrote a play on the subject (*Epitia*). Shakespeare knew some of these, possibly all.

believed in nothing; he was as cynical as Iago, as disillusioned as Macbeth, though he still retained, unlike the first, his sensitiveness, and, unlike the second, his hatred of cruelty, hypocrisy, and ingratitude'.[1] According to Sir Edmund Chambers, in *Measure for Measure* his 'remorseless analysis' 'probes the inmost being of man, and strips him naked'. 'It is the temper of the inquisitor': 'you can but shudder'.[2]

Prepare then to shudder, as you observe William Iago Torquemada Shakespeare at work. Shakespeare, for all the 'self-laceration', 'disgust', and 'general morbidity'[3] which is supposed to have obsessed him and his Jacobean contemporaries, removes from the play the really morbid scene of the heroine kissing the severed head of her supposed brother. Then, he divides the sorrows of the heroine between two characters, Isabel and Mariana. And the object of this duplication is, that, whatever their spiritual anguish, neither of them shall be placed in the 'really intolerable situation'[4] of poor Cassandra. Mariana has been contracted to Angelo formally by oath. It is vital to remember that, according to Elizabethan ideas, Angelo and Mariana are therefore man and wife. But Angelo has deserted Mariana. Now I grant that, according to our modern ideas, it is undignified for the deserted Mariana still to desire union with the husband who has scorned her. *We* may resent the elegiac and spaniel-like fidelity of Mariana of the Moated Grange. *But is that the attitude of the year 1604?* The tale of the deserted bride seeking her husband in disguise is old, approved, beloved. It is a mere anachronism to assume that Shakespeare, a practical dramatist, told this tale with some deep cynical and self-lacerating intention unintelligible to his audience, but now at last revealed to modern criticism. Shakespeare made Mariana gentle and dignified. She, in all shadow and silence, visits her husband in place of Isabel, to save Claudio's life.

And our twentieth-century critics are scandalized over the tale. This surprises me, a Late Victorian, brought up on the

---

[1] Op. cit., p. 122.   [2] Ibid., p. 213.
[3] J. DOVER WILSON, op. cit., pp. 117, 118.
[4] *Works of Shakespeare*, ed. G. L. KITTREDGE, p. 97.

Bible and Arthurian story. I did not know that our modern age was so proper. A Professor to-day cannot deliver a series of lectures on 'The Application of Thought to Textual Criticism' without its being reported as 'The Application of Thought to Sexual Criticism'. Yet this sex-obsessed age of ours is too modest to endure the old story of the substituted bride. I learnt at my Early Victorian mother's knee, how Jacob served seven years for Rachel: 'And it came to pass, that in the morning, behold, it was Leah',[1] and Jacob had to serve another seven years for his beloved. I did not exclaim: 'Oh, my mother, you are lacerating my feelings with this remorseless revelation of patriarchal polygamy.' A child could grasp the story of Jacob's service for Rachel, which 'seemed unto him but a few days, for the love he had to her'.

Sir Edmund Chambers is entitled to say that the story of the substituted bride 'does not commend itself to the modern conscience'. Jaques was entitled to say that he did not like the name of Rosalind. And Orlando was entitled to say, 'There was no thought of pleasing you when she was christened'. In the sixteenth century the story was a commonplace of romance, and Shakespeare used it in order to make more gentle one of the quite horrible situations of the pre-Shakespearean drama. There was a time when Shakespeare had not shrunk from staging the grossest horrors. It is to avoid them, that he now introduces the substitution which offends 'the modern conscience'.

It may be objected that Shakespeare is 'not for an age, but for all time', and that therefore he ought not to have condescended to use stories which, although current in his day, and although he made them less horrible, nevertheless would not appeal to future ages. But the great poets, Homer, Aeschylus, Sophocles, Dante, Shakespeare, speak to all time only through the language, conventions, and beliefs of their own age. How else?

A second fault of the old play is the crudity of the change from Cassandra's thirst for vengeance to her prayer for forgiveness. Shakespeare had permitted himself similar crudities

---

[1] Genesis XXIX, 25.

in the past. Now he sets to work to make the plot consistent: he does this by making it turn, from first to last, on the problem of punishment and forgiveness. It is Shakespeare's addition to the story that the Duke is distressed by this problem. Fearing lest his rule has been too lax, he deputes his office to Angelo, whilst remaining, disguised as a friar, to 'visit both prince and people'. And here critics, among them Sir Walter Raleigh[1] and Sir Arthur Quiller-Couch,[2] object. It is not seemly for a Duke to 'shirk his proper responsibility, and steal back incognito to play busybody and spy on his deputy'.

I am reminded of one of the first essays ever shown up to me, by a Japanese student, some thirty-five years ago. He objected to *The Merchant of Venice*. 'Sir Bassanio', he said, 'did not bring doctor in order that he tie up wound of friend. He did not recognize own spouse in masculine raiment.'

There was every reason for a Japanese student to be puzzled when suddenly introduced to the world of western romance, just as we in our turn are puzzled, when we first try to understand a translation of one of the *Nō* plays. But why do English critics to-day bring against *Measure for Measure* this kind of objection? They would be ashamed to bring it against Shakespeare's earlier comedies, or later romances.

Disguise and impersonation and misunderstanding are the very life of romantic comedy. The disguised monarch, who can learn the private affairs of his humblest subject, becomes a sort of earthly Providence, combining omniscience and omnipotence. That story has always had its appeal. 'Thus hath the wise magistrate done in all ages';[3] although obviously to introduce into our daily life this ancient habit of the benevolent monarch would be to incur deserved satire.

When Professor Raleigh complains that the Duke 'shirks his public duties', and when he likens him to a head of a college who 'tries to keep the love of the rebels by putting his ugly duties upon the shoulders of a deputy', is he not falling into the mistake which he deplores in other critics, that of being so

---

[1] *Shakespeare*, p. 167.
[2] New Cambridge Shakespeare, *Measure for Measure*, p. xxxiv.
[3] JONSON, *Bartholomew Fair*, II, i.

much more moral than Shakespeare himself? Is he not sub-
stituting for Shakespeare's Duke another, and a quite different
one? Bernard Shaw has rewritten the last act of *Cymbeline*, as
Shakespeare might have written it, if he had been post-Ibsen
and post-Shaw. And that is a legitimate thing to do, compared with the modern habit of keeping Shakespeare's text, but
putting upon it a construction which is post-Ibsen and post-
Shaw; imposing an outlook and a morality not Shakespeare's.

Obviously, it is wrong for the Master of a College deliberately
to put his unpopular duties upon the Vice-Master; and it would
be most improper for him to watch the result from the Porter's
Lodge, disguised as a scout. It would be equally improper
for a young lady to intervene in a law suit, by personating a
K.C.; and in this way we might moralize amiss every one of
Shakespeare's romantic plays. The question is not how Shaw
might have satirized the Duke, had he rewritten *Measure for
Measure*. The question is how Shakespeare meant us to see the
Duke; and since the Duke controls the whole action of the play,
we must see him as Shakespeare meant us to do, or misunder-
stand the play.

Shakespeare makes the Duke describe himself as one who has
ever loved the life removed; one who does not relish well the
loud applause of the people. Under his Friar's disguise, the
Duke is stung by Lucio's slanders into-defending himself as one
who, by the business he has helmed, 'shall appear to the envious
a scholar, a statesman and a soldier'. To make it quite clear
that we must take this seriously, Shakespeare makes Escalus,
immediately after, confirm the Duke's words by describing
him as

> One that, above all other strifes, contended especially to know
> himself. Rather rejoicing to see another merry, than merry
> at anything which professed to make him rejoice: a gentle-
> man of all temperance.

Isabel, in her moment of direst distress, remembers him as 'the
good Duke'. To Mariana he is, in his Friar's disguise, 'a man
of comfort', who has often stilled her 'brawling discontent'.
(This, of course, violates chronology, but Shakespeare never

bothered about that.) Angelo, in his moment of deepest humiliation, addresses the Duke with profound reverence and awe. If our moderns prefer to follow the 'fantastic' Lucio, and to regard the Duke cynically, they should remember that Lucio was but speaking according to the trick, and himself suggested a whipping as adequate punishment.

Shakespeare puts into the Duke's mouth a speech on Death which might have been uttered by Hamlet; and Shakespeare seems to have meant us to regard him as a man of Hamlet's thoughtful, scholarly type, but older, with much experience of government and of war: no longer 'courtier, soldier, scholar', but 'statesman, soldier, scholar'; yet still rather melancholy and distrustful of himself. Shakespeare, however, did not depict him with that intensity which makes his greatest characters come alive. The Duke remains somewhat impersonal, a controlling force; we never think of him by his name, Vincentio. But, though hardly a fully-realized character, he seems more than 'a puppet, cleverly painted and adroitly manipulated'.[1] Rather, he is the god in the machine: and we may concede that sometimes the machine creaks. But the Jacobeans did not mind if the machinery of their masques creaked a little, provided only it worked. And the Duke works: he is the source of the action of the play. Very truly he has been described as rather a power than a character.[2] So far from 'shirking his proper responsibility', he controls the fate of all the characters in the play.

The Duke is deeply distressed because, after fourteen years of his rule, his subjects are still no better than they ought to be. To the moralists who say that he ought to have announced publicly and personally his intention of himself inflicting a little experimental decapitation, it is answer enough that thereby the plot, which needs the Duke as a power in reserve, would have been wrecked. In the world of romantic story, in which alone he moves, the Duke has the long-established right of adopting a disguise and appointing a deputy; who will, as he knows, elect to exercise his office with severity.

[1] W. W. LAWRENCE, *Shakespeare's Problem Comedies*, 1931, p. 112.
[2] *The Times Literary Supplement*, 16 July 1931, p. 554.

Perhaps there may be a touch of irony when Shakespeare makes the Duke, who is to end as the lover of Isabel, begin by declaring that the dribbling dart of love cannot pierce a complete bosom. But there is nothing unfriendly in such irony. Of course it is part of the fun of the story (and good fun too) that the Duke has to listen to slander upon himself; has to keep his end up by giving himself a handsome testimonial; is frustrated by Lucio's 'Nay, friar, I am a kind of burr, I shall stick', when he tries to escape from his tormentor. But such are the inevitable misfortunes of the monarch in disguise; we do not honour King Alfred the less, because we enjoy his confusion when scolded for burning the cakes. Yet so great is the effect of persistent denigration, that even a wise critic, who is effectively defending the Duke, concedes to his detractors that he 'punished Lucio merely for poking fun at him behind his back'.[1] But that is not what Shakespeare wrote. Lucio, in the old days, had escaped marrying the mother of his child, by denying his parentage. The Duke, when he learns the truth, merely carries out his original plan of making Lucio marry the woman to whom he had promised marriage.[2] The Duke markedly does *not* punish Lucio for his slanders: the suggestion that he does so is merely one more instance of the extraordinary prejudice which critics cherish against all the people in this play. They christen it 'a dark comedy', and then darken the characters to justify their classification.

Not only does the Duke control the fate of all the characters; he profoundly alters the very nature of one: Angelo. The deputy, Angelo, is not so called for nothing. He *is* 'angel on the outward side' — an ascetic saint in the judgment of his fellow citizens, and despite the meanness of his spirit, nay, because of it, a saint in his own esteem. His soliloquies prove this, and Isabel at the end gives him some credit for sincerity.

Now Claudio and Juliet have lived together as man and wife, although their contract has been secret: it has 'lacked the denunciation of outward order'. (The contract between Angelo and Mariana, on the other hand, had been public,

---

[1] THALER, *Shakespeare's Silences*, p. 88.
[2] III. ii. 210, etc.; IV. iii. 180, etc.

and so had undoubtedly given them the rights of man and wife.) Angelo's puritanical revival of an ancient law, fourteen years out of date, renders Claudio's life forfeit. This Viennese law seems strange, but the Duke says the law is such. If we allow Portia to expound the even stranger law of Venice to the Duke and Magnificoes, we may surely allow the Duke of Vienna to understand the law of his own state. It is a postulate of the story.

Critics speak as if Shakespeare had imagined Claudio a self-indulgent boy, a 'poor weak soul'.[1] Yet it is only Angelo's retrospective revival which makes Claudio's offence capital. 'He hath but as offended in a dream', says the kindly Provost. He 'was worth five thousand of you all', says Mistress Overdone to Lucio and his friends. Claudio is first introduced, bearing himself with dignity under his sudden arrest. He sends his friend Lucio to his sister in her cloister, to beg her to intercede for him, because, he says,

> in her youth
> There is a prone and speechless dialect,
> Such as move men; beside, she hath prosperous art
> When she will play with reason and discourse,
> And well she can persuade.

Such descriptions of characters before they appear — perhaps before Shakespeare had written a word for them to speak — have surely a great weight. They show how Shakespeare wished the audience to see them. Isabel's characteristic when she does appear is exactly this mixture of winning silence with persuasive speech.

But before she can reach Angelo, his colleague Escalus has already interceded for Claudio, urging that, had time cohered with place, and place with wishing, Angelo might himself have fallen. Angelo replies:

> When I, that censure him, do so offend,
> Let mine own judgment pattern out my death,
> And nothing come in partial. Sir, he must die.

Isabel begins her pleading slowly and with characteristic

---

[1] E. K. CHAMBERS, op. cit., p. 209.

silences: then she grows eloquent, and to Angelo's stern refusal she at last replies:

> I would to Heaven I had your potency,
> And you were Isabel! Should it then be thus?
> No; I would tell what 'twere to be a judge,
> And what a prisoner.

Isabel has no notion as yet of the depth of sin which may have to be pardoned in Angelo. But there is 'dramatic irony' behind these two speeches, and we can forecast that in the end the places will be reversed: the fate of the convicted Angelo depending upon Isabel.

The phrase 'dramatic irony' may be misunderstood. Shakespeare, like Sophocles, puts into the mouths of his characters words which they speak in all sincerity, but which, as the play proceeds, will be found to have a deeper meaning than the speaker knew. Dramatic irony does *not* mean that, at every turn, we are justified in suspecting that Shakespeare may have meant the reverse of what he makes his characters say. When he does that ('honest Iago') he leaves us in no doubt. As a great American critic has put it: 'However much the *dramatis personae* mystify each other, the audience is never to be perplexed.'[1]

It is a marked feature of the plays which Shakespeare was producing about the same time as *Measure for Measure*, that their early scenes contain 'ironical', ominous lines, forecasting the conclusion:

BRABANTIO	She has deceived her father, and may thee.
OTHELLO	My life upon her faith. Honest Iago . . .

(Othello, I. ii)

LADY MACBETH A little water clears us of this deed.

(Macbeth, II. i)

> This is meant to forecast her later:
> 'What, will these hands ne'er be clean?'

(Macbeth, v. i)

EDMUND	Sir, I shall study deserving.
GLOSTER	He hath been out nine years, and away he shall again. (*Lear*, I. i)

[1] *Works of Shakespeare*, ed. G. L. KITTREDGE, p. 20.

But before Gloster can send him out again, Edmund lies dying with the words 'The wheel is come full circle'.

To Angelo and to Isabel the wheel will come full circle. Will Isabel then remember the pleas which she now pours forth? 'Well she can persuade.' Her marvellous and impassioned pleadings, unsurpassed anywhere in Shakespeare, are based on her Christian faith, and upon the Sermon on the Mount: all men are pardoned sinners, and *must* forgive:

> Why, all the souls that were, were forfeit once;
> And he that might the vantage best have took
> Found out the remedy.

'Judge not, that ye be not judged. For with what measure ye mete, it shall be measured to you again.' *Measure for Measure.* But how is the Sermon on the Mount to be reconciled with the practical necessities of government? That is the problem which puzzles people — and particularly perhaps young people — so much to-day. In the Tudor Age men met it by exalting Government. The King is 'the image of God's majesty': to him, and to his Government, the divine office of rule and punishment is committed. The private man must submit and forgive. Accordingly, Angelo appeals to his 'function': and there is real force in his answers to Isabel — if we remember, as we always must, that, for the purposes of the play, Claudio is supposed guilty of a capital offence.

Never does Shakespeare seem more passionately to identify himself with any of his characters than he does with Isabel, as she pleads for mercy against strict justice:

> O, it is excellent
> To have a giant's strength; but it is tyrannous
> To use it like a giant. . . .
> man, proud man,
> Drest in a little brief authority . . .
> like an angry ape
> Plays such fantastic tricks before high heaven
> As make the angels weep. . . .

'Man, proud man' is the man who, 'drest in authority', condemns his fellow men. The 'fantastic tricks' which such an
unforgiving man plays 'like an angry ape' make the angels
weep; because it is the function of angels to rejoice over one
sinner that repenteth. Yet portions of these lines are constantly
quoted,[1] divorced from their context, as if they were Shakespeare's
generalization about all actions of all mankind, when, in fact,
they are the words he gives to a distressed sister pleading before
a hard-hearted, proud, self-righteous authoritarian. To
Shakespeare, we are told, 'man is now no more than "an angry
Ape".' And so, Isabel's protest against the proud self-righteous
man who condemns his fellow men, is turned by the critics into
Shakespeare's proud, self-righteous condemnation of his fellow
men.

But the unforgiving Angelo is himself about to fall, though
not without a sincere struggle. More than one of Isabel's pleadings find a mark which she never meant:

> Go to your bosom;
> Knock there, and ask your heart what it doth know
> That's like my brother's fault . . .
> Hark how I'll bribe you . . .

Angelo has thought himself superior to human weakness,
because he is free from the vulgar vices of a Lucio. And the
'beauty of mind' of a distressed, noble woman throws him off
his balance.[2] If we fail to see the nobility of Isabel, we cannot
see the story as we should. The plot is rather like that of
Calderon's *Magician*, where the scholarly, austere Cipriano
is overthrown by speaking with the saintly Justina. Cipriano
sells himself literally to the Devil to gain his end by magic.
Angelo tempts Isabel in a second dialogue, as wonderful as the
first. In her innocence Isabel is slow to see Angelo's drift, and
it is only her confession of her own frailty that gives him a
chance of making himself clear. 'Nay,' Isabel says,

---

[1] E. K. CHAMBERS, op. cit., p. 213; J. DOVER WILSON, op. cit., p. 123; U. M.
ELLIS-FERMOR, op. cit., p. 261.
[2] Cf. JOHN MASEFIELD, *William Shakespeare*, p. 179.

call us ten times frail;
For we are soft as our complexions are,
And credulous to false prints.

If Shakespeare is depicting in Isabel the self-righteous prude which some critics would make of her, he goes strangely to work.

But when she perceives Angelo's meaning, Isabel decides without hesitation. Now whatever we think of that instant decision, it is certainly not un-Christian. Christianity could never have lived through its first three hundred years of persecution, if its ranks had not been stiffened by men and women who never hesitated in the choice between righteousness and the ties to their kinsfolk. We may call this fanaticism: but it was well understood in Shakespeare's day. Foxe's *Martyrs* was read by all; old people could still remember seeing the Smithfield fires; year after year saw the martyrdoms of Catholic men (and sometimes of Catholic women like the Ven. Margaret Clitherow). It was a stern age — an age such as the founder of Christianity had foreseen when he uttered his stern warnings. 'He that loveth father or mother more than me . . .' 'If any man come to me, and hate not his father, and mother, . . . and brethren and sisters, . . . he cannot be my disciple.'[1]

It is recorded of Linacre, the father of English medicine, that, albeit a priest, he opened his Greek New Testament for the first time late in life, and came on some of these hard sayings. 'Either this is not the Gospel', he said, 'or we are not Christians', and refusing to contemplate the second alternative, he flung the Book from him and returned to the study of medicine. Now it is open to us to say that we are not Christians: it is not open to us to say that Isabel is un-Christian. She goes to her brother, not because she hesitates, but that he may share with her the burden of her irrevocable decision. Claudio's first reply is, 'O heavens! it cannot be'; 'Thou shalt not do't.' But the very bravest of men have quailed, within the four walls of a prison cell, waiting for the axe next day. I am amazed at the way critics condemn Claudio, when he breaks down, and utters his

[1] Matthew x, 37; Luke xiv, 26.

288

second thoughts, 'Sweet sister, let me live'. Isabel overwhelms him in the furious speech which we all know. And I am even more amazed at the dislike which the critics feel for the tortured Isabel. But when they assure us that their feeling towards both his creatures was shared by the gentle Shakespeare, I am then most amazed of all.

It is admitted that no greater or more moving scenes had appeared on any stage, since the masterpieces of Attic drama ceased to be acted. Yet our critics tell us that Shakespeare wrote them in a mood of 'disillusionment and cynicism', 'self-laceration' and, strangest of all, 'weariness'.[1] 'A corroding atmosphere of moral suspicion'[2] hangs about this debate between 'the sainted Isabella, wrapt in her selfish chastity', and 'the wretched boy who in terror of death is ready to sacrifice his sister's honour'.[3] Isabel's chastity, they say, is 'rancid', and she is 'not by any means such a saint as she looks';[4] her inhumanity is pitiless, her virtue is self-indulgent, unimaginative, and self-absorbed.[5]

And yet, think of Rose Macaulay's war-poem, 'Many sisters to many brothers', and let us believe that a sister may suffer more in agony of mind than the brother can suffer in physical wounds or death. Shakespeare has made Isabel say to Claudio,

> O, were it but my life,
> I'ld throw it down for your deliverance
> As frankly as a pin.

It is standing the play on its head,[6] to say that Shakespeare wrote those words in irony and cynicism. How did he convey that to his audience? If such assumptions are allowed, we can prove anything we like, 'eight years together, dinners and suppers and sleeping-hours excepted'.

[1] J. DOVER WILSON, op. cit., pp. 116, 117.
[2] E. K. CHAMBERS, op. cit., p. 214.   [3] J. DOVER WILSON, op. cit., p. 116.
[4] New Cambridge Shakespeare, *Measure for Measure*, p. xxx.
[5] U. M. ELLIS-FERMOR, op. cit., pp. 261, 262.
[6] I borrow this very excellent phrase from W. W. Lawrence (p. 70). The brevity of a lecture compels me to pass over many points that a critic may think should have been more fully argued, but I do this the more cheerfully, because they have been already so fully discussed by Lawrence in his *Shakespeare's Problem Comedies*, 1931, and their moral emphasized in an excellent leading article in *The Times Literary Supplement* of 16 July 1931.

Isabel then, as Shakespeare sees her and asks us to see her, would frankly, joyously, give her life to save Claudio: and *'greater love hath no man than this'*. And now Claudio is asking for what she cannot give, and she bursts out in agony. Have the critics never seen a human soul or a human body in the extremity of torment? Physical torture Isabel thinks she could have stood without flinching. She has said so to Angelo:

> The impression of keen whips I'ld wear as rubies,
> And strip myself to death, as to a bed
> That longing have been sick for, ere I'ld yield
> My body up to shame.

To suppose that Shakespeare gave these burning words to Isabel so that we should perceive her to be selfish and cold, is to suppose that he did not know his job. The honour of her family and her religion are more to her than mere life, her own or Claudio's.

There are those, like Sir George Greenwood, who prefer to the character of Isabel that of the heroine of the original story — Cassandra, who was willing to endure all shame to save her brother's life. The New Cambridge Shakespeare quotes this dictum of Sir George with more approval than it would give to his other dicta.[1] And we may agree that from such a story a noble, if harrowing, tragedy might be made. There is no need to play the moralist, and to condemn either Cassandra or Isabel. 'Wisdom is justified of all her children.' Faced by a dire choice, different souls may make different decisions, which for each may be the right decision. Shakespeare has chosen to depict Isabel as one who cannot yield. And most of those who have criticized her, from Hazlitt downwards, agree that she cannot. And she has got to make that clear to Claudio. It is just here that her critics quarrel with her. Sir Arthur Quiller-Couch digs out Mrs. Charlotte Lennox from the obscurity of the mid-eighteenth century to tell us how the scene should have been written. Isabel, Charlotte says,

> should have made use of her superior understanding to reason down Claudio's fears, recall nobler ideas to his mind,

---

[1] p. xxxi.

teach him what was due to her honour and his own, and reconcile him to his approaching death by arguments drawn from that religion and virtue of which she made so high a profession.

'To reason down Claudio's fears!' 'By arguments drawn from religion and virtue!' Why, the Duke had just preached to Claudio the most eloquent Sermon Against the Fear of Death that has ever been written since Lucretius completed his Third Book. Claudio had expressed himself convinced; and then the Duke's discourse had shrivelled like a thread in the flame of Claudio's longing for life.

How will pi-jaw help Claudio? Shakespeare imagined Claudio as a good lad, but not, like his sister, devout; he doesn't keep devout company, exactly. Isabel 'well can persuade'. She is one of a few women in Shakespeare who can persuade. (Not Portia: 'The quality of mercy is not strain'd' produces no persuasion in the soul of Shylock.) Volumnia is a special case. The other great persuaders are: Isabel, Beatrice and Lady Macbeth. And they all use the same arguments — the arguments which, I expect, the first Cave-woman, when in dire straits, used to her Cave-man: You are a coward; You have no love or respect for me; I have no love for you.

Isabel is the most vehement of the three. Sisterly technique has its own rules; there is a peculiar freedom about the talk of those who have known each other from babyhood. And Isabel can appeal to the honour of the family. Escalus, when he first pleaded for Claudio, remembered his 'most noble father'. Isabel had exclaimed, when she first found Claudio firm,

> there my father's grave
> Did utter forth a voice.

And now she cries,

> Heaven shield my mother play'd my father fair.

Isabel appeals to the passion which, in an Elizabethan gentleman, may be presumed to be stronger than the fear of death — pride in his gentle birth and in the courage which should mark it. Don't people see that there are things about which we cannot argue calmly? The fierceness of Isabel's words is the measure of the agony of her soul. 'The fortress which parleys, the woman who parleys, is lost.' I grant that, at the end of a lifetime's training, a saint like Thomas More could smile on his daughter when she tempted him, 'What, Mistress Eve?' But the young martyrs are apt to be more stern, whether it be Cordelia or Antigone, the spitfire St. Eulalia, or St. Juliana putting the fear of death upon the Devil. Who but a pedant would blame them? And it is our fault if we don't see that Isabel is suffering martyrdom none the less because her torment is mental, not physical.

One of the most significant of Shakespeare's alterations of his original is to make the heroine a 'votarist of St. Clare'. At the root of the movement of St. Francis and St. Clare was the intense remembrance of the sufferings of Christ, in atonement for the sins of the whole world — the 'remedy' of which Isabel in vain reminds Angelo. Isabel, as a novice, is testing herself to see whether she is called to that utter renunciation which is the life of the 'poor Clare'. Whether she remains in the Convent or no, one who is contemplating such a life can no more be expected to sell herself into mortal sin, than a good soldier can be expected to sell a stronghold entrusted to him.

Imagine an officer and his subaltern commanded to hold to the uttermost a fortified post against rebels. In a sortie the rebels capture the subaltern, and threaten to shoot him unless the fort surrenders. The subaltern breaks down, and implores his commandant to save his life. I can imagine that the commandant would reply, firmly but gently, that surrender is impossible. But suppose the subaltern were his beloved younger brother, or his only son. I can imagine that then the commandant would reply to his son's appeal by passionate denunciation, telling him that he is a disgrace to his family. To discuss the matter calmly would lead to the surrender which he knows he must not make: his instinct would tell him that. So, at least, it seems to me in my ignorance. And when I find Shakespeare in his wisdom depicting the matter so, I don't see anything cynical about it.

Those who dislike the vehemence of Isabel would do well,

in Ben Jonson's phrase, to 'call forth Sophocles to us', and to ponder on the *Philoctetes*. In that play Neoptolemus is asked to sell his honour and betray his father's friend by a base lie, for the good of his country, and for the ultimate good of the friend who is to be deceived. Neoptolemus refuses indignantly, but he lets himself be drawn into discussion, and so sells his honour and his friend. But the anticipated good does not follow, and Neoptolemus has to make amends to his friend, though this means treason to the Greek army. The play is ending, with Neoptolemus deserting the army, and even contemplating war against his own countrymen, when the god appears from the machine to solve the knot. All this follows because Neoptolemus listens and debates when he hears the voice of the tempter: 'Now give thyself to me for one short, shameless day, and then, for the rest of thy time, be called of all mortals the most righteous.' We cannot argue with the tempter, when our own desires are already so much enlisted on his side. We can only refuse, instinctively, vehemently.

It is precisely the alternation of vehemence with silence which gives Isabel her individuality. When she first understands the drift of Angelo's temptation, the poor child flies at him with a pathetic attempt at blackmail: 'Sign me a present pardon for my brother, or . . . I'll tell the world . . .' When she is told that Angelo has slain Claudio, she exclaims:

> O, I will to him and pluck out his eyes!

Shakespeare sometimes puts his heroines in pairs, coupling the fierce, vehement girl with the gentle, swooning girl: Hermia with Helena, Beatrice with Hero, Isabel with Mariana. For all her silence and modesty, Isabel has the ferocity of the martyr. Yet I don't think Shakespeare disliked his vixens. Hermia has nails which can reach her enemy's eyes. Benedick foresaw a predestinate scratched face for the husband of Beatrice. Yet would any of us take Hero in to dinner, if we could get Beatrice, or go hiking through the Athenian forest with Helena, if we could get Hermia?

Critics ask, as does Sir Edmund Chambers, whether Isabel too 'has not had her ordeal, and in her turn failed', whether she was 'wholly justified in the eyes of her creator'. They are entitled to ask the question. But they ought to wait for the answer. The Duke enters, takes Claudio aside, and tells him there is no hope for him. And we find that Claudio, who before Isabel's outburst had been gripped by the mortal fear of death, is now again master of his soul:

> Let me ask my sister pardon. I am so out of love with life, that I will sue to be rid of it.

'Hold you there', says the Duke. Claudio does. Later, we see him quiet and self-possessed when the Provost shows him his death-warrant. To the Provost he is 'the most gentle Claudio': and to Shakespeare, the word 'gentle' is a word of very high praise, not consistent with any want of spirit.[1] 'Gentle' and 'most gentle' is how his worthy friends and fellows — Ben Jonson, Heminge, Condell — described Shakespeare. Claudio, 'most gentle' in his prison, has passed his ordeal well, showing quiet courage equally removed from the hilarity of a Posthumus and the insensibility of a Barnardine.

Mrs. Lennox says that Isabel ought to have taught Claudio what is due to her honour and his own. She has.

Now, if Isabel's speech had been intended to depict a 'cold' and 'remorseless' woman, 'all for saving her own soul', acting cruelly to her brother in the 'fiery ordeal' which (we are told) 'his frail soul proves ill-fitted to endure', why does Shakespeare show Claudio, far from resenting his sister's reproaches, only wishing to ask her pardon, and henceforth courageous and resolute? Why, above all, does Shakespeare make the Duke, when he overhears Isabel's whole speech, comment on the beauty of her goodness? This is intelligible only if Shakespeare means Isabel's speech to be an agonized outcry, working on her brother as no calm reasoning could have done. If Shakespeare's critics think they could have written the scene better, they are welcome to try; but it does not follow that Shakespeare was a disillusioned cynic because he did not write Isabel's speech as Charlotte Lennox would have done.

---

[1] 'He's gentle, and not fearful,' says Miranda to Prospero, warning him not to presume too much on Ferdinand's patience.

When the Duke suggests that Isabel may yet be able to save her brother, she replies, 'I have spirit to do any thing that appears not foul in the truth of my spirit.' And now Isabel's critics disapprove of her because of the 'businesslike' way in which she sets about saving her brother and assisting the Duke's plot. If Shakespeare's Jacobean audiences were as perverse as his modern critics, I can well understand how 'gloom and dejection' may have driven the poor man 'to the verge of madness', as critics assert that it did. That Shakespeare imagined Isabel as businesslike, should be clear to any one who studies with care her words in the earlier scenes. She is a sensible Elizabethan girl, with no nonsense about her, and she knows that it is no sin to bring husband and wife together.

So Mariana takes Isabel's place, to save Claudio's life.

Again, if Shakespeare meant us to regard Isabel cynically, why did he picture her not only as touching by her goodness both Angelo and the Duke, though to different issues, but even as awing the frivolous Lucio into sobriety and sympathy? To Lucio she is 'a thing ensky'd and sainted',

> an immortal spirit;
> And to be talk'd with in sincerity,
> As with a saint.

Sir Arthur disqualifies Lucio's evidence because Lucio is a sensualist, and sensualists, he says, habitually divide women into angels and those who are 'their animal prey'.[1] Even if that be true, could Shakespeare seriously expect his audience to grasp such a subtlety? Critics see Isabel 'hard as an icicle'.[2] If Shakespeare meant that, why did he make Lucio see her differently: 'O pretty Isabella, I am pale at mine heart to see thine eyes so red.'[3] Even a sensualist can tell when people's eyes are red.

Angelo's own words make it clear that it is his conviction of the innocence and goodness of Isabel which overthrows him.

As for Claudio — the critics may despise him, but Angelo

---

[1] New Cambridge Shakespeare, p. xxvii.
[2] U. M. ELLIS-FERMOR, op. cit., p. 262.
[3] IV. iii. 158.

knows better. He knows that Claudio is a plucky lad who, 'receiving a dishonour'd life with ransom of such shame', might take his revenge in time to come. So he commands Claudio's execution. The Duke, of course, prevents it, and continues to weave his toils round Angelo, till the moment when he will fall on him, and grind him to powder.

And, immediately, Angelo's remorse begins. He realizes what he really is: 'This deed unshapes me quite.' Yet his state is more gracious now, when he believes himself to be a perjured adulterer, than it was a few days before, when he believed himself to be a saint.

I pass over the agonies of Angelo's repentance. 'Dull to all proceedings', he fights to maintain all that is left him, the 'credent bulk' of a public esteem which has become a mockery to him. When Lucio brings the struggle to an end, by tearing the Friar's hood off the Duke, Angelo realizes that his master is one from whom no secrets are hid:

DUKE   Hast thou or word, or wit, or impudence,
       That yet can do thee office? . . .
ANGELO   O my dread lord,
       I should be guiltier than my guiltiness,
       To think I can be undiscernible,
       When I perceive your Grace, like power divine,
       Hath looked upon my passes.

A cold-hearted, self-righteous prig is brought to a sense of what he is, in the sight of his Master. A few hours before, Angelo had turned a deaf ear to the plea 'Why, all the souls that were, were forfeit once'. But now he can conceive no depth of guilt so deep as his own. 'Guiltier than my guiltiness.' It is like the repentance of Enobarbus, 'I am alone the villain of the earth', or of Posthumus,

                    it is I
       That all the abhorred things o' the earth amend
       By being worse than they.

For Angelo, as for Enobarbus and for Posthumus, nothing remains save a passionate prayer to be put out of his misery:

296

Then, good prince,
No longer session hold upon my shame,
But let my trial be mine own confession:
Immediate sentence then, and sequent death,
Is all the grace I beg.

Surely it is concerning repentance like this that it is written,
'There is joy in the presence of the angels of God'.

The ninety and nine just persons which need no repentance
naturally think otherwise. Coleridge began the outcry against
Measure for Measure, which he found 'the most painful — say
rather the only painful — part' of Shakespeare's genuine works.
The pardon of Angelo, he says, 'baffles the strong indignant
claim of justice — (for cruelty, with lust and damnable baseness,
cannot be forgiven, because we cannot conceive them as being
morally repented of)'.[1] Swinburne endorsed this judgment at
great length. Justice, he said, 'is buffeted, outraged, insulted,
struck in the face'. 'We are tricked out of our dole, defeated of
our due, lured and led on to look for some equitable and satisfy-
ing upshot, defrauded and derided and sent empty away.'[2]
Hazlitt could not allow Mariana to love Angelo 'whom we
hate'.[3] To enumerate the ninety-six other just persons would be
to write a bibliography of *Measure for Measure*, which is no part
of my intention. Rather I turn to Mariana as she implores
pardon for her husband. Coleridge thought the pardon and
marriage of Angelo not only unjust, but degrading to the character of woman. Yet repentance, intercession and forgiveness
are the stuff of Christianity and of the old stories of Christendom.
In the story which Calderon used, Cipriano, after selling himself
to the Devil in order to win Justina to his will, repents and dies
a martyr at her side, comforted by her words: 'So many stars
has not the Heaven, so many grains of sand the sea, not so many
sparks the fire, not so many motes the sunlight, as the sins which
He forgives.'

But the Duke again and again rejects Mariana's plea for
mercy. She turns at last to Isabel:

[1] *Notes on Shakespeare.* [2] *Study of Shakespeare.*
[3] *Characters of Shakespeare's Plays.*

> Sweet Isabel, take my part;
> Lend me your knees and all my life to come
> I'll lend you all my life to do you service.

Isabel stands silent.

It is many years ago that I saw acted, within this building where we are now met, Calderon's *Life is a Dream*, in the version of Edward Fitzgerald. In that play Basilio, King of Poland, has learnt from his study of the stars that his new-born son will end by trampling on his father's head. So Prince Segismund is kept, from his birth, in a cruel prison, not knowing who he is. But his father, relenting, determines to test whether he has read the stars aright: so he brings Segismund drugged to the palace. There Segismund awakes to find himself heir to the throne of Poland; but he abuses his one day of power, and is carried back in sleep again to his prison, to be told that all that he has seen and done that day has been a dream. Yet later the mutinous army releases him. Segismund marches at the head of the army, not knowing whether he dreams or no, and his victories end with the King Basilio kneeling humbled at the feet of his wronged son.

What will Segismund now do? Has he learnt how to forgive, the greatest thing that can be learnt from the Dream which is called Life?

It is not often that one can see a classical masterpiece acted without knowing how it will end. Whether it was the acting of Miss Margaret Halstan, who took the part of the boy-prince, or the stage production of Mr. Poel, I have never since felt the suspense of a great scene as I felt that. I like to think that those who first saw Shakespeare's play acted at the Christmas revels of 1604 may perhaps have felt such a suspense. The title, *Measure for Measure*, gave them no clue as to the ending.

A second time Mariana appeals:

> Isabel,
> Sweet Isabel, do yet but kneel by me;
> Hold up your hands, say nothing, I'll speak all.

Still Isabel stands silent, whilst Mariana pleads on pitifully:

> They say, best men are moulded out of faults;
> And, for the most, become much more the better
> For being a little bad: so may my husband.

At her third appeal,

> O Isabel, will you not lend a knee?

Isabel kneels at the feet of the Duke.

While Isabel is pleading for his life, Angelo is longing for death. Escalus turns to him, regretting his fall. Angelo only says:

> I am sorry that such sorrow I procure:
> And so deep sticks it in my penitent heart,
> That I crave death more willingly than mercy;
> 'Tis my deserving, and I do entreat it.

The wheel is come full circle.

Only two days before, Angelo had rejected the plea of mercy for Claudio with the words

> When I, that censure him, do so offend,
> Let mine own judgment pattern out my death.

And Isabel had longed for the potency of Angelo that she might 'tell what 'twere to be a judge, and what a prisoner'. Later we have seen Angelo 'unshaped' by his remorse, though still confident that he will escape undetected, whilst Isabel longs to 'pluck out his eyes', and is promised revenges to her heart on 'this wretch' who has murdered her brother. And now Angelo, publicly shamed, longing for death, faces an Isabel who can bring herself to say, after an agony of silent struggle, 'let him not die'. It was not in a spirit of 'weariness, cynicism, and disgust' that the Master Craftsman made the whirligig of time bring in revenges like these.

Isabel's sufferings are over. The Provost produces the muffled Claudio. Sister meets brother with that 'prone and speechless dialect' which moves, or should move, men.

Sir Edmund Chambers asks, Why does the Duke conceal

from Isabel in her grief the knowledge that her brother yet lives? Sir Walter Raleigh asked the same question thirty years ago. His answer was that the reason is dramatic; the crisis must be kept for the end. And, as a piece of stagecraft, the ending justifies itself; it is magnificent. But Sir Edmund Chambers is surely right when he says that a play dealing seriously with the problems of life must be taken seriously; the Duke, he thinks, symbolizes the workings of Providence. Is not such treatment of Providence, then, he asks, ironical?

The Duke certainly reminds us of the ways of Providence. And we feel so in the great final scene, where Mariana is imploring the silent Isabel to intercede for Angelo. Why, then, does the Duke gather up all his authority, as former Friar and present Monarch, and crash it, with a lie, in the path Isabel must tread?

> Should she kneel down in mercy of this fact,
> Her brother's ghost his paved bed would break,
> And take her hence in horror.

Yet all this time the Duke is keeping her brother in reserve, to produce him when Isabel shall have fulfilled her destiny, by making intercession for the man she most hates.

If we are thinking of the Duke as a character in the play, this is difficult to understand. Equally difficult is it to understand the Hermione of the last scene in the *Winter's Tale*. We cannot imagine the wronged queen of the first three acts shamming death, and tormenting her husband with sixteen years of remorse. There is, of course, the dramatic effect; but is there not also something more? Is there not something symbolic of a mysterious power, when, in the *Alcestis*, Heracles seems to torment Admetus before he restores his wife to him?

> It was the crowning grace of that great heart,
> To keep back joy, procrastinate the truth.[1]

If it be said that this torturing of Isabel,

> To make her heavenly comforts of despair
> When it is least expected,

---

[1] BROWNING, *Balaustion's Adventure*.

is unbearably cruel, I can only reply that life undoubtedly *is* sometimes like that. There are some souls (Isabel is one) for whom it is decreed that no trial, however agonizing, no pain, however atrocious, is to be spared them. Nevertheless, it is also true that there is no trial so agonizing, no pain so atrocious, but that some souls can rise above it, as Isabel does when, despite the Duke's stern warning, she kneels at his feet to intercede for Angelo.

Is it then true, as Sir Arthur Quiller-Couch says, that Isabel writes no lesson on the dark walls, and that they teach none to her soul? Or is it true when Sir Edmund Chambers echoes the complaint of Coleridge, and says that *Measure for Measure* 'just perplexes and offends', because there is no poetic justice? Is it true that 'to no profit of righteousness has Isabella's white soul been dragged through the mire'?

I know that many readers find a stumbling-block in this culminating scene, in Isabel's pleading for Angelo. Why should she plead, they ask, for her brother's murderer?

We must be prepared to accept the postulates of Shakespeare's plays, as we do, for example, of Sophocles' *Oedipus Tyrannus*. And, generally, we are so prepared: we accept the caskets and the pound of flesh, King Lear's love test and Prospero's art. It is a postulate of our story that Claudio has committed a capital offence. Angelo has not committed a crime in letting the law take its course upon Claudio; he has not committed a crime in his union with Mariana, to whom he has been publicly betrothed; those are assumptions on which the play is based. Angelo would be despicable if he put forward any such plea for himself, and he does not. But the fact remains that Angelo's sin has been, not in act, but in thought, and human law cannot take cognizance of thought: 'thoughts are no subjects'. Besides, Isabel is conscious that, however innocently, she herself has been the cause of Angelo's fall:

> I partly think
> A due sincerity govern'd his deeds,
> Till he did look on me; since it is so,
> Let him not die.

301

And Angelo is penitent. There can be no doubt what the words of the Sermon on the Mount demand: 'Judge not, and ye shall not be judged.' That had been Isabel's plea for Claudio. It is a test of her sincerity, if she can put forward a plea for mercy for her dearest foe, as well as for him whom she dearly loves.

Criticism of *Measure for Measure*, from Coleridge downwards, has amounted to this: 'There is a limit to human charity.' 'There is', says Chesterton's Father Brown, 'and that is the real difference between human charity and Christian charity.' Isabel had said the same:

> O, think on that;
> And mercy then will breathe within your lips
> Like man new made.

Shakespeare has so manipulated the story as to make it end in Isabel showing more than human charity to Angelo, whilst at the same time he has avoided, by the introduction of Mariana, the error, which he found in his crude original, of wedding Isabel to Angelo.

Yet we are told that in *Measure for Measure* 'the evidence of Shakespeare's profound disillusionment and discouragement of spirit is plain enough', that 'the searchlight of irony is thrown upon the paths of Providence itself'.[1]

The way in which the Duke, an earthly Providence, tortures Isabel till he wrings her agonized forgiveness out of her, reminds us of the way in which, in Shakespeare's contemporary tragedies, Providence seems to ordain that no suffering is spared to Lear or Cordelia, to Othello or Desdemona. It is very terrible. But it cannot be called, as it often is called, un-Christian, or 'an indictment of man's maker', or 'a definite arraignment of the scheme of things', or 'the final victory of evil'.[2] For in that case the representation would leave us desperate or rebellious. And it does not.[3] Lear and Othello, Cordelia and Desdemona rise 'superior to the world in which they appear'.[4] That wise critic, A. C. Bradley, has said:

[1] E. K. CHAMBERS in the *Encyclopaedia Britannica* (1911), xxiv, 785.
[2] Idem, *Shakespeare: A Survey*, pp. 215, 220, 231, 247.
[3] A. C. BRADLEY, *Shakespearean Tragedy*, p. 26.   [4] Ibid., p. 324.

The extremity of the disproportion between prosperity and goodness first shocks us, and then flashes on us the conviction that our whole attitude in asking or expecting that goodness should be prosperous is wrong; that, if only we could see things as they are, we should see that the outward is nothing and the inward is all.[1]

It is a thought which is difficult to express, and Bradley felt his own statement to be 'exaggerated and too explicit'. But the thought that 'Whosoever will lose his life shall find it', or, as Kent in the stocks puts it, 'Nothing almost sees miracles but misery', was, perhaps, more generally understood by the Englishmen of Shakespeare's day than it is now. Mr. Bettenham, Reader of Gray's Inn, was wont to say 'that virtuous men were like some herbs and spices, that give not their sweet smell, till they be broken and crushed'. And Francis Bacon, of the same Inn, put this doctrine into his Essay *Of Adversity*, to show that 'Prosperity is the blessing of the Old Testament; adversity is the blessing of the New, which carrieth the greater benediction, and the clearer revelation of God's favour'.

And I heard A. E. Housman, who, of all men I have known, was sternest in refusing to break his proud reserve, say in his first lecture:

> Fortitude and continence and honesty are not commended to us on the ground that they conduce, as on the whole they do conduce, to material success, nor yet on the ground that they will be rewarded hereafter: those whose office it is to exhort mankind to virtue are ashamed to degrade the cause they plead by proffering such lures as these.

Forty-one years later, in his last great public utterance, in which he bade us 'Farewell for ever', he quoted: 'Whosoever will save his life shall lose it, and whosoever will lose his life shall find it.' 'That', he said, 'is the most important truth which has ever been uttered, and the greatest discovery ever made in the moral world; but I do not find in it anything which I should call poetical.'[2]

---

[1] A. C. BRADLEY, *Shakespearean Tragedy*, p. 326.
[2] *Introductory Lecture*, 1892, p. 36; *Name and Nature of Poetry*, 1933, p. 36.

Now it would take me altogether out of my depth, to discuss whether there is anything poetical in those words. But it can surely be contended that Shakespearean tragedy is an expression *in poetry* of that 'most important truth which has ever been uttered'. And so, equally, is *Measure for Measure* an expression of 'the greatest discovery ever made in the moral world': the highly unpleasant discovery that there are things more important, for oneself and for others, than avoiding death and pain.

That, of course, is not a Christian discovery. One of the founders of modern Japan uttered it in two lines of Chinese verse, as he was led to execution, speaking with a loud voice, so that he might take farewell of his friend without implicating him by turning his head:

> It is better to be a crystal and be broken
> Than to remain perfect like a tile upon the housetop.

It is not Christian: but it is a foundation upon which Christianity, in common with every other religion worth the name, is built.

Measure for Measure is a play of forgiveness, more distinctly even than *The Tempest*. Isabel forgives in her moment of direst loss: Prospero only when he has recovered his Dukedom. Isabel urges forgiveness because a Christian must forgive: Prospero forgives because he does not condescend to torment his enemies further. And the contrast applies also to those forgiven. Angelo longs for death, because the Duke, '*like power divine*', has seen his sinfulness. Sebastian and Antonio learn from Prospero, when he forgives them, that besides their crimes against him, he knows also how they have plotted to kill their king; to the pardoned Sebastian, just as to Angelo, there naturally seems to be something superhuman in such knowledge; but Sebastian expresses his conviction differently from Angelo:

> The devil speaks in him.

'No!' says Prospero; and then he turns to his brother Antonio:

304

For you, most wicked Sir, whom to call brother
Would even infect my mouth, I do forgive
Thy rankest fault . . .

Antonio makes no answer to this forgiveness. But he and
Sebastian, unabashed, continue their joyless jests to the end.

Now, when we mark how evil, and its forgiveness, is depicted
in *Measure for Measure* in 1604, can we agree that Shakespeare's
philosophy about 1604 was 'obviously not a Christian philosophy'?
On the contrary, it seems to me more definitely Christian than
that of *The Tempest*, though I don't deny that the philosophy of
the Romances can also be called Christian. I would not deny
that, on the whole, Shakespeare's last plays *are* 'happy dreams',
'symbols of an optimistic faith in the beneficent dispositions of
an ordering Providence'.[1] But I see no ground to believe that
there is any 'complete breach' between the mood of 1604 and
that of 1611, or that we must assume a 'conversion', caused by
'a serious illness which may have been a nervous breakdown,
and on the other hand may have been merely the plague'.[2]

We are told that the low-comedy characters of *Measure for
Measure* are 'unwholesome company': that whereas Shakespeare, in Falstaff and his associates, had represented sin as
'human', he now represents it as 'devilish'.[3] But is this really so?
Surely the answer was given by Sir Walter Raleigh years ago.
These characters in *Measure for Measure* 'are live men, pleasant
to Shakespeare'. Pompey is 'one of those humble, cheerful
beings, willing to help in anything that is going forward, who
are the mainstay of human affairs . . . Froth is an amiable,
feather-headed young gentleman — to dislike him would argue
an ill-nature, and a small one . . . This world of Vienna, as
Shakespeare paints it, is not a black world; it is a weak world,
full of little vanities and stupidities, regardful of custom, fond
of pleasure, idle, and abundantly human.'[4]

As to Barnardine, his creator came to love him so much that
he had not the heart to decapitate him, although Barnardine
was only created to be decapitated.

[1] E. K. CHAMBERS, in the *Encyclopaedia Britannica* (1911), xxiv, 785.
[2] Idem, *William Shakespeare*, 1930, i, 86, 274.
[3] Idem, *Shakespeare: A Survey*, 1935, p. 211.   [4] *Shakespeare*, p. 166.

In *Measure for Measure* sin is not represented as 'devilish': it is represented as sinful, and that is necessitated by the serious and earnest character of the whole play. Yet the sinners do not altogether forfeit our sympathy. And when the unmasked Duke finally taxes Lucio with his slanders, he is not unequal to the occasion:

> Faith, my lord, I spoke it but according to the trick. If you will hang me for it, you may; but I had rather it would please you I might be whipt.

This, then, is how Shakespeare treats the barbarous old story of *Promos and Cassandra*, removing its morbid details, harmonizing its crudities, giving humanity and humour to its low characters, turning it into a consistent tale of intercession for sin, repentance from and forgiveness of crime. Yet *Measure for Measure* is adduced as the supreme proof that, about 1603, Shakespeare was in a mood of 'self-laceration, weariness, discord, cynicism, and disgust.'[1] He has been in that mood for the two years since the execution of Essex, and will remain in it for another four or five. This dominant mood of gloom and dejection will bring him on one occasion to the verge of madness, and lead him to write dramas greater than any other man ever wrote save Aeschylus and Sophocles alone. Then in 1608 Sir Edmund Chambers will cure him of his seven years of 'profound disillusionment and discouragement of spirit' by giving him either the plague, or (alternatively) a nervous break-down.

I hear a gentle voice from Stratford murmur

Good frend, for Jesus sake forbeare.

Yet the critics have one final kick at *Measure for Measure*. More Papistical than the Pope, they feel outraged that Isabel should 'throw her novitiate headdress over the mill'[2] and marry the Duke. Even the sober A. C. Bradley thought that here Shakespeare lent himself to 'a scandalous proceeding'.[3] Yet

---

[1] J. DOVER WILSON, op. cit., p. 117.
[2] New Cambridge Shakespeare, p. xxxi.
[3] *Shakespearean Tragedy*, p. 78.

Isabel is a novice, and her business as a novice is to learn her Creator's intentions for her future. Whether she ought to return to the cloister from which she has been so urgently summoned rests with her creator — William Shakespeare. And he leaves her silent, and us guessing. For myself, I am satisfied that Isabel will do her duty in that state of life unto which it shall please William Shakespeare to call her, whether as abbess or duchess.

Yet in Shakespeare's greatest plays, his greatest characters, for all their individuality, have also an imaginative, a symbolic suggestion. It is so in *The Tempest*, it is so in *Hamlet*. Thus also in the person of Lear, not only a helpless old man, but Paternity and Royalty are outraged; and 'Glamis hath murder'd Sleep'. No woman in Shakespeare is more individual than Isabel: silent yet eloquent, sternly righteous yet capable of infinite forgiveness, a very saint and a very vixen. But, first and last, she 'stands for' mercy.[1] The Duke is first shown to us as a governor perplexed about justice, puzzled in his search for righteousness, seeking above all things to know himself; and he becomes the arbiter of the destinies of everyone in the play. Is it altogether fanciful to remember once again that *Measure for Measure* was acted before the court at Christmas, 1604: that when Isabel at the beginning urges her plea for mercy (which she also makes good at the end) it is on the ground that

> He that might the vantage best have took
> Found out the remedy.

The day before *Measure for Measure* was acted, the finding out of that remedy was being commemorated. All sober criticism must remember the part which the accepted theology played in the thought of Shakespeare's day; that the Feast of the Nativity was — is — the union of Divine Mercy and of Divine Righteousness, and was — is — celebrated in the Christmas psalm:

> Mercy and truth are met together: righteousness and peace have kissed each other.

Shakespeare's audience expected a marriage at the end: and,

[1] This does not make her allegorical, any more than Beowulf is an allegory because, as W. P. Ker says, he 'stands for' valour.

though it may be an accident, the marriage of Isabel and the Duke makes a good ending to a Christmas play.

But I hear my Japanese student objecting: 'I imagine Lady Duchess can not be other than embarrassed, when she welcome Mr. Angel to marriage meal.'

We have no business to imagine any such thing. The play is over. But, if we must go by imaginations, I will imagine with you. I imagine that, as they moved off the stage two and two, the Duke and Isabel, Claudio and Juliet, Angelo and Mariana, Abhorson and Barnardine bringing up the rear, Isabel broke silence, and said softly to the Duke, 'Give me pardon that I, your vassal, should now beseech that you do intend the Lord Angelo for your swift ambassador to London. England is the place where the poor man will suffer least embarrassment, for in England they are such prudes that they rarely read and more rarely act *Measure for Measure*; although, my Duke' — and here Isabel turns to him with her 'heavenly and yielding'[1] smile — 'although you and I are agreed that, to us, it is the wisest of all Shakespeare's comedies.'

And, to conclude. I have no excuse, save a love of Shakespeare, for trespassing on the specialist field of Shakespeare study. But it was a high adventure to leave Beowulf alone for a while in his contest with Grendel and the Dragon, and to do battle on behalf of pretty Isabel. Further, I have sought to rescue William Shakespeare from his seven years' imprisonment in the pestiferous Cave of Despair, albeit thereby I have had to joust against Sir Arthur and Sir Edmund and the Lady Una Britomartis Ellis-Fermor, backed by all those spells which the Wizard professor of the North, the Prince of the Power of the Air, can weave from his chair amid the mists of high Dunedin. I realize how deeply fixed, by generations of repetition, is the dogma of Shakespeare's disillusioned early Jacobean period, 'in the Depths'. That is my excuse for venturing to repeat the protest, eloquently made in this place three years ago by Professor Sisson, in his discourse on 'The Mythical Sorrows of Shakespeare'.

---

[1] W. W. LAWRENCE, *Shakespeare's Problem Comedies*, p. 107. And may I here, once again, express my indebtedness to that great American scholar.

I submit that *Measure for Measure,* whilst it is akin to the tragedies with which it is contemporary, has also a likeness to those 'Romances' with which Shakespeare crowned his work. It is, indeed, for the continuity of Shakespeare that I am pleading. 'Shakespeare's career is the career of an artist.' Let us study his plays as the works of art which we know them to be, rather than weave baseless conjectures concerning details of a biography which we can never know. No one formula can summarize Shakespeare's life for us. Yet instead of always seeing him as suddenly plunged into the Depths, then raised by some convulsion to the Heights, might we not sometimes think of his career as a continuous progress to the Heights? We can trace the steady advance of Shakespeare's art, from *Henry VI* and *Richard III* to *Othello, Lear,* or *Macbeth*; or from the *Two Gentlemen* to *The Tempest.* We can also trace, I believe, the growth of a faith in the power of goodness, the growth of a belief that even in the valley of the shadow of death souls like Cordelia or Desdemona need fear no evil, that the beauty of such souls is Truth. It may be that Shakespeare felt the shadow closing upon him, when he made Prospero return to his Milan where

> Every third thought shall be my grave.

Yet no one has rightly felt *The Tempest* to be pessimistic or gloomy.

That is all we know, and all we need to know. The real story is so wonderful that we can only mar it by groundless biographical conjectures. Our knowledge 'can only be increased by minute and patient study, by the rejection of surmise about him, and by the constant public playing of his plays, in the Shakespearean manner, by actors who will neither mutilate nor distort what the great mind strove to make just'.[1]

I deprecate attempts to define Shakespeare's theological beliefs or unbeliefs. But from his earliest plays to his latest, he shows a belief in forgiveness as the virtue by which human goodness draws nearest to the divine:

[1] JOHN MASEFIELD, *William Shakespeare*, p. 251.

Who by repentance is not satisfied
Is nor of heaven nor earth, for these are pleased.[1]

And so far from agreeing that when he wrote *Measure for Measure* 'he quite obviously believed in nothing', I submit that it is precisely the depth of his belief in forgiveness which has puzzled, in their judgment of that play, so many of his greatest critics, from Coleridge and Hazlitt and Swinburne, down to the present day. *Measure for Measure* shows 'the drama of strong characters taking up and transforming the fanciful products of an earlier world, the inventions of minds not deeply or especially interested in character'. The great poet (in the words of Aristotle, quoted by W. P. Ker) 'gets over the unreason by the grace and skill of his handling'.[2] Grace and skill have transformed *Promos and Cassandra* into a noble drama on the theme 'Judge not: for with what measure ye mete it shall be measured to you again'. It is that which matters, rather than any surviving traces of the original 'unreason'.

This series of Academy Shakespeare lectures was initiated by the great ambassador of France, Jusserand, who crossed the Atlantic from Washington in 1911 to tell us 'What to expect of Shakespeare'. He gave me (it is twenty-six years ago) the copy of his inaugural lecture now on the table before me. It is inscribed 'To R. W. Chambers, who knows how to fight a good fight.' I have tried to fight a good fight this afternoon. I believe that *Measure for Measure* and *The Tempest* are Shakespeare's greatest plays of forgiveness. It is for forgiveness I would ask, if I have hurt the feelings of any of the great English scholars from whom I have ventured to differ. And I shall receive it, for I know their generosity.

As you from crimes would pardon'd be,
Let your indulgence set me free.

[1] *Two Gentlemen of Verona*, v. iv. 79. [2] *Epic and Romance*, p. 37.

X

RUSKIN (AND OTHERS) ON BYRON[1]

THROUGHOUT that long period during which the reputation of Byron was steadily sinking, Ruskin was his warmest champion.

Such other defenders as Byron had were often defending, not Byron, but his politics. Their championship may in the long run do Byron disservice. For the politics of the early nineteenth century have passed into history, but Byron's poetry is a living thing, by no means to be studied merely from the historical standpoint. Yet to ignore politics altogether is impossible when dealing with the mightiest of English political satirists. Swinburne has some reason when he says 'We find little really living or really praiseworthy work of Byron's which has not in it some direct or indirect touch of political emotion'. The statesmanship of Byron remains a subject on which, in the words of Sir Arthur Quiller-Couch, 'some thought will be usefully expended'.

Now, although Ruskin is attracted by Byron's treatment of state affairs, he is not attracted from the party point of view, but by the things which are independent of party and of time. He sees in the verse which Bryon wrote on political matters humanity, sincerity, courage, and, above all, poetry. Thus Ruskin was not only one of a small minority of defenders of Byron, but his defence was very unlike that of some of his most eminent comrades in that minority.

At the time of Byron's death, most people, however unwillingly, believed in his power. The young Carlyle wrote that 'the noblest spirit in Europe' had sunk. Only nine years later Carlyle was thundering 'Close thy Byron: open thy Goethe'. But people were still reading their Byron, as this command shows. Another ten years, and Thackeray attacks Byron, but he admits that in doing so he is 'denying the public gods'. In the

---

[1] For some very helpful criticisms I have to thank Sir Herbert Grierson, who was in the chair when this paper was read to the Edinburgh Branch of the English Association (4 Dec., 1925), and Professor George Gordon, who has been good enough to look through the proof-sheets.

course of a journey from Cornhill to Cairo, Michael Angelo Titmarsh arrives at Athens. The ancient glories of Athens do not kindle him, and he has a contempt for the poor modern kingdom. He cannot tolerate Byron's eye for exotic beauty:

> Lord Byron wrote more cant of this sort than any poet I know of. Think of 'the peasant girls with dark blue eyes' of the Rhine — the brown-faced, flat-nosed, thick-lipped, dirty wenches! Think of 'filling high a cup of Samian wine'; small beer is nectar compared to it, and Byron himself always drank gin. That man never wrote from his heart. He got up rapture and enthusiasm with an eye to the public ... The Great Public admires Greece and Byron ... Well, woe be to the man who denies the public gods!

This was written in 1845. We may perhaps reckon the middle of the century as the date when the tide turned: for already in 1853 Charles Kingsley, when he defends Byron, feels that the public is against him. That does not deter the spirited and chivalrous Kingsley from wielding his bludgeon with all the reckless violence of a just man fighting a losing battle:

> What has put Byron out of favour with the public of late, is not his faults, but his excellences. His artistic good taste, his classical polish, his sound shrewd sense, his hatred of cant, his insight into humbug, above all, his shallow, pitiable habit of being always intelligible: these are the sins which condemn him in the eyes of a mesmerizing, table-turning, spirit-rapping, Spiritualizing, Romanizing generation.[1] ...

Even Ruskin, in the same year (1853) showed a (quite temporary) irritation with the hero of his boyhood.[2]

So, by the fourth quarter of the Nineteenth Century, Byron's reputation had sunk to its lowest. Those, like Browning or Swinburne, who began by praising, ended by denouncing. Matthew Arnold's great defence of 1881 made many damaging concessions, but nevertheless it raised violent opposition, and gave rise to what has been described as a 'pogrom' against Byron.

[1] 'Thoughts on Shelley and Byron', in *Fraser's Magazine*, Nov., 1853.
[2] *Lectures on Architecture, Works*, xii, 55.

Arnold's advocacy seemed to Ruskin so lukewarm that he was driven to protest against his 'mangled misrepresentation'. And, indeed, mid-Victorian propriety seems to have prevented both Matthew Arnold and John Morley from doing justice to Byron's greatest things. Arnold's selection from Byron's works, a selection running to nearly three hundred pages, omits the meeting of Michael and Satan before the gate of Heaven. Arnold seems to find the *Vision of Judgment* too blasphemous to be quoted, save for a few stanzas attacking the government of George III — always a safe subject. Morley, we shall find, ignores the *Vision of Judgment* and *Don Juan*, save for a passing allusion to their 'wit'; although it is particularly as 'the poet of the Revolution' that he is considering Byron.

Now Ruskin is concerned with Byron as a poet and thinker, not with Byron as the representative of any particular section of political thought.

In fact, the difference in 'political doctrine' between Byron and Ruskin is very marked. Byron is one of the earliest of English 'Liberals': indeed, the first example of 'Liberal' in the political sense which we find in the *Oxford Dictionary* is 'The Liberal, Verse and Prose from the South.[1] Ruskin, when asked to define his political opinion, wrote, 'I hate all Liberalism as I do Beelzebub'.[2] Or, again, speaking of the absurdity of party politics, Ruskin says:

Consider the ridiculousness of the division of parties into 'Liberal' and 'Conservative'. There is no opposition whatever between these two kinds of men. There is opposition between Liberals and Illiberals; that is to say, between people who desire liberty, and who dislike it. I am a violent Illiberal; but it does not follow that I must be a Conservative. A Conservative is a person who wishes to keep things as they are; and he is opposed to a Destructive, who wishes to destroy them, or to an Innovator, who wishes to alter them. Now, though I am an Illiberal, there are many things I should like to destroy. I should like to destroy most of the railroads in England, and all the railroads in Wales. I should like to

---

[1] Although the terms 'Liberal' and 'Tory' were not at this date regarded as mutually exclusive.

[2] *Works,* xxxiv, p. 549.

destroy and rebuild the Houses of Parliament, the National Gallery, and the East end of London; and to destroy, without rebuilding, the new town of Edinburgh, the north suburb of Geneva, and the city of New York. Thus in many things I am the reverse of Conservative; nay, there are some long-established things which I hope to see changed before I die; but I want still to keep the fields of England green, and her cheeks red; and that girls should be taught to curtsey, and boys to take their hats off, when a Professor or otherwise dignified person passes by; and that Kings should keep their crowns on their heads, and Bishops their croziers in their hands; and should duly recognize the significance of the crown, and the use of the crook.

As you would find it thus impossible to class me justly in either party, so you would find it impossible to class any person whatever, who has clear and developed political opinions, and who could define them accurately.[1]

Yet it was natural that Byron's defenders should so largely have spoken from the party platform. For, till Byron's day, there had been a conspiracy among great English writers to ensure that the Whig dogs did not have the best of it. The Whigs had been satirized by Dryden; they had been denounced by Johnson ('Dear Bathurst', said Johnson, 'was a man to my very heart's content: he hated a fool, and he hated a rogue, and he hated a Whig: he was a very good hater'). The circle of Pope was hostile. Swift and Burke, beginning as Whigs, lived to carry havoc into the camp of their friends. Addison's wish to be fair led him to spend all his powers on Sir Roger, so that the greatest Whig writer of the Eighteenth Century is remembered for having drawn the most noble picture of the Tory country gentleman. This is as it should be: for the Whigs prided themselves on being more broad-minded than their adversaries: 'Tories own no argument but force', whilst 'Whigs allow no force but argument'. But from the party point of view it was bad business. The French Revolution seemed for the moment to redress matters; but very soon Coleridge, Southey, and Wordsworth were being reviled as 'renegades'. Byron was the first to stand firm. Apostasy, he says, is fashion-

[1] xxvii, p. 14.

able, but 'I still retain my "buff and blue".' (Buff and blue were the colours of the Whig Club of Charles James Fox — the tradition is retained[1] in the buff and blue of the *Edinburgh Review*.) Then, after Byron, we have the Whig tradition in English literature, eminent from many points of view, but especially in the field of History, both Political and Literary. Mid-Victorian Whigs and Liberals would have been the most ungrateful of men if they had not been prepared to defend Byron.

But Mid-Victorian Liberalism was nothing if not proper: and Byron was nothing if not shocking. It was a difficult problem.

John Morley's *Essay* is the best example of the official 'progressive' defence of Byron. The defence begins by heralding Byron as 'the poet of the Revolution': he is a shining exception to that profound antipathy to ideas usual in England, and above all to that 'hostility to generous aspirations' which characterizes the English aristocracy. So long as we can discourse of 'progress' and 'friends of progress', all is well: when we come to Byron, and above all to Byron's poetry, John Morley's troubles begin; and after about forty pages the horrid truth comes out — Byron wrote *Don Juan*. Still, his case is not hopeless; Byron also wrote highly regular dramas; there is *Marino Faliero, Doge of Venice*, from which some fine blank verse passages can be instanced on 'freedom', and even passages showing that Byron 'was not dead to the beauty of domestic sentiment' and that he (sometimes) 'appreciated the conditions of the family':

> The united tenderness and dignity of Faliero's words to Angiolina, before he goes to the meeting of the conspirators, would, if there were nothing else, be enough to show how rightly in his better moods the poet appreciated the conditions of the family. Unfortunately the better moods were not fixed, and we had *Don Juan*, where the wit and colour and power served to make an anti-social and licentious sentiment attractive to puny creatures, who were thankful to have their

[1] Written in 1925. In 1938 these once familiar colours have become a mere memory of the older generation.

lasciviousness so gaily adorned. As for Great Britain, she deserved *Don Juan*. A nation, whose disrespect for all ideas and aspirations that cannot be supported by a text, nor circulated by a religious tract society, was systematic, and where consequently the understanding was least protected against sensual sophisms, received no more than a just chastisement in 'the literature of Satan'. Here again, in the licence of this literature, we see the finger of the Revolution, and of that egoism which makes the passions of the individual his own law. Let us condemn and pass on, homily undelivered.[1]

And so, after further quotation from *Marino Faliero*, Morley closes his case for Byron. He urges, very truly, that Byron glorified freedom in tones that stirred the hearts of men. But he takes care to draw his examples from *Childe Harold*, not *Don Juan*.

You see the essence of the defence: it consists in an attack on the Great Britain of Byron's age. Byron's greatest poetry is ignored or repudiated: the *Vision of Judgment* ignored except for one passing allusion to its 'wit'; *Don Juan* deliberately rejected: 'condemn and pass on': terribly shocking — but the Great Britain of Byron's day deserved it.

Other apologists have followed the same line. They represent the first thirty years of the nineteenth century as an age of black reaction and shameless apostasy, with a Tory government always in power; so that, against such a background, the figures of Byron and Shelley become, if not snow-white, at any rate only a rather pale grey. The advocates of Byron or the advocates of Shelley contrast their heroes with 'Southey the renegade'; with Coleridge 'wrecked in a mist of opium'[2] (a more stimulating variant is 'tottering through opium to Highgate'[3]). Even Wordsworth does not escape:

> Just for a handful of silver he left us,
> Just for a riband to stick in his coat.

[1] JOHN MORLEY, *Byron*, in *Critical Miscellanies*, p. 166.
[2] Matthew Arnold.
[3] Sir Arthur Quiller-Couch.

And so the 'friends of progress' retreat in good order, carrying off Byron and Shelley under cover of this fire directed upon the politics of the contemporaries of their heroes. (Much of the ammunition is drawn, by the way, from that *Don Juan* which John Morley insists upon our condemning.) Unfortunately, at this moment the advocates of Shelley open an attack upon the 'lecherous', 'selfish' 'cad', Byron, whilst Byron's bodyguard retaliate upon the 'ineffectual', 'unsubstantial' Shelley. And so that noble company of early nineteenth-century poets is treated like the family of a deceased Turkish sultan. All but one of the royal children must be strangled with the bowstring, in order that the undisputed succession of the Commander of the Faithful may be assured.

Professor Chew, in his recent survey of what has been written upon Byron — a book to which every student of Byron is indebted — speaks of Morley's *Essay* as 'the finest study of Byron that has ever been written'. And indeed, the attack upon the age of George III and George IV has continued to be popular to the present time. Mrs. Campbell in her study of Shelley writes:

> And that Lamb should have been a drunkard, Coleridge an opium-eater, and Byron a libertine; that Wordsworth should have got so completely wearied out so early, and Keats have been so tremulous and hypersensitive that he at least laid himself open to the attacks of a mortal malady — all such things are symptoms of the age.

Mrs. Campbell has summed up this view in one phrase, when she speaks of Shelley withdrawing from England, after having 'tried in vain to cleanse the Georgian stables'. One of the liveliest examples of this offensive-defensive on behalf of Shelley and Byron is that of Sir Arthur Quiller-Couch, inaugurating the annual Byron Lectureship at Nottingham:

> I will ask you to consider this one point upon which some thought will be usefully expended, whether you apply it to the Europe of to-day, again staggering — blinded, almost broken — out of a stupendous war upon human liberty, or prefer to narrow it backwards down and upon an academic

theme, 'The Romantic Revival in English Poetry'. If, and
while, you so narrow it, I yet beg you to reflect that, of its
pioneers, Coleridge tottered through opium to Highgate;
Wordsworth, after a few glorious years, settled to live
comfortably beside the cataracts of the Lake Country that
had haunted him like a passion — and ended with Ecclesiastical Sonnets and Sonnets in Defence of Capital Punishment;
Southey, the Pantisocrat, turned renegade and kept in long
domesticity *his* home fires burning with duplicate proofs of
articles betraying his old faith. But, of the ensuing rank of
rebels, the great ones — Shelley, Keats, Landor, Byron —
for various reasons found England no place for them,
departed into exile, and in exile died. Let us weigh their
names to-day against those of Frere, Castlereagh, Gifford,
Lockhart, ask which were — after all and on the whole — in
the right, and beware how *we* persecute for opinion.[1]

Now, should respect for Byron or Shelley involve our
thinking of Coleridge and Southey, under the Castlereagh
administration, as an 'opium-eater' and a 'renegade', under
the administration of a 'jackal'?

To the question which side was right, I would suggest the
answer: 'At bottom, both: "It is not impossible that Truth
may have more shapes than one." ' Take the quarrel in its
most extreme form: Byron and Shelley as against Castlereagh.
In the autumn of 1818, Shelley was dreaming of the brotherhood of man, and beginning *Prometheus*; Byron, crusading
against tyranny and war, was writing the *Dedication* to *Don Juan*,
denouncing Castlereagh 'the tool', 'a bungler even in its dis-
gusting trade'; and all the time, on the shores of Erie and
Ontario, the war-ships were being broken up, because Castlereagh and Monroe had laid peace on the Great Lakes which
separate Canada from the United States, after negotiations
among the most potent for good in all history.[2]

It may be doubted whether we are helped to a correct
understanding either of Byron or of the England of Byron's
day, by the dictum of John Morley, that 'it is one of the

[1] *Studies in Literature, Second Series*, p. 18.
[2] See J. M. CALLAHAN, *Neutrality of the American Lakes*, 1898, *Johns Hopkins
Studies*, Series 16, 1-4.

singular facts in the history of literature' that Byron, the poet of the Revolution should have been born in England, and an English aristocrat. The English aristocracy of Byron's day included a good many liberal Whigs and liberal Tories. It may be objected that the principles of these liberal patricians were not of the purest democratic type. But, for the matter of that, neither were those of Byron himself. It was Byron who, in 1821, spoke of democracy as the worst of all forms of government: 'for what is (in fact) democracy? an Aristocracy of Blackguards'.[1] And, anyway, Byron did not depart into exile, and in exile die, because he was persecuted for opinion. Byron had too much courage to have found that England was no place for him, merely because his politics were not those of the majority. Those who suggest that Byron allowed himself to be driven from England because his politics were Whig, are, however unconsciously, reflecting on Byron's manhood, and on the common sense of the England of his age. England was ruled by an aristocracy far too 'broad and strongly based' to have made a practice of persecuting its own members merely for eccentricities of opinion.

Let us look at the facts.

Byron's maiden speech in the House of Lords was directed against a cruel law which made the wrecking of machinery a capital crime. To realize the position, we must keep in mind the ferocity of the penal code which the Nineteenth Century had inherited from the Eighteenth, and that a nation fighting a desperate war naturally tends rather to increase than to relax the severity of its discipline. All the more admirable therefore is Byron's opposition, in a noble speech. 'What we call "a mob",' he says, 'often speaks the sentiments of the people':

> A mob may be better reduced to reason by a mixture of conciliation and firmness than by additional irritation and redoubled penalties. Are we aware of our obligations to a mob? It is the mob that labour in your fields and serve in your houses — that man your navy and recruit your army — that have enabled you to defy all the world. . . .[2]

[1] *Letters and Journals*, v, pp. 405-6.   [2] Ibid., ii, p. 428.

The speech received the welcome it deserved. Byron writes a week later, telling of the compliments paid to him in the course of the debate, and continuing:

> I have had many marvellous eulogies repeated to me since, in person and by proxy, from divers persons *ministerial* — yea *ministerial*! — as well as oppositionists; of them I shall only mention Sir F. Burdett. *He* says it is the best speech by a *lord* since the '*Lord* knows when', probably from a fellow-feeling in the sentiments. Lord H[olland] tells me I shall beat them all if I persevere; and Lord G[renville] remarked that the construction of some of my periods are very like *Burke's*!! And so much for vanity. I spoke very violent sentences with a sort of modest impudence, abused everything and everybody, and put the Lord Chancellor very much out of humour: and if I may believe what I hear, have not lost any character by the experiment.[1]

Two days after this speech, *Childe Harold* appeared, with marked defiance of public opinion. It was a time when enthusiasm for our allies in the Peninsula had been stimulated by victory. Yet Byron tells us quite frankly how he loathes the Portuguese; he jeers at Scott's 'worthless lay', in which Beresford's victory at Albuera had been celebrated, and continues:

> Enough of Battle's minions! let them play
> Their game of lives, and barter breath for fame:
> Fame that will scarce reanimate their clay,
> Though thousands fall to deck some single name.
> In sooth 'twere sad to thwart their noble aim
> Who strike, blest hirelings! for their country's good,
> And die, that living might have proved her shame; . . .[2]

Yet this, and much more of the same kind, was addressed to a nation 'convinced' (in Wordsworth's phrase) 'that the cause is the most righteous cause in which, since the opposition of the Greek Republics to the Persian invader at Thermopylae and Marathon, sword ever was drawn!'

I will not stop to ask who was in the right here; though I

---

[1] ii, p. 104.   [2] I, 44.

do not know why those who believe that Napoleon was waging 'a stupendous war upon human liberty' should reserve their sympathy for those who sympathized with Napoleon, and their censure for those who, like Castlereagh, resisted him.

To call men who had fallen for their country 'hirelings', 'that living might have proved her shame', was provocative. Yet Byron was not 'persecuted'. On the contrary, he awoke and found himself famous; *Childe Harold* went through five editions before the year was out; and Byron became the darling of society.

If Byron did not follow up his early successes in the House of Lords, it was not because he was 'persecuted for opinion'; it was, he himself tells us, owing partly to 'dissipation', and partly to 'haughty and reserved opinions'; that is, to a temperament which made him rather a critic of political life than an actor in it. This critical temperament naturally became emphasized when, after his quarrel with Lady Byron and his withdrawal from England, Byron 'simplified his politics into an utter detestation of all existing governments'.

Byron's temperament drove him into opposition. And we may be thankful that this was so; for only in opposition could his powers find full scope.

He is the mightiest of English political satirists: and the gift of political satire is certainly not given to man in order that he may bolster up those in authority, and beat the under dog. A caricaturist ought to be in opposition. It is here that Byron has his great advantage over Dryden. Dryden, by instinct, sought for and respected authority, and, however he may conceal the fact, in *Absalom* and his other satires, Dryden is kicking the fallen. But Byron was born for opposition. So, it is quite consistent that, in his *Hours of Idleness*, he should have celebrated the memory of earlier Byrons who had held Newstead against the victorious party in the Civil Wars. So persistently is he in opposition that, if his enemies had been overthrown and revolutionary governments established in their place, he would soon have been attacking the new governors as vigorously as he had attacked the old. At least, so he says himself: 'I was born for opposition' —

But then 't is mostly on the weaker side;
So that I verily believe if they
Who now are basking in their full-blown pride
Were shaken down, and 'dogs had had their day',
Though at the first I might perchance deride
Their tumble, I should turn the other way
And wax an ultra-royalist in Loyalty,
Because I hate even democratic Royalty.[1]

Byron was, as Scott said, 'a patrician on principle', and 'the pleasure of displaying his wit and satire against individuals in office' had, Scott thought, much to do with his political views. But we cannot all be patrician satirists in opposition. The world's work has got to be done. 'An utter detestation of all existing governments' is a splendid platform for a political caricaturist, but it is not so firm a foundation for the work of His Majesty's Secretary of State for Foreign Affairs. So we must avoid the inference that, because Byron 'was born for opposition', therefore Castlereagh must have been in the wrong. 'Europe was staggering out of a stupendous war upon human liberty.' But surely the essential thing is, that the attack upon human liberty *was* defeated — and this had been due largely to Castlereagh: some historians say 'due to him more than to any other single man'.[2] It had required some courage to win that war: 'Napoleon could lose whole armies with impunity . . . Five thousand British troops beaten and captured would have brought any British Minister's head perilously near to the block.'[3] For there was an Opposition, waiting to take bitter advantage of any slip ministers might make. Six days before Waterloo, Byron writes of the preparation Castlereagh was making to meet the emergency: 'C**h is preparing his head for the pike, on which we shall see it carried before he has done.'[4] And when the news of Waterloo came through, 'After an instant's pause, Lord Byron replied, "I am damned sorry for it"; and then, after another slight

---

[1] *Don Juan*, xv, 23.
[2] WEBSTER, *Foreign Policy of Castlereagh*, 1925, p. 31.
[3] FORTESCUE, *British Statesman of the Great War*, 1911, p. 278.
[4] *Letters and Journals*, iii, p. 205.

pause, he added, "I didn't know but I might live to see Lord Castlereagh's head on a pole. But I suppose I shan't now." [1] After the Peace, Castlereagh worked incessantly for seven years; he defined his object as being 'to bring back the world to peaceful habits'. To him, admittedly, is largely due the fact that France was not dismembered: that the foundations were laid of peace in Europe for a generation, and of permanent peace with America and with France. 'Castlereagh undoubtedly gave up his life to the cause of international peace.' [2] In doing this he had, of course, to cultivate the friendship of many governments which Byron and his friends 'utterly detested'. He was a peacemaker who received from Shelley such beatitude as this:

> Let Fear and Disquiet and Strife
> Spread thy Couch in the chamber of Life!
> Marry Ruin, thou tyrant! and God be thy guide
> To the bed of the bride!

Every word of Shelley's appalling and hideous curse came home. The storm of persistent hatred and persecution, the ever-present possibility of assassination, the pressure of work, and a responsibility for the peace of Europe which, as he said, was 'more than he could bear'; these things did their work upon Castlereagh. As he was about to undertake the fresh responsibility of the conference of Verona, Wellington had to say, 'I am bound to warn you that you cannot be in your right mind'. Castlereagh covered his face with his hands, and said, 'Since you say so, I fear it must be so'. It is one of the tragic scenes of history: ennobled by 'the simple strength and honesty of these two great men'. [3] After some days of sickness, Castlereagh, in a fit of delirium, took his own life. Friends of progress raised a cheer as his body was borne to burial, and Byron gloated over his suicide with a horrible glee in three epigrams which he published in the *Liberal*, and in a fourth, too filthy to be published anywhere.

[1] TICKNOR, *Life*, i, p. 60.
[2] WEBSTER, p. 502.
[3] FORTESCUE, *British Statesmen*, p. 271.

Yes, by all means 'let us beware how we persecute for opinion'. But which was the persecutor, and which the persecuted? And why, after a century, is the memory of Castlereagh still assailed?

Yet Byron was indisputably a humane man, and his relations with Scott show how chivalrous he could be in dealing with men of politics and temper different from his own. Byron and Shelley misunderstood both Castlereagh and Southey. We owe the *Vision of Judgment* to Byron's misunderstanding of Southey, and therefore must say with the tolerant Kent, 'I cannot wish the fault undone, the issue of it being so proper'. But more profit is to be got out of thinking of Byron's friendship with Scott, based as it was upon mutual knowledge, than by giving historic value to his libels upon Castlereagh or Southey. Some of these libels are great literature, and some are not, but they are none of them a sound basis for history. Yet they have been repeated for a century, and are often repeated to-day by historians of literature; who, indeed, go farther. Byron had a deep admiration for the courage of Castlereagh,[1] albeit, as in an Icelandic blood-feud, this genuine admiration was combined with relentless hatred. Defenders of Byron to-day think it necessary to call Castlereagh a 'jackal'.[2]

I am sometimes reminded of the kind-hearted epicure who was worried when a humanitarian explained to him how a goose was made to suffer in the process of preparing *pâté de foie gras*. The epicure had an interview with his cook, and decided never to put the poor goose to this pain again, especially as his cook assured him that he could get an equally good *pâté* by subjecting two ducks to the same treatment. If we must talk about persecution, it is time some attention was paid to the persecution suffered by the Tory duck, as well as by the Liberal goose.

It is not only individuals, but a whole generation of Englishmen, who are wronged by the denunciation of the first thirty years of the nineteenth century as an age of base and mean ideals, rendering England no place for people like Byron or

---

[1] *Letters and Journals*, iv, p. 282.
[2] QUILLER-COUCH, *Studies in Literature, Second Series*, p. 16.

Shelley. Only when we have cleared away these misconceptions can we understand the relations of Ruskin, the child of a middle-class Tory home of this period, to Byron, its dominating figure.

During the war of 1914-18 some people found comfort and support in Wordsworth's *Sonnets dedicated to Liberty*, or the Tract on the *Convention of Cintra*. Seldom has the heroic temper, as found among a people battling for liberty, been better stated. And the temper was widespread, at some moments at least. Listen to Wordsworth, speaking of the expeditionary force departing to the Peninsula, with prayers and blessings 'as widely spread as they were fervent and intense':

> That army had been sent upon a service which appealed so strongly to all that was human in the heart of this nation, that there was scarcely a gallant father of a family who had not his moments of regret that he was not a soldier by profession, which might have made it his duty to accompany it.

Our allies had been generously succoured. Here it is Byron, a grudging and hostile witness, who is speaking:

> When the Portuguese suffered under the retreat of the French, every arm [in Britain] was stretched out, every hand was opened, from the rich man's largess to the widow's mite, all was bestowed, to enable them to rebuild their villages and replenish their granaries.[1]

When the victory was won, it was the privilege of the British leaders to save France from dismemberment and ruin. Of course it was Britain's interest to be generous, but it was something to have statesmen with sufficient breadth and restraint to see this. Typical of this is the story of the excursion which, in 1815, Lord and Lady Castlereagh had arranged for some of the allied magnates in Paris. The ladies grew tired, and one of Castlereagh's young diplomatists was sent to a village in quest of donkeys. He returned defeated. Blücher nodded to an aide-de-camp, and soon three times the requisite number of donkeys appeared, driven by half a dozen Prussian hussars, and followed by the screaming population. Sir Walter Scott, who was one of the party, tells the tale:

[1] *Letters and Journals*, ii, p. 428.

And an angry man was Blucher when Lord Castlereagh condescended to go among them, all smiles, and sent them back with more napoleons than perhaps the fee-simple of the whole stud was worth.

France had been the 'natural enemy' of Britain for centuries: there had been two wars with America in one generation. Castlereagh placed our relations with both countries upon a footing of enduring peace which has lasted to our own day, and of which it is for this generation to make what use it will.

It is pleasant to think that when, this week,[1] the Treaty of Locarno was signed at the Foreign Office, the portrait of Castlereagh was brought from the House of Lords, in order that the picture of the man who gave his life for the cause of peace in 1822 might look down upon the work of the pacificators of 1925.

Such achievements in war and peace are sufficient to entitle a generation to the gratitude of all posterity, had there been nothing else. But, in the midst of all this, England succeeded in carrying through the greatest reform in the history of the world. England abolished her own slave trade, and, since only international action could complete this reform, it became a main object of English foreign policy to persuade other nations to do the same. How many of us realized that, in 1817, Castlereagh persuaded Spain to abolish the slave trade by a bribe of £400,000, and that the Commons footed the bill? This is one of many things we learn from Professor Webster's illuminating volume.

I am not forgetting that, at the very time of the Abolition of Slavery, the Industrial Revolution was preparing new and horrible problems for humanitarians. But our gratitude to the English Abolitionists ought to be all the greater: for what would have been the plight of the world, if the Industrial Revolution had come upon it with the slave trade unchecked; if mines and factories had been manned by imported slave labour, leaving Europe with a colour problem, in addition to all her other troubles? And strangely enough, those who most

[1] This paper was read on 4 Dec., 1925.

bitterly attack the period of the 'Georgian Stables' lavish their abuse upon Southey 'the renegade' — Southey 'betraying his old faith' — Southey 'who abandoned all the causes which he had once enthusiastically supported'. Yet Southey was the first of a little group of Tory humanitarians, who raised a constant protest against the evils of the Industrial Revolution.[1] To this group Wordsworth too belongs: '*Right of a human Creature to be exempt from being considered as a mere Instrument. The condition of multitudes deplored from want of due respect to this truth on the part of their superiors in society. Earnest wish expressed for a System of National Education established universally by Government. Glorious effects of this foretold.*' The value of some of these topics as poetry may be open to dispute, but as a programme for social reform in 1814 they need no defence.

The age was one of steadily growing humanity, as is proved by the mitigation, during the reign of George IV, of the horrors of the earlier Criminal Law. If we are to judge it by its favourite literature, it was the age of the Waverley Novels, and the age which was gradually coming to the conclusion (in spite of Byron's opposition) that Wordsworth was one of the greatest of all English poets. Such an age cannot have been an age of base ideals. As to *Don Juan*, it is rather hard to judge an age by a satire upon it. Nevertheless, let us take *Don Juan*. When Juan's fortunes reach their lowest ebb, and he is exposed for sale in the slave-market of Constantinople, he meets there — his fellow in distress — his first English acquaintance, the soldier of fortune Johnson, with 'an English look' and

With resolution in his dark grey eye,

cool, unconquerable, humorously cheerful, compassionate, reckless concerning his own fate:

---

[1] There were, of course, other protesters. But the importance of Southey is emphasized alike by our own constitutional historian, and by the thoroughgoing German socialist. Compare DICEY, *Law and Opinion in England*, Sec. ed., 1914, pp. 223-5, with MAX BEER, *History of British Socialism*, 1919, vol. i, *passim*. 'Wordsworth, Coleridge, and Southey became, in the course of time, the spiritual leaders of the new conservatism, imbuing it with a sense of social righteousness and love of the people. They are the fathers of the Tory Democracy and Christian social reform' (Beer, i, p. 122).

But seeing at his elbow a mere lad,
　Of a high spirit evidently, though
At present weighed down by a doom which had
　O'erthrown even men, he soon began to show
A kind of blunt compassion for the sad
　Lot of so young a partner in the woe,
Which for himself he seemed to deem no worse
Than any other scrape, a thing of course.

'My boy', said he, 'amidst this motley crew
　Of Georgians, Russians, Nubians, and what not,
All ragamuffins, differing but in hue;
　With whom it is our luck to cast our lot,
The only gentlemen seem I and you;
　So let us be acquainted, as we ought:
If it could yield you any consolation
'T would give me pleasure. — Pray what is your nation?'[1]

And so, when Juan hints his story, he gives him a rough comfort:

'And these are things which ask a tender tear,
　Such as I, too, would shed if in your place:
I cried upon my first wife's dying day,
And also when my second ran away;

'My third' — 'Your third!' quoth Juan, turning round,
　'You scarcely can be thirty: have you three?'
'No — only two at present above ground:
　Surely 'tis nothing wonderful to see
One person thrice in holy wedlock bound!'
　'Well then, your third', said Juan, 'what did she?
She did not run away too — did she, sir?'
'No faith' — 'What then?' 'I ran away from her.'

Johnson may be a bigamist and a wife deserter. But a better
story of a comrade in a tight place[2] was never told. Later
Juan comes to England:

Besides (alas! his taste — forgive and pity!)
At *first* he did not think the women pretty.

---

[1] v, 12, *seq.*

[2] MACNEILE DIXON quotes Professor Santayana's description of the Englishman as 'the ideal comrade in a tight place': *The Englishman*, p. 63.

I say at *first* — for he found out at *last*,
  But by degrees, that they were fairer far
Than the more glowing dames whose lot is cast
  Beneath the influence of the Eastern star.[1]

Let this be the reply to Thackeray's maledictions.
And then there comes the picture of Aurora Raby:

Juan knew nought of such a character
  High, yet resembling not his lost Haidée. . . .

We must not overlook these passages, where the exiled satirist becomes enthusiastic at the thought of his countrymen and country-women. We expect him to curse, and we find him, like Balaam on the top of Peor, 'altogether blessing'.

If we prefer to judge the age from a quieter satirist than Byron — take Jane Austen. The age of Jane Austen can score some points, I submit, when we compare it with the age of Fielding or of Smollett, to say nothing of that of Wycherley and Etheredge. Byron bears witness to the change:

There now are no Squire Westerns as of old,
And our Sophias are not so emphatic.

Instead, we have women like Emma Woodhouse, and efficient, conscientious country gentlemen like Mr. Knightley. When Juan first lands in England, and rolls along the smooth turn-pike road, the face of the country is no less glorious than the character of some of its women turns out to be later:

On! on! through meadows, managed like a garden,
  A paradise of hops and high production.

Mr. Knightley of Donwell Abbey, and his brother John Knightley of Brunswick Square, are types of the country gentleman and man of affairs, to whose ability and industry we owe it that the country had survived the economic struggle with Napoleon.

And mention of Brunswick Square reminds us of another man who lived there, till he moved to Herne Hill — Mr. John James

[1] xii, 68.

Ruskin, engaged upon building up a business in sherry, and with the help of his wife bringing up an only son in the hope that he would end as a bishop, if not an archbishop, of the Established Church. At the age of twelve, discipline was so far relaxed that young Ruskin was allowed to drink wine, taken to the theatre, and began to have dinner with his father and mother: at dessert his father would read some favourite book, 'at last, the shipwreck in *Don Juan* — of which, finding me rightly appreciative, my father went on with nearly all the rest. I recollect that he and my mother looked across the table at each other with something of alarm, when, on asking me, a few *festas* afterwards, what we should have for after-dinner reading, I instantly answered "Juan and Haidée". My selection was not adopted. . . . But by the end of . . . 1834 [when Ruskin was fifteen] I knew my Byron pretty well all through.'[1]

So among the 'puny creatures, who', if we are to believe John Morley, 'were thankful to have their lasciviousness so gaily adorned', we must number Mr. and Mrs. John James Ruskin and their boy of twelve.

The pious Tory household of 1830 'deserved its *Don Juan*', I think, better than the enlightened Liberal of 1870. At any rate the Ruskins knew better how to use *Don Juan*. That Byron should be such a favourite in the Ruskin family is a curious commentary upon that connexion between Byron and Evangelicalism which Professor Grierson has emphasized. One of the many points of sympathy between Ruskin and Byron lies in the intimate knowledge of the Old Testament which each possessed. They had both been through and through[2] it before they were eight years old: and that left its permanent mark, in spite of all later changes.

Anyway, Ruskin was brought up on the Bible and Byron, and 'my mother', he says, 'was no more afraid of my turning out a corsair or a Giaour than a — Solomon'.

I am not pretending that Byron was the favourite reading of every strict Evangelical about 1830; on the contrary, Ruskin

---

[1] xxxv, p. 142.
[2] Byron says 'through and through' (*Letters and Journals*, v, p. 391). Ruskin's mother took him 'at least six times straight through the Bible', *Praeterita*, p. 164.

soon had the powerful stimulus of opposition to confirm him
in his love of Byron. Ruskin was sent to be taught by the Rev.
Thomas Dale (afterwards Dean Dale). I have the strongest
reasons for not speaking disrespectfully of the Rev. Thomas
Dale, for he was the first Professor of English in University
College, London (and indeed in England). Having warned his
students not to read Byron, the professor seems then to have
set them to write an essay. The essay which Ruskin wrote for
him on *Fiction* is still extant. I have never met with a better
instance of the undergraduate pulling his professor's leg: or if
I have, it has been wasted upon me. But this is not the place
to give an account of it.[1]

When a boy, Ruskin had resolved that Byron should be his
master in verse; and Byron *is* his master, though not in verse.
Byron's *Don Juan* and Ruskin's *Fors Clavigera* are alike in this:
they are periodic addresses to the nation on whatever topic
the spirit might dictate: addresses to a nation quite unconvinced and largely hostile — manifestoes like those of the
Hebrew prophets. The position of prophet is a trying one,
but Ruskin finds comfort in the woes of his predecessor. In
1870 John Morley had written that 'for no Englishman now
does Byron hold the highest place' — the place of 'the author
to whom we turn at all moments for inspiration and encouragement'. Now this is precisely the place which Byron does
occupy for Ruskin, and more emphatically than ever in the
year 1880, when he wrote *Fiction, Fair and Foul*.

For fully twenty years Ruskin had been moved by that
'volcanic instinct of justice' which he recognized as the motive
power of himself, of Byron, and of very few others: 'conviction
that about ninety-nine hundredths of whatever at present is,
is wrong, conviction making us ... declarers of political
doctrine monstrous to the ears of mercenary mankind'. Ruskin
had published *Unto this Last* in the *Cornhill*, and was condemned
as 'a babbler, a fanatic, and a heretic', till Thackeray, the
editor, had to tell him that his articles were so unanimously
condemned and disliked that he could only admit one more.[2]
Froude had given him another chance in *Fraser's Magazine*,

---

[1] See below, p. 347, etc. [2] COLLINGWOOD, p. 156.

where *Munera Pulveris* appeared. Again universal condemnation of his 'hopeless rubbish', and when the fourth number appeared Ruskin had been again gagged: even his father had disapproved. Again and again Ruskin had preached to an unheeding generation. Then he began the periodical publication of that colossal protest, *Fors Clavigera*: kept it up unaided for seven years, till he broke down under the strain in 1878: steadied himself, and continued his war with the world in 1880. All this had been done in the midst of private and personal griefs, till his 'conclusive' sorrow brought, as Carlyle noted, 'thick quiet despair on the personal question' which made him determined 'to go ahead all the more with fire and sword on the universal one'.[1]

And so, in 1880, Ruskin turns for encouragement to Byron, admiring the way Byron stands up in the face of a 'mercenary mankind', and refuses to be cowed, browbeaten, or silenced; refuses to despair either of himself or of the republic. It is this which makes *Don Juan* one of the heroic things in English literature, ranking with the *Battle of Maldon* or *Samson Agonistes*. Byron was thinking of himself when at the outset he described how poor Don José was brought low by his own frailties, and by a wife addicted to mathematics:

> Whate'er might be his worthlessness or worth,
>   Poor fellow! he had many things to wound him.
> Let's own — since it can do no good on earth —
>   It was a trying moment that which found him
> Standing alone beside his desolate hearth,
>   Where all his household gods lay shivered round him:
> No choice was left his feelings or his pride,
> Save Death or Doctors' Commons — so he died.[2]

Byron had stood with his household gods shivered, with 'deliberate desolation piled upon him', overwhelmed with remorse, and with the whole nation-crying shame. But he did not die. He faced his enemies like this:

[1] *New Letters*, 1904, ii, p. 293.
[2] i, 36.

Dogs, or men! for I flatter you in saying
   That ye are dogs — your betters far — ye may
Read, or read not, what I am now essaying
   To show ye what ye are in every way.
As little as the moon stops for the baying
   Of wolves, will the bright Muse withdraw one ray
From out her skies — then howl your idle wrath!
While still she silvers o'er your gloomy path.[1]

Or again:

For I will teach, if possible, the stones
To rise against Earth's tyrants.[2]

Or again:

And I will war, at least in words (and — should
   My chance so happen — deeds), with all who war
With Thought; — and of Thought's foes by far most rude,
   Tyrants and sycophants have been and are.
I know not who may conquer: if I could
   Have such a prescience, it should be no bar
To this my plain, sworn, downright detestation
Of every despotism in every nation.[3]

Secondly, Ruskin is attracted to Byron by his conviction of
his sincerity, 'that he confessed — in some sort even proclaimed
defiantly — the naughtiness of his life':

The first thing you have got to do, in reading Byron to
purpose, is to remember his motto, 'Trust Byron'. You
always may; and the more, that he takes some little pleasure
at first in offending you. But all he says is true, nevertheless,
though what worst of himself there is to tell, he insists upon
at once; and what good there may be, mostly leaves you to
find out. To the end of his life, he had a schoolboy's love of
getting into mischief: and a general instinct for never doing
anything he was bid; which extends up even as far as the
commandments themselves. But he never either recom-
mends you to break them, or equivocates in the smallest
degree to himself about what they *are*.[4]

[1] vii, 7.   [2] viii, 135.   [3] ix, 24.
[4] *Works*, xxxiv, p. 361. See also xxxvi, p. 574.

The third, and the greatest, tie between Byron and Ruskin lay in their humanity. Both men could be cruel when their passions were roused, but few have had such a hatred of the infliction of pain.[1]

Scott, Byron, and Ruskin are the three greatest dog-lovers of English literature. Hence their sympathy. For it is easier for a camel to go through the eye of a needle than for one dog-lover to believe that another dog-lover could ever do anything very wrong. Every one knows the story of Byron's dogs, particularly of Boatswain, whose epitaph declares him to possess 'all the virtues of man without his vices'. Before Byron went abroad he arranged that he, his dog, and his old servant Joe Murray should rest in the same tomb. 'If I was sure his lordship would come here, I should like it well enough', said old Joe (perhaps fearing the rival claims of Westminster Abbey), 'but I should not like to be alone with the dog.' 'If Byron were only in Venice now', wrote Ruskin in 1869, 'I think we should have got on with each other.'[2] Of course they would: they would have told each other dog stories, and Ruskin would have carried off Byron to the Scuola degli Schiavoni to inspect Carpaccio's picture of St. Jerome's dog 'watching his master translating the Bible, with highest complacency of approval',[3] 'though not, of course, understanding the full import of his master's literary work'.[4]

This sympathy between Ruskin and Byron makes Ruskin find in Byron what has been so often denied him (as e.g. by John Morley), the power of hitting upon the 'chance epithet of telling felicity', or 'the phrase that opens to us hidden lights'. Here is Ruskin's praise of a passage from a fine poem which has not many admirers, *The Island*:

Some very wicked people — mutineers, in fact — have retired, misanthropically, into an unfrequented part of the country, and there find themselves safe indeed, but extremely thirsty. Whereupon Byron thus gives them to drink:

---

[1] In 1822 the first act against cruelty to animals was passed. In his humanity, as in other things, Byron belongs to his age.
[2] xxxvi, p. 574.   [3] xxiv, p. 230.   [4] xxix, p. 36.

A little stream came tumbling from the height
And straggling into ocean as it might.
Its bounding crystal frolicked in the ray
And gushed from cliff to crag with saltless spray,
Close on the wild wide ocean, — yet as pure
And fresh as Innocence; and more secure.
Its silver torrent glittered o'er the deep
As the shy chamois' eye o'erlooks the steep,
While, far below, the vast and sullen swell
Of Ocean's Alpine azure rose and fell.

Now, I beg, with such authority as an old workman may take concerning his trade ... to assure the reader that here *is* entirely first-rate literary work. Though Lucifer himself had written it, the thing is itself good, and not only so, but unsurpassably good, the closing line being probably the best concerning the sea yet written by the race of the sea-kings. I tell you this, mind you, in my old name and faculty of 'author of *Modern Painters*' — having looked at a waterfall or two in my time, and not unfrequently at a wave, and got some things fairly well said, though I say it, concerning both; and on such standing, or reclination, do farther certify you that neither I in my weakness, nor Byron in his might, could either of us have said one right word of these lovely and mighty things, but that we both of us had in our hearts reverence for the laws of God, and pity for the creatures of earth.[1]

How far Byron 'had in his heart reverence for the laws of God', we will not discuss: that he had 'pity for the creatures of earth' is beyond dispute.

This humanity made both Ruskin and Byron resent what seemed like intentional cruelty towards themselves. But Byron was protected by his sense of humour:

But I, the mildest, meekest of mankind
  Like Moses, or Melancthon, who have ne'er
Done anything exceedingly unkind, —
  And (though I could not now and then forbear
Following the bent of body or of mind)
  Have always had a tendency to spare, —

[1] xxxiv, p. 333.

Why do they call me Misanthrope? Because
They hate me, not I them: — and here we'll pause. [1]

Youth and reckless humour carried Byron on; but Ruskin, an
older man, broke down under the strain of prophesying to an
unconvinced generation. Another illness interrupted his study
of Byron, and it remains a fragment.

So we may fall back upon his schoolboy Essay, with its
declaration that Byron 'in the vastness of their epic imaginations' is surpassed by Milton and Homer alone. In writing
this sentence, Ruskin was no doubt thinking primarily of
annoying the Rev. Dr. Dale. He may have been thinking
of the great meeting of Michael and Satan before the gate of
Heaven; that episode which Matthew Arnold did not venture
to include in his Selections from Byron.

It was upon this passage that Ruskin in 1880 proposed to
dilate ('to examine what facts lie at the root of Byron's imagination of that contest between the powers of good and evil').
That promise he was never to carry out. But we can see how
the humanity and the heroism of it attracted him — the
humanity which is essential to the greatest thing in heroic
story, whether in an Icelandic Saga or in Homer:

> Priam, son of Dardanus, wondered at Achilles, how great he
> was and how goodly: for he was like unto the gods. And
> Achilles marvelled at Priam, son of Dardanus, beholding his
> noble bearing, and hearing his speech.

It may even be said that Byron succeeds where Milton fails,
For whatever sympathy Milton may cause us to have for Satan.
he will allow no such weakness to his archangels. Accordingly,
when Satan is brought face to face with Gabriel, Gabriel taunts
him with his loss of Heaven, with the folly which has overthrown him, and finally calls him a liar.

> Gabriel . . .
> Disdainfully, half smiling, thus replied:
> O loss of one in Heaven to judge of wise
> Since Satan fell, whom folly overthrew. . . .

[1] ix, 21.

Byron knew his Bible better, perhaps, than Milton. Anyway he knew that archangels do not behave like that: for 'Michael the archangel, when, contending with the Devil, he disputed about the body of Moses, durst not bring against him a railing accusation'. But Byron's Michael shows much more than mere self-control, when, not the body of Moses, but the soul of George III, is in dispute. The angelic caravan has brought the old man with an old soul, both extremely blind, to the gate of Heaven, and seated him on a cloud:

> But bringing up the rear of this bright host
>   A Spirit of a different aspect waved
> His wings, like thunder-clouds above some coast
>   Whose barren beach with frequent wrecks is paved;
> His brow was like the deep when tempest-tossed;
>   Fierce and unfathomable thoughts engraved
> Eternal wrath on his immortal face,
> And *where* he gazed a bloom pervaded space.
>
> As he drew near, he gazed upon the gate
>   Ne'er to be entered more by him or Sin,
> With such a glance of supernatural hate,
>   As made Saint Peter wish himself within;

Then the gate flies asunder:

> And from the gate thrown open issued beaming
>   A beautiful and mighty thing of Light,
> Radiant with glory, like a banner streaming
>   Victorious from some world-o'erthrowing fight: . . .
>
> The Cherubs and the Saints bowed down before
>   That arch-angelic Hierarch, the first
> Of Essences angelical who wore
>   The aspect of a god; but this ne'er nursed
> Pride in his heavenly bosom, in whose core
>   No thought, save for his Maker's service, durst
> Intrude, however glorified and high;
> He knew him but the Viceroy of the sky.

He and the sombre, silent Spirit met —
   They knew each other both for good and ill;
Such was their power, that neither could forget
   His formal friend and future foe; but still
There was a high, immortal, proud regret
   In either's eye, as if 'twere less their will
Than destiny to make the eternal years
Their date of war, and their 'Champ Clos' the spheres. . . .

The spirits were in neutral space, before
   The gate of Heaven; like eastern thresholds is
The place where Death's grand cause is argued o'er,
   And souls dispatched to that world or to this;
And therefore Michael and the other wore
   A civil aspect: though they did not kiss,
Yet still between his Darkness and his Brightness
There passed a mutual glance of great politeness.

There are those who tell us that the twenty-fourth book of the *Iliad* was added by a later poet, who could not leave the story with Achilles and Priam unreconciled. To supplement Milton by depicting the courtesies of Michael and Satan was an adventure hardly less high than to bring Achilles and Priam face to face. We can see why the boy Ruskin classed together Homer, Milton, and Byron, and how, throughout life, he was attracted by the humanity which made Michael bow to Satan 'not too low, but kindly'.

For indeed the age of Scott and Byron was an age of very noble humanity. A great historian has drawn our attention to the fact that the actual Helen Walker, the prototype of the imaginary Jeanie Deans, after having obtained the pardon for her sister, had to struggle back to Scotland on foot, and only just arrived in time to save her sister's life. It was impossible for Scott to tell the story so. That is some measure of the difference between the humanity of 1736 and of 1818. This humanity is the more noteworthy because fate had concentrated upon the age of Wordsworth, Scott, Byron, and Shelley two blows, more than usually demoralizing. It was bad enough that the high hopes of the French Revolution should have been frustrated. Wordsworth (and in great measure also the ordinary Englishman) 'believed that a benignant spirit was abroad; and the September massacres were the comment of destiny on that belief. He expected to see the power of the one or few abolished; and Napoleon arose to mock his expectations.'[1] When the clash resulting from the French Revolution had to be met at the same time as that resulting from the Agricultural and Industrial Revolution, brave men might well have quailed. To Bacon *philanthropia* had been a very simple thing: if learning could but be advanced, and inventions multiplied, the relief of man's estate must follow. That great philanthropist, Jonathan Swift, saw more clearly. He saw that, if men learned to fly, they would use that knowledge to throw things from the clouds upon their fellow men; and the King of Brobdingnag knows where to place a science which teaches impotent and grovelling mankind how to blow each other to the skies. Still, that magnanimous monarch has no doubts as to agricultural improvements: the man who can make two ears of corn, or two blades of grass, grow upon a spot where only one grew before — he is the true benefactor. In that faith the gentry of England had gone ahead. But by 1830 they were beginning to find that though two ears of corn were growing where one had grown before, and a hundred cotton shirts being made where one had been made before, it was not clear that men were either better fed or better clothed. Would-be benefactors of mankind had some excuse, if they grew peevish; even if at times they attacked each other, as Oliver in his mortal swoon struck Roland at Roncesvalles:

> li oil li sunt trublet
> Ne loinz ne pres ne poet vedeir si cler
> Que reconoisse nisun hume mortel.

When Macaulay, in 1830, made his attack on Southey, because Southey had attacked the way in which the Industrial Revolution was being conducted, both were good men, honestly seeking the welfare of the whole nation.

A very real humanity marks all the great writers, and many

[1] RALEIGH, *Wordsworth*, p. 53.

at least of the great statesmen of the time. It marks Shelley with his passion for reforming mankind, and Wordsworth, alike in the more easy hopes of his youth, and in his later and humbler mood 'that was to seek comfort for itself from the old man on the moor'. It marks Keats, rejoicing over the dancing-class in Cumberland: 'There was as fine a row of boys and girls as you ever saw. I never felt so near the glory of Patriotism, the glory of making by any means a country happier. This is what I like better than scenery.' We see it in Byron, taking advantage of his independence to hazard everything for the sake of Greece; and not less in Castlereagh, sorrowfully admitting that he dare not 'endanger the fate of the present generation', and, for the sake of Greece, risk another European war. We see it in the magnificent charity of Scott, friend alike of Castlereagh and of Byron — Scott whom the very pig ran after with squeals of embarrassing affection.[1] We see it in Charles Lamb, defending his friend Leigh Hunt to his friend Southey, and we see it in the correspondence which followed between Lamb and Southey, a model for all time to those who become involved in controversy with their friends. We see this humanity in Sir Ralph Abercromby, anxious, as he was carried dying off the field, lest the soldier's blanket placed under his head should not get back to its rightful owner; or in the British army of the Peninsula, so trained by Wellington, that when at last it entered France, it caused a sensation among the French peasantry (which has lasted for three generations)[2] by paying double for the cattle taken. And once again we see it in Keats, 'so tremulous and hypersensitive' (as Mrs. Campbell has it) that finding a big butcher ill-treating a kitten, he fought him (scientifically) for nearly an hour till the butcher had to be assisted home.

It was in this age that England saved herself by her exertions, and Europe by her example. England has helped Europe by her exertions often, but we have to go back to the age of Bede

---

[1] LOCKHART, 1837, v, 9.
[2] See TREVELYAN, *British History in the Nineteenth Century*, pp. 99, 126. The French (Sir Walter Scott wrote from Paris on 6 Sept., 1815) 'submit with sad civility to the extortions of the Prussians and the Russians, and avenge themselves at the expense of the English, whom they charge three prices for everything, because they are the only people who pay at all'. LOCKHART, 1837, III, 365.

and Boniface to find a time when the example of England had been so useful to Europe. A parallel between Byron and the Venerable Bede might be pressed too far: but there are two points of resemblance. If we except Shakespeare, then of writers born in England, Byron seems most likely to rival Bede in the length of time during which his influence abroad will last. And, in the case alike of Bede and of Byron, the writer owed much of his influence to the fact that the Englishmen of his age were good Europeans, and had deserved well of the Continent. The England of Scott and Wordsworth had problems enough to solve. But when we are told that such a land was 'no place for' righteous persons like Shelley or Byron, we may remember that Byron himself did not think so:

> Yet was I born where men are proud to be
> Not without cause.

We may turn to Shelley's Sonnet on *England in 1819* for information about Shelley, but hardly for a fair view of the England of that year. It was the year of Ruskin's birth: and Ruskin grew up, a product of the 'Georgian stables', to carry on through a long life his struggle for humanity. And perhaps more than to any one other age, Ruskin turns for help and encouragement to this generation, to the great and humane men of 1798 to 1830: to Wordsworth, to Scott, and equally to Byron.

XI

PHILOLOGISTS AT
UNIVERSITY COLLEGE, LONDON[1]

I. THE BEGINNINGS: 1828-1889

IN English, the word Philology is ambiguous: it was once used, in its widest sense, for a love of all polite literature; it included 'all humane liberal studies'. Even when used in a narrower sense, Philology was wont to cover the study of literature, just as much as of grammar. But nowadays Philology is often limited to comparative grammar, and to the science of linguistics which is based upon it.

Now, in speaking of Philology at University College, I wish to use the word in the older, broader, and more correct sense, including the study of literature as well as the study of language. University College was the first place in England where chairs were established in the Language and Literature of England and of other modern countries; and within these walls the study of language has never been divorced from the study of literature.

But about the time of our foundation, startling new discoveries had just been made in the comparative study of languages, so that comparative philology in the narrower sense *does* play a very important part in the history of our chairs. Whether a teacher of language and literature were really wide-awake or no, could in some measure be tested, in 1828, by the interest he took, or did not take, in these new discoveries. Nowadays comparative philology seems to many people a dry and repulsive study: it has become highly specialized and carefully mapped out. But in 1828 it meant the study of unexplored fields. The comparative philologist was like Ulysses (not the Ulysses of Homer but the Ulysses of Dante) when he got outside the old confined Mediterranean and rowed on to explore the ocean beyond. No one knew what he might find. Scoffers may say that my parallel is all too true — that students

[1] A Centenary Address, delivered 2 May, 1927, in University College, London.

of comparative language, like Ulysses, found only the mountain of Purgatory — Grimm's Law, Verner's Law, Grassmann's Law, rising in successive terraces of horror — and were then overwhelmed beneath the waves of a study which has become so vast that even the specialists cannot remember its complexities.

These discoveries of comparative philology were only one portion of the great discovery of the nineteenth century: the historical or evolutionary point of view. It was left to that century to 'discover the idea of development or evolution as pervading the whole Universe.'[1]

Previous generations had regarded languages as starting ready made from the Tower of Babel, just as they had regarded species of animals as emerging ready made from the Garden of Eden. Of course people had realized that certain languages were related: the common use of the terms High Dutch and Low Dutch shows that everybody felt that the languages of Austria and of Holland were only branches of one speech. Dante noticed that French, Italian, and Provençal had many words in common.[2] Therefore, he argued, they must be dialects of one speech, not languages due to the confusion of tongues at Babel. Dante thought that if the difference between French and Italian had been due to God confounding the original tongue of mankind, the confusion must have been more absolute: it would be disrespectful to Omnipotence, he felt, to suppose that God could have made so imperfect a job of it.

Dante also realized how languages changed. Here again he worked the thing out from fundamental principles: 'Since man is a most unstable and changeable animal, no human speech can be permanent and continuous.' And so, when Dante meets Cacciaguida in Heaven, his great-great-grandfather addresses him 'not in this our modern tongue, but with a voice more sweet and soft'.[3]

Hebrew, Dante thought, was the original tongue of mankind,[4] and Hebrew alone had remained unchanged,

---

[1] JESPERSEN, *Language, its nature, development, and origin*, 1922, p. 32.
[2] *De Vulgari Eloquentia*, I, 8 etc.   [3] *Paradiso*, XVI, 32-3.
[4] But as to this Dante changed his mind. See *Paradiso*, XXVI, 124-6.

handed down by the tiny minority who refused to have anything to do with the building of the Tower. But Dante was
ahead of his time. He alludes to the foolish people who are
convinced that their own particular dialect must have been the
original speech of Adam. Yet many centuries after the time
of Dante, André Kempe, in a treatise on the language of
Paradise, maintained that God spoke to Adam in Swedish,
Adam replied in Danish, and the serpent spoke to Eve in
French. (I have this, I ought to say, on the authority of
Professor Max Müller: an authority not as great as it once was.
I have failed to find André Kempe's dissertation in the British
Museum; but then our national collection is notoriously defec-
tive in early Scandinavian treatises on Paradise.)

It was the opening up of India and the discovery of Sanscrit
by European, and especially English, scholars at the end of the
eighteenth century which brought about a new view. Before the
eighteenth century closed, Sir William Jones had published
the famous statement that Sanscrit, Greek, and Latin must have
all 'sprung from some common source, which, perhaps, no
longer exists'. 'There is a similar reason, though not quite so
forcible', he continued, 'for supposing that both the Gothic and
the Celtic had the same origin with the Sanscrit; and the Old
Persian might be added to the same family.' But it was not till
the nineteenth century was well on its way that a group of
continental scholars created a new science of language by
following up the path thus indicated. Prominent among this
group was Rasmus Rask, the son of a Danish peasant. Rask
possessed that amazing gift of tongues which enables a man to
pick up any language he hears spoken: a gift which, to those
of us who have not got it, is as unintelligible as the ability to
play twelve simultaneous games of chess blindfold. And he
possessed, what does not necessarily go with this first gift, an
intensely scientific mind. Rask's early life was spent in wander-
ings which carried him as far as Iceland and as far as India. If
he had merely noted that there was a relationship between the
different languages he met, he would have done no more than
Sir William Jones and many others had done. But the great

discovery of Rask was this. He found that the changes by which the languages had become differentiated from each other were not mere accidental and unaccountable corruptions, but that they took place according to certain fixed rules, and that these rules could be stated. Faint traces of this had been perceived before: it had been noted, for example, how often, when you find a 'p' in Latin (pes), you have an 'f' in the corresponding Germanic word (fuss).[1] But, in this treatise on the Origin of the Old Norse or Icelandic Tongue,[2] Rask formulated a whole series of correspondences as between Greek and Latin sounds on the one side and Icelandic on the other. Four years later Grimm developed these rules, adding a large number of illustrations. These illustrations were so convincing, and made such an impression upon European scholars, that the series of sound shifting has since been known as Grimm's law. It might just as properly be called Rask's rule.

Exactly what Grimm's law means is not always understood. I have been told in an examination paper that 'The Early Germanic Tribes decided to shift their consonants at the instigation of a man called Grimm'. The importance of the discovery of Rask and Grimm lay in their perception that changes of sounds took place in accordance with certain definite rules. Grimm's law was only the first of a number of similar discoveries. Thus the science of etymology was founded. Up to that time etymology had been a matter of guess-work, and there had been little by which to decide that one man's guess was better than another's. Etymology had in fact been a study where 'the consonants counted for very little and the vowels for nothing at all'. Now it became scientific.

Three great continental scholars, Bopp, Grimm, and Rask, laid the foundations of this new science, and each of them had a disciple who introduced his discoveries into England. Bopp's disciple came first. His name was Friedrich August Rosen, and

---

[1] In this connection, one of the most interesting early contributions to Philology is the article on WILKINS' *Sanscrit Grammar*, contributed to the *Edinburgh Review* by ALEXANDER HAMILTON in January, 1809. See article by the writer and F. NORMAN in *Studies in English Philology in honour of F. Klaeber*, 1929.

[2] Undersögelse om det gamle Nordiske eller Islandske Sprogs Oprindelse, af R. K. Rask. Kjöbenhavn, 1818, p. 169.

he began his work in 1828, at University College, as Professor of Oriental Languages. He taught within our walls Hindustani, Persian, Arabic, and Sanscrit, and he did this at the age of twenty-three. Further, he helped to catalogue the Syriac manuscripts in the British Museum, did any amount of pot-boiling for his living, popularized philology in the Penny Cyclopaedia, and yet found time to build up a solid reputation as a Sanscrit scholar before his early death at the age of thirty-two: a man of genius, prematurely cut off. Our College remembers him with peculiar sorrow and pride, as it remembers Arthur Strong, a worker in the same field, or Walter Seton, a worker in very different fields, but all alike in this, that their fiery spirit burnt itself out so soon, but not before they had, in a short time, fulfilled a long time.

And, in this short time, Rosen managed to introduce his classical colleagues here — all of them recruited when young men of about thirty — to the mysteries of the new philology, and, as we shall see, Key, Long and Malden carried on the tradition.[1]

A little later, John Mitchell Kemble, the friend of Tennyson and one of the Cambridge 'apostles', studied under Grimm in Germany; and he, together with Benjamin Thorpe, who had studied under Rask at Copenhagen, introduced the new methods of Comparative Philology into the teaching of Anglo-Saxon. In 1834, in a review of Thorpe's *Analecta*, Kemble praised Thorpe, and at the same time indicated that the old-fashioned, easy-going Anglo-Saxon professors at Oxford did not know their business; that, in fact, had they been schoolboys, they would have incurred 'a liberal application of ferula or direr birch'. Oxford retaliated by denouncing 'Germanised Englishmen who return from the Continent surcharged not only with gloomy ideas on divinity, but also upon philology'. Kemble retorted, 'These things may do at Oxford, but they will not do at Göttingen, at Munich, and at Cambridge.' This quarrel was not, as has sometimes been said, a mere unprofitable dispute between Oxford and Cambridge;[2] really it was a

---

[1] See DONALDSON, *The New Cratylus*, third edit., 1859, vii, 55.
[2] Cf. C. H. FIRTH, *The School of English Language and Literature*, Oxford, 1909.

quarrel between the old and the new view in philology. What is important to *us* is, that Kemble expressed quite clearly his expectation that the University of London, and King's College, would study Anglo-Saxon philology from such an excellent textbook as Thorpe's *Analecta*, in honourable contradistinction to the antiquated methods of Oxford.[1]

It was a compliment that the English department of University College, London, had as yet done nothing to deserve. In his inaugural lecture in 1828, Dr. Dale, our first Professor of English Language and Literature, shows entire ignorance of the exciting discoveries which Germans and Danes had been making, and of which he might have learnt from his fellow professor, Rosen, as his colleagues in Greek and Latin did later. But Dale is not interested in the new philology. What Dale is interested in, is the morals of his class. In the course of the lectures, he says,

> which it will be my duty to deliver, I shall invariably aim to impart moral, as well as intellectual instruction. These I can never consent to separate, for it has been the business of my life to combine them; and did I consider the union incompatible with my office in this University, I should not address you now. But in all my lectures I shall esteem it my duty — and I trust shall find it my delight — to inculcate lessons of virtue.

It is obvious that no man could long live up to this standard in University College: after two years, Dr. Dale ceased to find delight in inculcating lessons of virtue here. He left us, to find a new, and, I trust, a more moral home, as first Professor of English Language and Literature in King's College, London.

I will devote a few sentences to Dr. Dale, for it would be unfilial to pass too hastily over the first occupant of both our chairs. And much can be learnt about Dale from the works of John Ruskin: for Ruskin was a pupil of Dale's. Dale had the same contemptuous opinion of Scottish learning which Dr. Johnson professed. So, when Ruskin showed him his Latin Grammar by Alexander Adam, Dale threw it back at him with

[1] 'It is an excellent class-book for the London University and King's College.' *Gentleman's Magazine*, 1834, I, pp. 392-3.

a fierce bang upon his desk, saying, 'That's a *Scotch* thing'.[1]
In that one action, says Ruskin, 'he rejected himself from being
my master'.[2] It was just fifty years after Ruskin's parents had
sent him to attend Dale's lectures at King's, that Ruskin
recorded his recollections:[3]

> The lectures (says Ruskin) were on Early English Literature,
> of which, though I had never read a word of any before Pope,
> I thought myself already a much better judge than Mr. Dale.
> His quotation of 'Knut the King came sailing by' stayed
> with me; and I think that was about all I learnt during the
> summer.

But Ruskin's memory had played him false. Seven years after
Ruskin had given this summary of Dale's lectures, Dale's grand-
daughter extracted from her grandfather's desk an Essay which
Ruskin had written for him in that year 1836. It shows, as
Ruskin's boyish letters also show, that he paid more attention
to his professor's instruction than he remembered fifty years
later.

In later life, after Ruskin had become Slade Professor of Fine
Art at Oxford, he held very sound views as to the position of the
Professor in a well-ordered Commonwealth:

> Girls (he said) should be taught to curtsey, and boys to take
> their hats off, when a Professor (or otherwise dignified person)
> passes by.[4]

Now, observe the boy Ruskin taking off his hat to Professor
Dale.

In the same year that Ruskin became his student, Dale edited
a text-book for the use of his classes. It was adapted from an
American text-book by the Rev. John Todd (an interesting
example of that connection between the first professors of this
College and the American Universities, of which it would be
easy to multiply examples).[5] Dale's edition of the *Student's
Guide* carries out his principle of 'imparting moral as well as

[1] *Works*, Library Edition, xxxiv, p. 365.
[2] xxxv, p. 83.   [3] xxxv, p. 178.   [4] xxvii, p. 14.
[5] For Long and Key, see BRUCE, *History of the University of Virginia*, 1818-19,
esp. vol. II.

intellectual instruction'. The student is warned against Byron
— then at the height of his popularity:

> Lord Byron will quickly pass from notice, and is doomed to be
> exiled from the libraries of all virtuous men. It is a blessing
> to the world that what is putrid must soon pass away. The
> carcase hung in chains will be gazed at for a short time in
> horror; but men will soon turn their eyes away, and remove
> even the gallows on which it swung.

The subject of Ruskin's Essay is, 'Does the perusal of works of
fiction act favourably or unfavourably on the moral character'
— and all we know of Dale suggests that the subject was dictated
by the professor. Ruskin adroitly gets on to Scott, makes a
traverse from Scott to Byron, and proceeds to discuss the effect
of Byron on the moral character. He discovers that no human
being can be 'of soul so dead' as not to feel that he is a better
man, his ideas higher, his heart purer, his feelings nobler, after
reading Byron. But—

> There *are* animals who neither have felt this inspiration
> themselves nor believe that others can feel it . . . They actually
> appear to imagine that *they! they!!*, yes, *they!!!* will be able to
> wipe away his memory from the earth . . . These foul snails
> . . . are inferior to the slug in this respect, that their slime
> can neither shine nor injure . . . Who does not feel indignation
> mingled with his scorn of these Grub Street reptiles, even
> although the dust of a single year will overwhelm them for
> ever, and the impotence of their life be equalled by the
> oblivion of their death![1]

If Dr. Dale has not left us any contribution to philology, he has
at least left us a useful example — in the phrase which Saxo
Grammaticus applies to his heroes when they achieve victory by
doubtful means, 'an example more useful than honourable'.
I would ask my fellow-teachers to note the advantages which
accrue from leaving their students' essays unread for fifty-seven
years. If Dale had returned this essay to Ruskin at once,
Ruskin would have thrown it away, and it would have been
lost to the world.

[1] I, pp. 374-5.

Dale was succeeded in this College by Blair, and Blair by Rogers; the tenure of both was very short, and I may apply to them the useful and well-worn phrase of Thucydides, that, so far as my researches have gone, they do not seem to have done anything very remarkable. But it is a different story with regard to the next holder of the chair, Robert Gordon Latham.

Latham was an eccentric genius with a vast range of knowledge, and he had worked at Philology in Germany and Scandinavia. Rosen had died not long before Latham became professor here, but Latham associated himself with Key and Malden, who were carrying on Rosen's work, and were establishing the Philological Society on a firm basis.

The Philological Society had begun as a student society of this College, almost as soon as the College itself began. But it came under the influence of the Professors, and then, in 1842, the Society became a national, instead of a University, body. The three professors of University College — Latham, Key and Malden — remained prominent; but they associated with themselves any philologists living in London, Richard Garnett the elder, Edwin Guest, and others. They began the publication of a periodical — the *Proceedings* (later called *Transactions*) which remains to-day, the oldest purely philological periodical still running in England.

So, within a very few years of its foundation, this College first created, and then for many years took the main share in carrying on, the Philological Society.

Severe things have been said of English scholarship during this period. I quote the words of A. E. Housman, who describes the age as marked by 'the emancipation of human incapacity':

. . . After 1825 . . . our own great age of scholarship, begun in 1691 by Bentley's *Epistola ad Millium*, was ended by the successive strokes of doom which consigned Dobree and Elmsley to the grave, and Blomfield to the bishopric of Chester. England disappeared from the fellowship of nations for the next forty years: Badham, the one English scholar of the mid-century whose reputation crossed the Channel, received from abroad the praises of Duebner and Nauck and Cobet, but at home was excluded from academical preferment, set to teach

boys at Birmingham, and finally transported to the antipodes: his countrymen, having turned their backs on Europe
and science and the past, sat down to banquet on mutual
approbation, to produce the Classical Museum and the
Bibliotheca Classica, and to perish without a name.[1]

Now this hits us rather hard; for Long, the editor of the
Bibliotheca Classica, was our first professor of Greek and our second
professor of Latin. Professor Housman, when speaking of the
inferiority of English scholarship in the middle of the century
was, of course, thinking specially of the editing of classical texts.
In the field of Comparative Philology there is, it must be owned,
something of the same inferiority, if we compare our native
record with that of the great scholars of Germany. But in this
field, credit has to be allowed to University College and the
Philological Society, for what they did to keep the study alive
in England; and we ought also to reckon it to the credit of our
early professors that they did not allow the acknowledged
eminence of Germany in this branch of learning to rob them
of their right to their own judgment. The most famous instance
of this was the refusal of Latham to assent (without evidence)
to the dogma that the primitive Aryans originated in Asia. This
scepticism was stigmatized at the time, by a continental scholar,
as lunacy only possible to one who lived in a country of cranks.
During the generation after Latham put his heresy forward, it
generally grew more popular, till at last it became the orthodox
view. Latham was then on his death-bed: Theodore Watts
Dunton has told how he hastened to his bedside with the news.
Latham could hardly speak, but he could still understand. 'A
look of joy went sunning over his worn face', but he could only
utter the one word 'Late'.

Latham's extraordinary powers had been too erratic to bring
him success. As a controversialist he delivered himself into the
enemy's hands when he printed some cuneiform characters and,
through careless proof-reading, allowed them to go out to a
critical world upside down. And his last years were saddened
by incapacitating illness.

[1] MANILIUS, I, xlii.

351

A man of many troubles was Latham — troubles for which the world was answerable sometimes, and sometimes Latham — but the moment he got among that golden gorse of Wimbledon Common (for the sight of which Linnaeus before him had thanked God) or the bracken of Richmond Park, he forgot them all ... Latham knew the exact spot alongside Beverley Brook where any flower might be found at any season of the year: to him a flower was an actual sympathetic presence that appealed not only to his emotions, but to his intellect, for he knew its family, its descent, its ancestral transmissions.[1]

But if Latham died with his promise unfulfilled, the Philological Society had extraordinary good fortune in the vitality of Dr. Frederick Furnivall, who entered on the duties of secretary jointly with Professor Key in 1853, at the age of twenty-eight, and only laid down his duties in his eighty-sixth year, three weeks before his death. Those of us who were present at that meeting of the Society will not easily forget it:

... to see this old man, who knew how near death was, listening to the paper with the zeal of one who had years of study still before him. He was terribly changed from the Furnivall of a year ago; his cheeks were sunken and colourless, his feet moved painfully; yet life burnt in his eyes with a vehemence that was almost dreadful. Infirm as he was, no one dared offer to go home with him, and he made the journey to Primrose Hill alone.[2]

Furnivall was always a free lance:

His work as a student (says W. P. Ker) was another example of what is fortunately not rare in England, the pursuit and the diffusion of knowledge apart from any elaborate organisation of research. Much of the best historical work in England has been done by unprofessional hands, and Furnivall worked as an independent adventurer. No doubt his work had many of the faults which are prevented in the best-regulated schools, but it had always the spring and energy of a life unimpeded by routine.[3]

[1] THEODORE WATTS (DUNTON) in the *Athenaeum*, March 17, 1888, p. 340.
[2] FRANCIS BICKLEY, in *F. J. Furnivall: a Record*, 1911, p. 2.
[3] The same, p. 94.

Though Furnivall had neither place nor pay in any University, though his only teaching post was that of a volunteer at the Working Men's College, he belonged to us, from the day he entered our College in 1841 till that evening, seventy years later, when he walked out of our doors for the last time.

As a student, Furnivall kept a very conscientious diary. I will give you one day from it: the life of a student of U.C.L. from midnight to midnight:

Friday, May 13, 1842.

[A Party] Had some ices; danced; had supper at ½ past 1; danced (a country dance,) etc.; took a cab to Walshe's [where he lived] at ½ past 3; read, etc., went to bed. Got up at 20^m to 8; had breakfast; attended Prof. De Morgan's lecture on Mathematics till 20^m past 10; wrote in my Sermon book for an hour; put some plants into my book of Botanical Specimens; attended Prof. Malden's lecture on Greek till 20^m to 2; arranged my plants; had dinner; Tom Graham called and chatted till 3; dressed; ... attended Prof. Potter's lecture on Natural Philosophy till 5, and Dr. Lindley's examination on Botany till quarter to 6; had a parcel from home, unpacked it; Charles was better; dried plants till 8; Dr. Scratchley came to tea; finished dressing; took a cab at 20^m past 9 to Mr. Grahame's; had some coffee; danced, had ices; quadrilled and waltzed; had supper: Fine day.[1]

Shortly after Furnivall became secretary, the Philological Society was joined by Herbert Coleridge and by Trench, not yet an Archbishop, but a professor at King's College. Owing to their enthusiasm, the chief aim of the Society became the supplementing of the imperfect English dictionaries, and this aim was soon changed into a plan for the creation of a New English Dictionary. The death of Coleridge and the absorption of Trench in other work left Furnivall in charge of this, and he toiled for fifteen years at the head of a devoted band of volunteers, amid much disappointment. In the end, Oxford shouldered the task. Two or three times every year, the Society met to hear of the progress of the Dictionary, and during the first fifty years Furnivall was always present. The Early English

[1] Life by JOHN MUNRO, in *F. J. Furnivall: a Record*, 1911, p. x.

Text Society was a by-product of the Dictionary, for it was found that there was practically no Middle English material to work on.

I pass from the work of Furnivall, and the others who succeeded Latham in the Philological Society, to Latham's successors in the chair of English in this College. The chair had one or two transient occupants, of whom Arthur Hugh Clough is much the most famous. Clough had thrown up his fellowship at Oriel: he felt that he could not honestly stay in an Oxford which demanded from its students a belief in the Thirty-Nine Articles. It was natural that he should come to University College, free from all religious tests. But he was not to be one of those Oxford men who have found a new home here. 'Though not bound by any verbal obligations', Clough's biographer tells us, 'he found himself expected to express agreement with the opinions of the new set among whom he had fallen, and this was no more possible to him here than it had been at Oxford.'[1] We find Clough writing to Thomas Arnold (the younger), 'Intolerance, O Tom, is not confined to the cloisters of Oxford'.[2] He had visions of the Oxford he had left:

> Yet hadst thou alway visions of our light,
>> And long with men of care thou couldst not stay,
>> And soon thy foot resumed its wandering way,
> Left human haunt, and on alone till night.

Were the 'men of care' the professors of University College? I have often wondered. Words even more unkind have been spoken of us: Matthew Arnold's 'men of care' is mild compared with the words of a contemporary Cambridge don denouncing

> Gower Street's cursed Academy and such like stinking vermin.

Anyway, in less than three years Clough gave place to David Masson. Masson was much happier, and stayed much longer, but he too passed on, and found his life-work at Edinburgh. Then came Henry Morley, and he came to stay.

[1] *Poems and Prose Remains* of Arthur Hugh Clough, 1869, *Memoir*, I, p. 39.
[2] The same, I, p. 164.
[3] R. SHILLETO. See WHIBLEY, *In Cap and Gown*, 1890, p. 228.

Morley had been trained at King's College, London, as a doctor, but he cared more for poetry than medicine, and he was too soft-hearted to insist upon being paid by the Black Country labourers among whom his practice lay. So he abandoned physic, and returned to King's College, as lecturer on English in the Evening School. Upon the lectures which he gave at King's was based the first edition of his *English Writers*. In this work sections on the History of the English Language alternate with sections on the History of English Literature. The book is an attempt 'to tell, with something of the sustained interest of national biography, the story of the English mind'. This work justly made Morley's reputation, and as King's stole Dr. Dale from us, we bettered the example by stealing Morley from King's. Subsequently Morley recast his book on a much larger scale, bringing the story of English letters down to the death of Shakespeare. Monumental works of this kind are nowadays undertaken by a large group of scholars, as in the Cambridge Histories. The great advantage of Morley's book is that it bears the stamp of one mind and of one character: this gives it a permanent interest and value such as no compilation can have. W. P. Ker, his successor, wrote of Morley:

> It is impossible to separate Mr. Morley's teaching from his character. What he gave to his students was the incitement of his own energy, his unselfishness, and his belief in the inexhaustible value of his subject.

The list of Morley's students includes Walter Raleigh, the first professor of English Literature in Oxford; George Aitken, remembered for his work on Steele and other Eighteenth-Century writers, for his labours at the Board of Education, and his devoted loyalty to this College; Sir Frank Heath, Sir Gregory Foster, and Sir Israel Gollancz.

So the teaching of Philology in this College, from the standpoint of English, continued to flourish: when we pass to the Classical languages it has to be admitted that difficulties increased. The prestige of the older Universities drew students away to centres where the teaching of Greek had a tradition of more than three centuries behind it, from the time when

Erasmus, according to Gibbon, 'learned Greek at Oxford and taught it at Cambridge'.[1] (I much doubt if Erasmus *did* learn Greek at Oxford: but I will not discuss that problem now.) My point is that, during the earlier years of our existence, certain classes of men, excluded by the tests from the older Universities, had come from all over England to the only place in England where they could get education: as the tests were removed, and as newer Universities grew up in the provinces, this ceased to be the case. The competition of Oxford and Cambridge hit the teaching of Classics more severely than the teaching of subjects like English or Science, which were more peculiarly our own.

Our first great teachers of the Classics held office for nearly half a century: although his duties as Head Master of University College School took so much of his time, Key held the chair, first of Latin, then of Comparative Grammar, till he died in harness in 1876. Malden held the Professorship of Greek till the same year, dying a few days after the election of his successor. A Malden Medal was established to commemorate him, to be given to a third year student with a creditable knowledge of Greek. There have been years when difficulties have been encountered in finding that student, till W. P. Ker solved the problem in his courageous way by the ruling '*Any* knowledge of Greek is creditable'.

Key was succeeded in his chair of Comparative Grammar (after an interregnum of four years) by Postgate. (The title of the chair was at the same time changed from Comparative Grammar to Comparative Philology.) But there was so little enthusiasm for the subject that I am afraid Postgate, eminent scholar and fine teacher as he was, sometimes found great difficulties in forming a class. A professor of this College, I have been told, used to maintain that the first duty of a teacher was to reduce his class to one: then he could begin to teach. Postgate's first duty was to raise his class to one; then *he* could begin to teach. One year I constituted Prof. Postgate's class. The Beadle watched the Comparative Philology Class emerge from the room. He then came up to me with the question, 'Does Prof.

[1] *Decline and Fall*, cap. 66. (vi. p. 431, 1788).

Postgate come all the way down from Cambridge to lecture to *you*?'

Despite discouragement, Postgate held the chair for thirty years, before he left us in 1910 to become Professor of Latin at Liverpool. But, through the Philological Society, Postgate continued his connection with us, and the last lecture of his which I ever attended was his speech as President of the Philological Society.

So in Classics there was no lack of distinguished teachers, but it is not surprising if, with so few students, the teachers tended to drift off, after a few years, to the older Universities. John (afterwards Sir John) Seeley left us to earn fame as Professor of Modern History at Cambridge: his successor Robinson Ellis left to become Corpus Professor of Latin at Oxford. Alfred Goodwin overworked himself, combining the Greek and Latin chairs in his last years. But his discouragements were great, for the students in Classics had become in very great measure mere birds of passage — boys who had left school, and were putting in a few terms before going to Oxford or Cambridge. Goodwin never knew whether the disciples of one term would be the disciples of the next. There seemed a danger that in some important departments of the Arts Faculty, professors and students alike might come to regard themselves as merely filling in time till they could pass to a real University.

So, when Morley in 1889 resigned the chair of English which he had held with great distinction to the end, he left the College with a very strong Faculty of Science and an Arts Faculty strong in subjects like Mathematics, Logic, Statistics and Political Economy. But apart from Morley, the teaching of language here had become very thin. History had a distinguished teacher in E. S. Beesly, one of the 'three persons and no God' of the Positivist faith. But we saw little of him. Beesly used to come into his lecture room at 2 o'clock every Thursday, take off his hat and comforter, give us one lecture on Ancient History, one on Modern History, put on his comforter and hat, walk out; and that was all we saw of him till next week. I was the only member of his class who sat for his examination. As he handed me the paper, he said that he wished to catch an early train, and indicated a time, before that officially fixed for the termination of the examination, when he would be glad to receive my script. I managed to get all I knew about History down in the curtailed time, and handed my script to Beesly with a look of injured and aggrieved erudition. The First Prize in Ancient History and the First Prize in Modern History are to-day two of my most cherished possessions.

XII

PHILOLOGISTS AT
UNIVERSITY COLLEGE, LONDON

II. PLATT, HOUSMAN AND KER: 1889-1922

THERE has, therefore, seldom been a more momentous decision in this College than the appointment of the successor to Morley's chair. The fate of the Arts Faculty hung upon it. If the man appointed had merely regarded the post as a stepping-stone to some more lucrative professorship, and had failed to identify himself with the College, it might have been all over with the Arts Faculty for many years.

The successor chosen was a young scholar born in Glasgow, W. P. Ker. Some time after he was appointed, the Glasgow chair of English (a more valuable one than his own) fell vacant. It was expected that Ker would return to his native town. When Ker's father suggested that his son might prefer to stick to University College, an indignant Glaswegian retorted, 'Mon, he's no a limpet.' Ker, however, proved a limpet, for thirty-three years.

Ker had not held the chair three years when the College was shocked by the death of Alfred Goodwin. Goodwin's Latin chair passed to A. E. Housman, his Greek chair to William Wyse. Wyse regarded the shortcomings of his small and unfit flock rather with sorrow than with anger; after two years of disillusionment, he returned to Trinity College, Cambridge, to find students less unworthy of his standard of scholarship. (It is a pleasure, after thirty years, for an old student to pay a tribute of respect to his exact and patient teaching.)

The journey in the opposite direction from Trinity College, Cambridge, to University College, London, was made by Wyse's successor, Arthur Platt (though Platt had left Trinity some time before). Platt has told me that Wyse warned him that he must not expect too much of us.

And, as I look back, there seems a strange incongruity between those two mighty scholars, Platt and Housman, and the tiny and, I fear, immature classes they had at first to teach. Indeed, as I read again Housman's sentence about the great scholar Badham being set to teach boys, I have an uneasy feeling that he was thinking of another great scholar teaching boys. If he meant us, the thunder rolled harmlessly over our heads, for though we were mostly under eighteen, it would never have occurred to us that we were boys.

So, within five years, the College had recruited Ker, Housman, and Platt: and although Housman in the end left us, still for seventeen years they were together here. Students crowded to the Arts Dinners to hear the three speeches, so different and so delightful: or to meetings of the Literary Society, to see the one pulling the leg of the other.

ARTHUR PLATT

Although like Ker in the depth and width of his scholarship, Platt externally was very different. He came to University College

> wearing all that weight
> Of learning lightly like a flower.

He largely created the social life of the College Staff. The crowd that now surges in the Staff Smoking Room between the hours of one and two has developed from the group which Platt persuaded to meet after lunch, in the room to which he gave up his personal claim in order that it might become a meeting place for the staff. His chair was in the centre of the room, and there he sat for more than a quarter of a century, instructing Chemists in the Humanities and teaching Zoologists wisdom.

He was an omnivorous reader — I quote Professor Butler — in many languages. He had read the whole of Calderon's

360

plays, and the great poets of Persia, was steeped in Dante, and had produced a number of ingenious emendations of the corrupt text of Jane Austen, whose novels he knew almost by heart.

When Ker had just published, and presented to the College Library, his two volumes of selections from Dryden's prose, and the volumes had been placed upon the shelf in the common room reserved for books recently added to the Library: 'I saw them in the common room,' said Platt to Ker, 'but I did not look at them.' 'That is hypocrisy,' retorted Ker. 'No,' said Platt, 'I had bought and read a copy of my own, so why should I look at the Library copy?' 'That,' said W. P. K., 'is a bigger lie than the first.' It was, however, quite true; and how many professors of Greek would trouble to read Dryden's critical prose?

The most brilliant of all Goodwin's pupils, Mrs. Craigie (John Oliver Hobbes), had applied to *her* professor the lines:

He was a scholar, and a ripe and good one . . .
Lofty and sour to them that loved him not,
But to those men that sought him, sweet as summer.

No lines could better describe Platt than the first and the third; whether the second is equally applicable, we in University College shall never know, for there has never been any one who loved him not.

Children as well as grown-ups, and animals as well as mankind. I remember seeing in the giraffe house at the Zoo a crowd of children watching a giraffe, its neck stretched to capacity, rubbing its head backwards and forwards, like a cat, on the head of a visitor. The object of this somewhat embarrassing affection turned his head: it was Platt. At one time he was going about with three distinct wounds inflicted by the mistaken enthusiasm of his dumb friends at the Zoo. There was a goat who loved to bring his horns thwack against the bars of his cage. Platt used to relieve the monotony of that goat's existence by slyly putting his fingers inside the cage. Once only did the goat win the game, and Platt's finger was bound up for weeks.

His fun was a contrast to the grave friendliness with which

Ker would gaze upon the animals: a small girl knew Ker as 'Infessor Ker who takes care of the animals at the Zoo.' 'But what will all the animals do, Mummy?' was her remark when she was told that Ker, like the prophets of old, had gone up a mountain and would be seen no more.

Soon after Platt's death Housman wrote of him:

> In Platt's company one felt that one was not an educated man. His work was most esteemed by the few who could best appraise it, but he was so gay and unpretentious that vulgar judgments underrated him ... We have lost as genuine and straightforward a mind and character as can ever have been born into the world, and a delightful creature whom it is a precious treasure to have known.

We owe to Ker[1] the preservation of a distich which Housman threw out in praise of Platt's scholarly gaiety — a distich which otherwise might have been lost from the corpus of Housman's poems:

> Philology was tame, and dull, and flat;
> God said, 'Let there be larks', and there was Platt!

A small volume of English essays — mainly papers which he read to the College Literary Society — was published after his death, with an introduction by Housman which is one of the most extraordinary tributes ever paid by one great scholar to another. In giving me permission to quote these words, Mr. Edward Platt, Platt's only son, writes of Housman: 'As I knew him, when he used to come and see my parents, he seemed a genial person without any trace of malice.' The same happy geniality came out in a very striking way in the letters which Housman sent from Cambridge to Mrs. Platt.

In estimating Platt as a scholar, Housman dwells particularly upon his knowledge of Greek metre. 'Metrical science, upon the death of Elmsley, had deserted its native isle and taken flight to the Continent.' But

> Platt was one of the very few Englishmen who in the last hundred years have advanced the study, and among those

[1] See *The Times*, 9 Nov., 1936. (Francis Pember).

few he was the foremost. In conjectural emendation, like Dawes and Elmsley, he was shrewd and dexterous enough, but not, like Bentley and Porson, eminent. In literary comment he did not expatiate, although, or rather because, he was the most lettered scholar of his time. He stuck to business as a scholar should, and preferred, as a man of letters will, the dry to the watery. He knew better than to conceive himself that rarest of all the great works of God, a literary critic; but such remarks on literature as he did let fall were very different stuff from the usual flummery of the cobbler who is ambitious to go beyond his last.

As a teacher, he proved assiduous, patient, and effective:

Only an oaf could help learning from him and liking him; and with his best students he formed enduring ties, and would inveigle them into reading Dante or Cervantes with him at his house of an evening after they had taken their degrees. Outside his own class-room he was a centre and fount of the general life of the College, most of all in the Musical Society and among his colleagues in the smoking-room after luncheon. Nearer to his house he made another circle of friends. He was a Fellow of the Zoological Society, frequented its Gardens, and inspired a romantic passion in their resident population. There was a leopard which at Platt's approach would almost ooze through the bars of its cage to establish contact with the beloved object; the gnu, if it saw him on the opposite side of its broad enclosure, would walk all the way across to have its forelock pulled.

Then follows a passage which, besides depicting Platt, as no one else could have depicted him, reveals Housman himself:

That he wrote little was the direct and natural consequence of his extraordinary capacity and the variety of his interests and attainments. He would rather improve himself than instruct others. He wrote on subjects where he could make definite and original contributions to the advancement of learning: otherwise he preferred to read. Greek was his trade, but the home in which he dwelt was great literature, whether its language were Greek, Latin, English, French, Italian, Spanish, German, or Persian. The best authors were his study, but his reading ran far beyond them; his curiosity

363

invaded holes and corners, and his taste ranged from the
Divine Comedy to *Jorrocks's Jaunts*. He followed his inclinations
and read for his own delight, with a keen and natural relish,
not a dutiful and obedient admiration of the things which are
admired by the wise and good. Nor were his studies warped
and narrowed by ambition. A scholar who means to build
himself a monument must spend much of his life in acquiring
knowledge which for its own sake is not worth having, and
in reading books which do not in themselves deserve to be
read; *at illa iacent multa et praeclara relicta.*

Music was a rival of literature in his affections, and his
knowledge of the art and its history was almost an expert's.
He followed with interest and understanding the progress of
discovery in the natural sciences, and his acquaintance with
zoology in particular was such as few laymen can boast. In
conclusion it is proper to mention his vices. He was addicted
to tobacco and indifferent to wine, and he would squander
long summer days on watching the game of cricket.

His happy and useful life is over, and now begins the steady
encroachment of oblivion, as those who remember him are
in their turn summoned away. This record will not preserve,
perhaps none could preserve, more than an indistinct and
lifeless image of the friend who is lost to us: good, kind, bright,
unselfish, and as honest as the day; versatile without shallow-
ness, accomplished without ostentation, a treasury of hidden
knowledge which only accident brought to light, but which
accident brought to light perpetually, and which astonished
us so often that astonishment lost its nature and we should
have wondered more if wonders had failed. Yet what most
eludes description is not the excellence of his gifts but the
singularity of his essential being, his utter unlikeness to any
other creature in the world.

A. E. HOUSMAN

In estimating Platt's Greek scholarship, Housman speaks as one having authority. After his appointment with us to the Professorship of Latin, he almost ceased to write upon Greek, because, as he said later, 'I found that I could not attain to excellence in both'. But his earlier work had been as much on the Greek as on the Latin poets. When, in 1892, at the age of 33, he applied for the Latin chair at University College, it was with a proviso that, should it be conferred on another, he would ask to be considered as an applicant for the Professorship of Greek. He closed his application with the words: 'If I am honoured by your choice I shall give my best endeavours to the fulfilment of my duties and to the maintenance of accurate learning in University College.'

A more unconventional sentence in the application was, 'in 1881 I failed to obtain honours in the Final School of Litterae Humaniores'. This mishap, following the ability he had shown as a boy at Bromsgrove School, and his First in Moderations in 1879, had been one more example of that defect of the examination system which led to the dictum of Professor Raleigh: 'The nightingale got no prize at the poultry show.' A. W. Pollard, Housman's fellow-scholar at St. John Baptist's College, Oxford, has said: 'For a man who was, if not already a great scholar, at least a great scholar in the making, it was psychologically impossible to make the best of his knowledge on subjects in which he had lost interest.' He was too proud to do second-class work; and so he showed up no answers to many of the questions set; thus, as he later put it without malice, he left his examiners no option.

But consciousness of having disappointed his family at a time of need left its mark on him. The reminiscences of his sister, Mrs. Katharine E. Symons, and of his brother Laurence have now made clear what those who knew him had always felt, that he was 'a different man to the self-absorbed, self-contained personality that he chose to present to the world — and that

365

most of those who have written about him present also to the
world'. On his twelfth birthday he had lost his mother, and his
sister writes that this cruel loss

> seems to have roused in him an early resentment against
> nature's relentless ways of destruction. His own death made
> evident the faithful memories of her which he never ceased to
> cherish. Every scrap of writing that he had received from
> her or about her was preserved; and right on from the day
> of her death he maintained an enduring attachment to the
> family who supported him through his bitter hour; year by
> year, whenever possible, he visited them till death took them,
> too, away.[1]

Two years later, he had promised his stepmother to help her
in her task of looking after his six younger brothers and sisters;
and the loyalty with which he kept his word is clear from the
memoirs of both sister and brother. In the year after his Oxford
disaster, a small family legacy accrued. 'His share A.E.H.
never touched, but devoted it to helping the home that was in
sore need.' But, his brother writes, 'when he came back [from
Oxford], and for a good many years afterwards, we ceased to
know him — mainly, if not entirely, because he was determined
not to be known'.

Housman qualified for a Pass Degree, and obtained a Higher
Division Clerkship in the Patent Office. Much later, his answer
to the question what he did there was: 'As little as possible.'
That he was remembered among his fellow clerks for his gift of
sarcastic repartee, I know; of his ability as a clerk tradition does
not speak unanimously. But Mr. Gow writes, 'I have been
assured by one who was with him in the Office that he was a
very efficient public servant', and this is confirmed by the fact
that he came to University College, London, with an ability in
affairs which was quickly recognized and utilized by his colleagues.

His work at the Patent Office had left him with long evenings,
largely devoted to 'ancient literature and critical science',
and his contributions to learned journals had brought him a
reputation which, in the year before he joined us, led to dis-

[1] *Supplement* to *The Bromsgrovian*, p. 10.

cussions in the *Journal of Education* as to how this 'wandering son' of Oxford, not named, but very clearly indicated, had come by his plough.

Hopes that he might be speedily called home were also expressed; however, it was not Oxford, but University College, London, which 'lifted him out of the gutter', as he unkindly described H.M. Patent Office. To us belongs the credit which Mohammed gave to the old and plain widow Kadijah, as against the brilliant and beautiful Ayesha: 'She believed in me when none else would believe; in the whole world I had but one friend, and she was that.'

Housman's reputation as scholar and poet will make men, for many generations to come, wish to know something of him. For the Cambridge period Mr. Gow has drawn a wonderful portrait, and other Cambridge friends have spoken; whilst his brother and sister have told us something of the deep silent undercurrent of family relationships.[1] But memories of his ten years at the Patent Office have almost entirely perished, and I wish, before they also perish, to record (if I can) memories of the admiration, tempered by awe, which his students and younger colleagues felt in London. For there he was brought into much closer contact with undergraduates than was the case later, in Cambridge.

In thinking of Housman, my mind constantly goes back to his first academic discourse, the Introductory Lecture delivered before the Faculties of Arts and Laws and of Science in University College on 3 October, 1892. In those days it was customary to begin the session with an address delivered by one of the professors to his colleagues and to the assembled students, and this duty fell naturally to Housman as the latest accession to the staff. He discussed the dogma that the study of the Humanities transforms and beautifies man's inner nature by culture. He stated his belief that the proportion of the human race adapted

[1] See *A. E. Housman, a sketch, together with a list of his writings, and indexes to his classical papers*, by A. S. F. Gow, Cambridge, 1936; *A. E. H., some Poems, some Letters and a Personal Memoir by his brother*, LAURENCE HOUSMAN, 1937; *Supplement* to *The Bromsgrovian*, 1936 (American edit., 1937); *Memories of A. E. Housman* by Mrs. E. W. SYMONS in *The Edwardian*, Bath, Sept. and Dec., 1936; F. W. OLIVER in the *University College Magazine*, March, 1937; PERCY WITHERS in *The New Statesman*, 9 May, 1936, pp. 700-2.

by nature for such study of the Classics was not large. (The size of the classes he found waiting for him at University College must have confirmed him in this view.) And, he continued,

> I am quite sure that the proportion of the human race on whom the Classics will confer that benefit can attain the desired end without that minute and accurate study of the classical tongues which affords Latin Professors their only excuse for existing.

When we heard these sentences spoken we thought (in our folly) that the speaker would be a lenient censor of our Latin proses. But this was not so. Housman's remarks were so caustic as to paralyse his women students. But what, I think, hurt them more was the fact that, having reduced Miss Brown, Miss Jones and Miss Robinson to tears, Housman professed, when he met them next week, not to know which was Miss Brown, which Miss Jones, and which Miss Robinson. When, after nineteen years of teaching, Housman left us to take the Latin chair at Cambridge, he apologized to his assembled students, past and present, for this lack of memory. A certain Dartmoor shepherd had, just at that time, attained a place in history by getting into prison and out of it. This Dartmoor shepherd knew the faces of all his sheep. Housman admitted that *he* did not. 'But then', he said, 'if I had remembered all your faces, I might have forgotten more important things' — not, he hastened to explain, things more important in themselves, but more important to him; had he burdened his memory by the distinction between Miss Jones and Miss Robinson, he might have forgotten that between the second and the fourth declension.

During the same period, Housman was correcting his fellow-scholars, especially in his prefaces to his *Manilius* (1903) and *Juvenal* (1905), with no more regard for their feelings than he showed for ours. But we at least had the wit to see (as some of the fellow-scholars had not) that the castigation was deserved. 'We did not mind him making us cry', said one of his women students,[1] who has herself since earned a reputation for exactitude in other fields of scholarship, 'because we knew he was just.'

---

[1] Dr. E. V. Hitchcock.

Housman worked steadily during the London terms, against the length of which he protested with some success; 'Twelve weeks on end is not nice', he wrote. When he left us, he said that he hoped to be remembered (like Augustus who found Rome brick and left her marble) as the man who found us with an Easter vacation of four weeks and left us with one of five.

But I chiefly remember the scrupulous care with which he went through the 'proses' and 'unseens' of classes quite unworthy of him. When I told an American classical teacher something of the careful tuition I had received from him in 1892-4 (the first two years of his University teaching) she said, 'I feel as if I was sitting next to somebody who had touched God'. I was able to report to Housman at dinner, a few months before he died, this blasphemous tribute to his scholarship, and equally, I think, to his poetry. I am sure he enjoyed it, for he enjoyed expressions of American esteem. To a young American admirer who, some years earlier, had sent him a collection of opinions upon his poems, obtained from a number of American authors, he had replied, 'You are always kind and friendly, and your anthology of opinions ought to foster my self-esteem, and smooth my descent to the grave.' He later explained to his correspondent 'the impropriety of your conduct in writing, as you seem to have done, to ask famous writers their opinions of me'. He added, 'I hope that some of them, at any rate, have ignored your letters.' Yet later still he wrote to the same correspondent that the reputation which his poems brought him 'though it gives me no lively pleasure, is something like a mattress interposed between me and the hard ground'.

The last of these letters to the very young and guileless friend whom he had never seen[1] was written nine days before his death. They prove that Housman showed to the end that mixture of sarcastic reproof with friendly good humour which marked his relations with his undergraduate students from the time when he had first come among us, more than forty-three years earlier. It was not only that he was 'a thorough and sympathetic teacher'; he had shown himself to be that during the few months

[1] Mr. Houston Martin. The letters are printed in *The Yale Review*, Winter, 1937, pp. 283 etc.

of his teaching at Bromsgrove, between leaving Oxford and beginning work at the Patent Office. But his affability to his students was astonishing — I mean that, however severe his criticism of our work might be, he was willing to meet us in the College Literary Society and at Arts Dinners, and to break a lance with any professor, any junior teacher, or any student who was reckless enough to challenge him. Housman has described the University College Literary Society:

> University College London, like many other colleges, is the abode of a Minotaur. This monster does not devour youths and maidens: it consists of them, and it preys for choice on the Professors within its reach. It is called a Literary Society, and in hopes of deserving the name it exacts a periodical tribute from those whom it supposes to be literate. Studious men who might be settling *Hoti*'s business and properly basing *Oun* are expected to provide amusing discourses on subjects of which they have no official knowledge and upon which they may not be entitled even to open their mouths. Platt, whose temper made him accessible, whose pen ran easily, and whose mind was richly stored, paid more of this blackmail than most of his colleagues, and grudged it less.

Housman himself, however, paid 'this blackmail' much more cheerfully than might be gathered from his own words; he read papers on Matthew Arnold, Burns, Swinburne, Tennyson, the Spasmodic School and Erasmus Darwin. He reminded me of Sir Lancelot in Tennyson's *Idylls of the King* — a comparison which, had I ventured to suggest it, would have brought down his fiercest wrath. Each paper at the Literary Society was followed by a discussion, and you could observe Housman

> at the tilt
> Strike down the lusty and long-practised knight,
> And let the younger and unskill'd go by
> To win his honour and to make his name.

In these debates Housman, like his colleague Ker, had the power which belongs to the great, as it belonged to Dr. Johnson: if his pistol missed fire he knocked you down with the butt end. He would make a retort which, from anybody else, would not have been altogether conclusive, but the effect of which as uttered by Housman was devastating. I remember papers, in which he spoke of Tennyson with some disrespect. He described the argument of *In Memoriam* as being that 'things must come right in the end, because it would be so very unpleasant if they did not', adding that, if God had answered Tennyson out of the whirlwind as he answered Job, he would have said, 'Who is this that darkeneth counsel by words without knowledge?' In the subsequent debate Platt, who was in the chair, followed his practice of dropping on any member of the audience to speak, and called on me. I excused myself on the ground that Housman had uttered not merely his own but God's opinion on Tennyson, and that though I was willing to debate with Housman, I could not debate with one who had come armed with God's judgment. So I sat down, quoting Job's excuse for his silence, 'Wherefore I abhor myself and repent in dust and ashes.' I felt somewhat complacently that I had escaped rather well. When Housman rose to reply he said that he could attach no importance to what Mr. Chambers said, since he had been credibly informed that Mr. Chambers read the *Church Times*.[1] I felt, and everyone in the room felt, that I had been entirely flattened out. To lay an adversary low by a reply which would have been ineffective in the mouth of a smaller man, is the mark of the great debater.

I remember another debate in which I sought to defend the *Idylls of the King* against Housman's strictures by submitting that at any rate, if the *Idylls* had not got the spirit of Mallory, they would interest future generations as showing the spirit of the Victorian age. Housman, in his reply, retorted: 'Then, in that case, people will judge that the Victorian age was an age flowing with milk and water.'

Housman's challenges to the lusty and long-practised knight were not always taken up. He read a paper on Burns when W. P. Ker was present, packed full of jibes at Scots and Scotsmen;

[1] My belief was, that this was after Housman's paper on Matthew Arnold, which had ended by some remarks in praise of Arnold as contrasted with Tennyson and Browning — more surprising then than they would be to-day. But it must have been after the Tennyson paper; for before that was destroyed the words 'Church Times' were observed pencilled on the back — a note for the reply, doubtless.

but Ker refused to be drawn. 'Forgiveness', Ker began, 'is the last refuge of malignity. I will not forgive Professor Housman.' And he sat down.

Housman himself sometimes declined battle, and I have reason to remember a case when he left Ker in possession of the field. I had just been appointed librarian, and, with some friends, made a pretty thorough search of the then very neglected College library, in the course of which we discovered fourteen additional boxes of manuscripts, till then unknown, of Jeremy Bentham, and an unknown Coverdale Bible. I reported this to the Library Committee, possibly with an excess of self-satisfaction which Housman thought ought to be discountenanced. 'Would it not be as well', said Housman, 'to sell the Coverdale, and buy some really useful books with the money?' 'Judas Iscariot once said something of that sort,' retorted Ker, and Housman left it at that.

Another occasion on which Housman refused a challenge was when his brother Laurence came to University College, to give a lecture on behalf of women's suffrage. At the end there were loud cries for Alfred to speak. He rose and said:

> Birds in their little nests agree:
> And 'tis a shameful sight,
> When children of one family
> Fall out, and chide, and fight.

He then sat down again. Such at least is my recollection; Mr. Laurence Housman remembers the lines rather differently. Yet I am inclined to think my version correct, for Dr. Watts' pious poems were well known to Housman from childhood, and were praised by him in his Cambridge lecture, *The Name and Nature of Poetry*.

Housman differed from Platt in the care he took that his papers, read before colleagues and students, should not be printed. He gave one of the earliest of the Foundation Orations of University College Union Society. He delighted his audience by anthropological conjectures as to the origin of such celebrations, telling us how the savage, when suffering from toothache, said, 'The ghost of my grandfather is punishing me for neglect', and proceeded to make propitiatory sacrifice. But, though it was customary to print these orations, Housman would not let his be published, either on this occasion, or on the later one when he spoke on Thomas Campbell. We noticed as Housman went on, that he continued tearing up little bits of paper: we noticed it because such nervous fidgetiness was unlike him. When the President, at the end, made the usual request for the manuscript, Housman replied that it had been destroyed. As the address proceeded, he had been tearing up each page of his discourse after the other.

If he allowed himself to be blackmailed for papers to student societies, he was equally generous in contributing to the College magazine. I remember extracting *The Parallelogram* from him in the year 1904, under a promise that the authorship should not be divulged. It was divulged, but not by me. There were subsequent contributions in 1906 and 1911. In 1935 a younger teacher asked me if I would request Housman's permission to reprint these, on a private press which we have at University College. I refused, but suggested that he should see Housman himself: Housman, I said, would suffer young fools gladly, but would not suffer old fools with equal gladness. My friend presented himself at Housman's rooms in Trinity, explaining why I thought that he, rather than I, was the person to make the request, and Housman gave us permission to reprint these three poems.[1]

Housman brought to us not only some experience of routine business, but also 'a power of leadership and decisive action in a time of crisis'. The words are those of his colleague F. W. Oliver, Professor of Botany. It had been the tradition of University College to do without any Academic Head. Under the rule of Deans, honorary officials who served for terms of two or three years only, and were helped only by a secretary more and more incapacitated by his increasing ill-health, the College got deeper and deeper into debt. Housman, says Oliver, became 'the spokesman and leader' of the professors. Like the Israelites of old, they at last asked of their Honorary President,

[1] See *English*, I, pp. 485-93, *The publication of A. E. Housman's comic poems*, by GEOFFREY TILLOTSON (1937).

Lord Reay, that they might have someone to rule over them (together with a new and more energetic secretary). Oliver writes:

> The critical day (*circa* Midsummer, 1900) on which these measures were adopted by the Council is still fresh in my mind, and how the President, Lord Reay (in the absence of the Secretary), detained Housman at the end of the meeting to draft the minutes, and how I discharged the humbler office of telegraphing on Housman's behalf to his friends who were awaiting him at Henley (it was regatta week) that he would be joining them at a later hour than arranged, but that they should 'keep supper' for him.[1]

But once the business affairs of the College had been put straight by a Principal and an energetic secretary, Housman went back 'with relief and thankfulness to his proper job'. He did not, like W. P. Ker, continue to play a large part in College and University affairs. But he was an energetic Treasurer of our Dining Club, and Oliver tells how his own 'rudiments of a taste in wines' were 'definitely cultivated and enlarged through contact with Housman'. Women were beginning to be appointed to the staff of the College. A proposal that they should be eligible for the Dining Club 'was killed by Housman's invective'.

Less than three years after Housman had joined us, William Ramsay, working in his improvised laboratories in the cellars of the College, startled the world when he (together with the then Lord Rayleigh) discovered argon. Ramsay's share in this discovery was to be celebrated by a dinner at University College, at which Sir Henry Roscoe was to have proposed the principal toast. To everyone's consternation, Roscoe, the day before, telegraphed an apology for absence. Oliver, who was making the arrangements and who had heard from an Oxford source of Housman as an after-dinner speaker, persuaded him to fill the gap. Housman's speech, undertaken, in Oliver's words, 'from kindness of heart for a colleague in adversity', was the success of the evening. From that time he was the refuge of those at University College who had to organize formal dinners. One to W. P. Ker was enlivened by Housman's

[1] *University College Magazine*, March, 1937.

imaginary biography of his victim. Ker, Housman asserted, being determined to teach English, had begun by learning to speak and write it: 'And I must say that he learnt it very well; in fact, if I could speak and write Latin as well as Ker speaks and writes English, I should hang myself in despair of ever finding on earth a sufficiently appreciative audience.'

The world knew little of Housman in those days, and we felt a possessive pride in him. We knew (when most people did not), 'The lads in their hundreds':

> The lads in their hundreds to Ludlow come in for the fair,
> > There's men from the barn and the forge and the mill and
> > > the fold,
> The lads for the girls and the lads for the liquor are there,
> > And there with the rest are the lads that will never be old.
>
> There's chaps from the town and the field and the till and the
> > > cart,
> > And many to count are the stalwart, and many the brave,
> And many the handsome of face and the handsome of heart,
> > And few that will carry their looks or their truth to the
> > > grave.
>
> I wish one could know them, I wish there were tokens to tell
> > The fortunate fellows that now you can never discern;
> And then one could talk with them friendly and wish them
> > > farewell,
> > And watch them depart on the way that they will not return.
>
> But now you may stare as you like and there's nothing to scan;
> > And brushing your elbow unguessed-at and not to be told
> They carry back bright to the coiner the mintage of man,
> > The lads that will die in their glory and never be old.

To the same number of the College magazine to which Housman contributed *The Parallelogram*, the editor, Gerald Gould, contributed his *Ballad of the B.A. Classes*. The Shropshire Lad is supposed to speak in his character of Professor of Latin:

The lads in their hundreds come up — (it's a twopenny fare
If you travel by tube, which myself I do not ever do) —
The lads for the Inter., the lads for the Final, are there,
    And there, with the rest, are the lads who will never get
                        through.

There are men from St. Pancras and Hampstead and Ham-
                        mersmith way,
(This catalogue-making is easy, and fills up the space) —
And many there are that have hopes of the Honours B.A.,
    And few that are likely to get a respectable place.

I'm glad one can know them; I'm glad there are tokens to tell
    The fellows who rot and who slack and who cut the Unseen,
Because then one can speak them sarcastic, and cause them to
                        — well,
    One can cause them to look as a rule most remarkably
                        green.

My students may come to my lectures or not as they please;
    But I know, if they don't, the result that is safe to ensue;
They will carry back bright to the Office the requisite fees —
    The lads who go up and come down and can never get
                        through.

This has not, of course, the bite of the later parody by Hugh
Kingsmill:

        What, still alive at twenty two,
        A clean upstanding chap like you . . .

The Cambridge parody, as Guy Boas says, is 'deadly to the
point'. The London parody is an undergraduate's affectionate
jest. Characteristically, Housman spoke of the Cambridge
parody as 'the best he had seen'.

Our admiration took the form of caricature as well as parody.
R. E. M. Wheeler writes, 'I used to employ a considerable
portion of Housman's lectures on Lucretius in producing
portraits of him in action — if his calm, level, imperturbable
tenue could be called action.' One result of these studies was
the caricature, 'Thomas Campbell begins to wish he hadn't.'

A STUDENT'S CARICATURE OF A. E. HOUSMAN
by R. E. Mortimer Wheeler

This appeared in the magazine when Housman (just before he left us in 1911) had consented to give the Foundation Oration on our founder Thomas Campbell. It is evidence of Housman's popularity that he was asked to deliver the Foundation Oration twice; it is evidence of his affability that he complied with this quite unprecedented request. Those who heard the oration will agree that Campbell had reason for the shiver which the artist has depicted. Housman's attitude, looking, as has been said, 'ominously down his nose', is exactly that which we knew, when someone, proposing his health after a students' dinner, or criticizing his papers at the Literary Society, had boldly assailed him. (References to the Shropshire Lad were generally barred; a favourite line of attack was some comparison between Housman and God.) The assailant was warmly cheered — then there was an icy silence as Housman rose to reply, the assailant began to wish he hadn't, and the audience waited in delighted expectation of seeing him butchered. Housman once complained to Platt that I had an unfair advantage over him in these bouts, because, as a member of the Church of England, I could treat the Almighty with an irreverence which would be resented in him, a professing Atheist.

Yet beneath all lay Housman's impenetrable reserve. There was something ironical in his sitting amid an enthusiastic crowd of students, all singing that he was 'a jolly good fellow'.

The date of the dinner when he came to the help of a colleague in adversity with his joyous speech on Ramsay was 22 March 1895: the very time concerning which he said, twenty-seven years later: 'I can no longer expect to be revisited by the continuous excitement under which in the early months of 1895 I wrote the greater part of my other book, nor indeed could I well sustain it if it came.' It is safe to assume that none of his colleagues suspected this 'continuous excitement'. He lectured till one or two o'clock: drank his pint of beer (the College beer has a good reputation) and went for his solitary walks, on Hampstead Heath or elsewhere.

Such reserve was sometimes hardly fair to his fellow-teachers. During the South African War, a 'Pro-Boer' Professor made

some disrespectful remarks about the English private soldier.
The result was a display of Housman's invective which surprised even us, as he let his tongue curl round his unfortunate
colleague. But we did not realize that Housman had lost his
beloved soldier brother, Sergeant George Herbert Housman,
who fell in a charge of mounted infantry in 1901. That, as we
now know, is the explanation of *Last Poems*, XVII:

> Oh I will sit me down and weep
> For bones in Africa.

Those who knew Housman, even superficially, will never agree
with the judgment (not uncommon among critics who never
knew him) that he was 'filled equally with admiration for the
soldier and with mockery for his trade'. Housman's irony was
liable to be misunderstood. Some have even misunderstood

> Followed their mercenary calling
> And took their wages and are dead.

His sister has written:

On his intellectual side, we allow him to have been intolerant;
on his human side, he was ready to humble himself before
the man who chose to go out to fight and risk his life in doing
so. It is a true story that is told of his sending all his available
money to the Chancellor of the Exchequer in 1914, because
he could give no other war-service. He first sent £100 to
help in equipping three nephews who had joined the Army,
and all the rest of his bank balance he sent to the Exchequer.

One of *Last Poems*, No. 32, may literally apply to himself
from its opening, 'When I would muse in boyhood', to its
termination:

> They sought and found six feet of ground,
> And there they died for me.[1]

And she tells how, when one of her sons was killed in Flanders
in 1915, he sent her 'Illic Jacet' (*Last Poems*, No. IV):

> Oh hard is the bed they have made him,
> And common the blanket and cheap;
> But there he will lie as they laid him;
> Where else could you trust him to sleep? . . .

[1] *Supplement* to *The Bromsgrovian*, p. 26.

Oh dark is the chamber and lonely,
    And lights and companions depart;
But lief will he lose them and only
    Behold the desire of his heart. . . .

She writes:

He said that he had written it some years earlier, but he
sent it to me because 'it is the function of poetry to harmonize
the sadness of the world'.
Does not that give a key to much of his poetry?[1]

Mrs. Symons has stated, with authority and knowledge, what
I think was felt instinctively by nearly all of us. Not by quite
all. Housman's reserve concealed his personal loss: but his
views on national affairs ought to have been well enough known
to save his 'Pro-Boer' colleague from the blunder he made.
Housman was no political partisan, yet he generally welcomed
a Conservative victory at a bye-election, 'because', he said,
'it will vex the kind of people I don't like'. When he took the
chair at a debate on Democratic Government he summed up
in favour of democracy, on the ground that it was difficult to
betray a Government you had yourself chosen. He instanced
cases where defeatists had welcomed the disasters of their own
autocratic government, because such disasters must lead to
revolution. 'Democracy does save you from horrors like that',
he said, and at the word 'horrors' a shudder seemed to pass
over him.

His public spirit was shown when, in the financial crisis of
1931, he repeated the action of 1914, and, in his brother's
words, 'came to the rescue so far as his means allowed'.

But this open-handedness was not confined to public affairs.
'Among his papers', his brother writes, 'I found frequent
evidence of his generosity, both moral and monetary (lenient in
the one case, lavish in the other) . . . His kindness of tone (he
kept copies of his replies) to those he had once befriended
never varied, even when he had to reject further applications
for aid.'

It is known how Housman, having heard that the gondolier

[1] The same, page 29

whom he had employed for many summers was attacked by a
fatal disease, rushed off to Venice and made 'all provision, with
legal security', for his comfort. Of Venice he wrote, 'Certainly
there is no place like it in the world: everything there is better
in reality than in memory.' But, he added significantly, 'I
shall not go there again.' This explains the last stanza in the
lines on the rebuilt Campanile in *More Poems*:

> It looks to north and south,
>   It looks to east and west;
> It guides to Lido mouth
>   The steersman of Triest.
>   Andrea, fare you well;
>   Venice farewell to thee.
>   The tower that stood and fell
>   Is not rebuilt in me.

His characteristics were generosity and kindness to the
young, concealed by an outward austerity. When I was a very
young and inexperienced librarian at University College, faced
by the task of getting into order a neglected library of a
hundred thousand volumes, Housman was one of the men to
whom I instinctively appealed for helpful advice. It was always
generously given: and if the advice was sometimes accompanied
by sarcasms, I had thoroughly deserved them; and, I hope, I
profited by them.

When, in 1911, Housman was appointed to the Kennedy
chair of Latin at Cambridge, we, his old students of the past
nineteen years, gave him a silver loving cup, with the inscription round it, 'Malt does more than Milton can to justify
God's ways to man.' It was then that he described his predecessor at Cambridge, J. E. B. Mayor, as a man who drank
like a fish — 'If drinking nothing but water might be so
described.' 'When they see me coming to Cambridge with
this cup', he said, 'they will understand that things are going
to be changed.' At the farewell dinner given to him by his
colleagues, he made a similar reference to Mayor's abstemious-
ness, and to the duty incumbent on his successor of changing
that tradition: 'Cambridge has seen many strange sights.

It has seen Wordsworth drunk and Porson sober. It is now destined to see a better scholar than Wordsworth and a better poet than Porson betwixt and between.'[1] He professed, by a polite fiction, that he was leaving us because of the rule, then just introduced, of superannuation at sixty-five. This of course would not have been binding upon appointments, like his, already made. But he asserted that he had been kept awake at nights, pondering what he should do between the age of sixty-five, when he would be morally, though not legally, compelled to retire, and the age of seventy, when he would become eligible for the old age pension (which also had recently been introduced). 'I have now found a refuge,' he said. 'Death, raving madness, or detected crime are the only enemies I have now to fear.'

He asked that, though retiring, he might be allowed to retain his membership of the Dining Club. But it was some years before he attended another dinner, and then again as our guest. He repeated the jest about having been compelled to leave London by fears of superannuation, and clinched it by adding: 'In Cambridge I have found what in every sense of the word I may describe as an asylum.' This has sometimes been repeated apart from its context. So repeated, it may appear pointless, or even rude. The underlying meaning is that in Cambridge he had found, what we, with all our goodwill, could never supply — a home. There is no doubt that Cambridge gave to Housman students more suited to his teaching, and his fellowship of Trinity gave him what London could not. No one who saw him at Cambridge could doubt that he was at last 'in his right setting'; and his brother confirms the belief that his Cambridge period was happier than any other since his break with Oxford.

Housman had made his reputation, by the publication of *A Shropshire Lad*, and of his two great prefaces, before he left us. But, so far as I know, he never had any student at University College worthy of his scholarship. But three things we, his

---

[1] There have been various versions of this published, but my recollection is confirmed by our Senior Tutor, Mr. Lawrence Solomon, and with trifling verbal variants by Sir Percy Nunn (Letter to *The Times*, 5 May, 1936, signed 'T.P.N.'). We were all three present.

students, got from him. They were things which even those who were not exact scholars could learn. 'In the lecture-room or out', says Mr. Gow, 'it was impossible to listen attentively to Housman for long without becoming aware that one was in contact with a mind of extraordinary distinction; and it is not only, or even chiefly, to professional scholars that such a contact is fascinating and exhilarating.'

Secondly, there was his love of truth. In 1903 he wrote that 'the faintest of all human passions is the love of truth.'[1] But the strength of that passion was clear in his first lecture, and all subsequent knowledge of him confirmed it. He admitted that this pursuit might be in some directions injurious to happiness, 'because it compels us to take leave of delusions which were pleasant while they lasted'. Nevertheless, he said, it must in the long run be better for a man to see things as they are. (He was to say the same thing eleven years later in the Preface to *Manilius*, when he denounced the man who believes that the text of ancient authors is generally sound, because he would feel uncomfortable if he did not believe it; 'just as he believes, on the same cogent evidence, that he is a fine fellow, and that he will rise again from the dead'.) And in this pursuit of truth all must join:

> There is no rivalry between the studies of Arts and Laws and Science but the rivalry of fellow-soldiers in striving which can most victoriously achieve the common end of all, to set back the frontier of darkness.
>
> It is the glory of God, says Solomon, to conceal a thing; but the honour of kings is to search out a matter. Kings have long abdicated that province; and we students are come into their inheritance; it is our honour to search out the things which God has concealed.[2]

It was this love of truth which made him so exact; 'accuracy', he wrote, 'is a duty and not a virtue'[3]; it was that also which made him so fierce a critic of those who 'mistook a wish for a reason'. Love of truth was not warped, in him, by prejudices, personal or national. He would admit, concerning the critics

[1] Manilius, I, xliii.
[2] *Introductory Lecture*, 1892, p. 41.   [3] Manilius, V, 105.

whom he most severely lashed, that God, pitying their ineptitudes, had occasionally inspired them with a bright idea. And in very much the same way he used to praise any good work his unworthy flock showed up, though it is to be feared that our bright ideas were few. He was suspected of prejudice against German learning. Those who are best qualified to speak on that subject do not think the charge justified. He said things equally severe about English scholarship: if he pilloried Germans more frequently than Englishmen, that was because they had done very much more work in the fields in which he laboured, and so afforded a broader target. Mr. Gow quotes from a letter which Housman wrote in 1919: 'I should say that for the last hundred years individual German scholars have been the superiors in genius as well as learning of all scholars outside Germany, except Madvig and Cobet.' Intellectually he was a good European. 'Patriotism', he said, 'in the sphere of intellect is an unmitigated nuisance.' He took an impish delight in poking fun at national self-complacency, whether English or German. In company with another young teacher, I once pestered him to give a testimonial to a student who wanted to teach English in Germany, although all that Housman knew of him was that his Latin proses had not been impeccable. After much importunity, Housman consented to write some flowing periods concluding, 'Mr. X is, in my opinion, eminently qualified to teach English in a German University.' He knew that no irony would be suspected.

The third thing of which one could not but be aware was Housman's grim courage in facing a world, the evil of which he felt more keenly than most. It was like the outlook of the Norsemen, as Ker has defined it, 'their last independent guess at the secret of the Universe', before they were absorbed in European culture. 'It is the assertion of the individual freedom against all the terrors and temptations of the world. It is absolute resistance, perfect because without hope.' 'As far as it goes, and as a working theory, it is absolutely impregnable.'

That is the spirit of his poem, 'The Sage to the Young Man' (a spirit which his reserve made him usually hide):

O youth whose heart is right,
  Whose loins are girt to gain
The hell-defended height
  Where Virtue beckons plain; ...

Well is thy war begun;
  Endure, be strong and strive;
But think not, O my son,
  To save thy soul alive. ...

How shouldst thou keep the prize?
  Thou wast not born for aye.
Content thee if thine eyes
  Behold it in thy day.

We may compare 'The Oracles' in *Last Poems* (XXV):

And he that stands will die for nought, and home there's no returning.
  The Spartans on the sea-wet rock sat down and combed
  their hair.

Housman rejected 'The Sage to the Young Man' from *A Shropshire Lad*; he allowed it to be published during the war, but anonymously. He said of 'The Oracles' that he did not admire it 'quite so much as some people do'. He said of his London Introductory Lecture that it was 'rhetorical and not wholly sincere'. There were indeed some provocative things in it, which I remember our discussing among ourselves after, and which, like some of the things in his papers before the Literary Society, were meant to arouse discussion. But in that lecture Housman, free at last from his Civil Service drudgery, 'let himself go', and spoke out what he felt passionately, in a way which none who heard could forget. As Mr. Gow says, 'nobody familiar with his work can doubt the sincerity of its central theme, the value of learning for its own sake'.

I believe that Housman was accurately described by Sir John Squire:[1]

His philosophy was not every man's, but he was utterly honest, anguished because 'men loved unkindness', and unable, though a naturally Christian soul, to find consolation.

[1] In a review of *More Poems* in the *Daily Telegraph*.

My belief in the accuracy of this description is not shaken —
it is confirmed — because I know that Housman would have
shown annoyance, could he have seen himself so described.

Of those who gathered to pay their farewell, in Trinity
College Chapel on 4 May, 1936, Housman's brother Laurence
and I were, I fancy, the only ones who had been present at his
first Academic discourse in 1892. Housman's address had been
a reply to the question: What is the good which we set before
us as our end in learning? He had dismissed with scorn the
utilitarian plea. Science will not make you rich. Men do not
become millionaires by their knowledge of Science, though
they do sometimes become so by other people's knowledge of
Science. Men do not transform and beautify their inner
nature by the study of the Classics, though they do learn not
to call the muse who is supposed to preside over dancing
Terpsitshoar. Why then pursue learning beyond the small
amount which will serve our turn? Housman had given the
answer in the words of Dante, words which were the favourite
quotation of Ker, who was sitting beside him as he spoke: the
words in which the aged Ulysses urges his aged companions,
in this brief vigil of their senses that remains, to make their
voyage of exploration beyond the pillars of Hercules:

'Consider of what seed ye are sprung: ye were not formed
to live like brutes, but to follow virtue and knowledge.'
For knowledge (Housman went on) resembles virtue in this,
and differs in this from other possessions, that it is not merely
a means of procuring good, but is good in itself simply: it is
not a coin which we pay down to purchase happiness, but
has happiness indissolubly bound up with it. Fortitude
and continence and honesty are not commended to us on the
ground that they conduce, as on the whole they do conduce,
to material success, nor yet on the ground that they will be
rewarded hereafter: those whose office it is to exhort mankind
to virtue are ashamed to degrade the cause they plead by
proffering such lures as these. And let us too disdain to take
lower ground in commending knowledge: let us insist that
the pursuit of knowledge, like the pursuit of righteousness,
is part of man's duty to himself; and remember the Scripture

where it is written: 'He that refuseth instruction despiseth his own soul.'

It was right that we should take our farewell of Housman in that Chapel which is associated with the memory of many other men who shared Housman's passion for truth. Looking across at us was the statue

> Of Newton with his prism and silent face,
> The marble index of a mind for ever
> Voyaging through strange seas of Thought, alone.

None had ever made the voyage in more utter loneliness than had Housman. It came rather as a surprise to learn that he had written a hymn to be sung at this time, and had chosen the music, a Melody by Melchior Vulpius, harmonized by J. S. Bach.

> O thou that from thy mansion
>   Through time and place to roam,
> Dost send abroad thy children,
>   And then dost call them home,
>
> That men and tribes and nations
>   And all thy hand hath made
> May shelter them from sunshine
>   In thine eternal shade:
>
> We now to peace and darkness
>   And earth and thee restore
> Thy creature that thou madest
>   And wilt cast forth no more.

W. P. KER

Ker was fortunate in that he was able to spend his first twenty-eight years, without any premature specialization, in laying a broad foundation for the work of a lifetime. He was born in 1855, educated at the Glasgow Academy and University, and went to Balliol (1874-8) with a Snell Exhibition, in ·the time of Jowett.

He surprised his friends by getting only a Second in Greats after his First in Mods. They accounted for it by saying that he was 'William the Silent'. (But his silences, says Lord Ernle, who was in his fourth year at Balliol when Ker was in his first, were more companionable than are the conversations of others.)

Mr. A. C. Bradley has recorded: 'I was a young don at Balliol then. W. P. was as good at philosophy as at history: yet we used to say to one another, "It would be ridiculous for W. P. to miss his First, but can he write enough?" '

But this academic misadventure did not seriously harm him. He took it with equanimity, and announced it to his sister with a stoicism which he said that he had learnt from Outalissi,

> 'Because I may not stain with grief
> The death-song of an Indian chief.'

The incident was swiftly made good by the Taylorian Scholarship in the year of his Final Schools, 1878, and in November, 1879, by the All Souls Fellowship. Lord Ernle was one of the two Fellows of All Souls told off to draft the examination papers, and report upon the candidates. 'Ker's work', he says, 'impressed me by the richness of its quality and the poverty of its quantity. Ker was elected, I think, unanimously.'

In 1878-9, Ker had served as assistant to W. Y. Sellar, Professor of Humanity in Edinburgh. This assistantship to Sellar was one of the most valued experiences of Ker's life. Mrs. MacCunn (Miss Florence Sellar) tells how, the summer before his work with her father was to begin, he came to visit them at Kenbank in Galloway.

He arrived late, a good-looking, grave, silent young man. He hardly gave one the impression of shyness, at least he was not at all disconcerted by my mother's audaciously witty sallies, but he did not fill up gaps in the conversation.

The next day two of us were sitting out on the lawn struggling, with enthusiasm but rather imperfect Italian, with the twenty-sixth canto of the *Inferno*. How it came about I cannot remember, but I do not forget the sound of his beautiful Italian when he took the book and began at the 90th line, the speech of Ulysses. It was a fitting introduction, though one could not know it at the time. He did not live to be 'vecchio e tarde', but like Ulysses he could not have outlived the desire for further adventures in unknown seas; to the end he too must have followed 'virtute e conoscenza'. He translated as he went along, simply and clearly bringing out the weirdness of the end, the wind blowing from the mountain island, the ship turning three times round and sinking by the bow. And then he quoted rather solemnly the last verses of the *Ship of the Fiend*, bringing out the awsomeness of that other shipwreck when

> He struck the main mast wi' his hand,
> The foremast wi' his knee;
> The gallant ship was broken in twain,
> And sank into the sea.

Ballads were then, as always, running in his head, snatches from them were frequent on his lips. . . .

I think we looked on him mainly as a humorist of a fine and unusual kind. My mother delighted in his dry comments, and my six-year-old brother used to borrow an eyeglass that he might invent catastrophic situations and Mr. Ker's demeanour under them.[1]

It was a dozen years later, and Ker had left Cardiff and had been for a year Professor of English Literature in University College, London, when Sellar, who had been working hard upon his book, *Horace and the Elegiac Poets*, fell ill, one September evening, with a chill, which led to his death a few weeks later. It was Sellar's wish that Ker should edit his unfinished work. Mrs. MacCunn permits me to publish a portion of the letter which Ker wrote after the death of her father:

. . . I cannot think of your father now with any other feeling than that of thanks and praise for all he has been to me and of great reverence in the face of all the mysteries. I have learned a great deal from your father; he thought

[1] *Our Friend W. P.*, p. 49.

worthily and justly about most things, especially the most
solemn things, and the memory of the good days I have spent
with him is enough to keep away all ignoble thoughts — or
so it seems to me.

In 1883, at the age of twenty-eight, Ker was one of the young
men appointed to professorships in the new University College
of Cardiff. It was hard, pioneering work, and he looked back
on it with keen pleasure. 'There is something good in education', he said, 'when it beats up a crew of adventurers, and puts
them in a stockade to hold it against the enemy.'

In 1889 Ker was appointed to the Quain Chair of English
in University College, London. Till his resignation of that
chair thirty-three years later, he spent most of the very long
London terms at his house, 95 Gower Street. But at the end
of each week 'he was always to be found at Oxford'.

Returning to London on Mondays, he gave every week an
extraordinary number of lectures and classes — in the earlier
years of his professorship as many as a dozen. In substance
and style they were quite different from those single public
lectures on isolated topics, by which alone he is widely known
as a lecturer. For long after each lecture Ker waited in his
class room, and there was always a line of students who loved
to come up, each for a few moments' talk.

In the early years of his professorship he had among his
students G. K. Chesterton and E. V. Lucas. Some thirty years
later, at the dinner when, upon his retirement, he was the guest
of his old students and friends, Ker reminded G. K. of a
lecture on Pope delivered at University College to a single
but ample student. (Most of his audience thought Ker was
exaggerating, but he was, as always, strictly accurate.)[1]

He said, the same evening, that he could not remember
'any serious row or difficulty' in all his experience as a lecturer.

[1] I have this (and the next anecdote) on the authority of the late Sir Ernest
Hodder-Williams, a fellow-student of my own and of Chesterton's. Ker's early
register, which he preserved, records Chesterton as the only student present at
the 'Intermediate Class B' on 12 December, 1893, the note 'Exam.' accounting
for the absence of the rest of the class of twenty-three.

But the classes, at any rate at this early date, were not too tame. It was at this time that Ker quelled a very rowdy class room by pointing slowly at a burly student, the ring-leader of revolt, and saying very quietly, 'Be good'.

My own first encounter with Ker (a sufficiently formidable one) was as a very young undergraduate, in the third session of his tenure of the chair at University College. We were reading *Piers Plowman*, and Ker was following his usual practice of translating a passage with comment, then from time to time pausing, and putting on a member of the class to construe. I had been copying down his dicta so energetically that I had got somewhat behind, and missed his last remark — which had been a warning not to fall into a certain error of translation. 'Mr. Chambers, will you construe?' Mr. Chambers did his best, and floundered into the very error against which the class had just been warned. Ker paused for a full minute, as if reconsidering the matter. Then, 'I still adhere, Mr. Chambers, to my original opinion, in spite of your contradiction.' E. V. Lucas was in the class, and I still remember his glee.

Ker's manner of lecturing to his students has been described by Professor B. Ifor Evans, one of the younger among them:

We will always remember him as he lectured to us: the low voice with its slow, emphatic delivery: pausing at times while he stood, his hand outstretched even as if in pain. We remember how the eyes would sparkle and the whole face lighten in anticipation of a stroke of wit, and the voice would grow even thinner and quieter than in the main discourse; how he would read and quote frequently, while the sounds would rise and fall through a wide range of tones. We remember how he taught us that life and work were a game to be played well, and with attention to the rules and to the other players. Examinations, he used to tell us, were a game to be tried between the examiners and examinees.

About one-third of Ker's thirty-three years of strenuous teaching in University College had passed, when the University of London was reorganized. After that, as Chairman of the Modern Languages Board, and, later, of the English Board, Ker took the leading part in moulding English studies throughout the University of London. It was not always an easy task. He was strong in his hatred, on the one hand, of any officialdom which seemed likely to hamper the School, and, on the other, of any slackness on the part of his colleagues on the Board. When he thought he detected either of these sins, he could be unusually (his victims may have thought unnecessarily) severe. A member of the Board who came late might be greeted with the words, 'Mr. —— has returned from his holiday.' The words look harmless: but those who watched the eyes and mouth of W. P. had a lesson in the meaning which harmless words may be made to convey.

But the building up of an Honours School of English was only one of his labours in London. He threw himself into the general work of the University, on the Senate, the Academic Council, and the Faculty, and on the Professorial Board of his College. He attended assiduously, spoke seldom, and then always very briefly, but with extraordinary effect. His conservatism was combined with a readiness for any development upon sound lines. During the difficult years of the reconstruction of the University of London he was, in the words of his tried and experienced colleague Gregory Foster, Provost of University College, 'a tower of strength to us, and he often exhibited with skill the pettiness of the claims of one or the other of the contending parties'.

The pettiness was sometimes sufficiently trying. Ker had been appointed to his professorship without age-limit. But when he reached the age of 65, some officious persons on the Senate began to discuss whether he ought not to retire voluntarily. After he *had* retired, Ker mentioned this to me. 'It's bloody,' I said. 'To call it bloody,' Ker replied, slowly and sadly, 'is fulsome flattery.'

His eagerness for any new adventure was shown by the energy with which, even during the distractions of the War, he undertook the work of organizing the teaching of Scandinavian in London. After some Swedes had been dining with him, he wrote: 'They are all very keen about getting Sweden better known over here, and I am hoping to be one of the instruments, under Providence.'

An early biographer of Sidney tells us that 'Such was the ubiquitariness of Sir Philip's mind that he could attend at the same time to all arts.' Ker could attend to all the literatures of Western Europe, and to the affairs of more than one University, with a thoroughness which made it difficult to believe that each of these interests was not first in his mind. 'I go to-day', he wrote on 12 May, 1922, 'to Aberystwyth, to give a lecture on Pope. You may think this exorbitant, but it saves me a meeting of school governors at Bow' (Ker represented University College on the governing board of the Stepney and Bow schools for twenty-six years). At another time he apologized for not coming to lunch: 'I am sorry I am prevented. A committee springs up at 1.45 to-morrow, and chokes my party.' How many were his duties, and how seriously he took them, few knew till, after his death, friend spoke with friend about him, and found that he had been working in all sorts of unexpected ways. Three fragments from letters, quoted by Professor MacCunn, show how sometimes the routine work, and especially the Committee work, had been telling upon him. To an invitation to undertake a fresh duty, he replied:

I have Sermons to preach in November, December, and January and February — I mean show pieces which take, each of them, a week at least to think about and compose — forby the College Lectures — and two engagements to write books, which are about my bed and my board (the promises I mean); and I am examining already in Oxford and Cambridge, and thinking of chucking it, too. No, sir. Justice is every man doing his own business, and mine is quite enough for me.

Some people are going about saying that The Absolute is a Committee. I do not believe this. But, if I were a Manichee, I could think that the evil half of the world might be expressed in that way.

Far from hence the Atlantic breaks in a warm bay, and there the sunlight in the happy glens is fair —

While here contorted angels of the Pit
In foul committee without end commit
To chattering words a tale that has no sense in it.

The demands upon his time made by all these things grew,
in the end, unbearable; and when he resigned his London chair
in 1922, he wrote, in answer to my plea that he should consent
to stay at least a year or two longer, 'It is nothing in the house
that is making me leave it — only the intolerable agenda of
committees.' The Directorship of Scandinavian Studies in
London, however, he retained to the last, for the thing dearest
of all to him was the study of what Scandinavia had contributed to the world. Almost his last words to the Provost of
University College were: 'I am anxious about Scandinavian
studies; they must be kept going.' In a letter, amid other
topics, he would suddenly break out with, 'Do not neglect the
Danish tongue.' He once told me how he was made free of
the Norwegian tongue. He and a friend, immediately after
landing, met a Norwegian boy, and began, in their best
Norwegian, to explain to him that they were not foreigners
(though they might look it) but Norse. The boy would make
no reply. When they had exhausted their eloquence, he stepped
up to them, shook hands, and walked away in silence.

What he himself felt about his teaching was expressed when,
less than three months before his death, he said farewell to
old friends and students who had met in University College
to hand over his portrait to the College, and to give him the
album containing their signatures:

> ... I ought, I know, to feel that all my past life is coming
> back in a vision, and that this present reality is somewhat
> unreal as compared with what is past — and I will not say
> that that is altogether different from my present state of
> feeling ... but I am just as much impressed with the reality
> of the present occasion, with the sense that I have had a
> successful life, and that this place, in which I have spent so
> much time, is going on.

Ker went on to speak of the Provost, Sir Gregory Foster, who
'represents, in all senses of the word, the teaching of Henry

Morley', and whom, he said, 'I cannot thank enough, or admire enough, for his help in the Department of English'. Foster had begun his University teaching as Ker's assistant, and, in one capacity or another, had continued right through to teach. Ker had deep respect for Heads of Colleges who, like Foster, or Peterson of McGill (another old friend) carried on with teaching or research despite administrative duties. 'There is nothing left me to wish for,' Ker said, 'nothing that I wish better in this theatre as I leave it. There, I have spoken my mind. It is not that I haven't many things to repent of; I do not believe that all my sentences have been full of life, or that they have all been grammatical.'

> I might go on with reminiscences and with good advice. My good advice is that of the Abbey of Thelema: 'Do what you like' — and of course be sure that you know what you like. That advice is supplemented with the note that those who are well nurtured have in them the mind of honour that keeps them in the right way. That is my advice. I have followed it as well as I could since I began to attend to books. My training was not in English philology, in which I must confess that I am an amateur; but that does not mean that I owe nothing to nobody for what English philology I may command, and I should like here to name one of my old friends, William Gow. . . .

Gow, he told us, had been a pupil of the great German teachers, Bartsch and Sievers and Zupitza:

> From Gow I got advice and instruction to make a beginning; before that I was given to other languages, and my preferences were for Italian and French and Middle High German rather than for Anglo-Saxon and Middle English. That is merely part of my memory, but it is part also of the history of this College, and I am glad to think that I have owed some of my life to a man who was my companion in Glasgow and afterwards spent time here. It was he who told me forty years ago that University College, London, was the most spirited place he had ever been in, and he had known many places of study and learning. . . .

> May I add the piece of advice not to forget Mr. Helweg's 'Danish Ballads'? These are my last words. Thank you.

A STUDENT'S SNAP-SHOT OF W. P. KER
(Taken about 1916)

The album of signatures contained an address:

> You have been so faithful and so loving to us, you have fought
> so stoutly for us, you have been so hearty in counselling of us,
> that we shall never forget your favour toward us.

We all felt, I think, that these words of the Pilgrims to Mr.
Greatheart were peculiarly appropriate to our leavetaking.
Not that we thought of it as final. We remembered that Mr.
Greatheart, when he left the company he had guided so long,
so faithfully and so lovingly, was yet to be a conductor to more
of the pilgrims. But it was not to be so. 'The next day, said
they, we will, if the day be clear, show you the Delectable
Mountains. And when thou comest there, from thence, said
they, thou mayest see to the gate of the Celestial City.'

An Oxford friend said of Ker's memory at All Souls: 'Nor
will the day ever come, even if the larger world neglect him,
when his wisdom is not understood, and his sayings are not
repeated, in the College which he loved.'

In University College, London, which he also loved, the
tradition of him seems to have grown stronger and stronger in
the years which have passed since he left us. It will continue
to be treasured, in the spirit which he himself expressed when
speaking of the book which records the lives of the alumni of
University College fallen in the war: 'I keep it for a memorial,
and for hope.'

Ker was slow to publish. He was forty-two when *Epic and
Romance* appeared in 1897. Till then, he had printed hardly
anything. It was not at once realized how great was the light
which *Epic and Romance* threw on problems which had been
puzzling scholars for many years. In *The Dark Ages* (1904)
and *English Literature: Medieval* (1912) he compressed into small
volumes much of the result of his vast reading. In 1905 a
number of his shorter writings were issued in a collected
volume, *Essays on Medieval Literature* (including his Introduction
to Berners' *Froissart*). His lectures as Professor of Poetry at
Oxford were issued in 1923 (*The Art of Poetry — Seven Lectures*,
1920-2). His many scattered lectures, delivered on different
occasions, were collected after his death (2 vols., ed. Charles

Whibley, 1925). Some series of lectures, delivered in University College, are being printed from notes taken at the time, with a short biographical introduction; *Form and Style in Poetry* has been already issued.

Ker's feelings on public affairs were an essential part of him — one cannot imagine them otherwise. 'Nothing modern', says Mr. Charles Whibley, 'affected him so deeply as did modern politics', and Mr. Whibley goes on to quote a characteristic letter written two days before Ker set out for his last journey to Italy:

> I went to Windsor Castle yesterday ... There are the flags of the disbanded Irish regiments, all together, looking very honourable, and each succeeding swarm of tourists is told what they are. I hope they will be remembered.

Characteristically, Ker never allowed political differences to stand in the way of friendship. Friends have spoken of his combination of strong conviction with humorous intolerance, and have compared it to that of Dr. Johnson. But even historians most sympathetic to Mr. Gladstone now recognize that Gladstone's acceptance of Parnell's claim to coerce Protestant Ulster into a new Ireland 'flew in the face of racial and political possibilities'.[1] When Ker said 'We have made lies our refuge and under falsehood we have hid ourselves', that was not intolerance, but his feeling that realities were being ignored. Just before the War, early in 1914, a colleague at University College said that if the Ulstermen insisted on being shot down, there was nothing for it but to shoot them. A friend expressed to Ker a doubt whether such language could be regarded as sane. 'It is always dangerous', said Ker, 'when you begin to doubt the sanity of your fellow-men'; but the tone in which he spoke showed that he shared the feeling of his friend.

Ker once said to Sellar's daughter, Mrs. MacCunn, that he had learnt his politics from his old chief. Sellar, a Liberal Unionist, once defined Liberalism as 'the desire that every one should, as much as possible, have his full share of all that is

[1] G. M. TREVELYAN, *History of England*, 1926, p. 688.

best.' Ker's teaching life — the six years spent holding the 'stockade' at Cardiff, the thirty-three years of toil in London, were passed in trying to bring 'a full share of all that is best' within the reach of as many people as possible. It was this which made him squander precious hours in going 'to a meeting of school governors at Bow'.

Ker was able to do this work without falling into the pits which wait for those who concern themselves with the spread of education in the democratic universities, because of his belief in all men and women — 'the workers in field and fold and farm, the shepherd on the hill, the fisherman in his boat, the cottager at his fireside, the Alpine guide, the peasant bringing in his beasts ... He had much love for the ordinary folk of the countryside ... and the friendly greetings that passed were heart-felt and without shadow of make-believe; "very pleasant", he notes, "to be recognized by the fishermen on the shore".'

After the War, and his silent grief for the young lives lost, he felt bitterly how little the Allied victory was able to bring about the new world for which we had hoped:

> vain seemed all the strength to him
> As golden convoys sunk at sea.

A letter from Zermatt (27 July, 1921), telling of happy mountain excursions, past and to come, has a sudden post-script, 'When you write, you can tell me whether our country of Great Britain is deeper or shallower in disgrace.'

This mood is, I think, reflected in the noble portrait of Ker by Mr. Wilson Steer, now in University College, London — a portrait which is not reproduced here, only because no repro-duction can do justice to its forceful colour. The face is that of a man thinking deeply on some subject not altogether pleasing to him, but through which he sees further than his fellows.

The bust at All Souls College (by Mr. John Tweed) shows Ker in a happier mood, and one which his friends will recognize as a more usual one. There is a replica of this in the library of University College, London, and another in the University of Glasgow.

In the earlier years of his teaching in London, Ker had very little assistance. Yet he read our essays with scrupulous care, and a keen eye for any meaningless verbiage. A student wrote that 'Chaucer's verse was a vehicle for the loftiest flights of the imagination'. Ker's note in the margin: 'A flying machine'. 'The *Faerie Queene* was the highest point English poetry had achieved'. Ker's note: 'But the *Faerie Queene* has magnitude.' There was the same unexpected and whimsical turn in his sayings. Walking along a precipitous cliff path at a seaside resort, he noticed where a Salvation Army enthusiast had chalked up 'Prepare to meet thy God'. 'Dear me', said Ker, 'and in such a narrow place too.'

A group were examining a case of stuffed birds. 'I rather think it's a magpie,' said the first. 'It's not my idea of a magpie,' replied the second. After a long silence, Ker's voice sounded, quietly but positively, 'It's God Almighty's idea of a magpie.'[1] Ker's silence could be intimidating. Mrs. John Richard Green told me how, when his *Dark Ages* came out, she had expressed her appreciation to him. Ker gazed at her, but did not help the conversation, till she stopped in some embarrassment. After a long pause, he said, 'Go on; I like it.'

How in the midst of his teaching and the even more exacting Committees, he managed to attend to all the literatures of Western Europe, no one will ever know. In inaugurating his Oxford lectures on Poetry, when he set out on 'his last adventure but one', he pointed out how poetry, unlike the other arts, is beset by 'the curse of Babel'. But, five years before, Mr. E. V. Lucas had written of him:

> He's read every book — by two candles so dim;
> And Babel in vain was frustrated for him.

It was sufficiently amazing that he knew the tongues and the literatures of all lands in Europe to the borders of the Slavs; more amazing that, with all this, 'he never gave up to an imagined necessity of toil the hours which he might dedicate to talk and to his friends'. Only exceptional health could have

---

[1] The first record of this story, without Ker's name, seems to be in a letter of York Powell, 30 June, 1903 (*Life* by OLIVER ELTON, I, 377). It must have been about this time that I first heard the story, but the bird had by then become a guillemot. It was not a woodcock, as stated in Elton's *Life*.

enabled him to do all he did. During his thirty-three years'
tenure of the Quain Chair he never missed a lecture from
illness. If any man ever carried out the Pauline precept,
'Whatsoever things are of good report: if there be any virtue,
if there be any praise, think on these things', it was W. P. Ker.
An old student, Gerald Gould, wrote of him, 'his love of
children, of dancing, rowing, climbing, of good wine' (for
there also the Pauline advice was heeded), 'and of good fellowship, was the same thing as his love of books'. He loved animals
too, and would gaze at them with a grave friendliness during
his constant visits to the Zoo. He was happy watching the
penguins, happy carrying his boots down the narrow street of
Zermatt to Burgener to be re-nailed. ('In Regent Street this
would not be quite proper, but here it is the swagger thing to
do.') It was this which made him such a guide and counsellor
to the young. 'I have accustomed myself,' one of them writes,
'to feel that I could not get on without him; now I shall have to.'

Ker not only shared the 'passion of the good and wise for
walking', but would admit only grudgingly the goodness and
the wisdom of some in whom that passion was wanting: 'He
is a good man; but he does not walk, and he does not drink;
he is no good to me.' When, in middle life, some of his friends
took to bicycling, he wrote, 'Can two walk together if one is on
wheels?' Dante, he said, 'must have been good at walking
tours'. He thought the more of Keats because of his long and
difficult walk to the Ross of Mull. But he regretted that he
had not been there to give good advice. 'I wish I had known
Keats. I think I could have told him some things. He ought
not to have gone so fast.'

As a walker 'there were occasions when he could be severe.
"No weakness, my friend!" — such was his rebuke, delivered
from an upright posture, with face firmly set towards the
journey's end, five miles still to go, to a too reposeful comrade
who had, poor soul, flung himself down on the heather to
snatch a rest, after two days, not of the shorter order, across
moors, crags, torrents, mountain paths and pathless wastes.'[1]

[1] *Our Friend, W. P.*, pp. 7-8.

Some of the most delightful passages in his letters are brief accounts of walks. Every friend must have received, at some time, descriptions of the countryside in England, or Scotland, or Norway, or Switzerland, like some of the following:

Chequers in 1917.

I went out to look at the world on Saturday last, stirred up by the editor of *The Times*, who proposed a burst for freedom. We took train to Great Missenden, and walked over Chiltern Hills, past Hampden House to Chequers, where we were taken in to lunch, and looked at relics. It is the country that the Whigs came from, and there is a lot of Cromwell at Chequers. A place like a story book — a large Jacobean house looking down a long valley, and a hill behind it — and when you walk up to the top you find yourself on the edge of steep slopes, and a wide prospect over the Vale of Aylesbury and further. We walked to Princes Risborough, with a lift from a farmer in his pony cart, and got a train to Oxford — and slept in it most of the way. It was a fine day — misty in the morning and clearing later. Plenty of good natural rough going, through woods and up and down hill — the steep side to the West in the afternoon, and beautiful gallery paths — grass — leading along a down.

To a friend at Molde:

Molde is one of the places I knew best in Norway, and one of the best places in the world. It was in the year 1887, I think, that I cut the hotel Sunday dinner, and walked up on to the moor till I saw the outer sea. I met with no enemy except a Mother Ptarmigan, who stood up and drummed with her wings while her little poults ran for shelter. I was misunderstood — I wished them no harm. In a later year I walked round by the road to the outer coast — there were roses a good part of the way. And later still, in 1904, I came in on board the North Cape steamer at 1 in the morning, when all was quiet, and all in the strange light of July thereabout. Pleasant to remember, and not at all 'distained' by what I have seen lately. (September, 1921.)

What he had seen lately had been his favourite haunts on either side of the Monte Rosa range above Zermatt, Valtournanche, and Macugnaga.

During the war he had remained in England, doing confidential work for the Admiralty during his vacations, not without some envy of those who could qualify for more active service. An archaeological colleague, Ernest Gardner, expert in Modern Greek, was serving with the navy in the Eastern Mediterranean, and had just been promoted Commander. 'If I had learnt bad Greek,' said Ker, sadly and slowly, 'instead of learning good Greek, I might have been a Commander.' With the peace, the passion for the mountains had returned, and in 1919 he recorded his joy at finding them again:

I have been travelling on the 'Munt of Muntjeu' (Mundiú-fjall), meaning the Alps. Walking by moonlight and most of the day after is worth while, and there is air to breathe. I will not write the sentimental journey, but I may say that the world looks very much as it used to do when I was in this country last — six years ago. Italy in the Alps is like Norway — the woods and hayfields among them, the high cows, and the cheeses. Macugnaga is the place for blaeberries: under Monte Rosa. I knew that before, but always in July, and was glad to find them still going well in August.

He writes from Zermatt, at the beginning of his holiday in 1921:

It is quite worth the trouble coming here. I started walking on Saturday afternoon, and was made at home for the night in the H. de la Gare at Stalden (N.B. — *Not* the Station hotel, but aloof, higher up). Sunday 7.30 on the road to Zermatt very cheerful. At St. Nicholas I found the two monuments I wanted — in church, Aus Ehrfurcht vor dem Allerheiligsten nicht ausspucken — in the hotel, *Rob Roy* (Tauchnitz, 1846) to read at breakfast. But I was interrupted by Gabriel Lochmatter (after breakfast, when I was considering Andrew Fairservice) and taken to see his wife and family. Gabriel was young 15 years ago when I came here for the first time; 14 years ago he took me and Thompson over to Macugnaga and back by the Monte Moro (and St. Joderhorn) to Saas — whence we did Fletschhorn and Laquinhorn *im gleichen Tage*, a very good expedition. But we were beaten down off the Alphubeljoch by bad weather, and since then I have only seen him at long intervals — I was glad to see him again. This afternoon he takes me and Godley to Trift, to start to-morrow early for Trifthorn and over to Mountet hut.

When, in 1922, he was at last free from the duties of his London Chair, he set off in the spirit of a released schoolboy. Here is a summary of a week's holiday, in which bad weather did not stop him from climbing the Finsteraarhorn:

> Hotel Monte Rosa, Zermatt
> 19 August, 1922

. . . Last week I was *out* for 7 days. No plans, and the weather diverting. What actually happened was

1. Stalden to Weissmies Hotel.

2. To Simplon: beaten down from Rossboden Pass by cloud: new way found over a grass pass resembling Cumberland.

3. To Eggishorn. We had meant Monte Leone, but the weather was against it: also preventing cross-country travel to Binn: so we walked down the Simplon road to Brieg.

4. A very fine day: Eggishorn to Aletsch glacier: Concordia hut: Grünhornlücke: Finsteraarhorn hut.

5. Guides at 3 called: the weather beastly, and went back to bed. N.B. it occurred to me that here was I, *the Professor on the Shelf*: the shelf of an Alpine Club hut, and wondering why. But at 6 Joseph Biner took me out into the cold windy world: over snow to the foot of rocks. I did not want to go farther, but he is a strong man. Afterwards he told me I had been so good to him that he couldn't let me off: and I am glad he took me on, for though the wind was horrible and the rocks cold, yet there were good rocks everywhere, shaking you, or rather not shaking but taking you, by the hand — being laid the right way. [A sketch of the rocks and the climber is inserted here.] And the top was sooner than I expected. That night we stayed at Concordia in great comfort — the best hotel I know for true rest.

6. Saturday morning — fine — back to Eggishorn Hotel. There Joseph left me to come home, and I stayed.

7. Sunday, 13th Aug. I did what no man has ever done — walked from the Eggishorn hotel down the Rhone valley

through Brieg to Visp. I rested hours over breakfast at Moerell reading Dante, *Paradiso*, and some time at Brieg over tea: the last five miles into Visp in the cool of the evening ... William Wordsworth is everywhere — he and Jones on the Simplon must have seen the waterfall where Joseph and I descended to find the high road. Going down to Brieg we took a bit of the old road, same as 1790.

Ker's love of the high mountains came to him comparatively late in life. He was 52 when, in 1908, he joined the Alpine Club, and he had then been climbing above the snow line for the three preceding seasons only. From then his devotion, though naturally interrupted by the War, was continuous. I am permitted to quote, from the *Alpine Journal*, the account of Ker as a mountaineer, written by A. D. Godley:

Ker came too late in life to the Alps to be ever a perfect master of mountaineering technique. But he was a man of great physical strength, and indomitable courage and perseverance; many walks and climbs among Scottish and English hills, in the years which he confessed to have been unregenerate, had inured him to hardship ... In 1921, being then 65 years of age, he crossed the Trifthorn from Zermatt to the Mountet, and returned two days after over the Rothhorn; rested for a day or so at Zermatt, then crossed the Matterhorn to the Italian hut; came back next day over the Furggenjoch to the Schwarzsee, had a night's rest, then climbed either Castor or Pollux — I forget which[1] — and returned to Zermatt with no appearance of excessive fatigue, after an outing which might have tried the strength of a man in the prime of life. After that, it could not be expected that bad weather would prevent him from climbing the Finsteraarhorn, in 1922; nor did it ... He idealized mountains; nothing in the whole business of mountaineering but seemed in a manner to him to have a kind of divine sanction; and the peasants who guided him ceased to be ordinary men, and became creatures divinely appointed to lead him into sacred places. Somehow in the Alps he seemed to be raised to a higher power. Merely to be on a climb or a high walk in noble scenery quickened his senses and his intellect. The Alps satisfied him, as great literature satisfied him.

[1] [It was Castor. — R. W. C.]

There was something peculiarly happy in the application to Ker (by a friend writing three days after his death) of the words of Torfrida, 'Which of you knows all the tongues from Lapland to Provence?' It is not only that Ker 'knew every dialect of them all, and more beside', but that, with all his knowledge, he had the spirit of Hereward the Wake. We think of his words about the epic hero: 'A gentleman adventurer on board his own ship, following out his own ideas, carrying his men with him by his own power of mind and temper'; and then of his presidential address to a society of students and scholars: 'I have been chosen one of the captains of a band of adventurers, whose province is the Ocean of stories, the Fortunate Isles of Romance, kingdoms of wonders beyond the farthest part of the voyage of Argo.'

Although we know how distressed he was by unhappy things in post-War politics, many friends will look back on the five years after the Armistice as the most wonderful time of Ker's life. So, at least, thought Florence and John MacCunn, who were among the first made and latest left of his intimate friends. 'When he was free to return to the familiar beautiful things', writes Mrs. MacCunn, 'it was with a heightened conviction of their Reality. A quotation from Gawain Douglas was frequently on his lips and on his pen in these last years: 'Quhilk to behold was plesance and half-wonder.' The light of this wonder lies on the [Oxford] lectures ... He was, in these last years, to have an aftermath of friendship ... friendships with young people. There were many of these friends. He had known most of them in the nursery.' And John MacCunn tells how 'At no period was he more alive in body or in mind.' He was thinking, in these years, 'of writing a book on the measures of modern poetry, from about the year 1100, when it begins in Provence'.

The leisure of this last year gave opportunity for travel in Italy, which the attractions of Scotland and the Alps had not allowed before. When he visited San Gemignano from Sienna, it was in a carriage with two horses rather than a motor, because he had made the journey in that way fifty years before. He replied to a student who had written to him from Cornwall,

'I should like to see the Ocean Stream again at the Land's End, after the tideless midland sea — which all the same is a very good sea to swim in.'

And it was thus, between England, Scotland, Italy, and the Alps, that he passed his year of freedom, in the spirit of an explorer, preparing for new things. It was about this time that he quoted *nos manet oceanus* as his favourite motto.

In one of the earliest lectures he gave in London he had contrasted the perfect conclusion of the *Commedia*, in which Dante sees all the scattered leaves of the Universe, ingathered in the depths of the Eternal Light, with the apparently accidental ending of some great English poems, particularly of *Piers Plowman*; which ending, he maintained, is nevertheless also right and just. In his farewell to his students on 2 May, 1923, he said, 'I was never very careful to find a peroration for my lectures. The conclusion in which nothing is concluded has always seemed to me the most admirable; and I am hoping to go on.'

The conclusion (in which nothing is concluded) came on the 17th of July, 1923. He was at Macugnaga, which he loved best of all places in the Alps, and on the Pizzo Bianco, 'to him, its Holy of Holies'. He was walking up, with his three goddaughters and the guide, 'in the starlight and into the dawn: a most beautiful clear morning, with Monte Rosa above, lit by the sun'. 'I thought this was the most beautiful spot in the world', he said, 'and now I know it.' The party had just started again after a short rest, with Ker as happy as ever, when he fell dead from heart failure.

He was buried in the little old churchyard of Macugnaga, among the guides, not far from the great lime tree which he loved.

Should the time come when a view of history prevails, broader than that which is usually held at present, Ker will be recognized as one of our great historians: an outstanding figure in that august procession which begins with the Venerable Bede. And the conception of history *is* broadening. From 'past politics' it has extended to 'the growth of political institutions'. But more is needed. 'History', says Mr. Tawney, 'if it is to keep in touch with reality, must devote as much attention to the forms of social and economic organization as to that of political institutions.' It must also pay attention to the development of literature and thought. 'It must also be international.' In the words of Matthew Arnold, which are prefixed to Ker's *Dark Ages*, Europe is 'for intellectual and spiritual purposes, one great confederation, bound to a joint action and working to a common result'. This truth, vital to the salvation of Europe, Ker never forgot; nor can his readers forget it.

It is right that Ker should lie buried, near his beloved tree, under the mountains where the French, the Italian, and the German tongues meet, in the heart of 'the Europe which he loved'.

NOTE

The 'Three pages' of *Sir Thomas More* and *The Merchant of Venice*

Professor Dover Wilson writes to me:

I think *The Merchant of Venice* is the one undoubted play of Shakespeare which deals primarily with the position of an alien in a state which permits his domicile under sufferance, and there are striking parallels of phrase and thought between *The Merchant* and More's speech; for example:

> Spurn you like dogs, and like as if that God
> Owed not nor made not you, nor that the elements
> Were not all appropriate to your comforts
> But chartered unto them —
>
> (More, ll. 135-8)

> . . . foot me as you spurn a stranger cur
> Over your threshold . . .
> 'Fair sir, you spit on me on Wednesday last;
> You spurn'd me such a day; another time
> You call'd me dog . . .'
> Hath not a Jew eyes? . . . warmed and cooled by the
> same winter and summer, as a Christian is?
>
> (Merchant, I. iii. 115, etc.; III. i. 60, etc.)

But most interesting of all to my thinking are the passages in which More appeals to the crowd's sense of pity and humanity for the 'wretched strangers'. These breathe the very spirit of *The Tempest*, and surely give one the clue to Shakespeare's attitude to the Jew in *The Merchant*. I don't mean of course that Shylock was meant to be anything but an appalling old man; he was made so, however, by man's 'momtanish inhumanity' to man.

This letter is written on a day when I am to deliver a public lecture on *The Merchant*, in the hope of raising a little money for academic refugees. Perhaps that distorts my judgment, but if there seems to you anything at all in this, it is yours to use.

Yours ever,
J. DOVER WILSON

Surely, if these be Shakespeare's words, they enforce yet once again Carlyle's vision of him as the spokesman of the English-speaking peoples. It is a hundred years ago, all but one, that Carlyle uttered his prophecy: 'England before long, this Island of ours, will hold but a small fraction of the English; in America, in New Holland, east and west to the very Antipodes, there will be a Saxondom covering great spaces of the Globe. And now, what is it that can keep all these together? . . . Wheresoever, under what sort of Parish-Constable soever, English men and women are, they will say to one another: "Yes, this Shakespeare is ours; we produced him, we speak and think by him".' 'The most common-sense politician', Carlyle concluded, 'may think of that'.

And so may the two hundred odd million people of English speech.

INDEX

INDEX

INDEX

Froissart, Jean, 73, 96
Froude, James Anthony, 172 *sq.*, 180, 331 *sq.*
Fuller, Thomas, on Bede's alleged residence at Cambridge, 46-7; on Langland, 94 *sq.*
Furnivall, F. J., 101, 352-4

GARDNER, PROF. ERNEST, 401
Garnett, Richard, the elder, 350
Gasquet, F. A., Abbot, 143 n.
Gawayne and the Green Knight, 56, 93, 144
George III, King, 313, 317, 337
Gibbon, Edward, 51, 356
Gifford, William, 318
Giles, Brother, 129 *sq.*
Gilson, J. P., 239 *sq.*
Gladstone, W. E., 396
Godley, A. D., 402 *sq.*
Goethe, John Morley on, 88
Gollancz, Sir Israel, 143 n., 355
Goodwin, Alfred, 357, 359
Gordon, George, 311
Gosse, Sir Edmund, 75
Gould, Gerald, 376, 399
Gow, A. S. F., 366 *sq.*, 382 *sq.*
—— William, 394
Grattan, Prof. J. H. G., 102, 121
Great Malvern, 99 *sq.*
Greatheart, Mr., 395
Green, John Richard, 15, 54, 101 *sq.*, 122, 164
—— Mrs. John Richard, 398
Greene, Robert, 252, 256
Greenwood, Sir George, 290
Greg, W. W., 210, 213, 233 n., 239 *sq.*
Gregory the Great, Pope, 30, 78, 106, 143
—— of Tours, 31, 32
Grenville, Sir Richard, 252
—— William Wyndham, Baron, 320
Grey, Lady Jane, 254
—— of Fallodon, Viscount, 166
Grierson, Sir H. J. C., 311, 330
Grimm, Jacob, 345
Grinæus, Simon, 178 *sq.*
Grocyn, William, 57
Guest, Edwin, 350
Guntram, King, 31

HADRIAN, ABBOT, 54
Hallam, Henry, 24
Halston, Miss Margaret, in the part of Segismund, 298
Hamilton, Alexander, philologist, 345 n.
Harington, Sir John, 244
Harpsfield, Nicholas, 173 *sq.*
Harris, John. Thomas More's Secretary, 178
Harrowing of Hell, the, 157
Hatfield House Manuscripts, quoted, 269
Hawkins, Sir John, 252
Hawkyn the Active Man, 151 *sq.*
Hazlitt, William, on *Measure for Measure,* 290, 297, 310
Heath, Sir Frank, 355
Helweg, J. H., 394
Heminge, John, 276, 294
Henri IV, King of France, 269
Henry VII, King of England, 193
—— VIII, King of England, 85 *sq.*, 96, 172 *sq.*, 193, 202, 254, 264
—— Prince of Wales, son of James I, 271
Hereward the Wake, 92; and Torfrida, 404
Hertford, Council of, 42
Heywood, Thomas, 213 *sq.*, 230 *sq.*, 249
Hilton, Walter, 103 *sq.*, 124, 151
Hjort, Grete. *See* Hort, Greta
Hobbes, John Oliver (Mrs. Craigie), 361
Hodder-Williams, Sir Ernest, 389
Holland, Henry Fox, third Baron, 320

Homer, 279, unity of, 23, 63; comparison of *Beowulf* with, 64-6; Byron and Homer, 336-8
Hooker, Richard, 41
Hopkins, Gerard Manley, 90, 94
Hort, Greta (Grete Hjort), 124, 243
Housman, A. E., 21; quoted 17, 20, 100, 303, 359, 365-86 *passim*; on English scholarship after 1825, 350-1; his fellowship with Arthur Platt, 362; his description of Platt, 362-4; his early life, 365-6; at University College, London, 367 *sq.*; his good humour towards the young, 369 *sq.*; F. W. Oliver on, 373-4; parody by Gerald Gould and caricature by R. E. M. Wheeler, 375-7; his soldier brother, 379 *sq.*; his gondolier, 379-80; his appointment at Cambridge, 380 *sq.*
—— George Herbert, 378
—— Laurence, 365 *sq.*, 372, 385
Hunt, James Henry Leigh, 340

'IMAGINATIVE' in *Piers Plowman,* 138 *sq.*
Imitation of Christ, The, 103
Imola, Benvenuto da. *See* Benvenuto da Imola
Ingeld, 59, 60
Irony, Dramatic. *See* Dramatic Irony
Isidore, Bede's translations from, 40.

JACOB AND RACHEL, story of, 279
James I, 193, 250, 267 *sq.*
—— Dr. Montague R., on the manuscripts of Bede, 46 and n.
Jarrow, 29, 35, 38, 41
Jerome, St., 48
John, St., Bede's translation of, 40
—— the Deacon, 144
Johnson, Dr. Samuel, 370, 396; quoted, 19, 26, 314
Joinville, Jean de, Seneschal of Champagne, 15
Jones, H. S. V., on 'Imaginative' in *Piers Plowman,* 138 n.
—— Sir William, 344
Jonson, Ben, quoted, 271, 273, 294
Jowett, Benjamin, 387
Julian of Norwich, Dame, 103, 147
Jusserand, J. J., on *Piers Plowman,* 108 *sq.*, 118, 169, 310
Juvencus, possible influence of, upon the Old English epic, 64

KEATS, 73, 317 *sq.*, 399
Kellett, E. E., 236 *sq.*
Kemble, John Mitchell, 346-7
Kempe, André, on the languages of Paradise, 344
Kempis, Thomas à. *See* Thomas à Kempis
Kent, Elizabeth Barton, the Holy Maid of, 185
Ker, W. P., 386-405 *passim*; *see also* 19, 21, 50, 101, 307 n., 359, 361, 362, 372, 374-5, 383, 385; as Quain Professor at University College, London, 389 *sq.*; 'the ubiquitariness of his mind', 392; his interest in Scandinavian things, 393; his interest in public affairs, 396; walking and climbing, 399-403; his last years, 404 *sq.*; on Bede, 26, 48; on *Beowulf* and the old English epic, 64; his judgment of *Beowulf* criticized, 68-9; on 'the spirit of the age', 72; 'Defeat is not refutation', 92; how great poets treat the 'unreason' of ancient stories, 310; on F. J. Furnivall, 352; on Henry Morley, 355; on 'a creditable knowledge of Greek', 356
Key, Thomas Hewitt, 346, 350, 352, 356
Kingsley, Charles, on Byron, 312
Kingsmill, Hugh, 376
Kipling, Rudyard, 106

411

INDEX

INDEX

414